...GERED SPECIES

MUST THEY DISAPPEAR?

ISSN 1549-5345

ENDANGERED SPECIES
MUST THEY DISAPPEAR?

Jennifer J. Yeh

INFORMATION PLUS® REFERENCE SERIES
Formerly published by Information Plus, Wylie, Texas

THOMSON

GALE

Detroit • New York • San Francisco • San Diego • New Haven, Conn. • Waterville, Maine • London • Munich

THOMSON
™
GALE

Endangered Species: Must They Disappear?
Jennifer J. Yeh
Paula Kepos, Series Editor

Project Editor
John McCoy

Editorial
Danielle Behr, Ellice Engdahl, Michael L. LaBlanc, Elizabeth Manar, Daniel Marowski, Charles B. Montney, Heather Price, Timothy J. Sisler

Permissions
William Sampson, Sue Rudolph, Edna Hedblad, Jacqueline Key, Lori Hines, Denise Buckley, Sheila Spencer

Composition and Electronic Prepress
Evi Seoud

Manufacturing
Keith Helmling

LIBRARY OF CONGRESS CATALOGING-IN-PUBLICATION DATA

ISBN 0-7876-5103-6 (set)
ISBN 0-7876-9071-6
ISSN 1549-5345

This title is also available as an e-book.
ISBN 0-7876-9269-7 (set)
Contact your Thomson Gale sales representative for ordering information.

Printed in the United States of America
10 9 8 7 6 5 4 3 2 1

TABLE OF CONTENTS

PREFACE

Endangered Species: Must They Disappear? is part of the Information Plus Reference Series. The purpose of each volume of the series is to present the latest facts on a topic of pressing concern in modern American life. These topics include today's most controversial and most studied social issues: abortion, capital punishment, care for the elderly, crime, health care, the environment, immigration, minorities, social welfare, women, youth, and many more. Although written especially for the high school and undergraduate student, this series is an excellent resource for anyone in need of factual information on current affairs.

By presenting the facts, it is Thomson Gale's intention to provide its readers with everything they need to reach an informed opinion on current issues. To that end, there is a particular emphasis in this series on the presentation of scientific studies, surveys, and statistics. These data are generally presented in the form of tables, charts, and other graphics placed within the text of each book. Every graphic is directly referred to and carefully explained in the text. The source of each graphic is presented within the graphic itself. The data used in these graphics are drawn from the most reputable and reliable sources, in particular from the various branches of the U.S. government and from major independent polling organizations. Every effort has been made to secure the most recent information available. The reader should bear in mind that many major studies take years to conduct, and that additional years often pass before the data from these studies are made available to the public. Therefore, in many cases the most recent information available in 2004 dated from 2001 or 2002. Older statistics are sometimes presented as well, if they are of particular interest and no more recent information exists.

Although statistics are a major focus of the Information Plus Reference Series, they are by no means its only content. Each book also presents the widely held positions and important ideas that shape how the book's subject is discussed in the United States. These positions are explained in detail and, where possible, in the words of their proponents. Some of the other material to be found in these books includes: historical background; descriptions of major events related to the subject; relevant laws and court cases; and examples of how these issues play out in American life. Some books also feature primary documents, or have pro and con debate sections giving the words and opinions of prominent Americans on both sides of a controversial topic. All material is presented in an even-handed and unbiased manner; the reader will never be encouraged to accept one view of an issue over another.

HOW TO USE THIS BOOK

The status of endangered species is an issue of concern both for many Americans and for people around the world. In particular, balancing biodiversity with economics has led to much controversy. This book looks at what has been done to protect endangered species in America and around the world, and examines the debate over what future actions are warranted.

Endangered Species: Must They Disappear? consists of eleven chapters and three appendices. Each chapter is devoted to a particular aspect of endangered species. For a summary of the information covered in each chapter, please see the synopses provided in the Table of Contents at the front of the book. Chapters generally begin with an overview of the basic facts and background information on the chapter's topic, then proceed to examine sub-topics of particular interest. For example, Chapter 2: Working Toward Species Conservation begins with an overview of the history of efforts to save endangered species from extinction. The process of listing species on the U.S. Endangered Species List, and the methods by which species on that list are actually protected, are examined in particular detail. Opposition to the Endangered Species Act is also discussed. The chapter then moves on to look at endangered species on federal lands, ecosystem conservation, international conservation efforts, and the role of zoos. Readers can find their way through a chapter by looking for the section and sub-section headings, which are clearly set off from the text. Or, they can refer to the book's extensive index if they already know what they are looking for.

Statistical Information

The tables and figures featured throughout *Endangered Species: Must They Disappear?* will be of particular use to the reader in learning about this issue. The tables and figures represent an extensive collection of the most recent and important statistics on endangered species, as well as related issues—for example, graphics in the book cover the number of endangered species and the reasons for their endangerment; the locations of National Parks; pesticide runoff threats; and medically useful plant species. The photographs illustrate some of the most threatened species on earth, including the Asian box turtle, the Texas horned lizard, and the red wolf. Thomson Gale believes that making this information available to the reader is the most important way in which we fulfill the goal of this book: to help readers understand the issues and controversies surrounding endangered species and reach their own conclusions about them.

Each table or figure has a unique identifier appearing above it, for ease of identification and reference. Titles for the tables and figures explain their purpose. At the end of each table or figure, the original source of the data is provided.

In order to help readers understand these often complicated statistics, all tables and figures are explained in the text. References in the text direct the reader to the relevant statistics. Furthermore, the contents of all tables and figures are fully indexed. Please see the opening section of the index at the back of this volume for a description of how to find tables and figures within it.

Appendices

In addition to the main body text and images, *Endangered Species: Must They Disappear?* has three appendices. The first is the Important Names and Addresses directory. Here the reader will find contact information for a number of government and private organizations that can provide further information on aspects of endangered species. The second appendix is the Resources section, which can also assist the reader in conducting his or her own research. In this section, the author and editors of *Endangered Species: Must They Disappear?* describe some of the sources that were most useful during the compilation of this book. The final appendix is the index. It has been greatly expanded from previous editions, and should make it even easier to find specific topics in this book.

ADVISORY BOARD CONTRIBUTIONS

The staff of Information Plus would like to extend their heartfelt appreciation to the Information Plus Advisory Board. This dedicated group of media professionals provides feedback on the series on an ongoing basis. Their comments allow the editorial staff who work on the project to continually make the series better and more user-friendly. Our top priorities are to produce the highest-quality and most useful books possible, and the Advisory Board's contributions to this process are invaluable.

The members of the Information Plus Advisory Board are:

- Kathleen R. Bonn, Librarian, Newbury Park High School, Newbury Park, California

- Madelyn Garner, Librarian, San Jacinto College— North Campus, Houston, Texas

- Anne Oxenrider, Media Specialist, Dundee High School, Dundee, Michigan

- Charles R. Rodgers, Director of Libraries, Pasco-Hernando Community College, Dade City, Florida

- James N. Zitzelsberger, Library Media Department Chairman, Oshkosh West High School, Oshkosh, Wisconsin

COMMENTS AND SUGGESTIONS

The editors of the Information Plus Reference Series welcome your feedback on *Endangered Species: Must They Disappear?* Please direct all correspondence to:

Editors
Information Plus Reference Series
27500 Drake Rd.
Farmington Hills, MI 48331-3535

CHAPTER 1
EXTINCTION AND ENDANGERED SPECIES

Earth is a biosphere, a globe richly supplied with different types of living organisms, including animals, plants, fungi, and bacteria. Living organisms are named and categorized according to a taxonomy, a hierarchical system of order based on the natural relationships among all types of life. "Species" is a term assigned to a level of the taxonomy in which grouped organisms are considered capable of interbreeding with one another. Various living species coexist in their environments, forming complex, interrelated communities. Because all species depend on others for nutrients, shelter, or other resources, the removal of even one species in a community can set off a chain reaction affecting many others. In recent decades, large numbers of species have disappeared. The consequences of this loss of biological diversity, or biodiversity, are not only manifold but difficult to predict.

WHAT ARE ENDANGERED SPECIES?

A species is described as extinct when no living members remain. Scientists know from their study of fossils that dinosaurs, mammoths, saber-toothed cats, and countless other animal and plant species that once lived on Earth no longer exist. These species have "died out," or gone extinct. Once a species is extinct, there is no way to bring it back.

The U.S. Fish and Wildlife Service, an agency of the federal government, defines endangered species as those that are at risk of extinction through all or a significant portion of their natural habitats. Threatened species are defined as those likely to become endangered in the foreseeable future. The Fish and Wildlife Service maintains a list of species that are endangered or threatened in the U.S. and abroad. Both endangered and threatened species are protected by laws aimed to save them from extinction. In many cases, recovery plans for endangered species have also been developed and implemented. These include measures designed to protect endangered and threatened species and to help their populations grow.

Nevertheless, scientists estimate that hundreds, or even thousands, of species are lost each year.

MASS EXTINCTION

In the billions of years since life began on Earth, species have formed, existed, and then become extinct. Scientists call the natural extinction of a few species per million years a background, or normal, rate. When the extinction rate doubles for many different groups of plants and animals at the same time, this is described as a mass extinction. Mass extinctions have occurred infrequently in Earth's history and, in general, have been attributed to major cataclysmic geological or astronomical events. Five mass extinctions have occurred in the last 600 million years. These episodes, known as the Big Five, occurred at the end of five geologic periods—the Ordovician (505–440 million years ago), Devonian (410–360 million years ago), Permian (286–245 million years ago), Triassic (245–208 million years ago), and Cretaceous (146–65 million years ago). After each mass extinction, the floral (plant) and faunal (animal) composition of the Earth changed drastically. The largest mass extinction on record occurred at the end of the Permian, when an estimated 90–95 percent of all species went extinct. The Cretaceous extinction is perhaps the most familiar—it was at the end of the Cretaceous that many species of dinosaurs went extinct. The Cretaceous extinction is hypothesized to have resulted from the collision of an asteroid with the earth.

The Sixth Mass Extinction?

According to biologists, plant and animal species are now disappearing at a rate of one per day. This suggests that we are currently in the midst of another mass extinction. Unlike previous mass extinctions, however, the current extinction does not appear to be associated with a cataclysmic physical event. Rather, the heightened extinction

TABLE 1.1

Extinct species in Illinois, Indiana, Iowa, Michigan, Minnesota, Missouri, Ohio, and Wisconsin

These are some of the animals that were once part of the fauna in this region but are now extinct.

Mammals

Eastern Elk *(Cervus canadensis canadensis)*
Formerly found in: United States east of Great Plains
Extinct in 1880

Birds

Carolina parakeet *(Conuropsis carolinensis carolinensis)*
Formerly found in: Southeastern United States
Extinct about 1920
Heath Hen *(Tympanuchus cupido cupido)*
Formerly found in: Eastern United States
Extinct in 1932
Passenger Pigeon *(Ectopistes migratorius)*
Formerly found in: Central and eastern North America
Extinct in 1914

Fish

Blackfin cisco
(Coregonus nigripinnis)
Formerly found in: Lakes Huron, Michigan, Ontario, and Superior
Extinct in 1960s
Blue pike
(Stizostedion vitreum glacum)
Formerly found in: Lakes Erie and Ontario
Declared extinct in 1983
Deepwater cisco
(Coregonus johannae)
Formerly found in: Lakes Huron and Michigan
Extinct in 1960s
Harelip sucker
(Lagochila lacera)
Found in a few clear streams of the upper Mississippi Valley; Scioto River in Ohio; Tennesse River in Georgia; White River in Arkansas; Lake Erie drainage, Blanchard and Auglaize Rivers in northwestern Ohio
Not seen since 1900
Longjaw cisco
(Coregonus alpenae)
Formerly found in: Lakes Erie, Huron, and Michigan
Declared extinct in 1983
Shortnose cisco
(Coregonus reighardi)
Formerly found in: Lakes Huron, Michigan, and Ontario
No individuals collected since 1985

Clams

Leafshell
(Epioblasma flexuosa)
Formerly found in: Alabama, Illinois, Indiana, Kentucky, Ohio, Tennessee
Has not been found alive in over 75 years and since 1988 has been considered extinct
Round combshell
(Epioblasma personata)
Formerly found in: Illinois, Indiana, Kentucky, Ohio
Has not been found alive in over 75 years and since 1988 has been considered extinct
Sampson's pearlymussel (Wabash riffleshell)
Epioblasma sampsonii
Formerly found in: Illinois, Indiana, Kentucky
Declared extinct in 1984
Scioto pigtoe
(Pleurobema bournianum)
Formerly found in: Ohio
Tennessee riffleshell
(Epioblasma propinqua)
Formerly found in: Alabama, Illinois, Indiana, Kentucky, Ohio, Tennessee
Has not been found alive in over 75 years and since 1988 has been considered extinct

rate has coincided with the success and spread of human beings. Researchers predict that as humans continue to alter natural ecosystems through destruction of natural habitats, pollution, introduction of non-native species, and global climate change, the extinction rate may eventually

TABLE 1.1

Extinct species in Illinois, Indiana, Iowa, Michigan, Minnesota, Missouri, Ohio, and Wisconsin [CONTINUED]

These are some of the animals that were once part of the fauna in this region, but are now extinct.

Plants

Bigleaf scurfpea
(Orbexilum macrophyllum)
Formerly found in: Indiana and Kentucky
Thismia americana (no common name)
Found in Illinois
Last seen in 1916; declared extinct in 1995

SOURCE: Extinct Species, in *U.S. Fish and Wildlife Service Region 3: Endangered Species*, U.S. Fish & Wildlife Service, Fort Snelling, MN, 2004 [Online] http://midwest.fws.gov/Endangered/lists/extinct.html [accessed February 24, 2004]

approach several hundred species per day. This would be a rate millions of times higher than normal background levels. The Worldwatch Institute, a think tank devoted to environmental issues, has suggested that, without effective intervention, more species of flora and fauna may disappear in one human lifetime than were lost in the mass extinction that wiped out the dinosaurs 65 million years ago.

The World Conservation Union (IUCN) reports that in the last 500 years, at least 816 species are known to have gone extinct as a result of human activity. The actual number is probably much higher. Table 1.1 lists some U.S. animal and plant species that are now extinct from the midwestern United States.

HOW MANY SPECIES ARE ENDANGERED?

Determining how many species of plants and animals are threatened or endangered is difficult. In fact, only a small fraction of the species in existence have even been identified and named, let alone studied in detail. Estimates of the total number of species on Earth range from 5 million to 100 million, with most estimates figuring around 10 million species worldwide. Of these, only about 1.75 million species have been named and described. According to the World Resources Institute, mammals, which are probably the best-studied group—and the one that includes humans—make up only 0.3 percent of all known organisms. Insects are a particularly rich biological group—over 750,000 insect species have been identified, with countless more to be described.

Since 1960 the World Conservation Union (IUCN), based in Gland, Switzerland, has compiled the *IUCN Red List of Threatened Species*, which aims to examine the status of biological species across the globe. The IUCN's most recent update on the status of plants and animals was published in 2003. Worldwide, in 2003, a total of 12,259 species examined were listed by the IUCN as either critically endangered, endangered, or vulnerable. These

TABLE 1.2

Endangered and threatened species and recovery plans, 2004

Group	Endangered U.S.	Endangered Foreign	Threatened U.S.	Threatened Foreign	Total species	U.S. species with recovery plans[2]
Mammals	69	251	9	17	346	55
Birds	77	175	14	6	272	78
Reptiles	14	64	22	15	115	33
Amphibians	12	8	9	1	30	14
Fishes	71	11	43	0	125	95
Clams	62	2	8	0	72	64
Snails	21	1	11	0	33	23
Insects	35	4	9	0	48	31
Arachnids	12	0	0	0	12	5
Crustaceans	18	0	3	0	21	13
Animal subtotal	391	516	128	39	1074	411
Flowering plants	569	1	144	0	714	577
Conifers and cycads	2	0	1	2	5	2
Ferns and allies	24	0	2	0	26	26
Lichens	2	0	0	0	2	2
Plant subtotal	597	1	147	2	747	607
Grand total	**988**	**517**	**275**	**41**	**1821**[1]	**1018**

Total U.S. endangered—988 (391 animals, 597 plants)
Total U.S. threatened—275 (128 animals, 147 plants)
Total U.S. species—1263 (519 animals,[3] 744 plants)

[1]There are 1853 total listings (1290 U.S.). A listing is an E or a T in the "status" column of the Lists of Endangered and Threatened Wildlife and Plants. The following types of listings are combined as single counts in the table above: species listed both as threatened and endangered (dual status), and subunits of a single species listed as distinct population segments. Only the endangered population is tallied for dual status populations (except for the following: olive ridley sea turtle; for which only the threatened U.S. population is tallied). The dual status U.S. species that are tallied as endangered are: chinook salmon, gray wolf, green sea turtle, piping plover, roseate tern, sockeye salmon, steelhead, Steller sea-lion. The dual status foreign species that are tallied as endangered are: argali, chimpanzee, leopard, saltwater crocodile. Distinct population segments tallied as one include: California tiger salamander, chinook salmon, chum salmon, coho salmon, gray wolf, steelhead. Entries that represent entire genera or families include: African viviparous toads, gibbons, lemurs, musk deer, Oahu tree snails, sifakas, uakari (all species).
[2]There are 539 distinct approved recovery plans. Some recovery plans cover more than one species, and a few species have separate plans covering different parts of their ranges. This count include only plans generated by the USFWS or jointly by the USFWS and NMFS, and includes only listed species that occur in the United States.
[3]9 animal species have dual status in the U.S.

SOURCE: "Summary of Listed Species: Species and Recovery Plans as of 02/09/2004," in *Threatened and Endangered Species System (TESS)*, U.S. Fish and Wildlife Service, Washington, DC 2004 [Online] http://ecos.fws.gov/tess_public/TESSBoxscore [accessed February 9, 2004]

included 5,483 animals (of 20,509 examined) and 6,774 plants (of 9,706 examined). Listed animals included:

- 1,130 of 4,789 mammals studied (24%)
- 1,194 of 9,932 birds studied (12%)
- 293 of 473 reptiles studied (62%)
- 157 of 401 amphibians studied (39%)
- 750 of 1,532 fish studied (49%)
- 553 of 768 insects studied (72%)
- 409 of 461 crustaceans studied (89%)
- 875 of 1897 snails studied (46%)
- several species in other groups

Endangered plants identified by the IUCN included:

- 36 of 39 true mosses (92%)
- 42 of 52 liverworts (81%)
- 11 of 13 club mosses (85%)
- 98 of 164 true ferns (60%)
- 152 of 618 conifers (25%)
- 151 of 288 cycads (52%)

- 5,768 of 7,734 dicotyledonous flowering plants (75%)
- 511 of 792 monocotyledon flowering plants (65%)

Among these are 58 plant and animal species which are already extinct in the wild and continue to persist only in captivity or cultivation. Furthermore, with the exception of birds and mammals, most biological groups have yet to be thoroughly assessed by the IUCN. Further study will likely result in many more species being added to the *Red List*.

Table 1.2 lists the number of species identified as threatened or endangered by the U.S. Fish and Wildlife Service under the Endangered Species Act as of February 1, 2004. Of the 1,853 species listed, 1,290 are found in the United States. Among these, 988 are endangered and 275 are threatened. More than half of the United States' endangered or threatened species are plant forms. Among animals, the greatest numbers of listed species occur among fish, birds, mammals, and insects. A majority of the endangered plants are flowering plants. However, the groups with the largest numbers of endangered species are simply those which are most well-studied.

Figure 1.1 shows the number of listed U.S. species per calendar year from 1980 to 2002. During the early 1980s

FIGURE 1.1

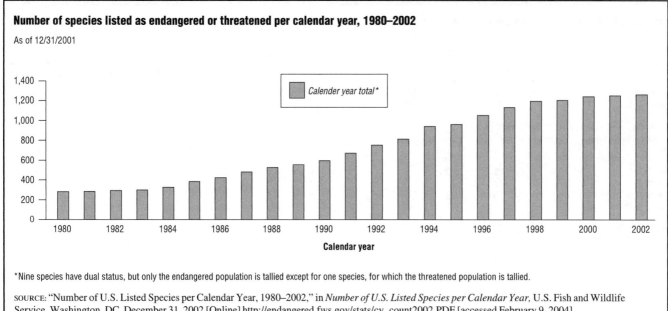

Number of species listed as endangered or threatened per calendar year, 1980–2002

As of 12/31/2001

*Nine species have dual status, but only the endangered population is tallied except for one species, for which the threatened population is tallied.

SOURCE: "Number of U.S. Listed Species per Calendar Year, 1980–2002," in *Number of U.S. Listed Species per Calendar Year,* U.S. Fish and Wildlife Service, Washington, DC, December 31, 2002 [Online] http://endangered.fws.gov/stats/cy_count2002.PDF [accessed February 9, 2004]

endangered and threatened species were listed at an average rate of 34 species per year. During the late 1980s and the first part of the 1990s the average rate exceeded 68 species per year. The plateau in listings during the late 1990s and early 2000s reflects, in part, budgetary constraints on listing activity at the U.S. Fish and Wildlife Service.

Within the United States, endangered and threatened species are not evenly distributed but clustered in specific geographical areas. Figure 1.2 shows the number of federally listed endangered and threatened species in each state on February 19, 2004. Regions where the number of threatened and endangered species is particularly high include southern Appalachia, Florida, the Southwest, California, and Hawaii. Hawaii harbors more threatened and endangered species than any other state, despite its small size. This is due largely to the fact that a significant proportion of the plant and animal life there is endemic—that is, found nowhere else on Earth.

Species Loss—Crisis or False Alarm?

Environmental issues, which have a tendency to pit conservation against business or economic development, are often hotly debated. With respect to current threats to biodiversity, some challengers argue that the scale of loss is not as great as we imagine. They point to uncertainty regarding the total number of species, as well as the geographic distributions of species. Other challengers claim that loss of habitat and disruption by human activity are not powerful enough to cause the massive extinction being documented. Still other challengers contend that extinction is inevitable, and that the Earth has experienced, and recovered from, mass extinctions before. They conclude that the current biodiversity loss, while huge, is not disastrous.

More commonly, however, opponents of conservation argue that "green" policies such as the U.S. Endangered Species Act place the needs of wildlife before those of humans. This was the central issue in one of the most bitter recent battles over an endangered species, that concerning protection of northern spotted owl habitat. (See Figure 1.3.) In 1990 declining populations resulted in the listing of the northern spotted owl as a threatened species. In 1992 the Fish and Wildlife Service set aside 7 million acres of forestland in the Pacific Northwest—both private and public—as critical habitat for the species. Logging was banned on federal lands within these areas. Loggers protested this ban, arguing that jobs would be lost. Supporters of the ban, on the other hand, claimed that most logging jobs had already been lost and that continued logging would preserve existing jobs only for a short time. Eventually, a compromise was reached in which logging was limited to trees under a certain size, leaving the mature growth for owl habitat. By early 1993 almost all old-growth logging on federal lands had been stopped by court action.

Why Save Endangered Species?

The conservation of species is important for many reasons. Species have both aesthetic and recreational value, as the tremendous popularity of zoos, wildlife safaris, recreational hiking, and wildlife watching (bird watching, whale watching, etc.) indicate. Wildlife also has educational and scientific value. In addition, because all species depend on other species for resources, the impact of a single lost species on an entire ecosystem may be immense—in addition to being difficult to predict. Scientists have shown that habitats with greater biodiversity are

FIGURE 1.2

Number of endangered or threatened species, by state or territory, 2004

Omits "similarity of appearance" and experimental populations. Does not map whales and non-nesting sea turtles in state coastal waters.

Washington 38 — Montana 15 — North Dakota 8 — Minnesota 13
Oregon 50 — Idaho 23 — Wyoming 15 — South Dakota 11 — Wisconsin 15 — Michigan 21
Nevada 37 — Utah 43 — Colorado 31 — Nebraska 13 — Iowa 14 — Illinois 26 — Indiana 27 — Ohio 25
California 288 — Arizona 54 — New Mexico 39 — Kansas 15 — Missouri 25 — Kentucky 42
Hawaii 312 — Alaska 7 — Oklahoma 19 — Arkansas 28 — Tennessee 83
Texas 81 — Louisiana 17 — Mississippi 29 — Alabama 90 — Georgia 54
Maine 11 — New Hampshire 8 — Vermont 10 — Massachusetts 18 — Rhode Island 15 — Connecticut 12 — New York 17 — New Jersey 16 — Pennsylvania 10 — Delaware 11 — Maryland 18 — DC 3 — West Virginia 20 — Virginia 55 — North Carolina 50 — South Carolina 32 — Florida 100

Outlying islands 17 — Puerto Rico 75 — U.S. Virgin Islands 13

Note: Total U.S. species is 1260. Numbers are not additive, because a species often occurs in multiple states.

SOURCE: "Listed Species Range by State/Territory as of Mon Feb 9 01:30:04 MST 2004," in *Threatened and Endangered Species System (TESS)*, U.S. Fish and Wildlife Service, Washington, DC, February 9, 2004 [Online] http://ecos.fws.gov/tess_public/TESSUsmap?status=listed [accessed February 9, 2004]

more stable—that is, they are better able to adjust to and recover from disturbances. This is because different species may perform overlapping functions in a biologically diverse ecosystem. Habitats with less diversity are more vulnerable, because a disturbance affecting one species may cause the entire network of interactions to collapse. Furthermore, many species have great economic value to human beings. Plants provide the genetic diversity used to breed new strains of agricultural crops, and many have been used to develop pharmaceutical products. Aside from the economic or utilitarian reasons for preserving species, however, many people think that humankind has a moral responsibility to maintain the Earth's biodiversity. When species are lost, the quality of all life is diminished.

ARE SOME SPECIES MORE IMPORTANT THAN OTHERS? Some species are particularly valued by scientists because they are the last remnants of once flourishing biological groups. Examples of these include the coelacanth, one of the few species (along with lungfish) that help to

document the transition from aquatic to terrestrial life in vertebrates, and the tuatara, a highly endangered reptile found only on New Zealand. The extinction of species that have no closely related species left on Earth represent particularly significant losses to the genetic diversity of the planet.

BIOLOGICAL INDICATOR SPECIES. The rapid rate of species loss should also concern human beings because many are dying out due to pollution and environmental degradation, problems that affect human health and well-being as well. Species that are particularly useful in reporting on the health of ecosystems are called biological indicator species. Environmental scientists rely on sensitive indicator species just as coal miners once relied on canaries to check air safety in underground tunnels, where dangerous gases frequently became concentrated enough to be poisonous. Miners carried a canary into the mineshaft, knowing that the air was safe to breathe as long as the canary lived. If the bird started to sicken, however, miners evacuated the tunnel. In the same way, the sudden

FIGURE 1.3

The northern spotted owl, which inhabits old-growth forests in the Pacific Northwest, was the subject of a lengthy battle pitting environmentalists against logging interests. *(U.S. Fish and Wildlife Service)*

FIGURE 1.4

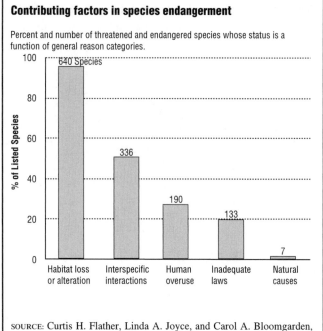

Contributing factors in species endangerment

Percent and number of threatened and endangered species whose status is a function of general reason categories.

SOURCE: Curtis H. Flather, Linda A. Joyce, and Carol A. Bloomgarden, "Contributing Factors in Species Endangerment," in *Species Endangerment Patterns in the United States,* U.S. Forest Service, Fort Collins, CO, 1994

deaths of large numbers of bald eagles and peregrine falcons warned people about the dangers of DDT, a powerful pesticide in wide use at the time. The disappearance of fish from various rivers, lakes, and seas also alerted people to the presence of dangerous chemicals in waters. During the final decades of the twentieth century, many scientists became concerned about the sudden disappearance of many amphibians, particularly frogs, all over the world. Most troubling was the fact that many species disappeared from protected parks and wildlife refuges, areas that appeared relatively pristine and undisturbed. Amphibians are believed to be particularly sensitive to environmental disturbances such as pollution because their skins are formed of living cells and readily absorb substances from the environment. Their decline is a suggestion that all may not be well.

FACTORS THAT CONTRIBUTE TO SPECIES ENDANGERMENT

Experts believe that the increasing loss and decline of species cannot be attributed to natural processes, but results

instead from the destructive effect of human activities. People hunt and collect wildlife. They destroy natural habitats by clearing trees and filling swamps for development. Aquatic habitats are altered or destroyed by the building of dams. Humans also poison habitats with polluting chemicals and industrial waste. Indeed, human activity is now causing changes in climate patterns on a global scale. In 1994, the Forest Service conducted a study of 667 listed species and identified the factors contributing to their endangerment. The breakdown is shown in Figure 1.4.

With each passing day, humans require more space and resources. The World Resources Institute has tracked the increase in global human population over the millennia. The human population has been growing with particular rapidity in recent centuries and passed the 6 billion mark in 1999. As of February 2004, the world population is estimated to be 6.4 billion. The large numbers of human beings puts tremendous pressure on other species. Americans, because they consume more energy and other resources than populations in other industrialized countries or in the developing world, have an even greater impact on the environment.

Habitat Destruction

Habitat destruction is probably the single most important factor leading to the endangerment of species. It plays a role in the decline of some 95 percent of federally listed threatened and endangered species. Habitat destruction has impacted nearly every type of habitat and all ecosystems.

Many types of human activity result in habitat destruction. Agriculture is a leading cause, with about 45 percent of the total land area in the U.S. used for farming. Besides causing the direct replacement of natural habitat with fields, agricultural activity also results in soil erosion, pollution from pesticides and fertilizers, and runoff into aquatic habitats. Agriculture has impacted forest, prairie, and wetland habitats in particular. Nearly 90 percent of wetland losses have resulted from drainage for agriculture. According to a study by Brian Czech, Paul R. Krausman, and Patrick K. Devers ("Economic associations among causes of species endangerment in the United States," *BioScience*, vol. 50, no. 7, 2000), the role of agriculture in the endangerment of species is greatest in the Southeast and California. However, agriculture impacts threatened and endangered species throughout the country, contributing to endangerment in thirty-five states.

Urban expansion has destroyed wild habitat areas as well, and is a primary factor in the endangerment of many plant species. As with agriculture, urbanization leads to the direct replacement of natural habitat. It also results in the depletion of local resources, such as water, which are important to many species. According to Czech, Krausman, and Devers, urbanization contributes to the endangerment of species in 31 states. The greatest impact is in California, Florida, and Texas, the three states that are urbanizing most rapidly. In contrast, only two species are endangered by urbanization in Utah, Nevada, and Idaho. The authors argue that this is because a large proportion of land in these states is public land and therefore not available for private development.

Logging, particularly the practice of clear-cutting forests, destroys important habitat for numerous species. Clear-cutting or extensive logging can also lead to significant erosion, harming both soils and aquatic habitats, which become blocked with soil.

Numerous other forms of human activity result in habitat destruction and degradation. Grazing by domestic livestock directly impacts numerous plant species, as well as animal species that compete with livestock. Mining destroys vegetation and soil, and also degrades habitat through pollution. Dams destroy aquatic habitats in rivers and streams. Finally, human recreational activity, particularly the use of off-road vehicles, results in the destruction of natural habitat. Czech, Krausman, and Devers show that recreational activity has a particularly detrimental effect on species in California, Hawaii, Florida, as well as species in the Mojave Desert, which includes portions of Arizona, California, Nevada, and Utah.

Habitat Fragmentation

Human land-use patterns often result in the fragmentation of natural habitat areas that are available to species. Studies have shown that habitat fragmentation is occur-ring in most habitat types. Habitat fragmentation can have significant effects on species. Small populations can become isolated, so that dispersal from one habitat patch to another is impossible. Smaller populations are also more likely to go extinct. Finally, because there are more "edges" when habitats are fragmented, there can be increased exposure to predators and increased vulnerability to disturbances associated with human activity.

Global Warming

The bulk of human energy requirements are obtained through the burning of fossil fuels. This results in the release of large amounts of carbon dioxide into the atmosphere. Increased levels of carbon dioxide create a "greenhouse effect," which results in warmer temperatures on Earth. A global temperature increase has been compellingly documented, and has already had important effects on ecosystems worldwide. Global warming is predicted to accelerate quickly if measures are not adopted to address it.

The warming of the Earth would alter habitats drastically, with serious consequences for numerous species. In places like Siberia and the northernmost regions of Canada, habitats such as tundra—permanently frozen land supporting only low-growing plant life such as mosses and lichens—and taiga—expanses of evergreen forests located immediately south of the tundra—are shrinking. Deserts are expanding. Forests and grasslands are beginning to shift towards more appropriate climate regimes. Animal and plant species that cannot shift their ranges quickly enough, or have no habitat to shift into, are dying out. Some plants and animals that are found in precise, narrow bands of temperature and humidity, such as monarch butterflies or edelweiss, are likely to find their habitats wiped out entirely. Global warming is already endangering some of the most diverse ecosystems on Earth, such as coral reefs and tropical cloud forests. The impact on endangered species, which are already in a fragile state, may be particularly great.

Pollution

Pollution is caused by the release of industrial and chemical wastes into the land, air, and water. It can damage habitats and kill or sicken animals and plants. Pollution comes from a wide variety of sources, including industrial plants, mining, automobiles, and agricultural products such as pesticides and fertilizers. Even animals that are not directly exposed to pollution can be affected, as the species that they rely on for food, shelter, or other purposes die out. According to Czech, Krausman, and Devers, pollution currently impacts a large number of species in the Southeast, particularly aquatic species such as fish or mussels.

Hunting and Trade

Humans have hunted numerous animal species to extinction, and hunting continues to be a major threat to

TABLE 1.3

Examples of invasive species, 2004

Terrestrial plants

Autumn olive *(Elaeagnus umbellata)*
Chinese tallow *(Sapium sebiferum)*
Downy brome *(Bromus tectorum)*
Garlic mustard *(Alliaria petiolata)*
Japanese honeysuckle *(Lonicera japonica)*
Japanese knotweed *(Polygonum cuspidatum)*
Kudzu *(Pueraria montana var. lobata)*
Leafy spurge *(Euphorbia esula)*
Mile-a-minute weed *(Polygonum perfoliatum)*
Multiflora rose *(Rosa multiflora)*
Musk thistle *(Carduus nutans)*
Russian knapweed *(Acroptilon repens)*
Russian olive *(Elaeagnus angustifolia)*
Saltcedar *(Tamarix spp.)*
Scotch broom *(Cytisus scoparius)*
Scotch thistle *(Onopordum acanthium)*
Spotted knapweed *(Centaurea maculosa)*
Tree of heaven *(Ailanthus altissima)*
Yellow star thistle *(Centaurea solstitialis)*

Terrestrial animals

Africanized honeybee *(Apis mellifera scutellata)*
Asian long-horned beetle *(Anoplophora glabripennis)*
Asian tiger mosquito *(Aedes albopictus)*
Brown tree snake *(Boiga irregularis)*
Cane toad *(Bufo marinus)*
Cactus moth *(Cactoblastis cactorum)*
Emerald ash borer *(Agrilus planipennis)*
European gypsy moth *(Lymantria dispar)*
European starling *(Sturnus vulgaris)*
Formosan subterranean termite *(Coptotermes formosanus)*
Glassy-winged sharpshooter *(Homalodisca coagulata)*
Hemlock, woolly adelgid *(Adelges tsugae)*
Red imported fire ant *(Solenopsis invicta)*
Wild boar *(Sus scrofa)*

TABLE 1.3

Examples of invasive species, 2004 [CONTINUED]

Aquatic & wetlands plants

Brazilian waterweed *(Egeria densa)*
Caulerpa, Mediterranean clone *(Caulerpa taxifolia)*
Common reed *(Phragmites australis)*
Eurasian water milfoil *(Myriophyllum spicatum)*
Giant hogweed *(Heracleum mantegazzianum)*
Giant reed *(Arundo donax)*
Giant salvinia *(Salvinia molesta)*
Hydrilla *(Hydrilla verticillata)*
Melaleuca *(Melaleuca quinquenervia)*
Purple loosestrife *(Lythrum salicaria)*
Water chestnut *(Trapa natans)*
Water hyacinth *(Eichhornia crassipes)*

Aquatic & wetlands animals

Alewife *(Alosa pseudoharengus)*
Asian swamp eel *(Monopterus albus)*
Bullfrog *(Rana catesbeiana)*
Eurasian ruffe *(Gymnocephalus cernuus)*
European green crab *(Carcinus maenas)*
Flathead catfish *(Pylodictus olivaris)*
Northern Snakehead *(Channa argus)*
Nutria *(Myocastor coypus)*
Round goby *(Neogobius melanostomus)*
Sea lamprey *(Petromyzon marinus)*
Veined rapa whelk *(Rapana venosa)*
Zebra mussel *(Dreissena polymorpha)*

Microbes

Exotic Newcastle disease *(Paramyxovirus)*
Fowlpox *(Avipoxvirus)*
Plum pox *(potyviruses: Potyviridae)*
Sudden oak death *(Phytophthora ramorum)*
West Nile virus *(Flavivirus)*
Whirling disease *(Myxobolus cerebralis)*

Note: This is not a list of all invasive species.

SOURCE: "Species Profiles," in *Invasive Species: Species Profiles,* U.S. Department of Agriculture, Washington, DC, 2004 [Online] http://www.invasivespecies.gov/profiles/main.shtml [accessed February 9, 2004]

some species. In the United States, gray wolves were nearly wiped out because they were considered a threat to livestock. The Caribbean monk seal was viewed as a competitor for fish, and exterminated. Other animals are hunted for the value of their hides, tusks, or horns, including elephants and rhinoceroses. Many rare or exotic species, such as parrots and other tropical birds, are taken from their natural habitats for the pet trade.

Invasive Species

Invasive species are those that have been introduced from their native habitat into a new, non-native habitat, and which cause environmental harm. Most introductions of invasive species are accidental, resulting from "stowaways" on ships and planes. Invasive species harm native species by competing with them for food and other resources, or by preying on them or parasitizing them. By 2000 about 50,000 species were believed to have been introduced into the United States alone. There are many types of invasive species, some of which are listed in Table 1.3. Figure 1.5 illustrates the effect of some invasive species on the habitats they have colonized. While there are sometimes beneficial effects from invasive species, most of the effects are harmful.

Some 35–46 percent of species listed by the U.S. Fish and Wildlife Service are endangered partly or entirely

because of invasive species. Similarly, the *2000 IUCN Red List of Threatened Species* suggested that invasive species affect 350 species of threatened birds (30 percent) and 361 species of threatened plants (15 percent). In fact, the IUCN found that the majority of bird extinctions since 1800 have been due to invasive species such as rats and snakes. In 2003 the IUCN reported that the unique flora and fauna of islands such as the Galapagos Islands, Hawaii, the Seychelles, the Falkland Islands, and the British Virgin Islands, have been devastated by invasive species. Human commensals—species that are used by and associated with humans—can be among the most destructive introduced species. In Hawaii, for example, grazing by feral pigs, goats, cattle, and sheep is responsible for the endangerment of numerous plants and birds.

Recognizing the threat posed by invasive species, President Bill Clinton signed Executive Order 13112 on Invasive Species in 1999. This order requires federal agencies to make every possible effort to control the spread of invasive species, and resulted in the formation of the Invasive Species Council, which drafted the first National Invasive Species Management Plan in January 2001. The plan emphasizes prevention of introduction of

FIGURE 1.5

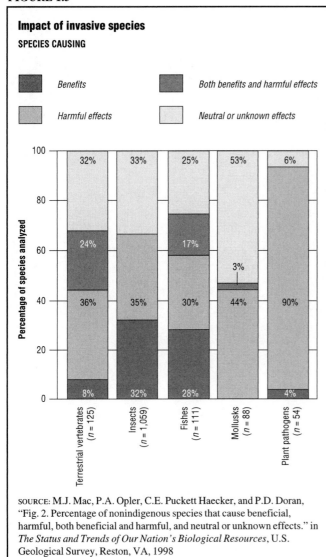

Impact of invasive species
SPECIES CAUSING

Benefits

Both benefits and harmful effects

Harmful effects

Neutral or unknown effects

SOURCE: M.J. Mac, P.A. Opler, C.E. Puckett Haecker, and P.D. Doran, "Fig. 2. Percentage of nonindigenous species that cause beneficial, harmful, both beneficial and harmful, and neutral or unknown effects." in *The Status and Trends of Our Nation's Biological Resources*, U.S. Geological Survey, Reston, VA, 1998

alien species, early detection of invasions, rapid response to them, and coordination of national and international efforts in management and control of these species. In the year 2000 federal agencies spent $631.5 million dealing with damage caused by invasive species or attempting to control them.

CHAPTER 2

WORKING TOWARD SPECIES CONSERVATION

Endangered species have different needs and require different conservation measures. Some fish are endangered only because of a history of overfishing. Halting or reducing fishing is sufficient for population recovery. In most cases, however, more active forms of intervention are necessary. The single most important conservation measure for many threatened and endangered species is habitat conservation or restoration. For some species, captive breeding followed by reintroduction into the wild may help increase numbers. In all cases, knowledge of the natural history of endangered species is essential to acquiring a better understanding of species' needs, as well as to the development of measures that will aid in conservation.

HISTORY OF SPECIES PROTECTION

Conservation has a long history. One of the oldest examples dates from 242 B.C.E. ("before the common era"), when the Indian emperor Asoka created nature reserves in Asia. Marco Polo reported that the Asian ruler Kublai Khan (A.D. 1215–1294) helped conserve bird and mammal species valued for hunting by banning hunting during their reproductive periods. He also helped to increase their numbers by planting food and providing protected cover areas. In South America, during the reign of the Inca kings, many species of seabirds were protected.

By the mid-nineteenth century many governments had developed an interest in wildlife conservation and an awareness of the need to protect natural habitats. In 1861 painters of the Barbizon school established the first French nature reserve, which covered nearly 3,458 acres of forest at Fontainebleau. Three years later the American government set aside the Yosemite Valley in California as a National Reserve. This became Yosemite National Park in 1890. Wyoming's Yellowstone Park was created in 1872 and became the first U.S. National Park.

Organizations and laws dedicated to the protection of species soon followed. In 1895 the first international

meeting for the protection of birds was held in Paris, and resulted in new laws protecting species in several countries. The first international conference for the protection of nature was held in 1913. The International Whaling Commission was established in 1946, and two years later, The World Conservation Union (IUCN) was founded as the International Union for the Protection of Nature. (In 1956 that organization became the International Union for Conservation of Nature and Natural Resources, or IUCN. In 1990 the name was shortened to IUCN-The World Conservation Union.) In 1961 a private conservation organization, the World Wildlife Fund (WWF), was founded. The Chinese giant panda was selected as the WWF symbol, not only because of the animal's great popularity, but also to reaffirm the international character of nature conservation, and to emphasize the independence of wildlife conservation from political differences. The Convention on International Trade in Endangered Species (CITES), an international treaty established to regulate commerce in wildlife, was first ratified in 1975 in an attempt to block both the import and export of endangered species and to regulate international trade in threatened species.

In the U.S., Congress passed the Endangered Species Preservation Act in 1966, and the first species were listed in 1967. (See Table 2.1.) This established a process for listing species as endangered and provided some measure of protection. The Endangered Species Conservation Act of 1969 provided protection to species facing worldwide extinction, prohibiting their import and sale within the U.S.

THE ENDANGERED SPECIES ACT OF 1973—A LANDMARK PROTECTION

The Endangered Species Act was passed by the U.S. Congress in 1973. It is generally considered one of the most far-reaching laws ever enacted by any nation for the preservation of wildlife. The passage of the Endangered Species Act resulted from alarm at the decline of numerous species

TABLE 2.1

First list of endangered species, 1967

In accordance with section 1(c) of the Endangered Species Preservation Act of October 15, 1966 (80 Stat. 926; 16 U.S.C. 668aa(c) I [the Secretary of the Interior] find after consulting the states, interested organizations, and individual scientists, that the following listed native fish and wildlife are threatened with extinction.

Mammals
- Indiana bat— *Myotis sodalis*
- Delmarva Peninsula fox squirrel—*Sciurus niger cinereus*
- Timber wolf—*Canis lupus lycaon*
- Red wolf —*Canis niger*
- San Joaquin kit fox—*Vulpes macrotis mutica*
- Grizzly bear —*Ursus horribilis*
- Black-footed ferret—*Mustela nigripes*
- Florida panther —*Felis concolor coryi*
- Caribbean monk seal—*Monachus tropicalis*
- Guadalupe fur seal —*Arctocephalus philippi townsendi*
- Florida manatee or Florida sea cow—*Trichechus manatus latirostris*
- Key deer—*Odocoileus virginianus clavium*
- Sonoran pronghorn —*Antilocapra americana sonoriensis*

Birds
- Hawaiian dark-rumped petrel—*Pterodroma phaeopygia sandwichensis*
- Hawaiian goose (nene)—*Branta sandvicensis*
- Aleutian Canada goose—*Branta canadensis leucopareia*
- Tule white-fronted goose—*Anser albifrons gambelli*
- Laysan duck—*Anas laysanensis*
- Hawaiian duck (or koloa)—*Anas wyvilliana*
- Mexican duck —*Anas diazi*
- California condor—*Gymnogyps californianus*
- Florida Everglade kite (Florida Snail Kite)—*Rostrhamus sociabilis plumbeus*
- Hawaiian hawk (or ii)—*Buteo solitarius*
- Southern bald eagle—*Haliaeetus t. leucocephalus*
- Attwater's greater prairie chicken—*Tympanuchus cupido attwateri*
- Masked bobwhite—*Colinus virginianus ridgwayi*
- Whooping crane —*Grus americana*
- Yuma clapper rail —*Rallus longirostris yumanensis*
- Hawaiian common gallinule—*Gallinula chloropus sandvicensis*
- Eskimo curlew —*Numenius borealis*
- Puerto Rican parrot—*Amazona vittata*
- American ivory-billed woodpecker—*Campephilus p. principalis*
- Hawaiian crow (or alala)—*Corvus hawaiiensis*
- Small Kauai thrush (puaiohi) —*Phaeornia pulmeri*
- Nihoa millerbird—*Acrocephalus kingi*
- Kauai oo (or oo aa) —*Moho braccatus*
- Crested honeycreeper (or akohekohe)—*Palmeria dolei*
- Akiapolaau—*Hemignathus wilsoni*
- Kauai akialoa —*Hemignathus procerus*
- Kauai nukupuu —*Hemignathus lucidus hanapepe*

- Laysan finchbill (Laysan Finch)—*Psittirostra c. cantans*
- Nihoa finchbill (Nihoa Finch)—*Psittirostra cantans ultima*
- Ou—*Psittirostra psittacea*
- Palila—*Psittirostra bailleui*
- Maui parrotbill—*Pseudonestor xanthophyrys*
- Bachman's warbler—*Vermivora bachmanii*
- Kirtland's warbler—*Dendroica kirtlandii*
- Dusky seaside sparrow—*Ammospiza nigrescens*
- Cape Sable sparrow—*Ammospiza mirabilis*

Reptiles and Amphibians
- American alligator—*Alligator mississippiensis*
- Blunt-nosed leopard lizard—*Crotaphytus wislizenii silus*
- San Francisco garter snake—*Thamnophis sirtalis tetrataenia*
- Santa Cruz long-toed salamander—*Ambystoma macrodactylum croceum*
- Texas blind salamander—*Typhlomolge rathbuni*
- Black toad, Inyo County toad—*Bufo exsul*

Fishes
- Shortnose sturgeon—*Acipenser brevirostrum*
- Longjaw cisco—*Coregonus alpenae*
- Paiute cutthroat trout—*Salmo clarki seleniris*
- Greenback cuttthroat trout—*Salmo clarki stomias*
- Montana Westslope cutthroat trout—*Salmo clarki*
- Gila trout—*Salmo gilae*
- Arizona (Apache) trout—*Salmo sp*
- Desert dace—*Eremichthys acros*
- Humpback chub—*Gila cypha*
- Little Colorado spinedace—*Lepidomeda vittata*
- Moapa dace—*Moapa coriacea*
- Colorado River squawfish—*Ptychocheilus lucius*
- Cui-ui —*Chasmistes cujus*
- Devils Hole pupfish— *Cyprinodon diabolis*
- Commanche Springs pupfish—*Cyprinodon elegans*
- Owens River pupfish —*Cyprinodon radiosus*
- Pahrump killifish—*Empetrichythys latos*
- Big Bend gambusia—*Gambusia gaigei*
- Clear Creek gambusia—*Gambusia heterochir*
- Gila topminnow—*Poeciliopsis occidentalis*
- Maryland darter—*Etheostoma sellare*
- Blue pike—*Stizostedion vitreum glaucum*

SOURCE: Stewart L. Udall, "Native Fish and Wildlife Endangered Species," in *Federal Register,* vol. 32, no. 48, March 11, 1967

---

worldwide, as well as from a recognition of the importance of preserving species diversity. The purpose of the Endangered Species Act is to identify species that are either endangered—at risk of extinction throughout all or a significant portion of their range—or threatened—likely to become endangered in the foreseeable future. With the exception of pest species, all animals and plants are eligible for listing under the Endangered Species Act. Listed species are protected without regard to either commercial or sport value.

The Endangered Species Act is administered by the U.S. Department of the Interior through the U.S. Fish and Wildlife Service. The U.S. Department of Commerce, through the National Marine Fisheries Service, is responsible for marine species.

The Endangered Species List

After passage of the Endangered Species Act, the Fish and Wildlife Service was inundated with petitions for

the listing of species—approximately 24,000 petitions were received in the first two years after passage. As of February 2004, there are 985 U.S. species (388 animals and 597 plants) and 517 foreign species (516 animals and 1 plant) listed as endangered, and 275 U.S. (128 animals and 147 plants) and 41 foreign species (39 animals and 2 plants) listed as threatened. Thousands of other species are being studied to see if they need to be added to the list.

The Listing Process

The process for listing a new species as endangered or threatened begins with a formal petition from a person or organization. (Figure 2.1 diagrams the petition process.) This petition is submitted to the Fish and Wildlife Service for terrestrial and freshwater species and to the National Marine Fisheries Service for marine species. All petitions must be backed by published scientific data supporting the need for listing. Within 90 days, the Fish and Wildlife Ser-

FIGURE 2.1

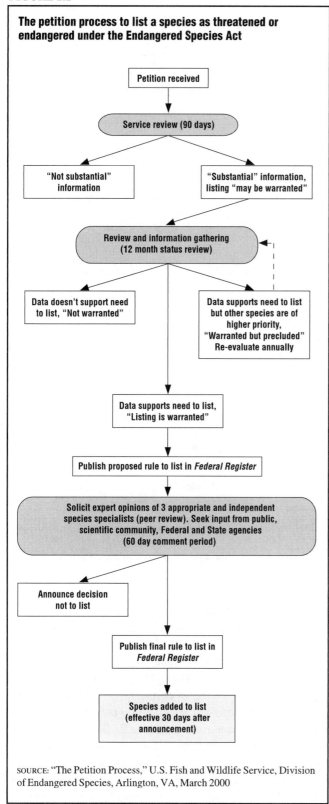

The petition process to list a species as threatened or endangered under the Endangered Species Act

Petition received

Service review (90 days)

"Not substantial" information

"Substantial" information, listing "may be warranted"

Review and information gathering (12 month status review)

Data doesn't support need to list, "Not warranted"

Data supports need to list but other species are of higher priority, "Warranted but precluded" Re-evaluate annually

Data supports need to list, "Listing is warranted"

Publish proposed rule to list in *Federal Register*

Solicit expert opinions of 3 appropriate and independent species specialists (peer review). Seek input from public, scientific community, Federal and State agencies (60 day comment period)

Announce decision not to list

Publish final rule to list in *Federal Register*

Species added to list (effective 30 days after announcement)

SOURCE: "The Petition Process," U.S. Fish and Wildlife Service, Division of Endangered Species, Arlington, VA, March 2000

vice or National Marine Fisheries Service determines whether there is "substantial information" to suggest that a species requires being listed under the Endangered Species Act. Approximately 65 percent of petitions for species are found to have substantial information to warrant further study, whereas 35 percent do not.

For petitions that present biological data suggesting that listing may be necessary, the Fish and Wildlife Service or National Marine Fisheries Service then performs a status review to determine whether listing is warranted. This process must be completed within 12 months. In the past, over half the petitions warrant action. Once it has been determined that action on a species is warranted, that species becomes a candidate species. Candidate species may immediately join the list of proposed species. However, in some cases, it may be decided that other candidate species have higher priority. If this is the case, the species is designated as "warranted but precluded," that is, immediate action is precluded by more urgent listing activity. Species that are listed as "warranted but precluded" are re-evaluated annually to confirm that listing continues to be warranted. These species continue to be re-evaluated until they either join the list of proposed species or until their status has improved sufficiently that they are no longer warranted for listing.

A species is officially proposed for listing through the publication of this action in the *Federal Register*. At this point, the Fish and Wildlife Service asks three independent biological experts to verify that the petitioned species requires listing under either threatened or endangered status. After that, input from the public, from other federal and state agencies, and from the scientific community is welcomed. This period of public comment lasts 60 days. Following the sixty-day period, the final rule regarding listing of the species is published in the *Federal Register*, and listing is effective thirty days after publication.

Figure 2.2 shows the number of species proposed for listing under the Endangered Species Act by state as of February 19, 2004, and these species are listed in Table 2.2. There were thirty-six U.S. proposed species in February 2004. (Three of these were proposed as threatened rather than endangered.) The Fish and Wildlife Service also keeps a list of candidate species (those for which there is scientific evidence warranting their proposal for listing, but which have yet to become proposed species). The Fish and Wildlife Service works with state wildlife agencies and other groups to help preserve and improve the status of candidate species, with the hope that populations may recover enough that species will not require listing. In February 2004 there were 256 U.S. candidate species recognized by the Fish and Wildlife Service. Figure 2.3 shows the number of candidate species per state.

After a species is listed, its condition and situation are reviewed at least every five years to decide whether it still requires government protection. Once the species is able to survive without government protection, it may be removed from the list.

Conserving Listed Species

Conservation efforts for protected species begin with the preparation of a recovery plan by the Fish and Wildlife

FIGURE 2.2

Proposed additions to the list of endangered and threatened species, by state or territory, 2004

Omits proposed "similarity of appearance" and experimental populations.

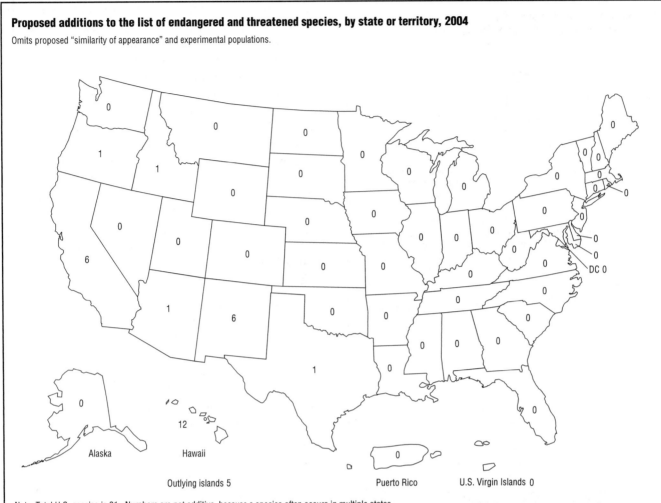

Note: Total U.S. species is 31. Numbers are not additive, because a species often occurs in multiple states.

SOURCE: "Proposed Species Range by State/Territory as of Tue Feb 10 01:30:32 MST 2004," in *Threatened and Endangered Species System (TESS)*, U.S. Fish and Wildlife Service, Washington, DC, 2004 [Online] http://ecos.fws.gov/tess_public/TESSUsmap?status=proposed [accessed February 10, 2004]

Service that details how the species will be protected and helped to thrive. This report also includes the estimated timeline for and cost of recovery. In many cases, recovery efforts include the designation of critical habitat—that is, areas of land, water, and air space that are used by threatened and endangered species for breeding, resting, and feeding. Critical habitat designation does not set up a refuge, and has no regulatory impact on private landowners unless they wish to take actions on their land that involve federal funding or permits. Species which have had critical habitat designated are listed in Table 2.3. For a small number of species, primarily mammals, birds, fish, and aquatic invertebrates, recovery efforts include the introduction of individuals into new areas. Species with so-called "experimental populations" are listed in Table 2.4.

The Endangered Species Act gives the government and its agencies the power to do whatever is necessary to protect a threatened or endangered species. However, budgetary constraints severely limit the action that can be taken. In 2004 the Fish and Wildlife Service had at its dis-

posal $9.8 million for the conservation of candidate species, $12.1 million for listing activity, $47.1 million for consultations with federal and private agencies to resolve potential issues, and $67.9 million for the recovery of listed species. How best to use these funds is contentious. In fact, in 2000, 50 percent of recovery expenditures were used to conserve only seven species (0.6 percent of listed species), and 90 percent of recovery expenditures were used to conserve 91 listed species (7.4 percent of all listed species). This means that very little effort goes towards the conservation of the large majority of endangered and threatened species. The ten species with the highest reported expenditure for 1998–2000 are shown in Table 2.5.

The number of species being added to the federal threatened and endangered species list is likely to continue to grow. Although vertebrate species dominated the list during the first years of the act, plants and invertebrate animals now make up a much greater proportion of listed species. (See Table 1.2 in Chapter 1.) These species are

TABLE 2.2

Species proposed to be added to the endangered or threatened list, 2004

Status	Species name
Mammals	
PE	Addax (Addax nasomaculatus)
PT	Bat, Mariana fruit (=Mariana flying fox) (Pteropus mariannus mariannus)
PE	Dugong (Dugong dugon)
PE	Fox, San Miguel Island (Urocyon littoralis littoralis)
PE	Fox, Santa Catalina Island (Urocyon littoralis catalinae)
PE	Fox, Santa Cruz Island (Urocyon littoralis santacruzae)
PE	Fox, Santa Rosa Island (Urocyon littoralis santarosae)
PE	Gazelle, dama (Gazella dama)
PE	Oryx, scimitar-horned (Oryx dammah)
Birds	
PE	White-eye, Rota bridled (Zosterops rotensis)
Amphibians	
PT	Salamander, California tiger (Ambystoma californiense)
Fishes	
PE	Chub, Cowhead Lake tui (Gila bicolor vaccaceps)
PE	Chub, Gila (Gila intermedia)
PT	Salmon, coho (Oncorhynchus (=Salmo) kisutch)
PE	Sturgeon, Beluga (Huso huso)
Snails	
PE	Snail, Koster's tryonia (Tryonia kosteri)
PE	Snail, Pecos assiminea (Assiminea pecos)
PE	Springsnail, Roswell (Pyrgulopsis roswellensis)
Insects	
PE	Butterfly, Sacramento Mountains checkerspot (Euphydryas anicia cloudcrofti)
PE	Pomace fly, [unnamed] (Drosophila aglaia)
PE	Pomace fly, [unnamed] (Drosophila differens)
PE	Pomace fly, [unnamed] (Drosophila hemipeza)
PE	Pomace fly, [unnamed] (Drosophila heteroneura)
PE	Pomace fly, [unnamed] (Drosophila montgomeryi)
PE	Pomace fly, [unnamed] (Drosophila mulli)
PE	Pomace fly, [unnamed] (Drosophila musaphila)
PE	Pomace fly, [unnamed] (Drosophila neoclavisetae)
PE	Pomace fly, [unnamed] (Drosophila obatai)
PE	Pomace fly, [unnamed] (Drosophila ochrobasis)
PE	Pomace fly, [unnamed] (Drosophila substenoptera)
PE	Pomace fly, [unnamed] (Drosophila tarphytrichia)
Crustaceans	
PE	Amphipod, Noel's (Gammarus desperatus)
Flowering plants	
PE	Peppergrass, Slick spot (Lepidium papilliferum)
PE	Nesogenes rotensis (No common name)
PE	Osmoxylon mariannense (No common name)
PE	Tabernaemontana rotensis (No common name)

Note: Proposed species count is 36 (excludes proposed "similarity of appearance" and experimental populations)
PE = proposed endangered
PT = proposed threatened

SOURCE: "Proposed Species as of 02/10/2004," in *Threatened and Endangered Species System (TESS)*, U.S. Fish and Wildlife Service, Washington, DC, 2004 [Online] http://ecos.fws.gov/tess_public/TESSWebpageNonlisted?listings =0&type=P [accessed February 10, 2004]

politically more difficult to defend than either mammals or birds, which are more inherently appealing to most Americans because of the "warm and fuzzy" factor. These circumstances raise questions about the continued feasibility of a species-by-species preservation strategy, and the Fish and Wildlife Service struggles under intense legal and political pressures to decide which species to protect first.

For its supporters, the Endangered Species Act has proved to be one of the most effective conservation laws ever enacted. Many Americans believe that the Endangered Species Act has saved many species from extinction. An estimated 40 percent of species on the list are either stable in population size or increasing in number. A few species have improved sufficiently to have their listing status changed. In Table 2.6, species whose status has been changed since listing under the Endangered Species Act are detailed. Many endangered species (E) have been reclassified as threatened (T), indicating that their status has improved since protection under the Endangered Species Act. Other species have declined in population, however, and have shifted from threatened to endangered.

Extinct, Recovered, and Down-Listed Species

Species may be removed from the Endangered Species List for three reasons:

1) The species has become extinct.

2) The species has recovered to such an extent that it is no longer threatened or endangered.

3) The original information warranting listing has been shown to be incorrect, or new information suggests that the species is not actually endangered or threatened.

As of February 2004, thirty-seven species that were once on the Endangered Species List had been removed from the list, or delisted. These species are shown in Table 2.7, along with the reason for being delisted. Of the species delisted, seven were removed from the list because they went extinct (two more were believed extinct), fifteen species were delisted because they were considered recovered, and fifteen species were delisted either because the original data was in error, because new information had been discovered, or because of taxonomic revision. Reclassification has been proposed for another twelve species, shown in Table 2.8. This includes the proposed delisting of species such as the bald eagle due to recovery.

Habitat Conservation Plans

Endangered and threatened species live and roam wherever they find suitable habitat, without regard to whether the land is federal or non-federal, or public or private. Many landowners fear being denied free use of their land because of laws protecting the endangered species that inhabit it. Recognizing this concern, Congress amended the Endangered Species Act in 1982 to allow for the creation of Habitat Conservation Plans (HCPs) governing land use or development. HCPs are generally partnerships drawn up by people at the local level, working with Fish and Wildlife Service officials. They frequently represent compromises between developers and environmentalists.

HCPs typically allow some individuals of a threatened or endangered species to be "taken" (harmed or killed) under a special authority called an incidental take permit. Included in the agreement is a "no surprise" provi-

FIGURE 2.3

Number of species that are candidates for the endangered or threatened list, by state or territory, 2004

Distributions reflect known historic range

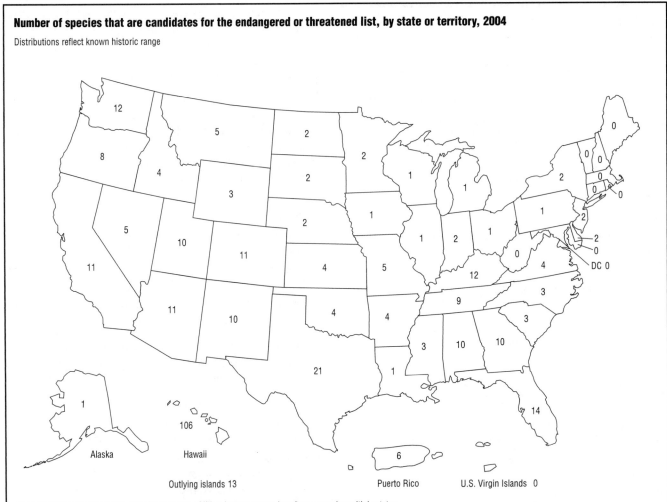

Note: Total U.S. species is 256. Numbers are not additive, because a species often occurs in multiple states.

SOURCE: "Candidate Species Range by State/Territory as of Tue Feb 10 01:30:54 MST 2004," in *Threatened and Endangered Species System (TESS)*, U.S. Fish and Wildlife Service, Washington, DC, 2004 [Online] http://ecos.fws.gov/tess_public/TESSUsmap?status=candidate [accessed February 10, 2004]

sion that assures landowners or developers that the overall cost of species protection measures will be limited to what has been agreed to under the HCP. In return, landowners make a long-term commitment to conservation as negotiated in the HCP. Many HCPs include the preservation of significant areas of habitat for endangered species. In 2003 a lawsuit brought by Spirit of the Sage Council challenged the "no surprise" policy, arguing that it allowed for too much damage to endangered species. The "no surprise" policy is now being reconsidered in the courts.

Although the HCP program was implemented in 1982, it was little used before 1992, with only fourteen permits issued in that time period. However, by 2002, there were 380 plans in place. HCPs now affect over 200 listed plant and animal species on over 20 million acres of land. The Fish and Wildlife Service maintains a list of approved Habitat Conservation Plans with the locations of the sites as well as data on the listed and unlisted species involved. HCPs have become an necessary tool in the negotiation of endangered species conservation.

A Habitat Conservation Plan for San Diego County

In 1997, after more than a decade of debate and negotiation, environmentalists and developers settled upon an HCP—the "Multispecies Conservation Plan"—for San Diego County. It is regarded by some experts as a possible national model. Under the HCP, certain undeveloped sections of land were permanently set aside as protected natural habitat, while other areas were opened to unrestricted development. Setting aside a connected (rather than fragmented) area of protected natural habitat is a crucial aspect of this HCP. The plan affects some eighty-five species of vulnerable plants and animals. The "Multispecies Conservation Plan" pleased environmentalists because of the creation of a large, permanent preserve for species protection. Developers were pleased that unrestricted development could proceed without costly legal challenges by environmentalists in defined areas.

Desert Tortoises and the Washington County HCP

In Washington County, Utah, an HCP was developed in 1996 to bridge differences between developers and conserva-

TABLE 2.3

Endangered or threatened species, February 2004

Status	Species name	Status	Species name
Mammals		**Amphibians**	
E	Bat, Indiana *(Myotis sodalis)*	T	Salamander, San Marcos *(Eurycea nana)*
E	Bat, Virginia big-eared *(Corynorhinus (=Plecotus) townsendii virginianus)*	E	Toad, arroyo (=arroyo southwestern) *(Bufo californicus (=microscaphus))*
E	Kangaroo rat, Fresno *(Dipodomys nitratoides exilis)*	E	Toad, Houston *(Bufo houstonensis)*
E	Kangaroo rat, Morro Bay *(Dipodomys heermanni morroensis)*	**Fishes**	
E	Kangaroo rat, San Bernardino Merriam's *(Dipodomys merriami parvus)*	T	Catfish, Yaqui *(Ictalurus pricei)*
E	Manatee, West Indian *(Trichechus manatus)*	E	Cavefish, Alabama *(Speoplatyrhinus poulsoni)*
E	Mouse, Alabama beach *(Peromyscus polionotus ammobates)*	E	Chub, bonytail *(Gila elegans)*
E	Mouse, Choctawhatchee beach *(Peromyscus polionotus allophrys)*	E	Chub, Borax Lake *(Gila boraxobius)*
E	Mouse, Perdido Key beach *(Peromyscus polionotus trissyllepsis)*	E	Chub, humpback *(Gila cypha)*
T	Mouse, Preble's meadow jumping *(Zapus hudsonius preblei)*	E	Chub, Owens tui *(Gila bicolor snyderi)*
E	Rice rat (lower Florida Keys) *(Oryzomys palustris natator)*	T	Chub, slender *(Erimystax cahni)*
E	Seal, Hawaiian monk *(Monachus schauinslandi)*	T	Chub, Sonora *(Gila ditaenia)*
E	Sea-lion, Steller (western population) *(Eumetopias jubatus)*	T	Chub, spotfin Entire *(Cyprinella monacha)*
T	Sea-lion, Steller (eastern population) *(Eumetopias jubatus)*	E	Chub, Virgin River *(Gila seminuda (=robusta))*
E	Sheep, bighorn (Peninsular California population) *(Ovis canadensis)*	E	Chub, Yaqui *(Gila purpurea)*
E	Squirrel, Mount Graham red *(Tamiasciurus hudsonicus grahamensis)*	E	Dace, Ash Meadows speckled *(Rhinichthys osculus nevadensis)*
E	Vole, Amargosa *(Microtus californicus scirpensis)*	T	Dace, desert *(Eremichthys acros)*
E	Whale, right *(Balaena glacialis* [including *australis*]*)*	E	Darter, amber *(Percina antesella)*
T	Wolf, gray, eastern distinct population segment *(Canis lupus)*	E	Darter, fountain *(Etheostoma fonticola)*
Birds		E	Darter, leopard *(Percina pantherina)*
E	Blackbird, yellow-shouldered *(Agelaius xanthomus)*	E	Darter, Maryland *(Etheostoma sellare)*
E	Condor, California (U.S.A. only) *(Gymnogyps californianus)*	T	Darter, Niangua *(Etheostoma nianguae)*
E	Crane, Mississippi sandhill *(Grus canadensis pulla)*	T	Darter, slackwater *(Etheostoma boschungi)*
E	Crane, whooping (except where XN) *(Grus americana)*	E	Gambusia, San Marcos *(Gambusia georgei)*
T	Eider, spectacled *(Somateria fischeri)*	E	Goby, tidewater Entire *(Eucyclogobius newberryi)*
T	Eider, Steller's (Alaska breeding population) *(Polysticta stelleri)*	E	Logperch, Conasauga *(Percina jenkinsi)*
E	Elepaio, Oahu *(Chasiempis sandwichensis ibidis)*	E	Madtom, smoky Entire *(Noturus baileyi)*
E	Flycatcher, southwestern willow *(Empidonax traillii extimus)*	T	Madtom, yellowfin (except where XN) *(Noturus flavipinnis)*
T	Gnatcatcher, coastal California *(Polioptila californica californica)*	T	Minnow, loach *(Tiaroga cobitis)*
E	Kite, Everglade snail (Florida population) *(Rostrhamus sociabilis plumbeus)*	E	Minnow, Rio Grande silvery *(Hybognathus amarus)*
T	Murrelet, marbled (California, Oregon, Washington) *(Brachyramphus marmoratus marmoratus)*	E	Pikeminnow (=squawfish), Colorado (except Salt and Verde River drainages, Arizona) *(Ptychocheilus lucius)*
T	Owl, Mexican spotted *(Strix occidentalis lucida)*	E	Pupfish, Ash Meadows Amargosa *(Cyprinodon nevadensis mionectes)*
T	Owl, northern spotted *(Strix occidentalis caurina)*	E	Pupfish, desert *(Cyprinodon macularius)*
E	Palila (honeycreeper) *(Loxioides bailleui)*	E	Pupfish, Leon Springs *(Cyprinodon bovinus)*
E	Plover, piping (Great Lakes watershed) *(Charadrius melodus)*	E	Salmon, chinook (winter Sacramento River) *(Oncorhynchus (=Salmo) tshawytscha)*
T	Plover, piping (except Great Lakes watershed) *(Charadrius melodus)*	E	Salmon, chinook (spring upper Columbia River) *(Oncorhynchus (=Salmo) tshawytscha)*
T	Plover, western snowy (Pacific coastal population) *(Charadrius alexandrinus nivosus)*	T	Salmon, chinook (upper Willamette River) *(Oncorhynchus (=Salmo) tshawytscha)*
E	Pygmy-owl, cactus ferruginous (Arizona population) *(Glaucidium brasilianum cactorum)*	T	Salmon, chinook (lower Columbia River) *(Oncorhynchus (=Salmo) tshawytscha)*
E	Sparrow, Cape Sable seaside *(Ammodramus maritimus mirabilis)*	T	Salmon, chinook (spring/summer Snake River) *(Oncorhynchus (=Salmo) tshawytscha)*
T	Towhee, Inyo California *(Pipilo crissalis eremophilus)*	T	Salmon, chinook (fall Snake River) *(Oncorhynchus (=Salmo) tshawytscha)*
E	Vireo, least Bell's *(Vireo bellii pusillus)*	T	Salmon, chinook (California Central Valley spring-run) *(Oncorhynchus (=Salmo) tshawytscha)*
Reptiles		T	Salmon, chinook (California coastal) *(Oncorhynchus (=Salmo) tshawytscha)*
E	Anole, Culebra Island giant *(Anolis roosevelti)*	T	Salmon, chinook (Puget Sound) *(Oncorhynchus (=Salmo) tshawytscha)*
T	Boa, Mona *(Epicrates monensis monensis)*	T	Salmon, chum (summer-run Hood Canal) *(Oncorhynchus (=Salmo) keta)*
E	Cooter (=turtle), northern redbelly (=Plymouth) *(Pseudemys rubriventris bangsi)*	T	Salmon, chum (Columbia River) *(Oncorhynchus (=Salmo) keta)*
E	Crocodile, American *(Crocodylus acutus)*	T	Salmon, coho (Oregon, California population) *(Oncorhynchus (=Salmo) kisutch)*
E	Gecko, Monito *(Sphaerodactylus micropithecus)*	E	Salmon, sockeye U.S.A. (Snake River, Idaho stock wherever found) *(Oncorhynchus (=Salmo) nerka)*
T	Iguana, Mona ground *(Cyclura stejnegeri)*	T	Salmon, sockeye U.S.A. (Ozette Lake, Washington) *(Oncorhynchus (=Salmo) nerka)*
E	Lizard, Coachella Valley fringe-toed *(Uma inornata)*	T	Shiner, Arkansas River (Arkansas River Basin) *(Notropis girardi)*
E	Lizard, St. Croix ground *(Ameiva polops)*	T	Shiner, beautiful *(Cyprinella formosa)*
T	Rattlesnake, New Mexican ridge-nosed *(Crotalus willardi obscurus)*	E	Shiner, Cape Fear *(Notropis mekistocholas)*
T	Sea turtle, green (except where endangered) *(Chelonia mydas)*	T	Shiner, Pecos bluntnose *(Notropis simus pecosensis)*
E	Sea turtle, hawksbill *(Eretmochelys imbricata)*	T	Silverside, Waccamaw *(Menidia extensa)*
E	Sea turtle, leatherback *(Dermochelys coriacea)*	T	Smelt, delta *(Hypomesus transpacificus)*
T	Snake, Concho water *(Nerodia paucimaculata)*	T	Spikedace *(Meda fulgida)*
T	Tortoise, desert (U.S.A., except in Sonoran Desert) *(Gopherus agassizii)*	T	Spinedace, Big Spring *(Lepidomeda mollispinis pratensis)*
T	Whipsnake (=striped racer), Alameda *(Masticophis lateralis euryxanthus)*	T	Spinedace, Little Colorado *(Lepidomeda vittata)*
Amphibians		E	Spinedace, White River *(Lepidomeda albivallis)*
T	Coqui, golden *(Eleutherodactylus jasperi)*	E	Springfish, Hiko White River *(Crenichthys baileyi grandis)*
T	Frog, California red-legged (subspecies range clarified) *(Rana aurora draytonii)*		

TABLE 2.3

Endangered or threatened species, February 2004 [CONTINUED]

Status	Species name	Status	Species name
Fishes		**Flowering plants**	
T	Springfish, Railroad Valley *(Crenichthys nevadae)*	E	'Akoko *(Chamaesyce kuwaleana)*
E	Springfish, White River *(Crenichthys baileyi baileyi)*	E	'Akoko *(Chamaesyce rockii)*
E	Steelhead (upper Columbia River Basin) *(Oncorhynchus (= Salmo) mykiss)*	E	'Akoko *(Euphorbia haeleeleana)*
E	Steelhead (southern California coast) *(Oncorhynchus (= Salmo) mykiss)*	E	Alani *(Melicope adscendens)*
T	Steelhead (middle Columbia River) *(Oncorhynchus (= Salmo) mykiss)*	E	Alani *(Melicope balloui)*
T	Steelhead (upper Willamette River) *(Oncorhynchus (= Salmo) mykiss)*	E	Alani *(Melicope haupuensis)*
T	Steelhead (central California coast) *(Oncorhynchus (= Salmo) mykiss)*	E	Alani *(Melicope knudsenii)*
T	Steelhead (Snake River Basin) *(Oncorhynchus (= Salmo) mykiss)*	E	Alani *(Melicope lydgatei)*
T	Steelhead (Central Valley California) *(Oncorhynchus (= Salmo) mykiss)*	E	Alani *(Melicope mucronulata)*
T	Steelhead (lower Columbia River) *(Oncorhynchus (= Salmo) mykiss)*	E	Alani *(Melicope ovalis)*
T	Steelhead (south central California coast) *(Oncorhynchus (= Salmo) mykiss)*	E	Alani *(Melicope pallida)*
T	Sturgeon, gulf *(Acipenser oxyrinchus desotoi)*	E	Alani *(Melicope quadrangularis)*
E	Sturgeon, white U.S.A. (Idaho, Montana), Canada (British Columbia), (Kootenai River system) *(Acipenser transmontanus)*	E	Alani *(Melicope reflexa)*
		E	Alani *(Melicope saint-johnii)*
E	Sucker, June *(Chasmistes liorus)*	E	Alani *(Melicope zahlbruckneri)*
E	Sucker, Modoc *(Catostomus microps)*	T	Amole, purple *(Chlorogalum purpureum)*
E	Sucker, razorback *(Xyrauchen texanus)*	E	'Anaunau *(Lepidium arbuscula)*
T	Sucker, Warner *(Catostomus warnerensis)*	E	'Anunu *(Sicyos alba)*
T	Trout, Little Kern golden *(Oncorhynchus aguabonita whitei)*	E	Aupaka *(Isodendrion hosakae)*
E	Woundfin (except Gila River drainage, Arizona, New Mexico) *(Plagopterus argentissimus)*	E	Aupaka *(Isodendrion laurifolium)*
		T	Aupaka *(Isodendrion longifolium)*
Clams		E	'Awikiwiki *(Canavalia molokaiensis)*
E	Elktoe, Appalachian *(Alasmidonta raveneliana)*	E	Awiwi *(Centaurium sebaeoides)*
E	Heelsplitter, Carolina *(Lasmigona decorata)*	E	Awiwi *(Hedyotis cookiana)*
		E	Bladderpod, San Bernardino Mountains *(Lesquerella kingii* ssp. *bernardina)*
Snails		E	Bladderpod, Zapata *(Lesquerella thamnophila)*
E	Snail, Morro shoulderband (=banded dune) *(Helminthoglypta walkeriana)*	T	Blazingstar, Ash Meadows *(Mentzelia leucophylla)*
T	Snail, Newcomb's *(Erinna newcombi)*	E	Bluegrass, Hawaiian *(Poa sandvicensis)*
		E	Bluegrass, Mann's *(Poa mannii)*
Insects		E	Buckwheat, cushenbury *(Eriogonum ovalifolium* var. *vineum)*
T	Beetle, delta green ground *(Elaphrus viridis)*	T	Centaury, spring-loving *(Centaurium namophilum)*
E	Beetle, Helotes mold *(Batrisodes venyivi)*	E	Checkermallow, Keck's *(Sidalcea keckii)*
T	Beetle, valley elderberry longhorn *(Desmocerus californicus dimorphus)*	E	Checkermallow, Wenatchee Mountains *(Sidalcea oregana* var. *calva)*
T	Butterfly, bay checkerspot *(Euphydryas editha bayensis)*	T	Daisy, Parish's *(Erigeron parishii)*
T	Butterfly, Oregon silverspot *(Speyeria zerene hippolyta)*	E	Evening primrose, Antioch Dunes *(Oenothera deltoides* ssp. *howellii)*
E	Butterfly, Palos Verdes blue *(Glaucopsyche lygdamus palosverdesensis)*	E	Fiddleneck, large-flowered *(Amsinckia grandiflora)*
E	Butterfly, Quino checkerspot *(Euphydryas editha quino (=E. e. wrighti))*	E	Geranium, Hawaiian red-flowered *(Geranium arboreum)*
E	Grasshopper, Zayante band-winged *(Trimerotropis infantilis)*	E	Goldfields, Contra Costa *(Lasthenia conjugens)*
E	Ground beetle, [unnamed] *(Rhadine exilis)*	E	Grass, Solano *(Tuctoria mucronata)*
E	Ground beetle, [unnamed] *(Rhadine infernalis)*	T	Groundsel, San Francisco Peaks *(Senecio franciscanus)*
E	Moth, Blackburn's sphinx *(Manduca blackburni)*	T	Gumplant, Ash Meadows *(Grindelia fraxino-pratensis)*
T	Naucorid, Ash Meadows *(Ambrysus amargosus)*	E	Haha *(Cyanea acuminata)*
		E	Haha *(Cyanea asarifolia)*
Arachnids		E	Haha *(Cyanea copelandii* ssp. *copelandii)*
E	Harvestman, Cokendolpher Cave *(Texella cokendolpheri)*	E	Haha *(Cyanea copelandii* ssp. *haleakalaensis)*
E	Meshweaver, Braken Bat Cave *(Cicurina venii)*	E	Haha *(Cyanea dunbarii)*
E	Meshweaver, Madla's Cave *(Cicurina madla)*	E	Haha *(Cyanea glabra)*
E	Meshweaver, Robber Baron Cave *(Cicurina baronia)*	E	Haha *(Cyanea grimesiana* ssp. *grimesiana)*
E	Spider, Kauai cave wolf or pe'e pe'e maka 'ole *(Adelocosa anops)*	E	Haha *(Cyanea grimesiana* ssp. *obatae)*
E	Spider, spruce-fir moss *(Microhexura montivaga)*	E	Haha *(Cyanea hamatiflora carlsonii)*
		E	Haha *(Cyanea hamatiflora* ssp. *hamatiflora)*
Crustaceans		E	Haha *(Cyanea humboldtiana)*
E	Amphipod, Kauai cave *(Spelaeorchestia koloana)*	E	Haha *(Cyanea koolauensis)*
E	Fairy shrimp, Conservancy *(Branchinecta conservatio)*	E	Haha *(Cyanea lobata)*
E	Fairy shrimp, longhorn *(Branchinecta longiantenna)*	E	Haha *(Cyanea longiflora)*
E	Fairy shrimp, Riverside *(Streptocephalus woottoni)*	E	Haha *(Cyanea macrostegia* ssp. *gibsonii)*
E	Fairy shrimp, San Diego *(Branchinecta sandiegonensis)*	E	Haha *(Cyanea mannii)*
T	Fairy shrimp, vernal pool *(Branchinecta lynchi)*	E	Haha *(Cyanea mceldowneyi)*
E	Shrimp, Kentucky cave *(Palaemonias ganteri)*	E	Haha *(Cyanea pinnatifida)*
E	Tadpole shrimp, vernal pool *(Lepidurus packardi)*	E	Haha *(Cyanea platyphylla)*
		E	Haha *(Cyanea procera)*
Flowering Plants		T	Haha *(Cyanea recta)*
E	A'e *(Zanthoxylum dipetalum* var. *tomentosum)*	E	Haha *(Cyanea remyi)*
E	A'e *(Zanthoxylum hawaiiense)*	E	Haha *(Cyanea shipmannii)*
T	Ahinahina *(Argyroxiphium sandwicense* ssp. *macrocephalum)*	E	Haha *(Cyanea stictophylla)*
E	'Aiakeakua, popolo *(Solanum sandwicense)*	E	Haha *(Cyanea st-johnii)*
E	'Aiea *(Nothocestrum breviflorum)*	E	Haha *(Cyanea superba)*
E	'Aiea *(Nothocestrum peltatum)*	E	Haha *(Cyanea truncata)*
E	'Akoko *(Chamaesyce celastroides* var. *kaenana)*	E	Haha *(Cyanea undulata)*
E	'Akoko *(Chamaesyce deppeana)*	E	Ha'iwale *(Cyrtandra crenata)*
E	'Akoko *(Chamaesyce herbstii)*	E	Ha'iwale *(Cyrtandra dentata)*

TABLE 2.3

Endangered or threatened species, February 2004 [CONTINUED]

Status	Species name	Status	Species name
Flowering plants		**Flowering plants**	
E	Haʻiwale *(Cyrtandra giffardii)*	E	Nehe *(Lipochaeta fauriei)*
T	Haʻiwale *(Cyrtandra limahuliensis)*	E	Nehe *(Lipochaeta kamolensis)*
E	Haʻiwale *(Cyrtandra munroi)*	E	Nehe *(Lipochaeta lobata var. leptophylla)*
E	Haʻiwale *(Cyrtandra polyantha)*	E	Nehe *(Lipochaeta micrantha)*
E	Haʻiwale *(Cyrtandra subumbellata)*	E	Nehe *(Lipochaeta tenuifolia)*
E	Haʻiwale *(Cyrtandra tintinnabula)*	E	Nehe *(Lipochaeta waimeaensis)*
E	Haʻiwale *(Cyrtandra viridiflora)*	E	Nioi *(Eugenia koolauensis)*
E	Hala pepe *(Pleomele hawaiiensis)*	E	Niterwort, Amargosa *(Nitrophila mohavensis)*
E	Hau kuahiwi *(Hibiscadelphus giffardianus)*	E	*Abutilon eremitopetalum* (No common name)
E	Hau kuahiwi *(Hibiscadelphus hualalaiensis)*	E	*Abutilon sandwicense* (No common name)
E	Hau kuahiwi *(Hibiscadelphus woodii)*	E	*Achyranthes mutica* (No common name)
T	Heather, mountain golden *(Hudsonia montana)*	E	*Alsinidendron obovatum* (No common name)
E	Heau *(Exocarpos luteolus)*	E	*Alsinidendron trinerve* (No common name)
E	Hedyotis, Na Pali beach *(Hedyotis st.-johnii)*	E	*Alsinidendron viscosum* (No common name)
E	Hibiscus, Clay's *(Hibiscus clayi)*	E	*Amaranthus brownii* (No common name)
E	Holei *(Ochrosia kilaueaensis)*	E	*Bonamia menziesii* (No common name)
E	Iliau, dwarf *(Wilkesia hobdyi)*	E	*Chamaesyce halemanui* (No common name)
E	Ischaemum, Hilo *(Ischaemum byrone)*	E	*Cyanea (= Rollandia) crispa* (No common name)
T	Ivesia, Ash Meadows *(Ivesia kingii var. eremica)*	E	*Delissea rhytidosperma* (No common name)
E	Kamakahala *(Labordia cyrtandrae)*	E	*Delissea undulata* (No common name)
E	Kamakahala *(Labordia lydgatei)*	E	*Gahnia lanaiensis* (No common name)
E	Kamakahala *(Labordia tinifolia var. wahiawaensis)*	E	*Gouania hillebrandii* (No common name)
E	Kamanomano *(Cenchrus agrimonioides)*	E	*Gouania meyenii* (No common name)
E	Kauila *(Colubrina oppositifolia)*	E	*Gouania vitifolia* (No common name)
E	Kaulu *(Pteralyxia kauaiensis)*	E	*Hedyotis degeneri* (No common name)
E	Kioʻele *(Hedyotis coriacea)*	E	*Hedyotis parvula* (No common name)
E	Kiponapona *(Phyllostegia racemosa)*	E	*Hesperomannia arborescens* (No common name)
E	Kohe malama malama o kanaloa *(Kanaloa kahoolawensis)*	E	*Hesperomannia arbuscula* (No common name)
E	Kokiʻo *(Kokia drynarioides)*	E	*Hesperomannia lydgatei* (No common name)
E	Kokiʻo *(Kokia kauaiensis)*	E	*Lobelia gaudichaudii* ssp. *koolauensis* (No common name)
E	Kokiʻo keʻokeʻo *(Hibiscus arnottianus ssp. immaculatus)*	E	*Lobelia monostachya* (No common name)
E	Kokiʻo keʻokeʻo *(Hibiscus waimeae ssp. hannerae)*	E	*Lobelia niihauensis* (No common name)
E	Kolea *(Myrsine juddii)*	E	*Lobelia oahuensis* (No common name)
T	Kolea *(Myrsine linearifolia)*	E	*Lysimachia filifolia* (No common name)
E	Koʻokoʻolau *(Bidens micrantha ssp. kalealaha)*	E	*Lysimachia lydgatei* (No common name)
E	Koʻokoʻolau *(Bidens wiebkei)*	E	*Lysimachia maxima* (No common name)
E	Kuahiwi laukahi *(Plantago hawaiensis)*	E	*Mariscus fauriei* (No common name)
E	Kuahiwi laukahi *(Plantago princeps)*	E	*Mariscus pennatiformis* (No common name)
E	Kuawawaenohu *(Alsinidendron lychnoides)*	E	*Munroidendron racemosum* (No common name)
E	Kula wahine noho *(Isodendrion pyrifolium)*	E	*Neraudia angulata* (No common name)
E	Kuluʻi *(Nototrichium humile)*	E	*Neraudia ovata* (No common name)
E	Larkspur, Baker's *(Delphinium bakeri)*	E	*Neraudia sericea* (No common name)
E	Larkspur, yellow *(Delphinium luteum)*	E	*Phyllostegia glabra var. lanaiensis* (No common name)
E	Lau ʻehu *(Panicum niihauense)*	E	*Phyllostegia hirsuta* (No common name)
E	Laulihilihi *(Schiedea stellarioides)*	E	*Phyllostegia kaalaensis* (No common name)
E	Liliwai *(Acaena exigua)*	E	*Phyllostegia knudsenii* (No common name)
E	Loʻulu *(Pritchardia affinis)*	E	*Phyllostegia mannii* (No common name)
E	Loʻulu *(Pritchardia kaalae)*	E	*Phyllostegia mollis* (No common name)
E	Loʻulu *(Pritchardia munroi)*	E	*Phyllostegia parviflora* (No common name)
E	Loʻulu *(Pritchardia napaliensis)*	E	*Phyllostegia velutina* (No common name)
E	Loʻulu *(Pritchardia remota)*	E	*Phyllostegia waimeae* (No common name)
E	Loʻulu *(Pritchardia schattaueri)*	E	*Phyllostegia warshaueri* (No common name)
E	Loʻulu *(Pritchardia viscosa)*	E	*Phyllostegia wawrana* (No common name)
E	Love grass, Fosberg's *(Eragrostis fosbergii)*	E	*Platanthera holochila* (No common name)
E	Mahoe *(Alectryon macrococcus)*	E	*Poa siphonoglossa* (No common name)
T	Makou *(Peucedanum sandwicense)*	E	*Remya kauaiensis* (No common name)
E	Maʻo hau hele, (=native yellow hibiscus) *(Hibiscus brackenridgei)*	E	*Remya montgomeryi* (No common name)
E	Maʻoliʻoli *(Schiedea apokremnos)*	E	*Sanicula mariversa* (No common name)
E	Maʻoliʻoli *(Schiedea kealiae)*	E	*Sanicula purpurea* (No common name)
E	Mapele *(Cyrtandra cyaneoides)*	E	*Schiedea haleakalensis* (No common name)
E	Meadowfoam, Butte County *(Limnanthes floccosa ssp. californica)*	E	*Schiedea helleri* (No common name)
E	Mehamehame *(Flueggea neowawraea)*	E	*Schiedea hookeri* (No common name)
E	Milk vetch, Ash meadows *(Astragalus phoenix)*	E	*Schiedea kaalae* (No common name)
T	Milk vetch, Cushenbury *(Astragalus albens)*	E	*Schiedea kauaiensis* (No common name)
E	Milk vetch, heliotrope *(Astragalus montii)*	E	*Schiedea lydgatei* (No common name)
T	Milkweed, Welsh's *(Asclepias welshii)*	E	*Schiedea membranacea* (No common name)
E	Naʻenaʻe *(Dubautia herbstobatae)*	E	*Schiedea nuttallii* (No common name)
E	Naʻenaʻe *(Dubautia latifolia)*	E	*Schiedea sarmentosa* (No common name)
E	Naʻenaʻe *(Dubautia pauciflorula)*	E	*Schiedea spergulina var. leiopoda* (No common name)
E	Naʻenaʻe *(Dubautia plantaginea ssp. humilis)*	E	*Schiedea spergulina var. spergulina* (No common name)
E	Nani waiʻaleʻale *(Viola kauaiensis var. wahiawaensis)*	E	*Schiedea verticillata* (No common name)
E	Nanu *(Gardenia mannii)*	E	*Silene alexandri* (No common name)

TABLE 2.3

Status	Species name	Status	Species name
Flowering plants		**Flowering plants**	
T	*Silene hawaiiensis* (No common name)	E	Pilo *(Hedyotis mannii)*
E	*Silene lanceolata* (No common name)	E	Po'e *(Portulaca sclerocarpa)*
E	*Silene perlmanii* (No common name)	E	Polygonum, Scotts Valley *(Polygonum hickmanii)*
E	*Spermolepis hawaiiensis* (No common name)	E	Popolo ku mai *(Solanum incompletum)*
E	*Stenogyne bifida* (No common name)	E	Pua 'ala *(Brighamia rockii)*
E	*Stenogyne campanulata* (No common name)	E	Pu'uka'a *(Cyperus trachysanthos)*
E	*Stenogyne kanehoana* (No common name)	E	Remya, Maui *(Remya mauiensis)*
E	*Tetramolopium arenarium* (No common name)	T	Seagrass, Johnson's *(Halophila johnsonii)*
E	*Tetramolopium filiforme* (No common name)	T	Sedge, Navajo *(Carex specuicola)*
E	*Tetramolopium lepidotum* ssp. *lepidotum* (No common name)	E	Silversword, Mauna Loa (=Ka'u) *(Argyroxiphium kauense)*
E	*Tetramolopium remyi* (No common name)	T	Spineflower, Monterey *(Chorizanthe pungens* var. *pungens)*
T	*Tetramolopium rockii* (No common name)	E	Spineflower, Robust (including Scotts Valley) *(Chorizanthe robusta*
E	*Trematolobelia singularis* (No common name)		[including vars. *robusta* and *hartwegii])*
E	*Vigna o-wahuensis* (No common name)	T	Spurge, Hoover's *(Chamaesyce hooveri)*
E	*Viola helenae* (No common name)	T	Sunray, Ash Meadows *(Enceliopsis nudicaulis* var. *corrugata)*
E	*Viola lanaiensis* (No common name)	E	Tarplant, Gaviota *(Hemizonia increscens* ssp. *villosa)*
E	*Viola oahuensis* (No common name)	T	Tarplant, Otay *(Deinandra* (= *Hemizonia) conjugens)*
E	*Xylosma crenatum* (No common name)	T	Tarplant, Santa Cruz *(Holocarpha macradenia)*
E	Nohoanu *(Geranium multiflorum)*	E	Thistle, La Graciosa *(Cirsium loncholepis)*
E	Oha *(Delissea rivularis)*	E	Tuctoria, Greene's *(Tuctoria greenei)*
E	Oha *(Delissea subcordata)*	E	Wahane *(Pritchardia aylmer-robinsonii)*
E	'Oha wai *(Clermontia drepanomorpha)*	E	Wallflower, Contra Costa *(Erysimum capitatum* var. *angustatum)*
E	'Oha wai *(Clermontia lindseyana)*	E	Water-umbel, Huachuca *(Lilaeopsis schaffneriana* var. *recurva)*
E	'Oha wai *(Clermontia oblongifolia* ssp. *brevipes)*	E	Wild-buckwheat, clay-loving *(Eriogonum pelinophilum)*
E	'Oha wai *(Clermontia oblongifolia* ssp. *mauiensis)*	T	Wild-buckwheat, gypsum *(Eriogonum gypsophilum)*
E	'Oha wai *(Clermontia peleana)*	E	Wild-rice, Texas *(Zizania texana)*
E	'Oha wai *(Clermontia pyrularia)*	E	Wire-lettuce, Malheur *(Stephanomeria malheurensis)*
E	'Oha wai *(Clermontia samuelii)*	E	Yerba santa, Lompoc *(Eriodictyon capitatum)*
E	Ohai *(Sesbania tomentosa)*		
E	'Ohe'ohe *(Tetraplasandra gymnocarpa)*	**Ferns and Allies**	
E	Olulu *(Brighamia insignis)*	E	Diellia, asplenium-leaved *(Diellia erecta)*
E	Opuhe *(Urera kaalae)*	E	Fern, pendant kihi *(Adenophorus periens)*
E	Orcutt grass, hairy *(Orcuttia pilosa)*	E	Ihi'ihi *(Marsilea villosa)*
E	Orcutt grass, Sacramento *(Orcuttia viscida)*	E	*Asplenium fragile* var. *insulare* (No common name)
T	Orcutt grass, San Joaquin *(Orcuttia inaequalis)*	E	*Diellia falcata* (No common name)
T	Orcutt grass, slender *(Orcuttia tenuis)*	E	*Diellia pallida* (No common name)
T	Owl's-clover, fleshy *(Castilleja campestris* ssp. *succulenta)*	E	*Diellia unisora* (No common name)
E	Oxytheca, cushenbury *(Oxytheca parishii* var. *goodmaniana)*	E	*Diplazium molokaiense* (No common name)
E	Pamakani *(Tetramolopium capillare)*	E	*Pteris lidgatei* (No common name)
E	Pamakani *(Viola chamissoniana* ssp. *chamissoniana)*	E	Pauoa *(Ctenitis squamigera)*
E	Panicgrass, Carter's *(Panicum faurie* var. *carteri)*	E	Wawae'iole *(Huperzia mannii)*
E	Penny-cress, Kneeland Prairie *(Thlaspi californicum)*	E	Wawae'iole *(Lycopodium* (= *Phlegmariurus) nutans)*
E	Pennyroyal, Todsen's *(Hedeoma todsenii)*		

Total number of species is 450.
E = endangered
T = threatened

SOURCE: Adapted from "Listed Species with Critical Habitat as of 02/10/2004," in *Threatened and Endangered Species System (TESS)*, U.S. Fish and Wildlife Service, Washington, DC, 2004 [Online] http://ecos.fws.gov/tess_public/TESSWebpageCrithab?nmfs=1&listings=1 [accessed February 10, 2004]

tionists concerned about the threatened desert tortoise. In 2001 an update on this HCP was published by the Fish and Wildlife Service. The Fish and Wildlife Service reported that a total of 1,500 acres of habitat were developed in Washington County after being cleared of tortoises—161 tortoises were legally "taken." The biological benefits of the HCP included the acquisition of a continuous area of habitat for desert tortoises administered by the Bureau of Land Management. This reserve was created through the exchange and purchase of land by the Bureau of Land Management. In addition, tortoises will be protected from other threats on the reserve. For example, grazing permits for reserve land have been retired, so cattle will no longer trample habitat and compete with tortoises for food. In addition, new restrictions were placed on the operation of off-road vehicles in the reserve, which damage habitats and sometimes hit tortoises. The development of

a nature education center is in the works. There are still a number of contentious issues. For example, some members of the public have demanded that more recreational opportunities be made available on the reserve. Also, the Bureau of Land Management needs to purchase more land to complete the reserve, difficult on its limited budget.

Opposition to the Endangered Species Act

Opponents of the Endangered Species Act believe the law violates private property rights and stifles economic growth by curbing development. They also charge that environmental protection often results in the loss of jobs and business profits.

One vocal critic of the Endangered Species Act is Thomas Lambert. In *The Endangered Species Act: A*

TABLE 2.4

Experimental populations, 2004

Inverted common name	Scientific name	Group code	Where listed
Bear, grizzly	Ursus arctos horribilis	Mammals	U.S.A. experimental non-essential (portions of ID and MT)
Ferret, black-footed	Mustela nigripes	Mammals	U.S.A. (specific portions of AZ, CO, MT, SD, UT, and WY)
Otter, southern sea	Enhydra lutris nereis	Mammals	All areas subject to U.S. jurisdiction south of Point Conception, CA
Squirrel, Delmarva Peninsula fox	Sciurus niger cinereus	Mammals	U.S.A. (DE—Sussex Co.)
Wolf, gray	Canis lupus	Mammals	U.S.A. (portions of AZ, NM, and TX)
Wolf, gray	Canis lupus	Mammals	U.S.A. (WV and portions of ID and MT)
Wolf, red	Canis rufus	Mammals	U.S.A. (portions of NC and TN)
Condor, California	Gymnogyps californianus	Birds	U.S.A. (specific portions of Arizona, Nevada, and Utah)
Crane, whooping	Grus americana	Birds	U.S.A. (AL, AR, GA, IL, IN, IA, KY, LA, MI, MN, MS, MO, NC, OH, SC, TN, VA, WI, WV)
Crane, whooping	Grus americana	Birds	U.S.A. (CO, ID, FL, NM, UT, and the western half of Wyoming)
Rail, Guam	Rallus owstoni	Birds	Rota
Chub, spotfin	Cyprinella monacha	Fishes	Tellico River, between the backwaters of the Tellico Reservoir and the Tellico Ranger Station, in Monroe County, Tennessee
Darter, duskytail	Etheostoma percnurum	Fishes	Tellico River, between the backwaters of the Tellico Reservoir and the Tellico Ranger Station, in Monroe County, Tennessee
Madtom, smoky	Noturus baileyi	Fishes	Tellico River, between the backwaters of the Tellico Reservoir and the Tellico Ranger Station, in Monroe County, Tennessee
Madtom, yellowfin	Noturus flavipinnis	Fishes	Tellico River, between the backwaters of the Tellico Reservoir and the Tellico Ranger Station, in Monroe County, Tennessee
Madtom, yellowfin	Noturus flavipinnis	Fishes	North Fork Holston River, VA, TN; South Fork Holston River, upstream to Fort Patrick Henry Dam, TN; Holston River downstream to John Sevier Detention Lake Dam, TN; and all tributaries thereto
Pikeminnow (=squawfish), Colorado	Ptychocheilus lucius	Fishes	Salt and Verde River drainages, AZ, NM
Woundfin	Plagopterus argentissimus	Fishes	Gila River drainage, AZ, NM
Bean, Cumberland (pearlymussel)	Villosa trabalis	Clams	U.S.A. (AL; the free-flowing reach of the Tennessee River from the base of Wilson Dam downstream to the backwaters of Pickwick Reservoir [about 12 RM (19 km)] and the lower 5 RM [8 km] of all tributaries to this reach in Colbert and Lauderdale Counties).
Blossom, tubercled (pearlymussel)	Epioblasma torulosa torulosa	Clams	U.S.A. (AL; the free-flowing reach of the Tennessee River from the base of Wilson Dam downstream to the backwaters of Pickwick Reservoir [about 12 RM (19 km)] and the lower 5 RM [8 km] of all tributaries to this reach in Colbert and Lauderdale Counties).
Blossom, turgid (pearlymussel)	Epioblasma turgidula	Clams	U.S.A. (AL; the free-flowing reach of the Tennessee River from the base of Wilson Dam downstream to the backwaters of Pickwick Reservoir [about 12 RM (19 km)] and the lower 5 RM [8 km] of all tributaries to this reach in Colbert and Lauderdale Counties).
Blossom, yellow (pearlymussel)	Epioblasma florentina florentina	Clams	U.S.A. (AL; the free-flowing reach of the Tennessee River from the base of Wilson Dam downstream to the backwaters of Pickwick Reservoir [about 12 RM (19 km)] and the lower 5 RM [8 km] of all tributaries to this reach in Colbert and Lauderdale Counties).
Catspaw (=purple cat's paw pearlymussel)	Epioblasma obliqua obliquata	Clams	U.S.A. (AL; the free-flowing reach of the Tennessee River from the base of Wilson Dam downstream to the backwaters of Pickwick Reservoir [about 12 RM (19 km)] and the lower 5 RM [8 km] of all tributaries to this reach in Colbert and Lauderdale Counties).
Clubshell	Pleurobema clava	Clams	U.S.A. (AL; the free-flowing reach of the Tennessee River from the base of Wilson Dam downstream to the backwaters of Pickwick Reservoir [about 12 RM (19 km)] and the lower 5 RM [8 km] of all tributaries to this reach in Colbert and Lauderdale Counties).
Combshell, Cumberlandian	Epioblasma brevidens	Clams	U.S.A. (AL; the free-flowing reach of the Tennessee River from the base of Wilson Dam downstream to the backwaters of Pickwick Reservoir [about 12 RM (19 km)] and the lower 5 RM [8 km] of all tributaries to this reach in Colbert and Lauderdale Counties).
Lampmussel, Alabama	Lampsilis virescens	Clams	U.S.A. (AL; the free-flowing reach of the Tennessee River from the base of Wilson Dam downstream to the backwaters of Pickwick Reservoir [about 12 RM (19 km)] and the lower 5 RM [8 km] of all tributaries to this reach in Colbert and Lauderdale Counties).
Mapleleaf, winged (mussel)	Quadrula fragosa	Clams	U.S.A. (AL; The free-flowing reach of the Tennessee River from the base of Wilson Dam downstream to the backwaters of Pickwick Reservoir [about 12 RM (19 km)] and the lower 5 RM [8 km] of all tributaries to this reach in Colbert and Lauderdale Counties).
Monkeyface, Cumberland (pearlymussel)	Quadrula intermedia	Clams	U.S.A. (AL; the free-flowing reach of the Tennessee River from the base of Wilson Dam ownstream to the backwaters of Pickwick Reservoir [about 12 RM (19 km)] and the lower 5 RM [8 km] of all tributaries to this reach in Colbert and Lauderdale Counties).
Pearlymussel, birdwing	Conradilla caelata	Clams	U.S.A. (AL; the free-flowing reach of the Tennessee River from the base of Wilson Dam downstream to the backwaters of Pickwick Reservoir [about 12 RM (19 km)] and the lower 5 RM [8 km] of all tributaries to this reach in Colbert and Lauderdale Counties).
Pearlymussel, cracking	Hemistena lata	Clams	U.S.A. (AL; the free-flowing reach of the Tennessee River from the base of Wilson Dam downstream to the backwaters of Pickwick Reservoir [about 12 RM (19 km)] and the lower 5 RM [8 km] of all tributaries to this reach in Colbert and Lauderdale Counties).
Pearlymussel, dromedary	Dromus dromas	Clams	U.S.A. (AL; the free-flowing reach of the Tennessee River from the base of Wilson Dam downstream to the backwaters of Pickwick Reservoir [about 12 RM (19 km)] and the lower 5 RM [8 km] of all tributaries to this reach in Colbert and Lauderdale Counties).

TABLE 2.4

Experimental populations, 2004 [CONTINUED]

Inverted common name	Scientific name	Group code	Where listed
Pigtoe, fine-rayed	Fusconaia cuneolus	Clams	U.S.A. (AL; the free-flowing reach of the Tennessee River from the base of Wilson Dam downstream to the backwaters of Pickwick Reservoir [about 12 RM (19 km)] and the lower 5 RM [8 km] of all tributaries to this reach in Colbert and Lauderdale Counties).
Pigtoe, shiny	Fusconaia cor	Clams	U.S.A. (AL; the free-flowing reach of the Tennessee River from the base of Wilson Dam downstream to the backwaters of Pickwick Reservoir [about 12 RM (19 km)] and the lower 5 RM [8 km] of all tributaries to this reach in Colbert and Lauderdale Counties).
River snail, Anthony's	Athearnia anthonyi	Snails	U.S.A. (AL; the free-flowing reach of the Tennessee River from the base of Wilson Dam downstream to the backwaters of Pickwick Reservoir [about 12 RM (19 km)] and the lower 5 RM [8 km] of all tributaries to this reach in Colbert and Lauderdale Counties).

SOURCE: Adapted from "Experimental Populations," in *Threatened and Endangered Species System (TESS)*, U.S. Fish and Wildlife Service, Washington, DC, 2004 [Online] http://ecos.fws.gov/tess_public/ TESSWebpageExpop [accessed February 11, 2004]

Train Wreck Ahead (St. Louis, MO: Center for the Study of American Business, 1995), Lambert argues that private property will become increasingly restricted under the act. This is because more species are continually being added to the threatened and endangered list, while few are removed from it. Lambert believes the best way to ensure that landowners are treated fairly is to require the federal government to compensate those whose property is devalued through Endangered Species Act land-use restrictions. That way, he says, regulators will be forced to weigh the costs and benefits of recovering a species much more thoroughly and sensibly than they do now.

Is the Endangered Species Act Enough?

Other critics argue, on the other hand, that the Endangered Species Act is not enough. These critics charge that species are often listed for protection so late in the slide to extinction that their populations have already become perilously small. In addition, the listing process can be extremely slow. A number of species have become extinct while federal authorities deliberated about listing action. Even some supporters of the Endangered Species Act believe that implementation of the act has been poor. In part, budget cuts are to blame. For example, in November 2000, the Fish and Wildlife Service announced that it would be unable to list any new species in 2001 because its budget would be entirely used up complying with court orders requiring designation of critical habitat for listed species. This continues to be a problem.

Other critics charge that the Endangered Species Act has failed in its central mission to preserve biodiversity. They argue that more must be done both to enforce the law and to supplement it. The Wilderness Society, an environmental advocacy organization, believes that the Endangered Species Act, even strengthened and fully funded, will not be sufficient to maintain biological diversity. It argues that conservation efforts must be ecosystem-based, and that the Endangered Species Act must be complemented with a biodiversity program which deals with units larger than single species.

FEDERAL LANDS AND WILDLIFE PROTECTION

The History of U.S. Land Management

In the United States' first century as a nation, the federal government owned about 80 percent of the nation's land. Beginning in 1785 the government began to survey and sell its land holdings to states, settlers, and railroad companies. By the end of the nineteenth century, the government had transferred most of its lands to private ownership. It also allowed private use of remaining federal lands. After several decades of rapid development and unrestricted use, much of the nation's lands and natural resources were significantly degraded. Responding to growing concerns, Congress slowly redefined the federal

TABLE 2.5

Endangered or threatened species with the highest reported expenditures, fiscal years 1998–2000

Species	Status	1998 Rank	1999 Rank	2000 Rank
Salmon, chinook	E, T	2, 3	1	1
Steelhead	E, T	5, 6, & 7	2	2
Salmon, coho	T	1	3	3
Salmon, chum	T	Not listed	4	5
Salmon, sockeye	E, T	4	5	4
Woodpecker, red-cockaded	E	8	6	7
Trout, bull	T	14, 152, & 187	7	8
Owl, northern spotted	T	9	8	14
Sea-lion, Steller	E, T	23	9	6
Crane, whooping	E	19	10	11
Flycatcher, southwestern willow	E	10	19	12
Sparrow, Cape Sable seaside	E	62	104	9
Manatee, West Indian	E	39	23	10

E = endangered
T = threatened

SOURCE: "Table 3. The 10 Species (Rank Shown in Bold) with the Highest Reported Expenditures for Fiscal Years 1998–2000," in *Three-Year Summary of Federal and State Endangered and Threatened Species Expenditures: Fiscal Years 1998–2000,* U.S. Fish and Wildlife Service, Washington, DC, November 2003

government's role in land management from temporary to permanent retention as well as active stewardship.

Half a century later, in the 1960s, increasing scientific and public concern about the declining condition of the country's natural resources led Congress to enact a number of laws to conserve both federal and nonfederal lands. These laws cover air, water, soil, plants, and animals. With increasing environmental legislation, the land management framework evolved into a complex collection of agencies, land units, and laws. Different agencies have different priorities, which are reflected in how they manage the resources under their care. The effects of these different missions are particularly evident in places where two agencies hold adjacent lands. For example, the National Park Service (Department of the Interior) oversees Yellowstone National Park, where timber harvesting is prohibited, whereas the U.S. Forest Service (Department of Agriculture) allows large areas to be clear-cut in the adjacent Targhee National Forest in Idaho.

The National Park System

The National Park System began with the establishment of Yellowstone National Park in 1872. By 2004

TABLE 2.6

Reclassified threatened and endangered species, February 2004

Current status	Species name	Status change
T	Argali (Kyrgyzstan, Mongolia, Tajikistan) *(Ovis ammon)*	06/23/1992: E→T
T	Birch, Virginia round-leaf *(Betula uber)*	11/16/1994: E→T
T	Bladderpod, Missouri *(Lesquerella filiformis)*	10/15/2003: E→T
E	Butterfly, Schaus swallowtail *(Heraclides aristodemus ponceanus)*	08/31/1984: T→E
T	Cactus, Siler pincushion *(Pediocactus (=Echinocactus, =Utahia) sileri)*	12/27/1993: E→T
T	Caiman, Yacare *(Caiman yacare)*	05/04/2000: E→T
E	Cavefish, Alabama *(Speoplatyrhinus poulsoni)*	09/28/1988: T→E
E	Chimpanzee (in the wild) *(Pan troglodytes)*	03/12/1990: T→E
T	Chimpanzee (captive) *(Pan troglodytes)*	03/12/1990: E→T
E	Chimpanzee, pygmy *(Pan paniscus)*	03/12/1990: T→E
T	Crocodile, Nile *(Crocodylus niloticus)*	09/30/1988: E→T, 09/23/1993: E→T, 06/17/1987: E→T
T	Crocodile, saltwater (Australia) *(Crocodylus porosus)*	06/24/1996: E→T
T	Daisy, Maguire *(Erigeron maguirei)*	06/19/1996: E→T
T	Darter, snail *(Percina tanasi)*	07/05/1984: E→T
E	Deer, Columbian white-tailed Columbia River distinct population segment *(Odocoileus virginianus leucurus)*	07/24/2003: E→T
T	Eagle, bald (lower 48 states) *(Haliaeetus leucocephalus)*	07/12/1995: E→T
T	Four-o'clock, MacFarlane's *(Mirabilis macfarlanei)*	03/15/1996: E→T
T	Leopard (Gabon to Kenya & southward) *(Panthera pardus)*	01/28/1982: E→T
T	Monarch, Tinian (old world flycatcher) *(Monarcha takatsukasae)*	04/06/1987: E→T
T	Pearlshell, Louisiana *(Margaritifera hembeli)*	09/24/1993: E→T
T	Pogonia, small whorled *(Isotria medeoloides)*	10/06/1994: E→T
T	Prairie dog, Utah *(Cynomys parvidens)*	05/29/1984: E→T
T	Salmon, chinook (fall Snake River) *(Oncorhynchus (=Salmo) tshawytscha)*	11/02/1994: T→E
T	Salmon, chinook (spring/summer Snake River) *(Oncorhynchus (=Salmo) tshawytscha)*	11/02/1994: T→E
E	Salmon, chinook (winter Sacramento River) *(Oncorhynchus (=Salmo) tshawytscha)*	03/23/1994: T→E
E	Sea lion, Steller (western population) *(Eumetopias jubatus)*	06/05/1997: T→E, 05/05/1997: T→E
T	Skullcap, large-flowered *(Scutellaria montana)*	01/14/2002: E→T
T	Trout, Apache *(Oncorhynchus apache)*	07/16/1975: E→T
T	Trout, greenback cutthroat *(Oncorhynchus clarki stomias)*	04/18/1978: E→T
T	Trout, Lahontan cutthroat *(Oncorhynchus clarki henshawi)*	07/16/1975: E→T
T	Trout, Paiute cutthroat *(Oncorhynchus clarki seleniris)*	07/16/1975: E→T
T	Wolf, gray, Western distinct population segment *(Canis lupus)*	04/01/2003: E→T
T	Wolf, gray, Eastern distinct population segment *(Canis lupus)*	04/01/2003: E→T, 03/09/1978: T→E

E = endangered
T = threatened

SOURCE: "Reclassified Threatened and Endangered Species as of 02/10/2004," in *Threatened and Endangered Species System (TESS)*, U.S. Fish and Wildlife Service, Washington, DC 2004 [Online] http://ecos.fws.gov/tess_public/TESSWebpageReclass [accessed February 10, 2004]

there were 384 national parks, monuments, preserves, memorials, historic sites, recreational areas, seashores, and other units that cover a total of more than 83 million acres. The National Park System has units in all U.S. states and territories with the exception of Delaware and the District of Columbia, American Samoa, Guam, Puerto Rico, and the Virgin Islands. In addition to preserving habitats that range from arctic tundra to tropical rain forest, the system protects representatives of more than half of North America's plant species and a large proportion of animal species. The map in Figure 2.4 shows the location and ranges of National Parks in the United States. The National Park Service is also responsible for encouraging public enjoyment of its natural areas. Balancing these objectives shapes the debate over how best to manage the National Parks. There were over 413 million visitations to National Parks in 2003, of which 266 million were recreational.

Working closely with the Fish and Wildlife Service, the National Park Service plays an important role in protecting and restoring threatened and endangered species. Three measures that the NPS takes to protect wildlife include:

1) Education of park visitors about species loss and the value of biodiversity.

2) Enforcement of laws related to protecting species under the Endangered Species Act.

3) Provision of a protected and undisturbed habitat for animals.

The National Parks have played a significant role in the return of several species, including red wolves and peregrine falcons. National Parks also contain designated critical habitat for numerous listed species. However, not all these are disclosed, in order to protect rare species from collectors, vandals, or curiosity seekers. In 2002 the Fish and Wildlife Service reported that 398 federally listed endangered species were found in National Parks. This represents nearly a third of all threatened and endangered U.S. species. Table 2.9 lists some of the types of endan-

TABLE 2.7

Delisted species report, February 2004

Date species listed	First date delisted	Species name	Reason delisted
03/11/1967	06/04/1987	Alligator, American *(Alligator mississippiensis)*	Recovered
11/06/1979	10/01/2003	Barberry, Truckee *(Berberis (=Mahonia) sonnei)*	Taxonomic revision
02/17/1984	02/06/1996	Bidens, cuneate *(Bidens cuneata)*	Taxonomic revision
08/27/1984	02/23/2004	Broadbill, Guam *(Myiagra freycineti)*	Believed extinct
04/28/1976	08/31/1984	Butterfly, Bahama swallowtail *(Heraclides andraemon bonhotei)*	Act amendment
10/26/1979	06/24/1999	Cactus, Lloyd's hedgehog *(Echinocereus lloydii)*	Taxonomic revision
11/07/1979	09/22/1993	Cactus, spineless hedgehog *(Echinocereus triglochidiatus* var. *inermis)*	Not a listable entity
09/17/1980	08/27/2002	Cinquefoil, Robbins' *(Potentilla robbinsiana)*	Recovered
03/11/1967	09/02/1983	Cisco, longjaw *(Coregonus alpenae)*	Extinct
03/11/1967	07/24/2003	Deer, Columbian white-tailed, Douglas County distinct population segment *(Odocoileus virginianus leucurus)*	Recovered, threats removed
06/02/1970	09/12/1985	Dove, Palau ground *(Gallicolumba canifrons)*	Recovered
03/11/1967	07/25/1978	Duck, Mexican (U.S.A. only) *(Anas "diazi")*	Taxonomi revision
06/02/1970	08/25/1999	Falcon, American peregrine *(Falco peregrinus anatum)*	Recovered
06/02/1970	10/05/1994	Falcon, Arctic peregrine *(Falco peregrinus tundrius)*	Recovered
06/02/1970	09/12/1985	Flycatcher, Palau fantail *(Rhipidura lepida)*	Recovered
04/30/1980	12/04/1987	Gambusia, Amistad *(Gambusia amistadensis)*	Extinct
04/29/1986	06/18/1993	Globeberry, Tumamoc *(Tumamoca macdougalii)*	New information discovered
03/11/1967	03/20/2001	Goose, Aleutian Canada *(Branta canadensis leucopareia)*	Recovered
10/11/1979	11/27/1989	Hedgehog cactus, purple-spined *(Echinocereus engelmannii* var. *purpureus)*	Taxonomic revision
12/30/1974	03/09/1995	Kangaroo, eastern gray *(Macropus giganteus)*	Recovered
12/30/1974	03/09/1995	Kangaroo, red *(Macropus rufus)*	Recovered
12/30/1974	03/09/1995	Kangaroo, western gray *(Macropus fuliginosus)*	Recovered
06/02/1977	02/23/2004	Mallard, Mariana *(Anas oustaleti)*	Believed extinct
04/26/1978	09/14/1989	Milk vetch, Rydberg *(Astragalus perianus)*	Recovered
06/02/1970	09/12/1985	Owl, Palau *(Pyroglaux podargina)*	Recovered
06/14/1976	01/09/1984	Pearlymussel, Sampson's *(Epioblasma sampsoni)*	Extinct
06/02/1970	02/04/1985	Pelican, brown (U.S. Atlantic coast, Florida, Alabama) *(Pelecanus occidentalis)*	Recovered
07/13/1982	09/22/1993	Pennyroyal, Mckittrick *(Hedeoma apiculatum)*	New information discovered
03/11/1967	09/02/1983	Pike, blue *(Stizostedion vitreum glaucum)*	Extinct
10/13/1970	01/15/1982	Pupfish, Tecopa *(Cyprinodon nevadensis calidae)*	Extinct
09/26/1986	02/28/2000	Shrew, Dismal Swamp southeastern *(Sorex longirostris fisheri)*	New information discovered
03/11/1967	12/12/1990	Sparrow, dusky seaside *(Ammodramus maritimus nigrescens)*	Extinct
06/04/1973	10/12/1983	Sparrow, Santa Barbara song *(Melospiza melodia graminea)*	Extinct
11/11/1977	11/22/1983	Treefrog, pine barrens (Florida population) *(Hyla andersonii)*	New information discovered
09/13/1996	04/26/2000	Trout, coastal cutthroat (Umpqua River) *(Oncorhynchus clarki clarki)*	Taxonomic revision
06/14/1976	02/29/1984	Turtle, Indian flap-shelled *(Lissemys punctata punctata)*	Erroneous data
06/02/1970	06/16/1994	Whale, gray (except where listed) *(Eschrichtius robustus)*	Recovered
03/11/1967	04/01/2003	Wolf, gray U.S.A. (delisting of all other lower 48 states or portions of lower 48 states not otherwise included in the 3 distinct population segments). *(Canis lupus)*	Taxonomic revision
07/19/1990	10/07/2003	Woolly star, Hoover's *(Eriastrum hooveri)*	New information discovered

SOURCE: "Delisted Species Report as of 02/10/2004," in *Threatened and Endangered Species System (TESS)*, U.S. Fish and Wildlife Service, Washington, DC 2004 [Online] http://ecos.fws.gov/tess_public/TESSWebpageDelisted?listings=0 [accessed February 10, 2004]

gered, threatened, proposed, and candidate species that are found within the National Park System. Parks that provide important habitat for disproportionately large numbers of endangered species are listed in Table 2.10. Several are in Hawaii and California, states that have a disproportionate number of listed threatened and endangered species.

The National Forests

The National Forests encompass more land than the National Park Service, including nearly 200 million acres in 155 national forests and 20 national grasslands. (See Table 2.11.) A map of the locations of U.S. National Forests is shown in Figure 2.5. In addition to forest and grassland areas, National Forest lands also include numerous lakes and ponds. National Forest land is, in general, not conserved to the same degree as National Park lands. For example, much logging occurs within these forests.

Within the Forest Service, the Threatened, Endangered, and Sensitive Species Program focuses on wildlife conservation. A total of 420, or 33 percent of, listed endangered or threatened species are found on National Forest lands. In addition 35 proposed species and 257 candidate species also make use of National Forest or Grassland habitats. The Forest Service has also designated over 2,900 species as sensitive, and has developed protective measures to help keep these species from becoming endangered.

TABLE 2.8

Species proposed for status change or delisting, February 2004

Status	Proposal date	Species name
AT	03/26/1998	Bat, Mariana fruit (=Mariana flying fox) *(Pteropus mariannus mariannus)*
AD	07/06/1999	Eagle, bald *(Haliaeetus leucocephalus)*
AD	05/22/2003	Frankenia, Johnston's *(Frankenia johnstonii)*
AT	08/05/1993	Hawk, Hawaiian (='Io) *(Buteo solitarius)*
AD	02/22/1999	Monarch, Tinian (old world flycatcher) *(Monarcha takatsukasae)*
AT	09/22/1993	Poolfish, Pahrump *(Empetrichthys latos)*
AT	pending	Salamander, California tiger *(Ambystoma californiense)*
AT	pending	Salamander, California tiger *(Ambystoma californiense)*
PT(S/A)	01/09/2001	Trout, Dolly Varden *(Salvelinus malma)*

AD=proposed delisting
AT=proposed reclassification to threatened
PT (SA)=proposed similarity of appearance to a threatened taxon

SOURCE: "Species Proposed for Status Change or Delisting as of 02/10/2004," in *Threatened and Endangered Species System*, U.S. Fish and Wildlife Service, Washington, DC, 2004 [Online] http://ecos.fws.gov/tess_public/ TESSWebpageProposedDr [accessed February 10, 2004]

TABLE 2.9

Endangered, threatened, proposed, and candidate species found in units of the National Park Service, June 1, 2001

Taxonomic group	Species
Plants	193
Invertebrates	43
Fish	40
Amphibians	4
Reptiles	19
Birds	53
Mammals	46
Total	**398**

SOURCE: Loyal A. Mehrhoff and Peter A. Dratch, "Table 1. Endangered, Threatened, Proposed, and Candidate Species Found in Units of the National Park Service," in "Endangered Species and the National Park Service," *Endangered Species Bulletin*, vol. XXVII, no. 1, U.S. Fish and Wildlife Service, Washington, DC, January/February 2002

The National Wildlife Refuge System

The National Wildlife Refuge System is the only network of federal lands and waters managed principally for the protection of fish and wildlife. In 1999, the total acreage in the system was well over 93 million. (See Table 2.12.) This includes 547 Wildlife Refuges; 38 Wetland Management Districts, which administer over 26,000 Waterfowl Protection Areas; and 50 Coordination Areas, which are jointly administered with a state wildlife agency. Figure 2.6 shows the distribution of units within the National Wildlife Refuge System.

The first unit of what would later become the refuge system was the Pelican Island Bird Reservation in Florida, established in 1903 to protect the dwindling populations of wading birds in Florida. Today the sixteen wildlife refuges in Alaska account for 83 percent of land in the refuge system. Yukon Delta, the largest of the Alaskan refuges, comprises 20 million acres. Approximately one-third of the total refuge acreage is wetland habitat, reflecting the importance of wetlands for wildlife survival.

Of the many species listed under the Endangered Species Act, a quarter have habitat on National Wildlife Refuges. Many other listed species use refuge lands on a temporary basis for breeding or migratory rest stops. A list of wildlife refuges established explicitly for endangered species appears, by state, along with the species of concern and the number of protected acres in Table 2.13. Lists of endangered animals and plants found within the National Wildlife Refuge System appear in Table 2.14 and Table 2.15 respectively. Virtually every species of bird in North America has been recorded in the refuge system. The wide variety of wildlife found on refuges also includes over 220 mammals, 250 reptiles and amphibians, and 200 fish species.

Funding limitations constrain efforts to manage wildlife refuges. The Fish and Wildlife Service reports that the refuge system's current annual funding is less than half the amount needed to meet established objectives. The 2004 budget for the system included $291.6 million for refuge operations and $99.9 million for refuge maintenance.

America's Wild Lands under Attack

Since the passage of the Wilderness Act in 1964, 630 areas have been designated wilderness. These cover a total of more than 103 million acres. Much of the designated land is located within the National Wildlife Refuge System under the management of the Fish and Wildlife Service. Table 2.16 shows the acreage of wilderness areas within the National Wildlife Refuges and National Fish Hatcheries Systems. Unlike National Parks, which are intended for use by large numbers of visitors, wilderness areas are intended to be pristine, with limited access and no amenities. True wilderness remains, for most humans, a place to visit only rarely. Nonetheless, the number of people using wilderness areas has increased steadily. Many visitors, as well as park managers, have wearied particularly of the intrusions of civilization—in the form of cell phones, snowmobiles, and aircraft—into wilderness areas.

Many national parks and monuments are suffering as well, in part because of the high volume of visitors. More than five million people visit the Grand Canyon each year. On a busy day, 6,500 vehicles compete for 2,000 parking spaces. By 2001, Grand Canyon, Zion, and Yosemite National Parks required visitors to use mass transit.

In 1997 the Wilderness Society listed "America's 10 Most Endangered Wild Lands." These were identified

FIGURE 2.4

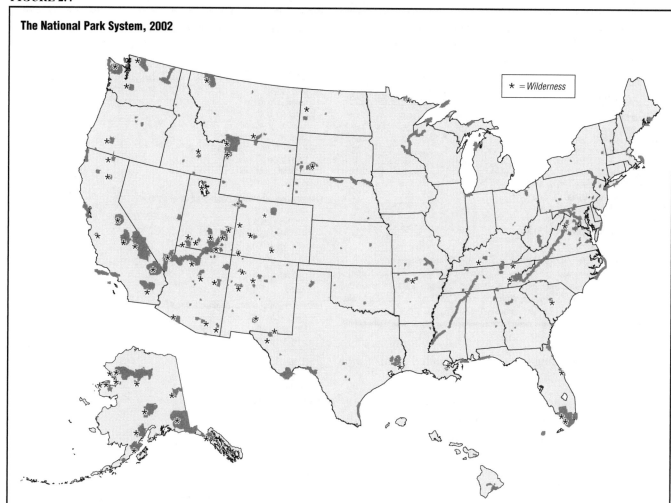

The National Park System, 2002

★ = Wilderness

SOURCE: Adapted from Loyal A. Mehrhoff and Peter A. Dratch, "The National Park System," in "Endangered Species and the National Park Service," *Endangered Species Bulletin*, vol. XXVII, no. 1, U.S. Fish and Wildlife Service, Washington, DC, January/February 2002 and "NPS Wilderness," in *Public Use Statistics Office*, National Park Service, U.S. Department of the Interior, Washington, DC [Online] http://www2.nature.nps.gov/stats/ [accessed February 10, 2004]

based on their natural resources, national significance, and the immediate threats to their integrity. Most are wildlife reserves. Among the ten were the Arctic National Wildlife Refuge (Alaska), Klamath Basin National Wildlife Refuge (Oregon/California), Snoqualmie Pass (Washington), Boundary Waters Canoe Area (Minnesota), and the Grand Staircase/Escalante National Monument (Utah). Also included were Owyhee Canyonlands (Idaho), Okefenokee National Wildlife Refuge (Georgia/Florida), Cabeza Prieta National Wildlife Refuge (Arizona), the Whitney Estate in New York, and California's Mojave Desert.

OIL DRILLING IN THE ARCTIC NATIONAL WILDLIFE REFUGE? The Arctic National Wildlife Refuge (ANWR) is the largest National Wildlife Refuge in the United States. It harbors the greatest number of plant and animal species of any park or refuge in the arctic, including a multitude of unique species such as caribou, musk oxen, polar bears, Arctic foxes, and snow geese. Because of the harsh climate, Arctic habitats are gener-

ally characterized by short food chains and extreme vulnerability to habitat disturbance. The majority of Arctic species already live "on the edge." Consequently, the decline of even a single species is likely to have dramatic effects on the entire community.

The protected status of the Arctic National Wildlife Refuge has been challenged by large oil companies and their political supporters. There has been interest in tapping the oil deposits in northern Alaska since the early 1900s. The area was first explored for oil and gas resources in the 1940s and 1950s. It was also in the 1950s, however, that people became aware of the ecological value of these lands, and a compromise was reached in which the northeastern part of the state was set aside as a wildlife range (later refuge), while drilling began—and continues—in the northwestern part of the state. Figure 2.7 shows the northern Alaskan refuge and oil drilling areas respectively. Production of oil and gas in the refuge area—the five percent of Alaska's North Slope not

TABLE 2.10

Areas in the National Park System with the largest numbers of endangered, threatened, proposed, and candidate species, June 1, 2001

National Park	Plants	Animals	Total
Haleakala National Park, Hawai'i	35	12	47
Hawaii Volcanoes National Park, Hawai'i	27	15	42
Channel Islands National Park, California	15	18	33
Golden Gate National Recreation Area, California	14	15	29
Santa Monica Mountains National Recreation Area, California	10	13	23
Kalaupapa National Historic Park, Hawai'i	15	7	22
Natchez Trace Parkway, Mississippi	8	12	20
Everglades National Park, Florida	7	12	19
Great Smoky Mountains National Park, Tennessee	4	12	16

SOURCE: Loyal A. Mehrhoff and Peter A. Dratch, "Table 2. Areas in the National Park System with the Largest Numbers of Endangered, Threatened, Proposed, and Candidate Species," in "Endangered Species and the National Park Service," *Endangered Species Bulletin,* vol. XXVII, no. 1, U.S. Fish and Wildlife Service, Washington, DC, January/February 2002

TABLE 2.11

National Forest Service acreage, 2004

Area kind	National Forest Service acreage
National totals	
National forests	187,860,217
Purchase units	359,351
National grasslands	3,839,167
Land utilization projects	1,876
Research and experimental areas	64,871
Other areas	295,814
National preserves	89,716
Totals	**192,511,012**
Western regional totals (Regions 1 through 6)	
National forests	141,121,533
Purchase units	12,244
National grasslands	3,800,985
Land utilization projects	1,834
Research and experimental areas	60,598
Other areas	108,431
National preserves	89,716
Totals	**145,195,341**
Eastern regional totals (Regions 8 and 9)	
National forests	24,757,779
Purchase units	347,107
National grasslands	38,182
Land utilization projects	42
Research and experimental areas	4,273
Other areas	187,383
Totals	**25,334,766**
Alaska region totals (Region 10)	
National forests	21,980,905
Totals	**21,980,905**

SOURCE: Adapted from "Table 1—National and Regional Areas Summary," in *Land Areas Report as of September 30, 2003,* U.S. Department of Agriculture Forest Service, Washington, DC, January 2004 [Online] http://www.fs.fed.us/land/staff/lar/LAR03/table1.htm [accessed February 10, 2004]

already open to drilling—was also prohibited at this time unless specifically authorized by Congress.

Environmentalists argue that studies by the Fish and Wildlife Service suggest that oil drilling in the refuge will harm many Arctic species, by taking over habitat, damaging habitats through pollution, interfering with species activities directly, or increasing opportunities for invasive species such as gulls and ravens through the availability of garbage as a food source.

When Republicans took control of Congress in 1995, they passed legislation to allow for drilling in ANWR. President Clinton vetoed this bill, saying, "I want to protect this biologically rich wilderness permanently." The succeeding administration under George W. Bush has been much more supportive of drilling in the refuge. Attention is now focused particularly on the "1002 Area" within the refuge, which some environmentalists consider one of the most ecologically diverse and valuable. Among the species that would be affected if drilling is permitted are polar bears, whose preferred sites for building dens are in the 1002 Area (see Figure 2.8) and caribou, which use this area for calving—giving birth to young (see Figure 2.9).

Since the terrorist attacks of September 11, 2001, Republican politicians have tried to emphasize the national security aspects of ANWR. They argue that America cannot be truly secure until it reduces its dependence on foreign oil, much of which comes from unstable regions of the world such as the Mideast. One enthusiastic supporter of drilling in ANWR is Walter J. Hickel, former Secretary of the Interior and twice-governor of Alaska. In an article titled, "ANWR Oil" (*The American Enterprise,* June 2002), Hickel states, "Over-dependence on foreign oil exposes us to energy blackmail and compromises our

ability to protect our citizens and assist our friends in times of crisis. Our goal as Americans must be to produce as much energy as we can for ourselves." Hickel goes on to state his belief that "[t]he very small portion of the refuge with oil potential can be explored and drilled without damaging the environment."

In August 2001 the House of Representatives again passed a bill allowing for drilling within the refuge. However, the Senate rejected this proposal in April 2002 and the refuge continues to be protected. In 2004 the Bush administration pressed again for oil drilling in ANWR, and included a drilling plan in its proposed 2005 budget. Oil drilling within ANWR will remain a bone of contention among politicians and the American public.

ECOSYSTEM CONSERVATION—AN ALTERNATIVE APPROACH

In the 1990s there was growing concern that traditional methods of species protection, using a species-by-species approach, were ineffective. Many alternatives were proposed. One of the most popular was a method variously termed the "habitat," "ecosystem," or "community" approach. The Fish and Wildlife Service defines an ecosys-

FIGURE 2.5

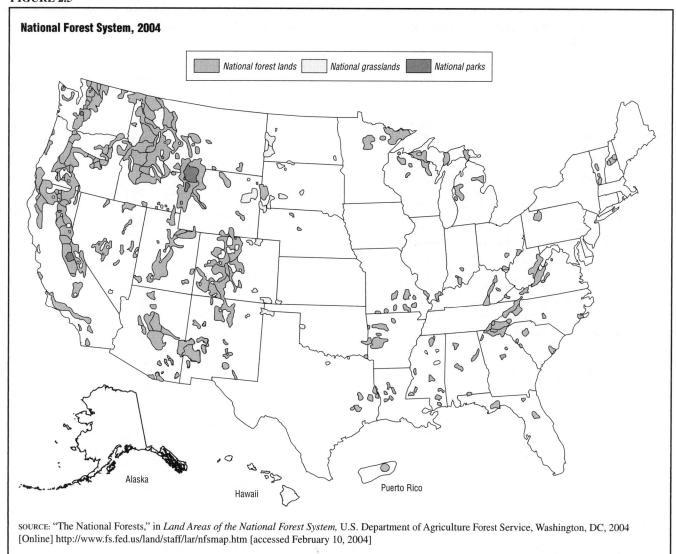

National Forest System, 2004

National forest lands National grasslands National parks

Alaska

Hawaii

Puerto Rico

SOURCE: "The National Forests," in *Land Areas of the National Forest System,* U.S. Department of Agriculture Forest Service, Washington, DC, 2004 [Online] http://www.fs.fed.us/land/staff/lar/nfsmap.htm [accessed February 10, 2004]

tem as a "geographic area including all the living organisms (people, plants, animals, and microorganisms), their physical surroundings (such as soil, water, and air), and the natural cycles that sustain them." Central to these approaches is a focus on conservation of large intact areas of habitat. It is hoped that by focusing on entire habitats, rather than individual species recovery, numerous species will be protected before they reach critically low population sizes.

The National Biological Service was created in 1993 by the Department of the Interior. This agency is responsible for gathering, analyzing, and disseminating biological information necessary for stewardship of the nation's resources. The National Biological Service conducted the first large-scale study of ecosystems in the United States and found that many U.S. ecosystems are imperiled. In 1996 the National Biological Service was integrated into the United States Geological Survey as the Biological Resources Division.

In 1993 the White House Office on Environmental Policy established the Interagency Ecosystem Manage-

ment Task Force to implement an ecosystem approach to environmental management. The task force included representatives from each of the four primary federal land-management agencies. A total of $700 million was appropriated to facilitate the implementations. The ambitious proposals included four pilot projects addressing conservation of old-growth forests of the Pacific Northwest, habitats in the Everglades and Florida Bay, the urban watershed of the Anacostia River in Maryland and the District of Columbia, and Alaska's Prince William Sound. However, due to budget cuts enacted by Congress in 1994, efforts on the projects were sidelined.

By the turn of the twenty-first century, however, progress had been made on a number of key ecosystem fronts:

• In the late 1990s the Clinton administration secured $1.2 billion for Everglades restoration and added 70,000 acres to the Everglades National Park.

• A budget appropriation of $250 million was designated for the preservation of the Headwaters Forest in

TABLE 2.12

Summary of National Wildlife Refuge System land holdings, as of September 30, 1999

(In acres)

Reserved From Public Domain	Acquired by Other Federal Agency	Devise or Gift	Purchased	Agreement, Easement or Lease	Total
82,085,483.61	2,717,198.55	664,254.82	4,532,441.93	3,605,242.69	93,604,621.6

SOURCE: "National Wildlife Refuge System Acreage," in *Annual Report of Lands under Control of the U.S. Fish and Wildlife Service, as of September 30, 1999,* U.S. Fish and Wildlife Service, Washington, DC, September 30, 1999 [Online] http://refugedata.fws.gov/databases/national.taf?_function= list&<@UserReferenceArgument>&_start=1 [accessed February 10, 2004]

Northern California, where 2,000-year-old redwoods stand. Additionally, $220 million was appropriated for the restoration of the California Bay-Delta ecosystem, including $30 million in water management funds for the Bay-Delta.

• Death Valley National Park, the largest National Park in the lower 48 states, was created.

• The Clinton administration successfully blocked congressional proposals to open the Arctic National Wildlife Refuge, located in Alaska, to oil drilling. A second attempt to open the refuge to drilling was defeated by the Senate in 2002.

Adaptive Management

Adaptive management describes a conservation strategy that involves active, experimental manipulation of the environment in order to restore damaged ecosystems. It is being pursued in a variety of primarily aquatic habitats, including the Florida Everglades, San Francisco Bay, and the Great Barrier Reef in Australia.

One of the oldest examples of adaptive management is an effort to restore Colorado River habitats by the Department of the Interior and the U.S. Bureau of Reclamation. Colorado River ecosystems were originally damaged by water control measures following the completion of the Glen Canyon Dam at the northern edge of the Grand Canyon in 1963. The dam was built to store water for portions of Colorado, New Mexico, Utah, and Wyoming, as well as to provide hydroelectric power. Water flow management has caused severe ecological damage in Glen Canyon National Recreation Area and Grand Canyon National Park. This includes large-scale erosion, including the loss of sandy beaches, invasion by non-native species, and the extinction of four species of native fish. Another native fish species, the humpback chub, is currently in serious decline, partly because of the purposeful introduction of predatory rainbow trout. The

TABLE 2.13

National Wildlife Refuges for endangered species, 2004

State	Unit name	Species of concern	Unit acreage
Alabama	Blowing Wind Cave National Wildlife Refuge	Indiana bat, gray bat	264
	Fern Cave National Wildlife Refuge	Indiana bat, gray bat	199
	Key Cave National Wildlife Refuge	Alabama cavefish, gray bat	1,060
	Watercress Darter National Wildlife Refuge	Watercress darter	7
Arkansas	Logan Cave National Wildlife Refuge	Cave crayfish, gray bat, Indiana bat, Ozark cavefish	124
Arizona	Buenos Aires National Wildlife Refuge	Masked bobwhite quail	116,585
	Leslie Canyon	Gila topminnow, Yaqui chub, peregrine falcon	2,765
	San Bernardino National Wildlife Refuge	Gila topminnow, Yaqui chub, Yaqui catfish, beautiful shiner, Huachuca water umbel	2,369
California	Antioch Dunes National Wildlife Refuge	Lange's metalmark butterfly, Antioch dunes evening-primrose, Contra Costa wallflower	55
	Bitter Creek National Wildlife Refuge	California condor	14,054
	Blue Ridge National Wildlife Refuge	California condor	897
	Castle Rock National Wildlife Refuge	Aleutian Canada goose	14
	Coachella Valley National Wildlife Refuge	Coachello Valley fringe-toed lizard	3,592
	Don Edwards San Francisco Bay National Wildlife Refuge	California clapper rail, California least tern, salt marsh harvest mouse	21,524
	Ellicott Slough National Wildlife Refuge	Santa Cruz long-toed salamander	139
	Hopper Mountain National Wildlife Refuge	California condor	2,471
	Sacramento River National Wildlife Refuge	Valley elderberry longhorn beetle, bald eagle, least Bell's vireo	7,884
	San Diego National Wildlife Refuge	San Diego fairy shrimp, San Diego mesa mint, Otay mesa mint, California orcutt grass, San Diego button celery	1,840
	San Joaquin River National Wildlife Refuge	Aleutian Canada goose	1,638
	Seal Beach National Wildlife Refuge	Light-footed clapper rail, California least tern	911
	Sweetwater Marsh National Wildlife Refuge	Light-footed clapper rail	316
	Tijuana Slough National Wildlife Refuge	Light-footed clapper rail	1,023

humpback chub has been listed as endangered since 1967 and has declined by 75 percent in the last 10 years alone.

As adaptive management is dependent on experimentation and manipulation, it can sometimes lead to unintended and unfortunate consequences. For example, an early effort at restoring Colorado River habitats involved sending huge amounts of water down the river. This was expected to lift sand from the river bottom and create sandy beaches, and did. However, the sand was quickly

TABLE 2.13

National Wildlife Refuges for endangered species, 2004 [CONTINUED]

State	Unit name	Species of concern	Unit acreage
Florida	Archie Carr National Wildlife Refuge	Loggerhead sea turtle, green sea turtle	29
	Crocodile Lake National Wildlife Refuge	American crocodile	6,686
	Crystal River National Wildlife Refuge	West Indian manatee	80
	Florida Panther National Wildlife Refuge	Florida panther	23,379
	Hobe Sound National Wildlife Refuge	Loggerhead sea turtle, green sea turtle	980
	Lake Wales Ridge National Wildlife Refuge	Florida scrub jay, snakeroot, scrub blazing star, Carter's mustard, papery whitlow wort, Florida bonamia, scrub lupine, highlands scrub hypericum, Garett's mint, scrub mint, pygmy gringe tree, wireweed, Florida ziziphus, scrub plum, eastern indigo snake, bluetail mole skink, sand skink	659
	National Key Deer Refuge	Key deer	8,542
	St. Johns National Wildlife Refuge	Dusky seaside sparrow	6,255
Hawaii	Hakalau Forest National Wildlife Refuge	Akepa, akiapolaau, 'o'u, Hawaiian hawk, Hawaiian creeper	32,730
	Hanalei National Wildlife Refuge	Hawaiian stilt, Hawaiian coot, Hawaiian moorhen, Hawaiian duck	917
	Huleia National Wildlife Refuge	Hawaiian stilt, Hawaiian coot, Hawaiian moorhen, Hawaiian duck	241
	James C. Campbell National Wildlife Refuge	Hawaiian stilt, Hawaiian coot, Hawaiian moorhen, Hawaiian duck	164
	Kakahaia National Wildlife Refuge	Hawaiian stilt, Hawaiian coot	45
	Kealia Pond National Wildlife Refuge	Hawaiian stilt, Hawaiian coot	691
	Pearl Harbor National Wildlife Refuge	Hawaiian stilt	61
Iowa	Driftless Area National Wildlife Refuge	Iowa Pleistocene snail	521
Massachusetts	Massasoit National Wildlife Refuge	Plymouth red-bellied turtle	184
Michigan	Kirtland's warbler Wildlife Management Area	Kirtland's warbler	6,535
Mississippi	Mississippi sandhill crane National Wildlife Refuge	Mississippi sandhill crane	19,713
Missouri	Ozark cavefish National Wildlife Refuge	Ozark cavefish	42
	Pilot Knob National Wildlife Refuge	Indiana bat	90
Nebraska	Karl E. Mundt National Wildlife Refuge	Bald eagle	19

TABLE 2.13

National Wildlife Refuges for endangered species, 2004 [CONTINUED]

State	Unit name	Species of concern	Unit acreage
Nevada	Ash Meadows National Wildlife Refuge	Devil's Hole pupfish, Warm Springs pupfish, Ash Meadows amargosa pupfish, Ash Meadows speckled dace, Ash Meadows naucorid, Ash Meadows blazing star, amargosa niterwort, Ash Meadows milk vetch, Ash Meadows sunray, Spring-loving centaury, Ash Meadows gumplant, Ash Meadows invesia	13,268
	Moapa Valley National Wildlife Refuge	Moapa dace	32
Oklahoma	Ozark Plateau National Wildlife Refuge	Ozark big-eared bat, gray bat	2,208
Oregon	Bear Valley National Wildlife Refuge	Bald eagle	4,200
	Julia Butler Hansen Refuge for Columbian White-tail Deer	Columbian white-tailed deer	2,750
	Nestucca Bay National Wildlife Refuge	Aleutian Canada goose	457
South Dakota	Karl E. Mundt National Wildlife Refuge	Bald eagle	1,044
Texas	Attwater Prairie Chicken National Wildlife Refuge	Attwater's greater prairie chicken	8,007
	Balcones Canyonlands National Wildlife Refuge	Black-capped vireo, Golden-cheeked warbler	14,144
Virgin Islands	Green Cay National Wildlife Refuge	St. Croix ground lizard	14
	Sandy Point National Wildlife Refuge	Leatherback sea turtle	327
Virginia	James River National Wildlife Refuge	Bald eagle	4,147
	Mason Neck National Wildlife Refuge	Bald eagle	2,276
Washington	Julia Butler Hansen Refuge for Columbian White-tail Deer	Columbian white-tailed deer	2,777
Wyoming	Mortenson Lake National Wildlife Refuge	Wyoming toad	1,776

SOURCE: "National Wildlife Refuges Established for Endangered Species," in *America's National Wildlife Refuge System,* U.S. Fish and Wildlife Service, Washington, DC, 2004 [Online] http://refuges.fws.gov/habitats/endSpRefuges.html [accessed February 10, 2004]

through the Grand Canyon for three months—this may kill rainbow trout eggs and reduce the numbers of this non-native species. Native fish species tend to inhabit side channels, and are less likely to be affected. There are also plans in place to warm water released from the dam, which the Fish and Wildlife Service believes would aid endangered native fish species.

INTERNATIONAL EFFORTS

The United Nations Environment Programme (UNEP) was established to address diverse environmental issues on an international level. Many of its conventions have been extremely valuable in protecting global biodiversity and natural resources. UNEP has also helped to regulate pollution and the use of toxic chemicals.

lost again to fluctuating river flows. In 2003 attention turned to the Paria River, which supplies the Colorado River with sand. The Paria feeds into the Colorado downstream of the Glen Canyon Dam, and it is hoped that a large pulse of floodwater from the dam following natural monsoon storms will carry sand to new beaches along the Colorado. Another plan underway at the end of 2003 called for the running of high fluctuating flows of water

FIGURE 2.6

National Wildlife Refuge System, 2004

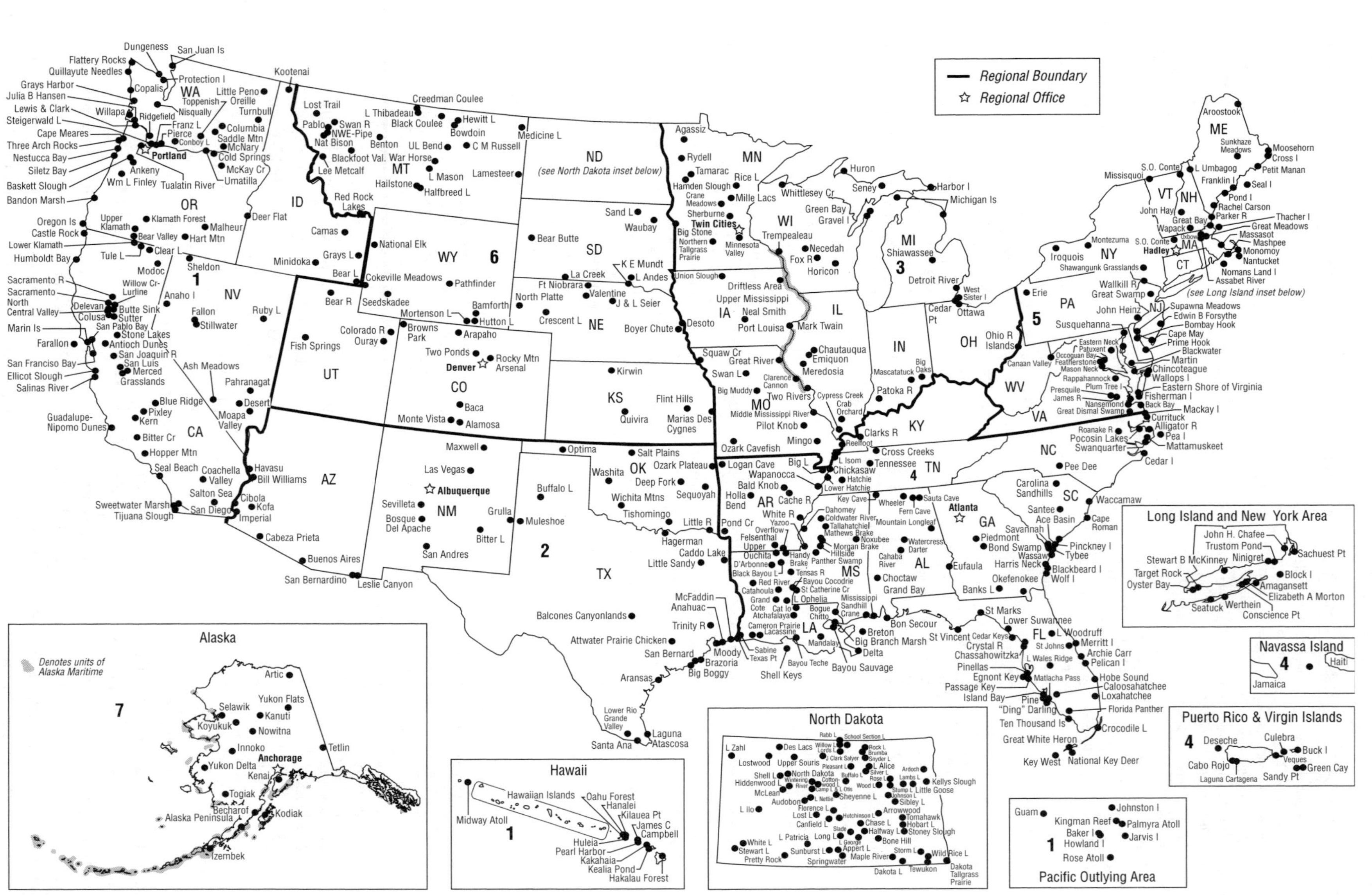

SOURCE: "National Wildlife Refuge System," in *National Wildlife Refuge System*, U.S. Fish and Wildlife Service, Washington, DC, September 30, 2003 [Online] http://refuges.fws.gov/pdfs/refugeMap0930_2003.pdf [accessed February 10, 2004]

TABLE 2.14

Threatened and endangered animal species found on the National Wildlife Refuge System, 2004

The following list includes all of the federally listed threatened and endangered animal species that are known to occur on units of the National Wildlife Refuge System.

Amphibians
- Frog, California red-legged
- Salamander, Cheat Mountain
- Salamander, Santa Cruz long-toed
- Toad, Arroyo
- Toad, Wyoming

Birds
- Akepa, Hawaii
- Akiapolaau
- Albatross, short-tailed
- Blackbird, Yellow-shouldered
- Bobwhite, masked (quail)
- Broadbill, Guam
- Caracara, Audubon's crested
- Condor, California
- Coot, Hawaiian
- Crane, Mississippi sandhill
- Crane, whooping
- Creeper, Hawaii
- Crow, Mariana
- Curlew, Eskimo
- Duck, Hawaiian
- Duck, Laysan
- Eider, spectacled
- Eider, Stellar's
- Elepaio, Ohau
- Falcon, Northern Aplomado
- Finch, Laysan
- Finch, Nihoa
- Flycatcher, Southwestern Willow
- Gnatcatcher, Coastal California
- Goose, Hawaiian (=nene)
- Hawk, Hawaiian
- Jay, Florida scrub
- Kingfisher, Guam Micronesian
- Kite, Everglade snail
- Millerbird, Nihoa
- Moorhen (=gallilnule), Hawaiian common
- Moorhen, Mariana common
- Murrelet, marbled
- 'O'u (honeycreeper)
- Owl, northern spotted
- Pelican, brown
- Plover, pipin
- Plover, western snowy (Pacific coastal)
- Prairie chicken, Attwater's greater
- Pygmy owl, cactus ferruginous
- Rail, California clapper
- Rail, light-footed clapper
- Rail, Yuma clapper
- Stilt, Hawaiian
- Stork, wood
- Swiftlet, Vanikoro
- Tern, California least
- Tern, least (interior)
- Tern, roseate
- Vireo, black-capped
- Vireo, least Bell's
- Warbler, Bachman's
- Warbler, golden-cheeked
- Warbler, Kirtland's
- White-eye, bridled
- Woodpecker, red-cockaded

Clams
- Clubshell
- Fanshell

- Mussel, ring pink (=golf stick pearly)
- Mussel, winged mapleleaf
- Pearlymussel, Higgin's eye
- Pearlymussel, orange-footed pimpleback
- Pearlymussel, pink mucket
- Pigtoe, rough
- Pocketbook, fat
- Riffleshell, northern

Crustaceans
- Cambarus aculabrum (crayfish with no common name)
- Fairy shrimp, riverside
- Fairy shrimp, San Diego
- Tadpole shrimp, vernal pool

Fishes
- Catfish, Yaqui
- Cavefish, Alabama
- Cavefish, Ozark
- Chub, bonytail
- Chub, humpback
- Chub, Oregon
- Chub, Yaqui
- Dace, Ash Meadows speckled
- Dace, Moapa
- Darter, watercress
- Gambusia, Pecos
- Goby, tidewater
- Madtom, Neosho
- Madtom, pygmy
- Minnow, Rio Grande silvery
- Poolfish (=killifish), Pahrump
- Pupfish, Ash Meadows Amargosa
- Pupfish, desert
- Pupfish, Devils Hole
- Pupfish, Warm Springs
- Salmon, Chinook
- Shiner, beautiful
- Shiner, Pecos bluntnose
- Shiner, Topeka
- Squawfish, Colorado
- Sturgeon, gulf
- Sturgeon, pallid
- Sturgeon, shortnose
- Sturgeon, white, Kootenai River population
- Sucker, Lost River
- Sucker, Razorback
- Sucker, short-nose
- Topminnow, Gila (including Yaqui)

Insects
- Beetle, American burying
- Beetle, valley elderberry longhorn
- Butterfly, Karner blue
- Butterfly, Lange's metalmark
- Butterfly, Quino checkerspot
- Butterfly, Schaus swallowtail
- Butterfly, Smith's blue
- Dragonfly, Hine's emerald
- Naucorid, Ash Meadows

Mammals
- Bat, gray
- Bat, Hawaiian hoary
- Bat, Indiana
- Bat, lesser (=Sanborn's) long-nosed
- Bat, little Mariana fruit
- Bat, Mariana Fruit

- Bat, Ozark big-eared
- Bear, grizzly
- Bear, Louisiana black
- Deer, Columbian white-tailed
- Deer, Key
- Ferret, black-footed
- Fox, San Joaquin kit
- Jaguar
- Jaguarundi
- Manatee, West Indian (Florida)
- Mouse, Alabama beach
- Mouse, Key Largo cotton
- Mouse, salt marsh harvest
- Mouse, southeastern beach
- Ocelot
- Panther, Florida
- Pronghorn, Sonoran
- Puma, eastern
- Rabbit, lower Keys
- Rabbit, riparian brush
- Rat, Morro Bay kangaroo
- Rat, rice (=silver rice)
- Rat, Tipton kangaroo
- Sea-lion, Steller (=northern)
- Seal, Hawaiian monk
- Squirrel, Delmarva Peninsula fox
- Squirrel, Virginia northern flying
- Whale, blue
- Whale, bowhead
- Whale, finback
- Whale, gray
- Whale, humpback
- Whale, right
- Whale, Sei
- Whale, sperm
- Wolf, gray
- Wolf, Mexican
- Wolf, red
- Woodrat, Key Largo

Reptiles
- Anole, Culebra Island giant
- Crocodile, American
- Lizard, blunt-nosed leopard
- Lizard, Coachella Valley fringe-toed
- Lizard, St. Croix ground
- Skink, blue-tailed mole
- Skink, sand
- Snake, Atlantic salt marsh
- Snake, Eastern indigo
- Snake, giant garter
- Snake, northern copperbelly water
- Tortoise, desert
- Tortoise, gopher
- Turtle, green sea
- Turtle, hawksbill sea
- Turtle, Kemp's (=Atlantic) ridley sea
- Turtle, leatherback sea
- Turtle, loggerhead sea
- Turtle, Plymouth redbelly
- Turtle, ringed map (=sawback)

Snails
- Snail, Iowa pleistocence
- Snail, Oahu tree
- Snail, Stock Island tree

SOURCE: "Threatened and Endangered Animal Species Found on the National Wildlife Refuge System," in *America's National Wildlife Refuge System*, U.S. Fish and Wildlife Service, Washington, DC, 2004 [Online] http://refuges.fws.gov/habitats/EndSpAnimals.html [accessed February 10, 2004]

TABLE 2.15

Threatened and endangered plant species found on the National Wildlife Refuge System, 2004

The following list includes all of the federally listed threatened and endangered plant species that are known to occur on units of the National Wildlife Refuge System. The species are listed in alphabetical order by scientific name.

- *Aconitum noveboracense*—northern wild monkshood
- *Aeschynomene virginica*—sensitive joint-vetch
- *Agalinis acuta*—sandplain gerardia
- *Amaranthus brownii*—Brown's pigweed
- *Amaranthus pumilus*—seabeach amaranth
- *Apios priceana*—Price's potato bean
- *Arenaria paludicola*—marsh sandwort
- *Aristida chasae*—no common name
- *Asclepias meadii*— Mead's milkweed
- *Asimina tetramera*— four-petal pawpaw
- *Asplenium scolopendrium* var. *americana*—American hart's-tongue fern
- *Astragalus phoenix*—Ash Meadows milk-vetch
- *Boltonia decurrens*—Decurrent false aster
- *Bonamia grandiflora*—Florida bonamia
- *Calyptranthes thomasiana*—Thomas' lidflower
- *Centaurium namophilum*—spring-loving centaury
- *Cereus eriophorus* var. *fragrans*—fragrant prickly apple
- *Cereus robinii*—Key tree-cactus
- *Chamaesyce garberi (= Euphorbia garberi)* Garber's spurge
- *Chamaesyce rockii*—'akoko
- *Chionanthus pygmaeus*—pygmy fringe-tree
- *Chorizante pungens* var *pungens*—Monterey spineflower
- *Cirsium pitcheri*—Pitcher's thistle
- *Clermontia pyrularia*—'oha wai
- *Clitoria fragrans*—Pigeon wings
- *Cordylanthus maritimus* ssp. *maritimus*—salt marsh bird's-beak
- *Cordylanthus palmatus*—palmate-bracted bird's-beak
- *Coryphantha sneedii* var. *robustispina*—Pima pineapple cactus
- *Coryphantha sneedii* var. *sneedii*—Sneed pincushion cactus
- *Cyanea acuminata*—haha
- *Cyanea humboldtiana*—haha
- *Cyanea koolauensis*—haha
- *Cyanea schipmanii*—haha
- *Cyrtandra subumbellata*—ha'iwale
- *Cyrtandra viridiflora*—ha'iwale
- *Dicerandra christmaii*—Garett's mint
- *Echinocereus fendleri* var. *kuenzleri*—Kuenzler hedgehog cactus
- *Enceliopsis nudicaulis* var. *corrugata*—Ash Meadows sunray
- *Eriogonum longifolium* var. *gnaphalifolium*—scrub buckwheat
- *Eryngium aristulatum* var. *parishii*—San Diego button celery
- *Erysimum capitatum* var. *angustatum*—Contra Costa wallflower
- *Eugenia woodburyana*—no common name
- *Frankenia johnstonii*—Johnston's frankenia
- *Gardenia manii*—nanu, Na'u
- *Goetzea elegans*—beautiful goetzea
- *Grindelia fraxino-pratensis*—Ash Meadows gumplant
- *Harrisia portorricensis*—Higo chumbo
- *Helianthus pardoxius*—Pecos sunflower
- *Helonias bullata*—Swamp pink
- *Hesperomanni arborescens*—no common name
- *Howellia aquatilus*—water howellia
- *Hymenoxys aculis* var. *glabra*—lakeside daisy
- *Iris lacustris*—Dwarf Lake iris
- *Isodendrion laurifolium*—aupaka
- *Ivesia kingii* var. *eremica*—Ash Meadows ivesia
- *Lespedeza leptosyachya*—prairie bush clover
- *Liatris ohlingerae*—scrub blazingstar
- *Lilaeopsis schaffneriana* var. *recurva*—Huachuca water umbel
- *Lobelia gaudichaudii* spp. *koolauensis*—no common name
- *Lobelia oahuensis*—no common name
- *Lomatium bradshawii*—Bradshaw's desert parsley
- *Manihot walkerae*—Walker's manioc
- *Mariscus pennatiformis* ssp. *bryanii*—no common name
- *Mentzelia leucophylla*—Ash Meadows blazing star
- *Nitrophila mohavensis*—Amargosa niterwort
- *Oenothera deltoides* ssp. *howellii*—Antioch Dunes evening primose
- *Orcuttia californica*—California orcutt grass
- *Oxypolis canbyi* — Canby's dropwort
- *Oxytropis campestris* var. *chartacea*—Fassett's locoweed
- *Paronychia chartacea (= Nyachia pulvinata)*—Papery whitlow wort
- *Penstemon haydenii*—blowout penstemon
- *Peperomia wheeleri*—Wheeler's peperomia
- *Phlegmariurus nutans*—wawae'iole
- *Phyllostegia hirsuta*—no common name
- *Phyllostegia racemosa*—kiponapona
- *Platanthera leucophaea*—eastern prairie fringed orchid
- *Platanthera praeclara*—western prairie fringed orchid
- *Pogogyne abramsii*—San Diego mesa mint
- *Pogogyne nudiuscula*—Otay mesa mint
- *Polygonella basiramia (=P. ciliata* var. *b.)*—Wireweed
- *Polystichum aleuticum*—Aleutian shield-fern
- *Pritchardia remota*—loulu
- *Prunus geniculata*—scrub plum
- *Pteris lydgatei*—no common name
- *Sanicula purpurea*—no common name
- *Sarracenia oreophila*—green pitcher plant
- *Schiedea verticillata*—whorled schiedea
- *Schwalbea americana*—American chaffseed
- *Sclerocactus glaucus*—Unita Basin hookless cactus
- *Sedum integrifolium leedyi*—Leedy's roseroot
- *Serianthes nelsonii*—Hayun lagu
- *Sesbania tomentosa*—'ohai
- *Sidalcea nelsoniana*—Nelson's checkermallow
- *Stahlia monosperma*—cobana negra
- *Tetraplasandra gymnocarpa*—no common name
- *Thymophylla tephroleuca*—ashy dogweed
- *Trifolium stoloniferum*—running buffalo clover
- *Viola oahuensis*—no common name

SOURCE: "Threatened and Endangered Plant Species Found on the National Wildlife Refuge System," in *America's National Wildlife Refuge System,* U.S. Fish and Wildlife Service, Washington, DC, 2004 [Online] http://refuges.fws.gov/habitats/EndSpPlants.html [accessed February 10, 2004]

Convention on Biological Diversity

The United Nations Convention on Biological Diversity was set up to conserve biodiversity and to promote the sustainable use of biodiversity. The Convention supports national efforts in the documentation and monitoring of biodiversity, the establishment of refuges and other protected areas, and the restoration of degraded ecosystems. It also supports goals related to the maintenance of traditional knowledge of sustainable resource use, the prevention of invasive species introductions, and the control of invasive species that are already present. Finally, it funds education programs promoting public awareness of the value of natural resources.

The Convention on International Trade in Endangered Species (CITES)

The Convention on International Trade in Endangered Species of Wild Fauna and Flora (CITES) is an international agreement administered under UNEP which regulates international trade in wildlife. CITES is perhaps the single most important international agreement relating to endangered species and has contributed critically to the protection of many threatened species. The international wildlife trade is estimated to involve hundreds of millions of specimens annually.

CITES was first drafted in 1963 at a meeting of the IUCN, and went into effect in 1975. As of 2004, CITES

TABLE 2.16

Wilderness areas in national wildlife refuges and national fish hatcheries, 2002

Wilderness Area: Service land designated by Congress to be managed as a unit of the National Wilderness Preservation System, in accordance with the terms of the Wilderness Act of 1964. All Service Wilderness Areas occur within National Wildlife Refuges, with the exception of the Mount Massive Wilderness Area which is located at the Leadville National Fish Hatchery (NFH).

State and unit	Wilderness name	Wilderness acres	Refuge acres	Public law Number	Public law Date
Alaska					
Alaska Maritime	Aleutian Islands	1,300,000.00	3,465,246.79	96–487	12-02-80
Alaska Maritime	Bering Sea	81,340.00	0.00	91–504	10-23-70
Alaska Maritime	Bogoslof	175.00	0.00	91–504	10-23-70
Alaska Maritime	Chamisso	455.00	0.00	93–632	01-03-75
Alaska Maritime	Forrester Island	2,832.00	0.00	91–504	10-23-70
Alaska Maritime	Hazy Island	32.00	0.00	91–504	10-23-70
Alaska Maritime	Semidi	250,000.00	0.00	96–487	12-02-80
Alaska Maritime	Simeonof	25,855.00	0.00	94–557	10-19-76
Alaska Maritime	St. Lazaria	65.00	0.00	91–504	10-23-70
Alaska Maritime	Tuxedni	5,566.00	0.00	91–504	10-23-70
Alaska Maritime	Unimak	910,000.00	0.00	96–487	12-02-80
Arctic	Mollie Beattie	8,000,000.00	19,285,922.40	96–487	12-02-80
Becharof	Becharof	400,000.00	1,200,017.75	96–487	12-02-80
Innoko	Innoko	1,240,000.00	3,850,321.21	96–487	12-02-80
Izembek	Izembek	307,981.76	311,075.78	96–487	12-02-80
Kenai	Kenai	1,354,247.0	1,908,178.23	96–487	12-02-80
Koyukuk	Koyukuk	400,000.00	3,550,000.53	96–487	12-02-80
Selawik	Selawik	240,000.00	2,150,002.01	96–487	12-02-80
Togiak	Togiak	2,270,799.79	4,098,740.94	96–487	12-02-80
Yukon Delta	Andreafsky	1,300,000.00	19,166,094.48	96–487	12-02-80
Yukon Delta	Nunivak	600,000.00	0.00	96–487	12-02-80
State total		**18,689,348.55**	**58,985,600.12**		
Arizona					
Cabreza Prieta	Cabreza Prieta	803,418.00	860,041.32	101–628	11-28-90
Havasu	Havasu	14,606.00	30,279.82	101–628	11-28-90
Imperial	Imperial	9,220.00	17,809.76	101–628	11-28-90
Kofa	Kofa	516,200.00	666,480.00	101–628	11-28-90
State total		**1,343,444.00**	**1,574,610.90**		
Arkansas					
Big Lake	Big Lake	2,143.80	11,036.10	94–557	10-19-76
State total		**2,143.80**	**11,036.10**		
California					
Farallon	Farallon	141.00	211.00	93–550	12-26-74
Havasu	Havasu	3,195.00	7,235.34	103–433	10-31-94
Imperial	Imperial	5,836.00	7,958.19	103–433	10-31-94
State total		**9,172.00**	**15,404.53**		
Colorado					
Leadville NFH	Mount Massive	2,560.00	3,065.88	96–560	12-22-80
State total		**2,560.00**	**3,065.88**		
Florida					
Cedar Keys	Cedar Keys	379.00	891.15	92–364	08-07-72
Chassahowitzka	Chassahowitzka	23,578.93	30,842.91	94–557	10-19-76
Great White Heron	Florida Keys	1,900.00	192,787.68	93–632	01-03-75
Island Bay	Island Bay	20.24	20.24	91–504	10-23-70
J.N. Ding Darling	J.N. Ding Darling	2,619.13	6,388.28	94–557	10-19-76
Key West	Florida Keys	2,019.00	208,308.17	93–632	01-03-75
Lake Woodruff	Lake Woodruff	1,066.00	21,559.02	94–557	10-19-76
National Key Deer	Florida Keys (1)	2,278.00	8,952.31	93–632	01-03-75
National Key Deer	Florida Keys (2)	0.00	0.00	97–211	06-30-82
Passage Key	Passage Key	36.37	63.87	91–504	10-23-70
Pelican Island	Pelican Island	5.50	5,375.93	91–504	10-23-70
St. Marks	St. Marks	17,350.00	67,623.07	93–632	01-03-75
State total		**51,252.17**	**542,812.58**		
Georgia					
Blackbeard Island	Blackbeard Island	3,000.00	5,617.64	93–632	10-23-70
Okefenokee	Okefenokee	353,981.00	391,401.99	93–429	10-01-74
Wolf Island	Wolf Island	5,125.82	5,125.82	93–632	01-03-75
State total		**362,106.82**	**402,145.45**		
Illinois					
Crab Orchard	Crab Orchard	4,050.00	43,888.52	94–557	10-19-76
State total		**4,050.00**	**43,888.52**		

TABLE 2.16

Wilderness areas in national wildlife refuges and national fish hatcheries, 2002 [CONTINUED]

Wilderness Area: Service land designated by Congress to be managed as a unit of the National Wilderness Preservation System, in accordance with the terms of the Wilderness Act of 1964. All Service Wilderness Areas occur within National Wildlife Refuges, with the exception of the Mount Massive Wilderness Area which is located at the Leadville National Fish Hatchery (NFH).

State and unit	Wilderness name	Wilderness acres	Refuge acres	Public law Number	Date
Louisiana					
Breton	Breton	5,000.00	9,047.00	93–632	01-01-75
Lacassine	Lacassine	3,345.60	34,378.77	94–557	10-19-76
State total		**8,345.60**	**43,425.77**		
Maine					
Moosehorn	Baring Unit	4,680.00	27,680,45	93–632	01-03-75
Moosehorn	Birch Islands Unit	6.00	0.00	91–504	10-23-70
Moosehorn	Edmunds Unit	2,706.00	0.00	91–504	10-23-70
State total		**7,392.00**	**27,680.45**		
Massachusetts					
Monomoy	Monomoy	2,420.00	2,701.85	91–504	10-23-70
State total		**2,420.00**	**2,701.85**		
Michigan					
Huron	Huron Islands	147.50	146.85	91–504	10-23-70
Michigan Islands	Michigan Islands	12.00	597.39	91–504	10-23-70
Seney	Seney	25,150.00	95,244.81	91–504	10-23-70
State total		**25,309.50**	**95,989.05**		
Minnesota					
Agassiz	Agassiz	4,000.00	61,500.93	94–557	10-19-76
Tamarac	Tamarac	2,180.00	35,191.38	94–557	10-19-76
State total		**6,180.00**	**96,692.31**		
Missouri					
Mingo	Mingo	7,730.00	21,745.86	94–557	10-19-76
State total		**7,730.00**	**21,745.86**		
Montana					
Medicine Lake	Medicine Lake	11,366.00	31,484.01	94–557	10-19-76
Red Rock Lakes	Red Rock Lakes	32,350.00	51,744.41	94–557	10-19-76
UL Bend	UL Bend (1)	20,819.00	56,049.56	94–557	10-19-76
UL Bend	UL Bend (2)	0.00	0.00	98–140	10-31-83
State total		**64,535.00**	**139,277.98**		
Nebraska					
Fort Niobrara	Fort Niobrara	4,635.00	19,132.53	94–557	10-19-76
State total		**4,635.00**	**19,132.53**		
New Jersey					
Edwin B. Forsythe	Brigantine	6,681.00	45,191.13	93–632	01-03-75
Great Swamp	Great Swamp	3,660.00	7,530.95	90–532	09-28-68
State total		**10,341.00**	**52,722.08**		
New Mexico					
Bitter lake	Salt Creek	9,621.00	26,608.64	91–504	10-23-70
Bosque Del Apache	Chupadea Unit	5,289.00	57,191.10	93–632	01-03-75
Bosque Del Apache	Indian Well Unit	5,139.00	0.00	93–632	01-03-75
Bosque Del Apache	Little San Pascual Unit	19,859.00	0.00	93–632	01-03-75
State total		**39,908.00**	**81,799.74**		
North Carolina					
Swanquarter	Swanquarter	8,784.93	16,411.09	94–557	10-19-76
State total		**8,784.93**	**16,411.09**		
North Dakota					
Chase Lake	Chase Lake	4,155.00	4,449.47	93–632	01-03-75
Lostwood	Lostwood	5,577.00	26,903.99	96–632	01-03-75
State total		**9,732.00**	**31,353.46**		
Ohio					
West Sister Island	West Sister Island	77.00	80.13	93–632	01-03-75
State total		**77.00**	**80.13**		
Oklahoma					
Wichita Mountains	Charons Garden Unit	5,723.00	59,019.60	91–50	10-23-70
Wichita Mountains	North Mountain Unit	2,847.00	0.00	91–504	10-23-70
State total		**8,570.00**	**59,019.60**		

safeguards approximately 5,000 animal species and 28,000 plant species worldwide. These are listed in three separate CITES appendices depending on degree of endangerment. Appendix I includes species that are in immediate danger of extinction. CITES generally prohibits international trade of these species. Appendix II lists species that are likely to become in danger of extinction without strict protection from international trade. Permits may be obtained

TABLE 2.16

Wilderness areas in national wildlife refuges and national fish hatcheries, 2002 [CONTINUED]

Wilderness Area: Service land designated by Congress to be managed as a unit of the National Wilderness Preservation System, in accordance with the terms of the Wilderness Act of 1964. All Service Wilderness Areas occur within National Wildlife Refuges, with the exception of the Mount Massive Wilderness Area which is located at the Leadville National Fish Hatchery (NFH).

State and unit	Wilderness name	Wilderness acres	Refuge acres	Public law Number	Public law Date
Oregon					
Oregon Islands	Oregon Islands (1)	21.00	1,079.61	91–504	10-23-70
Oregon Islands	Oregon Islands (2)	459.00	0.00	95–450	10-11-78
Oregon Islands	Oregon Islands (3)	445.06	0.00	104–333	11-12-96
Three Arch Rocks	Three Arch Rocks	15.00	15.00	91–504	10-23-70
State total		**940.06**	**1,095.61**		
South Carolina					
Cape Romain	Cape Romain	29,000.00	65,224.94	93–632	01-03-75
State total		**29,000.00**	**65,224.94**		
Washington					
Copalis	Washington Islands	60.80	60.80	91–504	10-23-70
Flattery Rocks	Washington Islands	125.00	125.00	91–504	10-23-70
Quillayute Needles	Washington Islands	300.20	300.20	91–504	10-23-70
San Juan Islands	San Juan Islands	353.00	448.53	94–557	10-19-76
State total		**839.00**	**934.53**		
Wisconsin					
Gravel Island	Wisconsin Islands	27.00	27.00	91–504	10-23-70
Green Bay	Wisconsin Islands	2.00	2.00	91–504	10-23-70
State total		**29.00**	**29.00**		
Grand total		**20,698,845.43**	**62,290,453.29**		

As of 9/30/2002

SOURCE: "Wilderness Areas in National Wildlife Refuges and National Fish Hatcheries," in *Division of Realty,* U.S. Fish and Wildlife Service, Washington, DC, September 30, 2002 [Online] http://realty.fws.gov/table10.html [accessed February 11, 2004]

for the trade of Appendix II species only if trade will not harm the survival prospects of the species in the wild. Appendix III lists species whose trade is regulated in one or more nations. Any member nation can list a species in Appendix III to request international cooperation in order to prevent unsustainable levels of international trade. Nations agree to abide by CITES rules voluntarily. In 2004 there were 164 nations party to the agreement.

Convention on Migratory Species of Wild Animals

The Convention on Migratory Species of Wild Animals (also known as the CMS or Bonn Convention) recognizes that certain migratory species cross national boundaries and require protection throughout their range. This convention aims to "conserve terrestrial, marine, and avian migratory species throughout their range." CMS was originally signed in Bonn, Germany in 1979 and went into force in November 1983. As of February 2004, 85 nations in Africa, Central and South America, Asia, Europe, and Oceania were involved in the agreement. The United States and several other nations are not official parties to the agreement but nonetheless abide by its rules.

CMS provides two levels of protection to migratory species. Appendix I species are endangered and strictly protected. There are currently 107 species in this category, including the Siberian crane, white-tailed eagle, hawksbill turtle, Mediterranean monk seal, and Dama gazelle.

FIGURE 2.7

Generalized view of land status by 1961

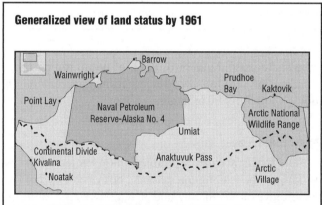

SOURCE: "Generalized view of land status by 1961," in *Potential Impacts of Proposed Oil and Gas Development on the Arctic Refuge's Coastal Plain: Historical Overview and Issues of Concern,* U.S. Fish and Wildlife Service, Fairbanks, AK, January 17, 2001 [Online] http://arctic.fws.gov/issues1.html [accessed February 11, 2004]

Appendix II lists species that are less severely threatened but would nonetheless benefit from international cooperative agreements. Appendix II agreements have been drawn up for groups such as European bats, Mediterranean and Black Sea cetaceans, Baltic and North Sea cetaceans, Wadden Sea seals, African-Eurasian migratory water birds, and marine turtles. In February 2004 the CMS announced the latest agreement to come into force, the Agreement on the Conservation of Albatrosses and

FIGURE 2.8

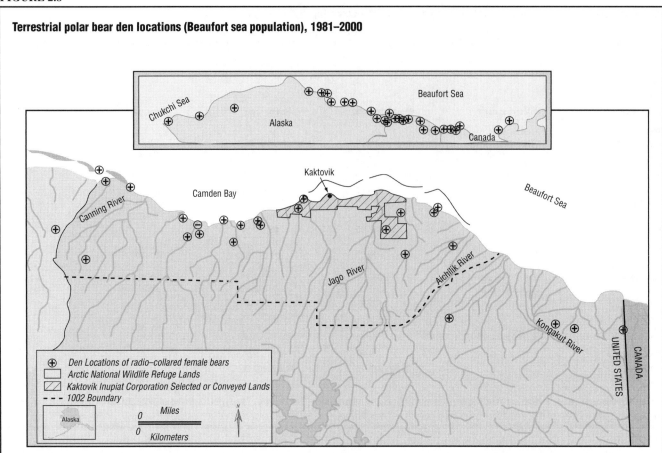

Terrestrial polar bear den locations (Beaufort sea population), 1981–2000

SOURCE: "Terrestrial Polar Bear Den Locations (Beaufort Sea Population) 1981–2000," in *Potential Impacts of Proposed Oil and Gas Development on the Arctic Refuge's Coastal Plain: Historical Overview and Issues of Concern*, U.S. Fish and Wildlife Service, Fairbanks, AK, January 17, 2001 [Online] http://arctic.fws.gov/issues1.html [accessed February 11, 2004]

Petrels. Because these birds are highly migratory, their conservation requires broad international agreements in addition to efforts by individual nations.

Protected Areas

The IUCN's World Commission on Protected Areas (WCPA) is the leading international body dedicated to the selection, establishment, and management of national parks and protected areas. It has helped set up many natural areas around the world for the protection of plant and animal species, and also maintains a database of protected areas. Protected areas often consist of a core zone where wildlife cannot legally be disturbed by human beings, surrounded by "buffer zones," transitional spaces that act as shields for the core zone. On the periphery are areas for managed human living. In 1998 there were 30,000 protected areas worldwide, covering 13.2 million square kilometers of land, freshwater habitat, and ocean. The terrestrial portion of the network, which is by far the largest, accounted for 11.7 million square kilometers—nearly 8 percent of the world's land area. A protected area is defined as "an area of land and/or sea especially dedicated to the protection and maintenance of biological

diversity, and of natural and associated cultural resources, and managed through legal or other effective means."

Conservation biology theory advocates that protected areas should be as large as possible in order to increase biological diversity and to buffer refuges from outside pressures. The world's largest protected areas are Greenland National Park (Greenland), Ar-Rub'al-khali Wildlife Management Area (Saudi Arabia), Great Barrier Reef Marine Park (Australia), Qiang Tang Nature Reserve (China), Cape Churchill Wildlife Management Area (Canada), and the Northern Wildlife Management Zone (Saudi Arabia).

ZOOS

Although some animal lovers object to caging wild species and keeping them in unnatural enclosures, zoos play one absolutely critical role—fostering interest in animal species, biodiversity, and conservation. In fact, the majority of zoo animals are not collected from the wild but bred in captivity. For example, among U.S. zoos, 90 percent of mammals and 74 percent of birds added to zoo collections since 1985 were born in captivity. Zoos have

FIGURE 2.9

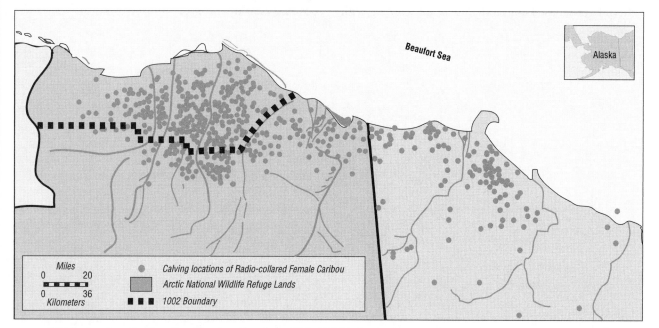

Calving locations of radio-collared female caribou during 1983–99

SOURCE: "Calving locations of radio-collared female caribou during 1983–1999," in *Potential Impacts of Proposed Oil and Gas Development on the Arctic Refuge's Coastal Plain: Historical Overview and Issues of Concern*, U.S. Fish and Wildlife Service, Fairbanks, AK, January 17, 2001 [Online] http://arctic.fws.gov/issues1.html [accessed February 11, 2004]

also contributed significantly to the survival of some highly endangered species through captive breeding efforts.

Captive Breeding

The majority of captive breeding efforts take place at zoos. Captive breeding has increased the number of many endangered species, and in several cases, saved them from certain extinction. Captive breeding has helped increase population sizes of species such as the California condor and the black-footed ferret. Both these species have thrived in captive breeding efforts, making reintroductions into wild habitat possible. Captive breeding offers the greatest hope for survival of additional species as well, including the highly endangered Florida panther. Although some species are notoriously difficult to breed in captivity, including the giant panda, many species have been bred in captivity, including over 3,000 species of vertebrates—some 19 percent of mammal species and 10 percent of bird species. A small selection of the many ongoing captive breeding efforts and the institutions leading the efforts include: the giant panda (San Diego Zoo) in California; Guam rail (Lincoln Park Zoological Gardens) in Chicago, Illinois; white rhinoceros (Fort Worth Zoological Park) in Texas; Mexican gray wolf (Arizona-Sonora Desert Museum) in Tucson, Arizona; wattled crane (Franklin Park Zoo) in Boston, Massachusetts; and the Chinese alligator (Bronx

Zoo) in New York. Species Survival Plans for captive breeding programs are organized by the American Zoo and Aquarium Association (AZA).

Captive breeding is not without its critics, however, who charge that it is costly, and that funds would be better used to conserve natural habitats. Critics also charge that captive breeding is able to focus only on a few charismatic species, and that it often gives the false impression that the battle against extinction is being won.

A New Role For Zoos

At one time, zoos kept animals tightly caged and in conditions that were unnatural and unhealthy. Today, however, many zoos have been redesigned to house animals in areas more similar to their natural habitats. For many people, a zoo is the only place to see wildlife, including endangered species. Many zoos have developed public education programs tying zoo exhibits to natural ecology. Some zoos have also evolved from being "menageries" for the pleasure of humans to living museums and ecological conservation centers for species.

Zoos and aquariums also constitute an extraordinary base of data for field conservation operations. The aim is to apply expertise on animal health, nutrition, handling, and reproduction to the needs of animals in the wild. The Bronx Zoo in New York is pioneering new efforts to extend its expertise into field study. With habitats for large animals becoming increasingly degraded, Bronx Zoo veterinarians are closely monitoring animal health in the field. Zoo resources are also being directed towards conservation. Bronx-based conservationists are working with national governments, local politicians, and international aid agencies to develop measures to preserve habitat and protect wildlife. One particular goal is to transfer technology and expertise to developing countries so that they can develop their own conservation efforts.

CHAPTER 3
GLOBAL CLIMATE CHANGE

Although large changes in climate are a natural part of Earth history, there is little doubt that human activities have caused observed patterns of global warming in the twentieth and twenty-first centuries. Global climate change has large implications for both humans and wildlife. Many threatened and endangered species, which already lead a precarious existence, are likely to suffer further declines. Global warming also threatens populations of species that were once relatively secure, and is likely to result in the endangerment of more species in the future.

A study of habitats comprising 20 percent of the earth's surface suggested that 15 to 37 percent of the world's species may be extinct by 2050 if recent warming trends continue ("Extinction Risk from Climate Change," *Nature,* no. 427, January 2004.) Summarizing his findings, ecologist Chris D. Thomas said, "The midrange estimate is that 24 percent of plants and animals will be committed to extinction by 2050. We're not talking about the occasional extinction—we're talking about 1.25 million species. It's a massive number."

CLIMATE CHANGE IN EARTH HISTORY

Over hundreds of millions of years, geological and astronomical forces have changed Earth's environment from hot to cold, wet to dry, and back again. Studies have shown that the climate has fluctuated between long periods of cold lasting 50,000 to 80,000 years and shorter periods of warmth lasting about 10,000 years. The Earth is in the midst of one of those warm periods now. These climate cycles are caused by tiny irregularities (known as Milankovitch Cycles) in the Earth's orbit around the sun. The climate of the past 10,000 years, during which human civilization developed, is a mere blip in a much larger history of climate change. However, human influences on the climate are significant, and effects are already being seen on species worldwide.

GLOBAL WARMING—THE RESULT OF HUMAN ACTIVITY

The Greenhouse Effect

Earth's climate is a delicate balance of energy input, chemical and biological processes, and physical phenomena. The Earth's atmosphere plays a critical role in planetary surface temperature. Some gases, such as carbon dioxide (CO_2) and methane (CH_4), absorb and maintain heat in the same way that glass traps heat in a greenhouse. These greenhouse gases in Earth's atmosphere allow temperatures to build up, keeping the planet warm and habitable to the life forms that have evolved here. This phenomenon is called the greenhouse effect. Figure 3.1 shows how the greenhouse effect causes elevation of surface temperatures on Earth.

The "natural greenhouse effect" creates a climate in which life can exist. It maintains the mean temperature of Earth's surface at approximately 33 degrees warmer than if natural greenhouse gases were not present. Without this process, Earth would be frigid and uninhabitable. However, an "enhanced greenhouse effect," sometimes called the "anthropogenic effect," refers to the increase in Earth's surface temperature due to human activity.

A Revolutionary Idea

Earth's atmosphere was compared to a glass vessel in 1827 by the French mathematician Jean-Baptiste Fourier. In the 1850s British physicist John Tyndall measured the heat-trapping properties of various components of the atmosphere. By the 1890s scientists had concluded that the great increase in combustion in the Industrial Revolution had the potential to change the atmosphere's load of carbon dioxide. In 1896 the Swedish chemist Svante Arrhenius made the revolutionary suggestion that the rapid increase in coal use during the Industrial Revolution could increase carbon dioxide concentrations and cause a gradual rise in temperatures. For almost six decades, his theory stirred little interest.

FIGURE 3.1

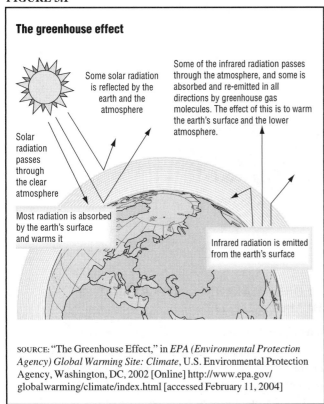

The greenhouse effect

Some solar radiation is reflected by the earth and the atmosphere

Some of the infrared radiation passes through the atmosphere, and some is absorbed and re-emitted in all directions by greenhouse gas molecules. The effect of this is to warm the earth's surface and the lower atmosphere.

Solar radiation passes through the clear atmosphere

Most radiation is absorbed by the earth's surface and warms it

Infrared radiation is emitted from the earth's surface

SOURCE: "The Greenhouse Effect," in *EPA (Environmental Protection Agency) Global Warming Site: Climate*, U.S. Environmental Protection Agency, Washington, DC, 2002 [Online] http://www.epa.gov/globalwarming/climate/index.html [accessed February 11, 2004]

Then in 1957 studies at the Scripps Institute of Oceanography in California showed that, in fact, half the carbon dioxide released by industry remained permanently trapped in the atmosphere. Atmospheric concentrations of carbon dioxide were shown to be at their highest level in 160,000 years.

More recent studies have provided evidence that levels of other greenhouse gases are also rising due to human activity:

- Methane (CH_4). Its atmospheric concentration is now about 150 times higher than in the pre-industrial era. Some estimates indicate that methane's concentration in the atmosphere could double again during the next 100 years.

- Nitrous oxide (N_2O). This gas comes from fertilizers used in agriculture, combustion of fossil fuels and solid waste, and industrial processes. Scientists estimate that there is 16 percent more nitrous oxide in the atmosphere presently than there was in 1750.

Man-made greenhouse gases, particularly fluorinated compounds, also contribute to global warming. These include:

- Chlorofluorocarbons (CFCs). The Montreal Protocol on Substances That Deplete the Ozone Layer phased out, with a few exceptions, the use of these popular aerosols, refrigerants, and solvents.

- Hydrochlorofluorocarbons (HCFCs). Designed as substitutes for the ozone-depleting CFCs, they have

about one-fifth the stratospheric ozone depletion potential of CFCs and most of the same uses.

- Hydrofluorocarbons (HFCs). These low-cost and often energy-efficient compounds are used in insulation, air conditioning, refrigeration, fire suppression, and medical metered dose inhalers.

Most man-made gases are present in the atmosphere now at concentrations about 25 percent greater than 150 years ago. The Intergovernmental Panel on Climate Change (IPCC) has documented increases in the levels of a number of greenhouse gases. The panel has conducted studies of ice cores obtained from Antarctica and Greenland—as ice gradually accumulates over millenia, it traps tiny air bubbles that yield information on past atmospheric conditions. Some of the ice cores examined required drilling to depths of thousands of feet.

Earth's Increasing Temperature

As of 2004 experts are almost certain that human-induced climate change is occurring due to increased levels of greenhouse gases. The IPCC, sponsored jointly by the United Nations Environmental Programme (UNEP) and the World Meteorological Organization, was formed to study climate change and to advise policymakers worldwide.

Evidence that global temperatures have been increasing comes from sources as diverse as fossils, corals, ancient ice, and growth rings in trees. The IPCC published a report in 2001 that shows global surface temperatures as measured by thermometers in the last 140 years. A marked rise of approximately one degree has occurred during the 140-year time course. There are extremely striking increases documented in the twentieth century. Data used to document these increases are derived from tree rings, corals, ice cores, and historical temperature records. Climate models suggest that the Earth will warm another two to six degrees between 2000 and 2100. If this happens, it will be the warmest Earth has been for millions of years.

Greenhouse Gases and Emission Trends

Total greenhouse gas emissions from 1991–2001 are shown in Figure 3.2. Emissions increased sharply through the 1990s, but dropped between 2000 and 2001. This drop is attributed to slow economic growth in the U.S. that year, as well as to reduced heating demands due to an unusually warm winter in 2001.

Although carbon dioxide is the primary driver of global warming, several other gases also impact temperatures significantly. Figure 3.3 shows U.S. greenhouse gas emission by type of gas in 2002.

CARBON DIOXIDE. Carbon dioxide, a naturally occurring component of Earth's atmosphere, is generally considered the major cause of global warming. Carbon is an essential component of all living organisms. The carbon

FIGURE 3.2

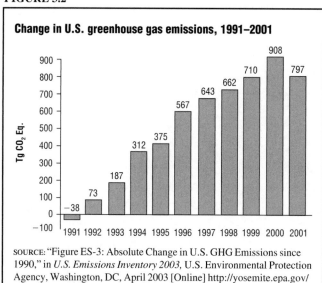

Change in U.S. greenhouse gas emissions, 1991–2001

SOURCE: "Figure ES-3: Absolute Change in U.S. GHG Emissions since 1990," in *U.S. Emissions Inventory 2003,* U.S. Environmental Protection Agency, Washington, DC, April 2003 [Online] http://yosemite.epa.gov/ oar/globalwarming.nsf/content/ResourceCenterPublicationsGHG EmissionsUSEmissionsInventory2003.html [accessed February 11, 2004]

FIGURE 3.3

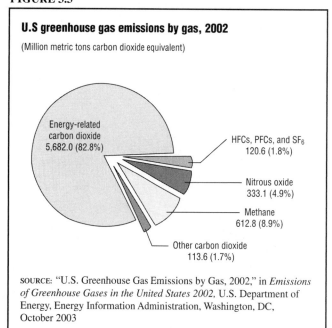

U.S greenhouse gas emissions by gas, 2002

(Million metric tons carbon dioxide equivalent)

SOURCE: "U.S. Greenhouse Gas Emissions by Gas, 2002," in *Emissions of Greenhouse Gases in the United States 2002,* U.S. Department of Energy, Energy Information Administration, Washington, DC, October 2003

cycle, which shows the movement of carbon from organic to inorganic forms, is illustrated in Figure 3.4. Plants perform the essential function of taking carbon dioxide from the atmosphere and converting it to organic matter, a form that can be used by other living species.

The Energy Information Administration of the U.S. Department of Energy reported in 2002 that carbon dioxide accounted for 82.8 percent of greenhouse gas emissions in the United States (shown in Figure 3.3). The burning of fossil fuels by industry and motor vehicles is by far the leading source of carbon dioxide, accounting for more than 96 percent of carbon dioxide emissions. (See Table 3.1 and Figure 3.5.) As populations and economies expand, they use ever-greater amounts of fossil fuels. Consequently, most carbon dioxide emission comes from the developed world.

Contributions from the developing world are expected to increase as these countries industrialize. (See Figure 3.6 and Figure 3.7.) The United States, despite having only 5 percent of the world's population, accounts for 25 percent of the world's energy use, making it the most carbon-intensive country on Earth. Figure 3.8 and Figure 3.9 document the sources of energy in the United States—the bulk is derived from fossil fuels (petroleum, natural gas, and coal).

METHANE. Methane is second only to carbon dioxide in its contribution to global warming, contributing 8.9 percent of greenhouse gases in 2002 (shown in Figure 3.3). While there is less methane than carbon dioxide in the atmosphere, scientists estimate that it may be 21 times more effective at trapping heat. Since the 1800s, the amount of methane in the atmosphere has more than doubled. Scientists attribute this rise to human sources,

including landfills, natural gas systems, agricultural activities, coal mining, and wastewater treatment. Sources of methane in 2001 are shown in Figure 3.10.

NITROUS OXIDE. Nitrous oxide is a greenhouse gas with natural biological sources as well as human sources. Although nitrous oxide makes up a much smaller portion of greenhouse gases than carbon dioxide (4.9 percent in 2002), it is as much as 310 times more powerful than carbon dioxide at trapping heat.

CHLOROFLUOROCARBONS. Chlorofluorocarbons (CFCs), an important class of modern industrial chemicals, caused some of the anthropogenic greenhouse effect and global warming experienced during the 1980s. CFCs are also responsible for depletion of the ozone layer in the stratosphere, which has resulted in increased levels of damaging ultraviolet radiation on Earth. The United States is the leading producer of CFCs. Beginning in the 1970s the United States and some other nations banned the use of CFCs in aerosol sprays. In 1987 leaders of many world nations met in Montreal, Canada, and agreed to cut CFC output by 50 percent by the year 2000. In 1989, 82 nations signed the Helsinki Declaration, pledging to completely phase out five CFCs.

Forests and Oceans as Carbon Sinks

Because plants naturally take in carbon dioxide from the atmosphere for photosynthesis, large forests act as sinks, or repositories, for carbon. There has been some debate about whether forests are capable of soaking up the excess carbon dioxide emitted through human activity. Some scientists have also argued that the increasing levels of carbon dioxide in the atmosphere might be better toler-

FIGURE 3.4

The carbon cycle

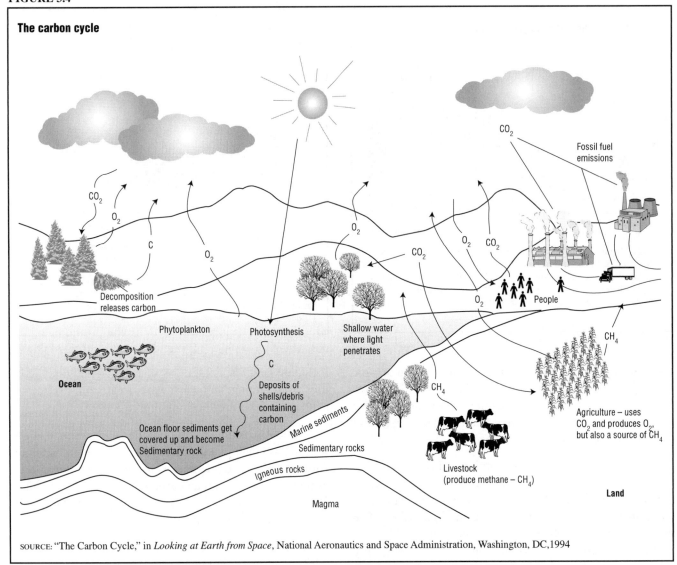

SOURCE: "The Carbon Cycle," in *Looking at Earth from Space*, National Aeronautics and Space Administration, Washington, DC, 1994

ated if not for the additional complicating factor of global deforestation. (See Figure 3.11.)

Oceans may also have a profound effect on climate change, both because of their tremendous heat storage capability and because they affect levels of atmospheric gases. The ocean is by far the largest reservoir of carbon in the carbon cycle. It holds approximately 50 times more carbon than the atmosphere and 20 times more than the terrestrial reservoir. Ocean currents also transport stored heat, causing heating and cooling in different parts of the world. It is still unclear, however, what effects oceans may have on global warming.

Other Factors Affecting the Global Climate

VOLCANOES. Volcanic activity, such as the 1991 eruption of Mount Pinatubo in the Philippines, can temporarily offset global warming. Volcanoes spew vast quantities of particles and gas into the atmosphere. Sulfur dioxide, a frequent product of eruptions, combines with water to form tiny super-cooled sulfuric acid droplets.

These create a long-lasting global haze that reflects sunlight, reducing the amount of heat absorbed and cooling the planet. (See Figure 3.12.) The effects of the Mount Pinatubo cloud—the largest volcanic cloud of the twentieth century—were felt for years. It not only blocked a significant portion of the impinging sunlight but affected wind and weather patterns. Weather anomalies such as cooler summers and warmer winters, as well as an overall cooling effect, were observed for several years. Similarly, the explosion of the El Chichon volcano in Mexico in 1982 depressed global temperatures for about four years.

CLOUDS. Clouds also contribute to global climate patterns. Clouds can either reflect sunlight, cooling the Earth, or cause the planet to retain heat. These differing effects depend largely on the brightness and thickness of the clouds in question. Marine stratocumulus clouds, which occur at low altitudes over the ocean, are known to reflect solar energy, resulting in a cooling of the Earth. (See Figure 3.13.) Other clouds, however, such as the cirrus clouds that occur at high altitudes, enhance global warming. A

TABLE 3.1

Trends in U.S. greenhouse gas emissions and sinks, 1990 and 1995–2001

Gas/source	1990	1995	1996	1997	1998	1999	2000	2001
CO$_2$	**5,003.7**	**5,334.4**	**5,514.8**	**5,595.4**	**5,614.2**	**5,680.7**	**5,883.1**	**5,794.8**
Fossil fuel combustion	4,814.8	5,141.5	5,325.8	5,400.0	5,420.5	5,488.8	5,692.2	5,614.9
Iron and steel production	85.4	74.4	68.3	71.9	67.4	64.4	65.8	59.1
Cement manufacture	33.3	36.8	37.1	38.3	39.2	40.0	41.2	41.4
Waste combustion	14.1	18.5	19.4	21.2	22.5	23.9	25.4	26.9
Ammonia manufacture & urea application	19.3	20.5	20.3	20.7	21.9	20.6	19.6	16.6
Lime manufacture	11.2	12.8	13.5	13.7	13.9	13.5	13.3	12.9
Natural gas flaring	5.5	8.7	8.2	7.6	6.3	6.7	5.5	5.2
Limestone and dolomite use	5.5	7.0	7.6	7.1	7.3	7.7	5.8	5.3
Aluminum production	6.3	5.3	5.6	5.6	5.8	5.9	5.4	4.1
Soda ash manufacture and consumption	4.1	4.3	4.2	4.4	4.3	4.2	4.2	4.1
Titanium dioxide production	1.3	1.7	1.7	1.8	1.8	1.9	1.9	1.9
Carbon dioxide consumption	0.9	1.1	1.1	1.2	1.2	1.2	1.2	1.3
Ferroalloys	2.0	1.9	2.0	2.0	2.0	2.0	1.7	1.3
Land-use change and forestry (sink)[1]	(1,072.8)	(1,064.2)	(1,061.0)	(840.6)	(830.5)	(841.1)	(834.6)	(838.1)
International bunker fuels[2]	113.9	101.0	102.3	109.9	112.9	105.3	99.3	97.3
CH$_4$	**644.0**	**650.0**	**636.8**	**629.5**	**622.7**	**615.5**	**613.4**	**605.9**
Landfills	212.1	216.1	212.1	207.5	202.4	203.7	205.8	202.9
Natural gas systems	122.0	127.2	127.4	126.0	124.0	120.3	121.2	117.3
Enteric fermentation	117.9	123.0	120.5	118.3	116.7	116.6	115.7	114.8
Coal mining	87.1	73.5	68.4	68.1	67.9	63.7	60.9	60.7
Manure management	31.3	36.2	34.9	36.6	39.0	38.9	38.2	38.9
Wastewater treatment	24.1	26.6	26.8	27.3	27.7	28.2	28.3	28.3
Petroleum systems	27.5	24.2	23.9	23.6	22.9	21.6	21.2	21.2
Rice cultivation	7.1	7.6	7.0	7.5	7.9	8.3	7.5	7.6
Stationary sources	8.1	8.5	8.7	7.5	7.2	7.4	7.6	7.4
Mobile sources	5.0	4.9	4.8	4.7	4.6	4.5	4.4	4.3
Petrochemical production	1.2	1.5	1.6	1.6	1.6	1.7	1.7	1.5
Field burning of agricultural residues	0.7	0.7	0.7	0.8	0.8	0.8	0.8	0.8
Silicon carbide production	+	+	+	+	+	+	+	+
International bunker fuels[2]	0.2	0.1	0.1	0.1	0.1	0.1	0.1	0.1
N$_2$O	**397.6**	**430.9**	**441.7**	**440.9**	**436.8**	**430.0**	**429.9**	**424.6**
Agricultural soil management	267.5	284.1	293.2	298.2	299.2	297.0	294.6	294.3
Mobile sources	50.6	60.9	60.7	60.3	59.7	58.8	57.5	54.8
Manure management	16.2	16.6	17.0	17.3	17.3	17.4	17.9	18.0
Nitric acid	17.8	19.9	20.7	21.2	20.9	20.1	19.1	17.6
Human sewage	12.7	13.9	14.1	14.4	14.6	15.1	15.1	15.3
Stationary combustion	12.5	13.2	13.8	13.7	13.7	13.7	14.3	14.2
Adipic acid	15.2	17.2	17.0	10.3	6.0	5.5	6.0	4.9
N$_2$O product usage	4.3	4.5	4.5	4.8	4.8	4.8	4.8	4.8
Field burning of agricultural residues	0.4	0.4	0.4	0.4	0.5	0.4	0.5	0.5
Waste combustion	0.3	0.3	0.3	0.3	0.2	0.2	0.2	0.2
International bunker fuels[2]	1.0	0.9	0.9	1.0	1.0	0.9	0.9	0.9
HFCs, PFCs, and SF$_6$	**94.4**	**99.5**	**113.6**	**116.8**	**127.6**	**120.3**	**121.0**	**111.0**
Substitution of ozone depleting substances	0.9	21.7	30.4	37.7	44.5	50.9	57.3	63.7
HCFC-22 production	35.0	27.0	31.1	30.0	40.2	30.4	29.8	19.8
Electrical transmission and distribution	32.1	27.5	27.7	25.2	20.9	16.4	15.4	15.3
Semiconductor manufacture	2.9	5.9	5.4	6.5	7.3	7.7	7.4	5.5
Aluminum production	18.1	11.8	12.5	11.0	9.0	8.9	7.9	4.1
Magnesium production and processing	5.4	5.6	6.5	6.3	5.8	6.0	3.2	2.5
Total	**6,139.6**	**6,514.9**	**6,707.0**	**6,782.6**	**6,801.3**	**6,849.5**	**7,047.4**	**6,936.2**
Net emissions (sources and sinks)	**5,066.8**	**5,450.7**	**5,646.0**	**5,942.0**	**5,970.9**	**6,008.5**	**6,212.7**	**6,098.1**

+Does not exceed 0.05 Tg CO$_2$ Eq.

[1]For the most recent years, a portion of the sink estimate is based on historical and projected data. Parentheses indicate negative values (or sequestration).

[2]Emissions from International Bunker Fuels are not included in totals.

Note: Totals may not sum due to independent rounding.

SOURCE: "Table ES-1: Recent Trends in U.S. Greenhouse Gas Emissions and Sinks (Tg CO$_2$ Eq.)," in *U.S. Emissions Inventory 2003,* U.S. Environmental Protection Agency, Washington, DC, April 2003 [Online] http://yosemite.epa.gov/oar/globalwarming.nsf/content/ResourceCenterPublicationsGHGEmissions USEmissionsInventory2003.html [accessed February 11, 2004]

2000 study at NASA's Goddard Institute for Space Studies reported that global warming results in the formation of thinner clouds that are less capable of reflecting sunlight.

SOLAR CYCLES. Finally, the sun itself is not an entirely steady source of energy. The sun has seasons, storms, and characteristic patterns of activity. Sunspots and flares appear in cycles of roughly eleven years, and may well contribute

to climate change on Earth. Future studies of each stage of this cycle are expected to produce a wealth of new data that will increase our understanding of these phenomena.

EFFECTS OF A WARMING CLIMATE

In 1990 the Intergovernmental Panel on Climate Change (IPCC) noted several early signs of climate

FIGURE 3.5

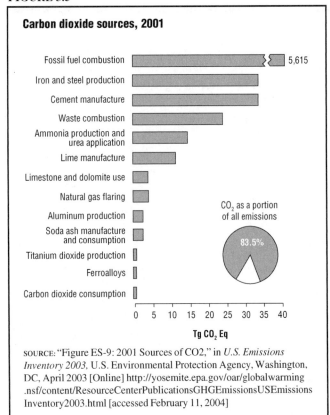

Carbon dioxide sources, 2001

Fossil fuel combustion — 5,615
Iron and steel production
Cement manufacture
Waste combustion
Ammonia production and urea application
Lime manufacture
Limestone and dolomite use
Natural gas flaring
Aluminum production
Soda ash manufacture and consumption
Titanium dioxide production
Ferroalloys
Carbon dioxide consumption

CO₂ as a portion of all emissions

83.5%

0 5 10 15 20 25 30 35 40

Tg CO₂ Eq

SOURCE: "Figure ES-9: 2001 Sources of CO2," in *U.S. Emissions Inventory 2003*, U.S. Environmental Protection Agency, Washington, DC, April 2003 [Online] http://yosemite.epa.gov/oar/globalwarming.nsf/content/ResourceCenterPublicationsGHGEmissionsUSEmissionsInventory2003.html [accessed February 11, 2004]

FIGURE 3.6

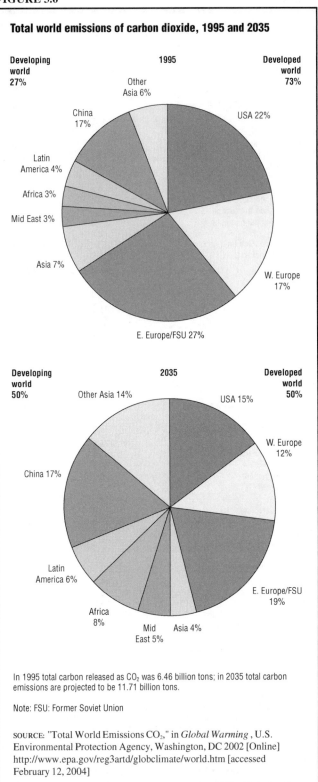

Total world emissions of carbon dioxide, 1995 and 2035

Developing world 27%   1995   Developed world 73%

Other Asia 6%
China 17%
Latin America 4%
Africa 3%
Mid East 3%
Asia 7%
USA 22%
W. Europe 17%
E. Europe/FSU 27%

Developing world 50%   2035   Developed world 50%

Other Asia 14%
China 17%
Latin America 6%
Africa 8%
Mid East 5%
Asia 4%
USA 15%
W. Europe 12%
E. Europe/FSU 19%

In 1995 total carbon released as CO₂ was 6.46 billion tons; in 2035 total carbon emissions are projected to be 11.71 billion tons.

Note: FSU: Former Soviet Union

SOURCE: "Total World Emissions CO₂," in *Global Warming*, U.S. Environmental Protection Agency, Washington, DC 2002 [Online] http://www.epa.gov/reg3artd/globclimate/world.htm [accessed February 12, 2004]

change in Earth's colder habitats. The average warm-season temperature in Alaska had increased three degrees in fifty years. Glaciers had receded and thinned by thirty feet in forty years. There was significantly less sea ice in the Bering Sea than in the 1950s. Permafrost had thawed, causing landslides, erosion, and local floods. Ice cellars in northern villages thawed, becoming useless. More precipitation fell as rain than snow, and snow melted faster, causing more running and standing water.

Since then, further evidence of global warming has been frequent and diverse:

• Heat waves and unusually warm weather have been reported at numerous locales, resulting in increased levels of human heat-related illness and death.

• Sea level rise, resulting from the expansion of warmer sea water and the melting of glaciers, is estimated at four to ten inches over the course of the twentieth century. Sea level rise has resulted in land inundation, coastal flooding, and erosion.

• Incidents of heavy snowstorms and rainfall have increased.

• Droughts have increased in frequency.

• Mountain glaciers have continued to shrink, and have disappeared in lower latitudes.

• Diseases formerly confined to tropical regions, including several mosquito-borne diseases, have increased their range to higher altitudes and latitudes.

• Spring arrives earlier in many places.

• Numerous biological species have shifted their ranges to occupy higher latitudes and higher elevations.

FIGURE 3.7

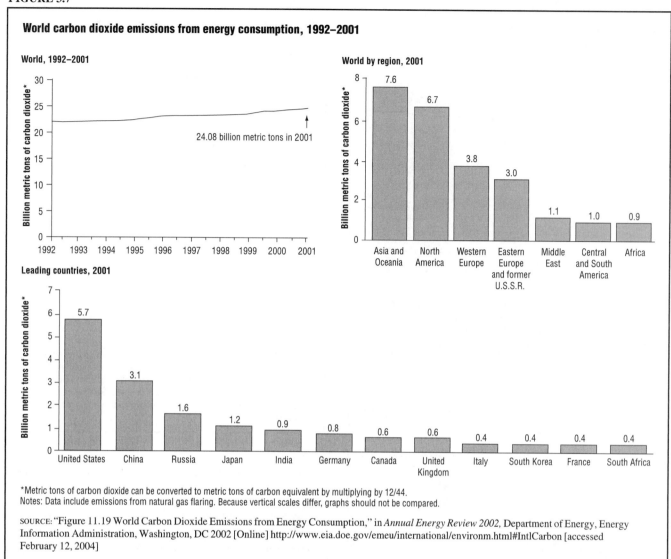

World carbon dioxide emissions from energy consumption, 1992–2001

World, 1992–2001

24.08 billion metric tons in 2001

World by region, 2001

Leading countries, 2001

*Metric tons of carbon dioxide can be converted to metric tons of carbon equivalent by multiplying by 12/44.
Notes: Data include emissions from natural gas flaring. Because vertical scales differ, graphs should not be compared.

SOURCE: "Figure 11.19 World Carbon Dioxide Emissions from Energy Consumption," in *Annual Energy Review 2002,* Department of Energy, Energy Information Administration, Washington, DC 2002 [Online] http://www.eia.doe.gov/emeu/international/environm.html#IntlCarbon [accessed February 12, 2004]

In March 2002, in what is perhaps the most dramatic event resulting from global warming to date, the giant Larsen B ice shelf collapsed off the coast of Antarctica. (See Figure 3.14.) Ice shelves are thick blocks of ice that are continuations of the ice sheets that cover the Antarctic continent. The Larsen B shelf was larger than the state of Rhode Island and likely had existed since the end of the last ice age 12,000 years ago.

Global temperatures are predicted to continue to rise. Some of the major effects of global climate change, and the likelihood of their occurrence, were listed by the IPCC in 2001. Many of these predictions have drastic consequences for humans as well as for wildlife.

Global Warming and Human Health

Higher temperatures alone are killing some people, particularly young and old people in urban areas. Over 250 died during a heat wave across the eastern United States in the summer of 1999. Most of these heat-related deaths occur directly from heat-induced strokes and heart attacks.

Air quality also deteriorates as temperatures rise. Hot, stagnant air contributes to the formation of atmospheric ozone, the main component of smog. Poor air quality also aggravates asthma and other respiratory diseases.

Higher temperatures and increased rainfall could create ideal conditions for the spread of a host of infectious diseases by insects, including mosquito-borne malaria, dengue fever, and encephalitis. Some tropical diseases have already spread beyond their old ranges, affecting people at higher altitudes and latitudes. For example, dengue fever, once restricted to altitudes below 3,300 feet, was reported at altitudes above 4,000 feet in Central America in 1999, at 5,600 feet in Mexico in 1998, and at 7,200 feet in the Andes Mountains of Columbia in 1998. Similarly, malaria was detected at high altitudes in Indonesia in 1997. Expansion of malarial ranges have also been reported in parts of Africa. West Nile virus-induced encephalitis, which is native to Egypt and Uganda, was first seen in the United States in 1999; by 2003 it had spread throughout the continental U.S., except for Oregon.

FIGURE 3.8

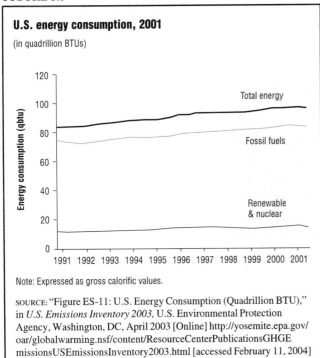

U.S. energy consumption, 2001

(in quadrillion BTUs)

Note: Expressed as gross calorific values.

SOURCE: "Figure ES-11: U.S. Energy Consumption (Quadrillion BTU)," in *U.S. Emissions Inventory 2003,* U.S. Environmental Protection Agency, Washington, DC, April 2003 [Online] http://yosemite.epa.gov/oar/globalwarming.nsf/content/ResourceCenterPublicationsGHGEmissionsUSEmissionsInventory2003.html [accessed February 11, 2004]

FIGURE 3.10

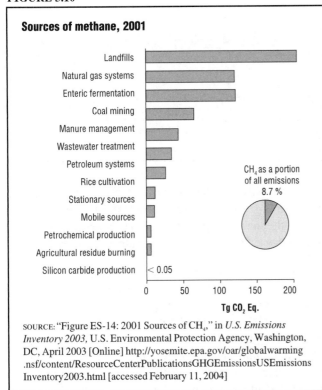

Sources of methane, 2001

SOURCE: "Figure ES-14: 2001 Sources of CH₄," in *U.S. Emissions Inventory 2003,* U.S. Environmental Protection Agency, Washington, DC, April 2003 [Online] http://yosemite.epa.gov/oar/globalwarming.nsf/content/ResourceCenterPublicationsGHGEmissionsUSEmissionsInventory2003.html [accessed February 11, 2004]

FIGURE 3.9

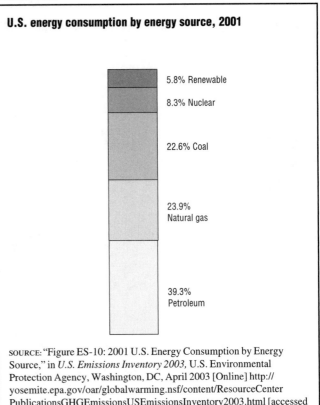

U.S. energy consumption by energy source, 2001

SOURCE: "Figure ES-10: 2001 U.S. Energy Consumption by Energy Source," in *U.S. Emissions Inventory 2003,* U.S. Environmental Protection Agency, Washington, DC, April 2003 [Online] http://yosemite.epa.gov/oar/globalwarming.nsf/content/ResourceCenterPublicationsGHGEmissionsUSEmissionsInventory2003.html [accessed February 11, 2004]

Sea Levels and Precipitation Patterns

The National Climatic Data Center reports that sea levels rose by as much as 10 inches in the twentieth century. The Climate Institute in Washington, D.C., forecasts a further rise of 8 inches by 2030 and 26 inches by 2100 if current trends continue. These would be caused by the expansion of seawater as it is warmed, as well as by melting glaciers and ice caps.

Rising sea levels would narrow or destroy beaches, flood wetland areas, and either submerge or require the costly fortification of shoreline property. Numerous coastal cities worldwide would be flooded. Rising waters would also intrude on inland rivers, destroying freshwater habitats, threatening human water supplies, and increasing the salt content of groundwater.

A warmer climate is also likely to shift the rain belt of the middle latitudes toward the poles, affecting rainfall patterns around the world. Wetter, more violent weather is projected for some regions. The opposite problem—too little water—could worsen in arid areas such as the Middle East and parts of Africa. Frequent droughts could plague North America and Asia as well. Some experts have suggested that "global warming" is too mild a term for an era marked by heat waves that will make certain regions virtually uninhabitable.

Decreasing Biological Diversity

Global biodiversity is also predicted to suffer from planetary warming. Certain ecosystems will shrink or be lost entirely, including cold-temperature habitats such as tundra, and specialized habitats such as coral reefs and coastal mangrove swamps. Other species expected to be heavily affected include those that require habitat within

FIGURE 3.11

The effect of forests on carbon dioxide concentrations

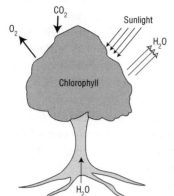

As plants and trees grow, photosynthesis — involving the interaction of sunlight, chlorophyll in green leaves, carbon dioxide (CO_2) and water (H_2O) — results in a net removal of CO_2 from the air and the release of oxygen (O_2) as a by-product. Also, moisture is released to the air through evapotranspiration.

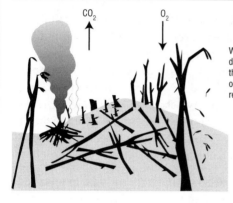

When forests die and decay, or are burned, the biomass is oxidized and CO_2 is returned to the air.

SOURCE: "Figure 2a" and "Figure 2b," in *Biosphere, NASA Facts*, National Aeronautics and Space Administration, Goddard Space Flight Center, Greenbelt, MD, April 1998

FIGURE 3.12

Potential effects of volcanic eruptions on climate and the surrounding environment

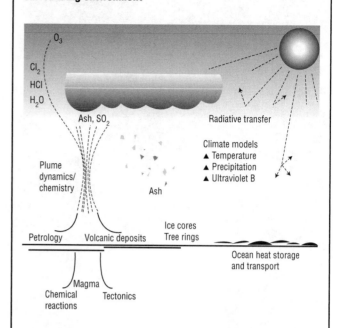

SOURCE: "Figure 1. Volcanism studies are an important aspect of climate research," in *Volcanoes and Global Climate Change, NASA Facts*, National Aeronautics and Space Administration, Goddard Space Flight Center, Greenbelt, MD, May 1998

FIGURE 3.13

Clouds and their effect on global temperature

The shortwave rays from the sun are scattered in a cloud. Many of the rays return to space. The resulting "cloud albedo forcing," taken by itself, tends to cause a cooling of the Earth.

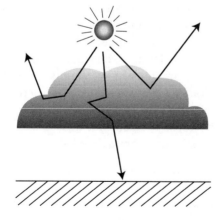

Longwave rays emitted by the Earth are absorbed and reemitted by a cloud, with some rays going to space and some going to the surface. Wavy arrows indicate longwave rays (distinguished from straight arrows, which indicate shortwave rays, as in the previous figure), and thicker arrows indicate more energy. The resulting "cloud greenhouse forcing," taken by itself, tends to cause a warming of the Earth.

SOURCE: "Figure 1" and "Figure 2," in *Clouds and the Energy Cycle, NASA Facts*, National Aeronautics and Space Administration, Goddard Space Flight Center, Greenbelt, MD, May 1998

FIGURE 3.14

Satellite photo of the Larsen B ice shelf retreating to the rock cliffs. (*AP/Wide World Photos*)

narrow bands of temperature and humidity, such as the monarch butterfly or the edelweiss flower.

Many ecosystems are expected to shift geographically toward more appropriate climate regimes. However, some species may be unable to migrate rapidly enough to cope with climate change at the projected rates. Species expected to be most successful, in fact, include opportunistic varieties such as weeds and pests. The EPA warned in 1988, "If current trends continue, it is likely that climate may change too quickly for many natural systems to adapt."

SPECIES RANGE SHIFTS. The ranges of most species depend, among other things, on temperature and climate. A number of plant and animal species have already shifted their geographic ranges in response to warming patterns. Range shifts have been reported in alpine plants, butterflies, birds, invertebrates, and mosquitoes.

A 1999 study by Dr. Camille Parmesan and colleagues showed that among surveyed European butterfly species, 63 percent had shifted their ranges northward. Moreover, these species had shifted their ranges by a distance corresponding to temperature rises on the European

continent. Dr. Parmesan also showed that one California species, Edith's checkerspot butterfly, has been disappearing from the southern parts of its range, as well as from lower-elevation habitats. Similarly, a 1999 study of bird species in the United Kingdom revealed that ranges have shifted north by an average of 12 miles. In the Olympic Mountains in the state of Washington, biologists reported in 1994 that sub-alpine forests have shifted to higher elevations previously characterized by alpine meadows. In Monterey Bay, California, a 1995 study showed that invertebrate species such as snails and starfish have shifted north as well. In Germany, a study of mollusk species showed that 20 percent of species had shifted their ranges. Range shifts of mosquitoes are supported by the occurrence of mosquito-borne diseases such as dengue fever at more northern latitudes and at higher altitudes.

DISAPPEARING SPECIES. Some species will be unable to shift their ranges in response to global warming. There may be physical barriers that are difficult or impossible to cross—mountains, perhaps, or oceans or other bodies of water. The species they depend on for food or other resources may not have shifted their ranges. Or, species may encounter new competitors or predators as they try to move into new habitats. These species are likely to decline with global warming.

Population declines have recently been reported in a number of habitats and species. Mangrove forests have been inundated by water due to rising sea levels and are dying. Arctic species are particularly vulnerable. An Arctic bird species, the black guillemot, is declining because of reductions in the amount of floating sea ice—ice formed by frozen saltwater. This has resulted in decreased food availability for guillemots as well as a reduction in the number of available nesting sites. Adelie penguin populations have declined dramatically in Antarctica, probably because of a reduction in sea ice, which not only provides penguin habitat but is essential to the penguins' primary food source, krill. In the Monteverde cloud forest of Costa Rica, where a unique, moist habitat is created by large amounts of water mist, an altitudinal rise in the cloud bank has resulted in the extinction of some twenty frog species as of 1999. Declines in lizard populations have also been documented, as well as altitudinal shifts by populations of birds and bats.

An issue of particular concern is the loss of plant species due to global warming. Plants are often less able to shift their ranges than are animals, which are mobile. As plants form the basis of most ecosystems, the loss of plant species will impact animals as well. Several factors may limit the ability of trees to shift their ranges. First, seed dispersal by wind or by birds may not be fast enough to keep pace with climate change. In addition, trees are long-lived species with long maturation times, and it takes a considerable amount of time for forests to become fully established in new areas. In terms of altitudinal shifts, soils at high altitudes tend to be poorer than at lower altitudes. Consequently, some species may not be able to colonize at higher elevations.

In the United States, the Forest Service believes that Eastern hemlock, yellow birch, beech, and sugar maple forests will gradually have to shift their ranges northward by 300 to 600 miles if projected warming trends become a reality. Several of these ecosystems are likely to be severely limited by warming, however, and are likely to die out, along with the wildlife they shelter. Studies by World Wildlife Fund International report that more than half the world's parks and reserves could be threatened by climate change. Some U.S. parks believed to be particularly vulnerable include the Florida Everglades, Yellowstone National Park, the Great Smoky Mountains, and Redwood National Park in California.

Global warming will also threaten ecosystems in unexpected ways. In 2002 extensive forest damage was reported on the Kenai Peninsula near Anchorage, Alaska. Over 38 million dead spruce trees, some of them over a hundred years old, were cleared from 4 million acres of forest habitat. The cause of this catastrophe was an explosion in the number of spruce bark beetles. Spruce bark beetles have always preyed on spruce trees in the Kenai Peninsula, but have been reproducing much more quickly because of warm temperatures. This represents the worst insect decimation of forests ever reported in North America.

CORAL BLEACHING. Coral reefs are among the ecosystems most immediately threatened by global warming. (See Figure 3.15.) Coral reef habitats are found in coastal marine waters in tropical areas, and are among the richest and most diverse of marine ecosystems. In fact, one-quarter of all marine species are found in coral reefs. The corals that form the basis of this ecosystem normally have a close relationship with different species of algae. This relationship benefits both members—the algae receive shelter and protection within the calcium carbonate skeletons of corals, and the corals receive nutrients from the algae. Coral bleaching occurs when the corals eject the algae with which they normally live. This process is called bleaching because the corals lose their normally bright colors and take on a stark, white appearance. Coral bleaching has been shown to result from unusually warm oceanic water temperatures. Coral may recover after a bleaching episode when temperatures cool down again and the algae return. However, if the ejected algae die during a bleaching episode, the corals are doomed as well.

Widespread coral bleaching was reported beginning in the 1990s. In the spring of 2002 coral bleaching affected numerous coral reef ecosystems, including the Great Barrier Reef off the coast of Australia, the largest coral reef in the world. This is the second major bleaching event in four years, and it is believed to be extending throughout tropical

FIGURE 3.15

Coral reefs are among the most diverse ecosystems in the world. They are also immediately threatened by global warming, which has caused unprecedented episodes of coral bleaching in recent years. *(AP/Wide World Photos)*

Pacific coral reef systems. Professor Ove Hoegh-Guldberg, a leading authority on corals and coral bleaching, predicts that if warming trends continue, all coral will be extinct—and the diverse coral reef ecosystems lost—by 2030.

TURTLES AND TEMPERATURE-DEPENDENT SEX DETERMINATION. Turtles and other reptiles, such as lizards and crocodilians, are characterized by an unusual sex determination system called temperature-dependent sex determination. This differs from the chromosomal system familiar in humans and other mammals, where two X chromosomes (XX) result in production of females and an X and a Y chromosome (XY) lead to males. In species with temperature-dependent sex determination, sex depends on the temperature at which egg development occurs.

Global climate change has resulted in skewed sex ratios in several turtle species. Generally, warmer temperatures favor the production of females in these species. Among loggerhead turtles in Florida, for example, females made up 87 to 99.9 percent of the hatchling population in 1992, depending on the precise nesting site used. This was traced to warmer sand temperatures on beaches. Among Mississippi painted turtles, almost 100 percent of hatchlings were female in 1994. Continued production of large numbers of females and few or no males could have drastic implications for many turtle populations.

INTERNATIONAL EFFORTS AND GLOBAL WARMING

In order to slow or halt global warming, many industrialized countries are committed to stabilizing or reducing carbon dioxide emissions. The first Bush administration (1989–1992) opposed precise deadlines for carbon dioxide limits, arguing that the extent of the problem was too uncertain to justify painful economic measures. When President Bill Clinton took office in 1993, he joined the European community in calling for overall emissions to be stabilized at 1990 levels by the year 2000. However, this goal was not met. The administration of George W. Bush has shown little desire to address the issue of global climate change. Oil interests in particular have vigorously opposed emissions standards, fearing that these will decrease demand for oil. Many environmentalists believe that fighting global warming will require advances in energy efficiency. Others have promoted a gradual shift from fossil-fuel burning to renewable energy, an idea most industrialized countries have been slow to embrace.

The Kyoto Protocol

The aim of the United Nations Framework Convention on Climate Change is to stabilize global atmospheric greenhouse gases at levels "that would prevent dangerous anthropogenic interference with the climate system." In December 1997 delegates from 166 countries met in Kyoto, Japan, to formulate a plan for reducing greenhouse gas emissions as the first step towards this goal. The task was more complicated and difficult than envisioned in 1995, when parties to the 1992 Rio climate change treaty decided that stronger action was necessary. The "simple" matter of deciding on a reduction target and creating a timetable for reductions broadened into contentious debate on several fronts.

Developed nations, such as the United States, argued that both industrialized and developing countries should be required to reduce greenhouse gas emissions. Developing countries, however, argued that because industrialized nations had caused most of the global warming, and were still emitting the bulk of global greenhouse gases, industrialized nations should bear most of the economic burden of the cleanup. It was ultimately decided that the Kyoto Protocol would address only emissions reductions for developed countries. There was also debate over whether development of carbon sinks—such as through the building of tree farms—could offset emissions targets. Many countries wanted sinks to be excluded, in part because their role in global warming has not been well studied and remains uncertain. However, the United States insisted on this carbon sink clause, which it argued would allow businesses low-cost means for complying with treaty requirements. Finally, the United States successfully battled to allow for emissions trading among nations. This permits businesses or countries to purchase less expensive emissions permits from foreign countries that do not need them, rather than cutting emissions.

In the end, the final version of the Kyoto Protocol called for industrialized nations to reduce emissions from 1990 levels by an average of 5 percent by 2008–2012. It was signed by over 170 nations, including the United States, which committed to legally binding emissions reductions of 7 percent below 1990 levels. European Union nations were required to reduce emission by 8 percent, Japan by 6 percent. However, ratification by 55 nations, jointly responsible for 55 percent of 1990 emissions, is required for the treaty to enter into force.

The United States has made no move towards ratifying the Kyoto Protocol since signing it. In fact, President Bush confirmed in March 2001 that the United States would withdraw from the Kyoto Protocol. Bush said that he believed the emissions reductions would be too costly. Christine Todd Whitman, Bush's appointed head of the Environmental Protection Agency, said, "We have no interest in implementing that treaty." The United States was responsible for 25 percent of global emissions in 1990, and it was widely believed that the treaty could not enter into force without U.S. ratification. Despite the withdrawal of the United States from the treaty, however, other countries, including the European Union, Japan, and Canada, have gone ahead with a modified version of the protocol. The Kyoto Protocol is one of several international treaties enjoying broad international support in which the United States has not participated. President Bush has since proposed alternative strategies for dealing with global warming based on tax incentives and volunteer emissions reductions by industry. These plans have been widely attacked as vague and unenforceable.

In June 2002 the Bush administration's *U.S. Climate Action Report 2002* (U.S. Department of State, May 2002) conceded first, that global warming exists and is largely the result of human activity, and second, that global warming will cause substantial and far-reaching effects in the United States. The Bush administration has voiced support for adapting to these changes rather than adopting serious measures to reduce greenhouse gas emissions. Soon after the release of the report, President Bush, when asked if he planned any new initiatives to combat global warming, responded, "No, I've laid out that very comprehensive initiative. I read the report put out by the bureaucracy. I do not support the Kyoto treaty. The Kyoto treaty would severely damage the United States economy, and I don't accept that. I accept the alternative we put out, that we can grow our economy and, at the same time, through technologies, improve our environment."

In December 2003 Vladimir Putin, the President of Russia, announced that Russia, the second largest producer of greenhouse gases after the United States, also would not ratify the Kyoto Protocol. However the European Union continues to be enthusiastic about the importance of the agreement, and announced in December 2003 that it was on target for meeting emissions reductions.

U.S. Public Opinion

A November 1997 Gallup Poll suggested that despite their concern about global climate change, Americans were unlikely to support strict measures regarding greenhouse gas emissions. Sixty-nine percent of respondents did not think global warming would be a threat in their own lifetimes, but 65 percent believed it would be a problem in their children's lifetimes. Even so, 48 percent said they were unwilling to reduce global warming if costs for energy went up. (However, 44 percent said they were willing to pay higher energy costs.) An even greater percentage—54 percent—said they would be unwilling to take steps to reduce global warming if unemployment would rise as a result.

Gallup conducted another survey on environmental attitudes in April 2001, coincident with the annual celebration of "Earth Day." Regarding global warming, most Americans surveyed said that they believe global warming's effects will be visible in their lifetimes. One-third of those surveyed said they worry about global warming "a great deal." In fact, a quarter of Americans believe that "immediate and drastic" action must be taken to help preserve environmental resources. A majority, 57 percent, also said that environmental concerns should take precedence over economic considerations when these clash, as they often do. Americans also disagree with several choices made by the Bush administration, in general favoring environmentally friendly choices on issues such as regulating industrial emissions, drilling in the Arctic National Wildlife Refuge, and participating in the Kyoto Protocol on global warming.

Finally, a March 2003 Gallup survey revealed that 75 percent of respondents favored increased enforcement of environmental regulation, and a similar proportion were in favor of mandatory controls on carbon dioxide emissions and other "greenhouse gas" emissions. Fifty-five percent were opposed to opening the Arctic National Wildlife Refuge to oil companies. However, in this poll, respondents were more evenly divided on the question of environmental concerns vs. energy supplies. Forty-nine percent agreed that environmental protection should be a priority even at the risk of limiting energy supplies, while 45 percent took the opposite position.

CHAPTER 4

ENDANGERED PLANTS AND ECOSYSTEMS

Well over half the threatened and endangered species listed with the U.S. Fish and Wildlife Service are plants. There are a total of 714 threatened and endangered flowering plants (713 U.S. species, 1 foreign species), 5 threatened and endangered conifers and cycads (3 U.S. species, 2 foreign species), 26 listed ferns and allied species (all U.S.), and 2 listed lichen species (both U.S.). Listed U.S. species are shown in Table 4.1, which lists flowering plants, and Table 4.2, which lists endangered conifers, ferns, and lichens. Because the status of most plant species has not been studied in detail, many more plants are probably in danger of extinction than appear on these lists.

Many factors contribute to the endangerment of plant species. Numerous species are the victims of habitat loss due to land and agricultural development. Others have declined due to pollution or habitat damage, or as a result of competition with invasive species. Still others have succumbed to introduced plant diseases. Finally, collectors or dealers often illegally seek rare, showy, or unusual plants, and have depleted populations through over-collection.

The preservation of plant species is important for many reasons. Not only are plants of aesthetic value, they are crucial components of every ecosystem on earth. Plants also serve several functions directly beneficial to humans. First, they provide genetic variation that is used in the breeding of new crop varieties—native plants provide genes that allow for adaptation to local environments, as well as resistance to pests, disease, or drought. In addition, plants are the source of numerous human medicines.

PLANTS IN DECLINE

The *1997 IUCN Red List of Threatened Plants* from the World Conservation Union represents the first global assessment of plants, and was the result of over 20 years of study by botanists, conservation organizations, botani-

cal gardens, and museums around the world. It revealed that 12.5 percent—one of every eight—of the world's plant species are in danger of extinction. In the United States, the figure is even higher, with 29 percent of the nation's 16,000 plant species threatened. Other findings included:

- Of the estimated 270,000 known species of vascular plants (ferns, conifers, and flowering plants, but not mosses, lichens, and algae), 33,798 species are in danger of extinction.

- Of the plant species at risk, 91 percent are found only in a single nation. These species are particularly vulnerable, having only limited options for recovery.

- Many plant species known to have medicinal value are at risk of disappearing. For example, 75 percent of species in the yew family, a source of cancer-fighting compounds, are threatened. Twelve percent of the willow family, from which aspirin is derived, are threatened.

- About 33 percent of the dipterocarps, a tree group that includes valuable timber species in Asia, are threatened.

- The loss of each species causes a loss of genetic material that could be used to produce stronger, healthier crops for human and animal consumption.

- Close relatives to many familiar plants are at risk of extinction, including 14 percent of the rose family and 32 percent of lilies and irises.

- Numerous species whose value has not yet been studied are at risk.

According to the *1997 IUCN Red List of Threatened Plants*, the primary reasons for plant endangerment are habitat loss and introduction of invasive species. The ten areas with the greatest percentage of threatened flora are St. Helena (41.2 percent), Mauritius (39.2 percent), Seychelles (31.2 percent), the United States (29 percent),

TABLE 4.1

Endangered and threatened species of flowering plants, February 2004

Status	Species name	Status	Species name
E	Sand verbena, large-fruited *(Abronia macrocarpa)*	E	Milk vetch, Ventura Marsh *(Astragalus pycnostachyus var. lanosissimus)*
E	*Abutilon eremitopetalum* (No common name)	E	Milk vetch, Jesup's *(Astragalus robbinsii var. jesupi)*
E	Koʻoloaʻula *(Abutilon menziesii)*	E	Milk vetch, coastal dunes *(Astragalus tener var. titi)*
E	*Abutilon sandwicense* (No common name)	E	Milk vetch, triple-ribbed *(Astragalus tricarinatus)*
E	Liliwai *(Acaena exigua)*	E	Cactus, star *(Astrophytum asterias)*
T	Thornmint, San Diego *(Acanthomintha ilicifolia)*	E	Crownscale, San Jacinto Valley *(Atriplex coronata var. notatior)*
E	Thornmint, San Mateo *(Acanthomintha obovata ssp. duttonii)*	E	*Auerodendron pauciflorum* (No common name)
E	*Achyranthes mutica* (No common name)	E	Ayenia, Texas *(Ayenia limitaris)*
E	Chaff flower, round-leaved *(Achyranthes splendens var. rotundata)*	T	Baccharis, Encinitas *(Baccharis vanessae)*
T	Monkshood, northern wild *(Aconitum noveboracense)*	E	Palo de ramon *(Banara vanderbiltii)*
T	Joint vetch, sensitive *(Aeschynomene virginica)*	E	Rattleweed, hairy *(Baptisia arachnifera)*
E	Gerardia, sandplain *(Agalinis acuta)*	E	Barberry, Nevin's *(Berberis nevinii)*
E	Agave, Arizona *(Agave arizonica)*	E	Barberry, island *(Berberis pinnata ssp. insularis)*
E	Mahoe *(Alectryon macrococcus)*	T	Birch, Virginia round-leaf *(Betula uber)*
E	Onion, Munz's *(Allium munzii)*	E	Koʻokoʻolau *(Bidens micrantha ssp. kalealaha)*
E	Alopecurus, Sonoma *(Alopecurus aequalis var. sonomensis)*	E	Koʻokoʻolau *(Bidens wiebkei)*
E	Kuawawaenohu *(Alsinidendron lychnoides)*	E	Sunshine, Sonoma *(Blennosperma bakeri)*
E	*Alsinidendron obovatum* (No common name)	T	Aster, decurrent false *(Boltonia decurrens)*
E	*Alsinidendron trinerve* (No common name)	T	Bonamia, Florida *(Bonamia grandiflora)*
E	*Alsinidendron viscosum* (No common name)	E	*Bonamia menziesii* (No common name)
E	*Amaranthus brownii* (No common name)	E	Olulu *(Brighamia insignis)*
T	Amaranth, seabeach *(Amaranthus pumilus)*	E	Pua ʻala *(Brighamia rockii)*
E	Ambrosia, south Texas *(Ambrosia cheiranthifolia)*	T	Brodiaea, thread-leaved *(Brodiaea filifolia)*
E	Ambrosia, San Diego *(Ambrosia pumila)*	T	Brodiaea, Chinese Camp *(Brodiaea pallida)*
E	Lead plant, crenulate *(Amorpha crenulata)*	E	Boxwood, Vahl's *(Buxus vahlii)*
T	Amphianthus, little *(Amphianthus pusillus)*	E	Uhiuhi *(Caesalpinia kavaiense)*
E	Fiddleneck, large-flowered *(Amsinckia grandiflora)*	E	Capa rosa *(Callicarpa ampla)*
E	Blue-star, Kearney's *(Amsonia kearneyana)*	E	Poppy mallow, Texas *(Callirhoe scabriuscula)*
E	Cactus, Tobusch fishhook *(Ancistrocactus tobuschii)*	T	Mariposa lily, Tiburon *(Calochortus tiburonensis)*
T	Potato bean, Price's *(Apios priceana)*	E	*Calyptranthes thomasiana* (No common name)
E	Rock cress, Hoffmann's *(Arabis hoffmannii)*	T	Pussypaws, Mariposa *(Calyptridium pulchellum)*
E	Rock cress, McDonald's *(Arabis mcdonaldiana)*	T	Manaca, palma de *(Calyptronoma rivalis)*
E	Rock cress, Braun's *(Arabis perstellata)*	E	Morning glory, Stebbins' *(Calystegia stebbinsii)*
E	Rock cress, shale barren *(Arabis serotina)*	T	Evening primrose, San Benito *(Camissonia benitensis)*
E	Bear-poppy, dwarf *(Arctomecon humilis)*	E	Bellflower, Brooksville *(Campanula robinsiae)*
E	Manzanita, Santa Rosa Island *(Arctostaphylos confertiflora)*	E	ʻAwikiwiki *(Canavalia molokaiensis)*
E	Manzanita, Del Mar *(Arctostaphylos glandulosa ssp. crassifolia)*	E	Bittercress, small-anthered *(Cardamine micranthera)*
E	Manzanita, Presidio *(Arctostaphylos hookeri var. ravenii)*	E	Sedge, white *(Carex albida)*
T	Manzanita, Morro *(Arctostaphylos morroensis)*	E	Sedge, golden *(Carex lutea)*
T	Manzanita, Ione *(Arctostaphylos myrtifolia)*	E	Sedge, Navajo *(Carex specuicola)*
T	Manzanita, pallid *(Arctostaphylos pallida)*	E	Paintbrush, Tiburon *(Castilleja affinis ssp. neglecta)*
E	Sandwort, Cumberland *(Arenaria cumberlandensis)*	T	Owl's clover, fleshy *(Castilleja campestris ssp. succulenta)*
E	Sandwort, marsh *(Arenaria paludicola)*	T	Paintbrush, ash-grey *(Castilleja cinerea)*
T	Sandwort, Bear Valley *(Arenaria ursina)*	E	Indian paintbrush, San Clemente Island *(Castilleja grisea)*
E	Poppy, Sacramento prickly *(Argemone pleiacantha ssp. pinnatisecta)*	T	Paintbrush, golden *(Castilleja levisecta)*
E	Silversword, Mauna Loa (=Kaʻu) *(Argyroxiphium kauense)*	E	Paintbrush, soft-leaved *(Castilleja mollis)*
T	ʻAhinahina *(Argyroxiphium sandwicense ssp. macrocephalum)*	E	*Catesbaea melanocarpa* (No common name)
E	ʻAhinahina *(Argyroxiphium sandwicense ssp. sandwicense)*	E	Jewelflower, California *(Caulanthus californicus)*
E	*Aristida chaseae* (No common name)	E	Ceanothus, coyote *(Ceanothus ferrisae)*
E	Pelos del diablo *(Aristida portoricensis)*	T	Ceanothus, Vail Lake *(Ceanothus ophiochilus)*
T	Milkweed, Mead's *(Asclepias meadii)*	E	Ceanothus, Pine Hill *(Ceanothus roderickii)*
T	Milkweed, Welsh's *(Asclepias welshii)*	E	Kamanomano *(Cenchrus agrimonioides)*
E	Pawpaw, four-petal *(Asimina tetramera)*	T	Century, spring-loving *(Centaurium namophilum)*
E	Milk vetch, Cushenbury *(Astragalus albens)*	E	Awiwi *(Centaurium sebaeoides)*
E	Milk vetch, Shivwitz *(Astragalus ampullarioides)*	E	Mountain mahogany, Catalina Island *(Cercocarpus traskiae)*
E	Milk vetch, Applegate's *(Astragalus applegatei)*	E	Prickly apple, fragrant *(Cereus eriophorus var. fragrans)*
E	Ground plum, Guthrie's (=Pyne's) *(Astragalus bibullatus)*	E	*Chamaecrista glandulosa var. mirabilis* (No common name)
E	Milk vetch, Braunton's *(Astragalus brauntonii)*	E	ʻAkoko *(Chamaesyce celastroides var. kaenana)*
E	Milk vetch, Clara Hunt's *(Astragalus clarianus)*	E	Spurge, deltoid *(Chamaesyce deltoidea ssp. deltoidea)*
E	Milk vetch, Sentry *(Astragalus cremnophylax var. cremnophylax)*	E	ʻAkoko *(Chamaesyce deppeana)*
T	Milk vetch, Deseret *(Astragalus desereticus)*	T	Spurge, Garber's *(Chamaesyce garberi)*
E	Milk vetch, Holmgren *(Astragalus holmgreniorum)*	E	*Chamaesyce halemanui* (No common name)
E	Milk vetch, Mancos *(Astragalus humillimus)*	E	ʻAkoko *(Chamaesyce herbstii)*
E	Milk vetch, Lane Mountain *(Astragalus jaegerianus)*	T	Spurge, Hoover's *(Chamaesyce hooveri)*
E	Milk vetch, Coachella Valley *(Astragalus lentiginosus var. coachellae)*	E	ʻAkoko *(Chamaesyce kuwaleana)*
T	Milk vetch, Fish Slough *(Astragalus lentiginosus var. piscinensis)*	E	ʻAkoko *(Chamaesyce rockii)*
T	Milk vetch, Peirson's *(Astragalus magdalenae var. peirsonii)*	E	ʻAkoko, Ewa Plains *(Chamaesyce skottsbergii var. kalaeloana)*
T	Milk vetch, heliotrope *(Astragalus montii)*	E	Fringe tree, pygmy *(Chionanthus pygmaeus)*
E	Milk vetch, Osterhout *(Astragalus osterhoutii)*	T	Amole, purple *(Chlorogalum purpureum)*
T	Milk vetch, Ash Meadows *(Astragalus phoenix)*	E	Spineflower, Howell's *(Chorizanthe howellii)*

Jamaica (22.5 percent), Turkey (21.7 percent), Spain (19.5 percent), French Polynesia (19.5 percent), Pitcairn (18.4 percent), and Reunion (18.1 percent). Note that islands are disproportionately represented in the top ten. This is primarily because islands are particularly vulnerable to invasive species.

TABLE 4.1

Endangered and threatened species of flowering plants, February 2004 [CONTINUED]

Status	Species name	Status	Species name
E	Spineflower, Orcutt's (*Chorizanthe orcuttiana*)	E	*Cyanea (= Rollandia) crispa* (No common name)
E	Spineflower, Ben Lomond (*Chorizanthe pungens* var. *hartwegiana*)	E	Haha (*Cyanea shipmannii*)
T	Spineflower, Monterey (*Chorizanthe pungens* var. *pungens*)	E	Haha (*Cyanea stictophylla*)
E	Spineflower, Robust (including Scotts Valley) (*Chorizanthe robusta* (incuding vars. *robusta* and *hartwegii*))	E	Haha (*Cyanea st-johnii*)
		E	Haha (*Cyanea superba*)
E	Spineflower, Sonoma (*Chorizanthe valida*)	E	Haha (*Cyanea truncata*)
E	Aster, Florida golden (*Chrysopsis floridana*)	E	Haha (*Cyanea undulata*)
E	Thistle, fountain (*Cirsium fontinale* var. *fontinale*)	T	Cycladenia, Jones (*Cycladenia jonesii* (= *humilis*))
E	Thistle, Chorro Creek bog (*Cirsium fontinale* var. *obispoense*)	E	Pu'uka'a (*Cyperus trachysanthos*)
E	Thistle, Suisun (*Cirsium hydrophilum* var. *hydrophilum*)	E	Ha'iwale (*Cyrtandra crenata*)
E	Thistle, La Graciosa (*Cirsium loncholepis*)	E	Mapele (*Cyrtandra cyaneoides*)
T	Thistle, Pitcher's (*Cirsium pitcheri*)	E	Ha'iwale (*Cyrtandra dentata*)
T	Thistle, Sacramento Mountains (*Cirsium vinaceum*)	E	Ha'iwale (*Cyrtandra giffardii*)
E	Clarkia, Presidio (*Clarkia franciscana*)	T	Ha'iwale (*Cyrtandra limahuliensis*)
E	Clarkia, Vine Hill (*Clarkia imbricata*)	E	Ha'iwale (*Cyrtandra munroi*)
E	Clarkia, Pismo (*Clarkia speciosa* ssp. *immaculata*)	E	Ha'iwale (*Cyrtandra polyantha*)
T	Clarkia, Springville (*Clarkia springvillensis*)	E	Ha'iwale (*Cyrtandra subumbellata*)
E	Leather flower, Morefield's (*Clematis morefieldii*)	E	Ha'iwale (*Cyrtandra tintinnabula*)
E	Leather flower, Alabama (*Clematis socialis*)	E	Ha'iwale (*Cyrtandra viridiflora*)
E	'Oha wai (*Clermontia drepanomorpha*)	E	Prairie-clover, leafy (*Dalea foliosa*)
E	'Oha wai (*Clermontia lindseyana*)	E	*Daphnopsis hellerana* (No common name)
E	'Oha wai (*Clermontia oblongifolia* ssp. *brevipes*)	E	Pawpaw, beautiful (*Deeringothamnus pulchellus*)
E	'Oha wai (*Clermontia oblongifolia* ssp. *mauiensis*)	E	Pawpaw, Rugel's (*Deeringothamnus rugelii*)
E	'Oha wai (*Clermontia peleana*)	T	Tarplant, Otay (*Deinandra (= Hemizonia) conjugens*)
E	'Oha wai (*Clermontia pyrularia*)	E	*Delissea rhytidosperma* (No common name)
E	'Oha wai (*Clermontia samuelii*)	E	Oha (*Delissea rivularis*)
T	Pigeon wings (*Clitoria fragrans*)	E	Oha (*Delissea subcordata*)
E	Kauila (*Colubrina oppositifolia*)	E	*Delissea undulata* (No common name)
E	Rosemary, short-leaved (*Conradina brevifolia*)	E	Larkspur, Baker's (*Delphinium bakeri*)
E	Rosemary, Etonia (*Conradina etonia*)	E	Larkspur, yellow (*Delphinium luteum*)
E	Rosemary, Apalachicola (*Conradina glabra*)	E	Larkspur, San Clemente Island (*Delphinium variegatum* ssp. *kinkiense*)
T	Rosemary, Cumberland (*Conradina verticillata*)	E	Mint, Garrett's (*Dicerandra christmanii*)
E	*Cordia bellonis* (No common name)	E	Mint, longspurred (*Dicerandra cornutissima*)
E	Bird's beak, salt marsh (*Cordylanthus maritimus* ssp. *maritimus*)	E	Mint, scrub (*Dicerandra frutescens*)
E	Bird's beak, soft (*Cordylanthus mollis* ssp. *mollis*)	E	Mint, Lakela's (*Dicerandra immaculata*)
E	Bird's beak, palmate-bracted (*Cordylanthus palmatus*)	E	Spineflower, slender-horned (*Dodecahema leptoceras*)
E	Bird's beak, Pennell's (*Cordylanthus tenuis* ssp. *capillaris*)	E	Na'ena'e (*Dubautia herbstobatae*)
E	Palo de nigua (*Cornutia obovata*)	E	Na'ena'e (*Dubautia latifolia*)
E	Cactus, Nellie cory (*Coryphantha minima*)	E	Na'ena'e (*Dubautia pauciflorula*)
T	Cory cactus, bunched (*Coryphantha ramillosa*)	E	Na'ena'e (*Dubautia plantaginea* ssp. *humilis*)
T	Cactus, Cochise pincushion (*Coryphantha robbinsorum*)	T	Dudleya, Conejo (*Dudleya abramsii* ssp. *parva*)
E	Cactus, Pima pineapple (*Coryphantha scheeri* var. *robustispina*)	T	Dudleya, marcescent (*Dudleya cymosa* ssp. *marcescens*)
T	Cactus, Lee pincushion (*Coryphantha sneedii* var. *leei*)	T	Dudleyea, Santa Monica Mountains (*Dudleya cymosa* ssp. *ovatifolia*)
E	Cactus, Sneed pincushion (*Coryphantha sneedii* var. *sneedii*)	T	Dudleya, Santa Cruz Island (*Dudleya nesiotica*)
E	*Cranichis ricartii* (No common name)	E	Dudleya, Santa Clara Valley (*Dudleya setchellii*)
E	Higuero de sierra (*Crescentia portoricensis*)	T	Liveforever, Laguna Beach (*Dudleya stolonifera*)
E	Harebells, Avon Park (*Crotalaria avonensis*)	E	Liveforever, Santa Barbara Island (*Dudleya traskiae*)
E	Cat's-eye, Terlingua Creek (*Cryptantha crassipes*)	T	Dudleya, Verity's (*Dudleya verityi*)
E	Gourd, Okeechobee (*Cucurbita okeechobeensis* ssp. *okeechobeensis*)	E	Coneflower, smooth (*Echinacea laevigata*)
E	Haha (*Cyanea acuminata*)	E	Coneflower, Tennessee purple (*Echinacea tennesseensis*)
E	Haha (*Cyanea asarifolia*)	E	Cactus, Nichol's Turk's head (*Echinocactus horizonthalonius* var. *nicholii*)
E	Haha (*Cyanea copelandii* ssp. *copelandii*)	T	Cactus, Chisos Mountain hedgehog (*Echinocereus chisoensis* var. *chisoensis*)
E	Haha (*Cyanea copelandii* ssp. *haleakalaensis*)		
E	Haha (*Cyanea dunbarii*)	E	Cactus, Kuenzler hedgehog (*Echinocereus fendleri* var. *kuenzleri*)
E	Haha (*Cyanea glabra*)	E	Cactus, black lace (*Echinocereus reichenbachii* var. *albertii*)
E	Haha (*Cyanea grimesiana* ssp. *grimesiana*)	E	Cactus, Arizona hedgehog (*Echinocereus triglochidiatus* var. *arizonicus*)
E	Haha (*Cyanea grimesiana* ssp. *obatae*)	E	Pitaya, Davis' green (*Echinocereus viridiflorus* var. *davisii*)
E	Haha (*Cyanea hamatiflora carlsonii*)	T	Cactus, Lloyd's Mariposa (*Echinomastus mariposensis*)
E	Haha (*Cyanea hamatiflora* ssp. *hamatiflora*)	T	Sunray, Ash Meadows (*Enceliopsis nudicaulis* var. *corrugata*)
E	Haha (*Cyanea humboldtiana*)	E	Love grass, Fosberg's (*Eragrostis fosbergii*)
E	Haha (*Cyanea koolauensis*)	E	Mallow, Kern (*Eremalche kernensis*)
E	Haha (*Cyanea lobata*)	E	Woolly star, Santa Ana River (*Eriastrum densifolium* ssp. *sanctorum*)
E	Haha (*Cyanea longiflora*)	E	Daisy, Willamette (*Erigeron decumbens* var. *decumbens*)
E	Haha (*Cyanea macrostegia* ssp. *gibsonii*)	T	Daisy, Maguire (*Erigeron maguirei*)
E	Haha (*Cyanea mannii*)	T	Daisy, Parish's (*Erigeron parishii*)
E	Haha (*Cyanea mceldowneyi*)	T	Fleabane, Zuni (*Erigeron rhizomatus*)
E	Haha (*Cyanea pinnatifida*)	E	Mountain balm, Indian Knob (*Eriodictyon altissimum*)
E	Haha (*Cyanea platyphylla*)	E	Yerba santa, Lompoc (*Eriodictyon capitatum*)
E	Haha (*Cyanea procera*)	E	Buckwheat, Ione (including Irish Hill) (*Eriogonum apricum* (including var. *postratum*))
T	Haha (*Cyanea recta*)		
E	Haha (*Cyanea remyi*)	T	Wild buckwheat, gypsum (*Eriogonum gypsophilum*)

However, the *1997 IUCN Red List of Threatened Plants* contains regional biases—assessments of flora in North America, Australia, and Southern Africa were more comprehensive than those for other regions. It is likely that significantly greater numbers of threatened plant species will be found in Asia, the Caribbean, South America, and the rest of Africa when these areas are fully studied.

TABLE 4.1

Endangered and threatened species of flowering plants, February 2004 [CONTINUED]

Status	Species name	Status	Species name
T	Wild buckwheat, southern mountain (*Eriogonum kennedyi* var. *austromontanum*)	E	Kauai hau kuahiwi (*Hibiscadelphus distans*)
T	Buckwheat, scrub (*Eriogonum longifolium* var. *gnaphalifolium*)	E	Hau kuahiwi (*Hibiscadelphus giffardianus*)
E	Buckwheat, cushenbury (*Eriogonum ovalifolium* var. *vineum*)	E	Hau kuahiwi (*Hibiscadelphus hualalaiensis*)
E	Buckwheat, steamboat (*Eriogonum ovalifolium* var. *williamsiae*)	E	Hau kuahiwi (*Hibiscadelphus woodii*)
E	Wild buckwheat, clay-loving (*Eriogonum pelinophilum*)	E	Koki'o ke'oke'o (*Hibiscus arnottianus* ssp. *immaculatus*)
E	Sunflower, San Mateo woolly (*Eriophyllum latilobum*)	E	Ma'o hau hele, (=native yellow hibiscus) (*Hibiscus brackenridgei*)
E	Button celery, San Diego (*Eryngium aristulatum* var. *parishii*)	E	Hibiscus, Clay's (*Hibiscus clayi*)
E	Thistle, Loch Lomond coyote (*Eryngium constancei*)	E	Koki'o ke'oke'o (*Hibiscus waimeae* ssp. *hannerae*)
E	Snakeroot (*Eryngium cuneifolium*)	E	Rush pea, slender (*Hoffmannseggia tenella*)
E	Wallflower, Contra Costa (*Erysimum capitatum* var. *angustatum*)	T	Tarplant, Santa Cruz (*Holocarpha macradenia*)
E	Wallflower, Menzies' (*Erysimum menziesii*)	T	Howellia, water (*Howellia aquatilis*)
E	Wallflower, Ben Lomond (*Erysimum teretifolium*)	T	Heather, mountain golden (*Hudsonia montana*)
E	Lily, Minnesota dwarf trout (*Erythronium propullans*)	T	Daisy, lakeside (*Hymenoxys herbacea*)
E	Uvillo (*Eugenia haematocarpa*)	T	Dawn flower, Texas prairie (*Hymenoxys texana*)
E	Nioi (*Eugenia koolauensis*)	E	Hypericum, highlands scrub (*Hypericum cumulicola*)
E	*Eugenia woodburyana* (No common name)	E	Holly, Cook's (*Ilex cookii*)
E	'Akoko (*Euphorbia haeleeleana*)	E	*Ilex sintenisii* (No common name)
T	Spurge, telephus (*Euphorbia telephioides*)	E	Mallow, Peter's Mountain (*Iliamna corei*)
T	Mustard, Penland alpine fen (*Eutrema penlandii*)	E	Ipomopsis, Holy Ghost (*Ipomopsis sancti-spiritus*)
E	Heau (*Exocarpos luteolus*)	T	Iris, dwarf lake (*Iris lacustris*)
E	Mehamehame (*Flueggea neowawraea*)	E	Ischaemum, Hilo (*Ischaemum byrone*)
E	Frankenia, Johnston's (*Frankenia johnstonii*)	E	Aupaka (*Isodendrion hosakae*)
E	Flannelbush, Pine Hill (*Fremontodendron californicum* ssp. *decumbens*)	E	Aupaka (*Isodendrion laurifolium*)
E	Flannelbush, Mexican (*Fremontodendron mexicanum*)	T	Aupaka (*Isodendrion longifolium*)
E	Fritillary, Gentner's (*Fritillaria gentneri*)	E	Kula wahine noho (*Isodendrion pyrifolium*)
E	*Gahnia lanaiensis* (No common name)	T	Pogonia, small whorled (*Isotria medeoloides*)
E	Milkpea, Small's (*Galactia smallii*)	T	Ivesia, Ash Meadows (*Ivesia kingii* var. *eremica*)
E	Bedstraw, island (*Galium buxifolium*)	E	Jacquemontia, beach (*Jacquemontia reclinata*)
E	Bedstraw, El Dorado (*Galium californicum* ssp. *sierrae*)	E	Walnut, West Indian or nogal (*Juglans jamaicensis*)
E	Gardenia (=Na'u), Hawaiian (*Gardenia brighamii*)	E	Water-willow, Cooley's (*Justicia cooleyi*)
E	Nanu (*Gardenia mannii*)	E	Kohe malama malama o kanaloa (*Kanaloa kahoolawensis*)
T	Butterfly plant, Colorado (*Gaura neomexicana* var. *coloradensis*)	E	Koki'o, Cooke's (*Kokia cookei*)
T	*Geocarpon minimum* (No common name)	E	Koki'o (*Kokia drynarioides*)
E	Geranium, Hawaiian red-flowered (*Geranium arboreum*)	E	Koki'o (*Kokia kauaiensis*)
E	Nohoanu (*Geranium multiflorum*)	E	Kamakahala (*Labordia cyrtandrae*)
T	*Gesneria pauciflora* (No common name)	E	Kamakahala (*Labordia lydgatei*)
E	Avens, spreading (*Geum radiatum*)	E	Kamakahala (*Labordia tinifolia* var. *lanaiensis*)
E	Gilia, Monterey (*Gilia tenuiflora* ssp. *arenaria*)	E	Kamakahala (*Labordia tinifolia* var. *wahiawaensis*)
E	Gilia, Hoffmann's slender-flowered (*Gilia tenuiflora* ssp. *hoffmannii*)	E	Kamakahala (*Labordia triflora*)
E	Goetzea, beautiful (*Goetzea elegans*)	E	Goldfields, Burke's (*Lasthenia burkei*)
E	*Gouania hillebrandii* (No common name)	E	Goldfields, Contra Costa (*Lasthenia conjugens*)
E	*Gouania meyenii* (No common name)	E	Layia, beach (*Layia carnosa*)
E	*Gouania vitifolia* (No common name)	E	*Lepanthes eltoroensis* (No common name)
T	Gumplant, Ash Meadows (*Grindelia fraxino-pratensis*)	E	'Anaunau (*Lepidium arbuscula*)
E	Stickseed, showy (*Hackelia venusta*)	E	Ridge-cress, Barneby (*Lepidium barnebyanum*)
T	Seagrass, Johnson's (*Halophila johnsonii*)	E	*Leptocereus grantianus* (No common name)
E	Honohono (*Haplostachys haplostachya*)	T	Bush clover, prairie (*Lespedeza leptostachya*)
E	Beauty, Harper's (*Harperocallis flava*)	T	Bladderpod, Dudley Bluffs (*Lesquerella congesta*)
T	Higo, chumbo (*Harrisia portoricensis*)	T	Bladderpod, Missouri (*Lesquerella filiformis*)
E	Pennyroyal, Todsen's (*Hedeoma todsenii*)	E	Bladderpod, San Bernardino Mountains (*Lesquerella kingii* ssp. *bernardina*)
E	Awiwi (*Hedyotis cookiana*)	T	Bladderpod, lyrate (*Lesquerella lyrata*)
E	Kio'ele (*Hedyotis coriacea*)	E	Bladderpod, white (*Lesquerella pallida*)
E	*Hedyotis degeneri* (No common name)	E	Bladderpod, Spring Creek (*Lesquerella perforata*)
E	Pilo (*Hedyotis mannii*)	E	Bladderpod, Zapata (*Lesquerella thamnophila*)
E	*Hedyotis parvula* (No common name)	E	Bladderpod, kodachrome (*Lesquerella tumulosa*)
E	Bluet, Roan Mountain (*Hedyotis purpurea* var. *montana*)	E	Lessingia, San Francisco (*Lessingia germanorum* (=*L.g.* var. *germanorum*))
E	Kopa (*Hedyotis schlechtendahliana* var. *remyi*)	T	Blazingstar, Heller's (*Liatris helleri*)
E	Hedyotis, Na Pali beach (*Hedyotis st.-johnii*)	E	Blazingstar, scrub (*Liatris ohlingerae*)
T	Sneezeweed, Virginia (*Helenium virginicum*)	E	Water-umbel, Huachuca (*Lilaeopsis schaffneriana* var. *recurva*)
T	Rush rose, island (*Helianthemum greenei*)	E	Lily, western (*Lilium occidentale*)
T	Sunflower, Eggert's (*Helianthus eggertii*)	E	Lily, Pitkin Marsh (*Lilium pardalinum* ssp. *pitkinense*)
T	Sunflower, Pecos (=puzzle, =paradox) (*Helianthus paradoxus*)	E	Meadowfoam, large-flowered wooly (*Limnanthes floccosa grandiflora*)
E	Sunflower, Schweinitz's (*Helianthus schweinitzii*)	E	Meadowfoam, Butte County (*Limnanthes floccosa* ssp. *californica*)
T	Pink, swamp (*Helonias bullata*)	E	Meadowfoam, Sebastopol (*Limnanthes vinculans*)
E	Tarplant, Gaviota (*Hemizonia increscens* ssp. *villosa*)	E	Pondberry (*Lindera melissifolia*)
T	Dwar flax, Marin (*Hesperolinon congestum*)	E	Nehe (*Lipochaeta fauriei*)
E	*Hesperomannia arborescens* (No common name)	E	Nehe (*Lipochaeta kamolensis*)
E	*Hesperomannia arbuscula* (No common name)	E	Nehe (*Lipochaeta lobata* var. *leptophylla*)
E	*Hesperomannia lydgatei* (No common name)	E	Nehe (*Lipochaeta micrantha*)
T	Heartleaf, dwarf-flowered (*Hexastylis naniflora*)	E	Nehe (*Lipochaeta tenuifolia*)
		E	*Lipochaeta venosa* (No common name)

Information from the *1997 IUCN Red List of Threatened Plants* is being incorporated into new versions of IUCN publications. The *2003 IUCN Red List of Threatened Species* currently lists 6,774 species of threatened plants. This is almost 70 percent of the 9,706 that have been examined. However, only about 4 percent of plant

Status	Species name	Status	Species name
E	Nehe (*Lipochaeta waimeaensis*)	E	Orcutt grass, hairy (*Orcuttia pilosa*)
E	Woodland-star, San Clemente Island (*Lithophragma maximum*)	T	Orcutt grass, slender (*Orcuttia tenuis*)
E	*Lobelia gaudichaudii* ssp. *koolauensis* (No common name)	E	Orcutt grass, Sacramento (*Orcuttia viscida*)
E	*Lobelia monostachya* (No common name)	E	Palo de rosa (*Ottoschulzia rhodoxylon*)
E	*Lobelia niihauensis* (No common name)	E	Dropwort, Canby's (*Oxypolis canbyi*)
E	*Lobelia oahuensis* (No common name)	E	Oxytheca, cushenbury (*Oxytheca parishii* var. *goodmaniana*)
E	Desert parsley, Bradshaw's (*Lomatium bradshawii*)	T	Locoweed, Fassett's (*Oxytropis campestris* var. *chartacea*)
E	Lomatium, Cook's (*Lomatium cookii*)	E	Panicgrass, Carter's (*Panicum fauriei* var. *carteri*)
E	Broom, San Clemente Island (*Lotus dendroideus* ssp. *traskiae*)	E	Lau 'ehu (*Panicum niihauense*)
E	Lupine, scrub (*Lupinus aridorum*)	T	Whitlow wort, papery (*Paronychia chartacea*)
E	Lupine, Nipomo Mesa (*Lupinus nipomensis*)	E	Stonecrop, Lake County (*Parvisedum leiocarpum*)
T	Lupine, Kincaid's (*Lupinus sulphureus* (= *oreganus*) ssp. *kincaidii* (= var. *kincaidii*))	E	Lousewort, Furbish (*Pedicularis furbishiae*)
E	Lupine, clover (*Lupinus tidestromii*)	E	Cactus, Brady pincushion (*Pediocactus bradyi*)
E	*Lyonia truncata* var. *proctorii* (No common name)	E	Cactus, San Rafael (*Pediocactus despainii*)
E	Loosestrife, rough-leaved (*Lysimachia asperulaefolia*)	T	Cactus, Siler pincushion (*Pediocactus* (= *Echinocactus*, = *Utahia*) *sileri*)
E	*Lysimachia filifolia* (No common name)	E	Cactus, Knowlton (*Pediocactus knowltonii*)
E	*Lysimachia lydgatei* (No common name)	E	Cactus, Peebles Navajo (*Pediocactus peeblesianus peeblesianus*)
E	*Lysimachia maxima* (No common name)	T	Cactus, Winkler (*Pediocactus winkleri*)
T	Birds in a nest, white (*Macbridea alba*)	E	Penstemon, blowout (*Penstemon haydenii*)
E	Bush mallow, San Clemente Island (*Malacothamnus clementinus*)	E	Beardtongue, Penland (*Penstemon penlandii*)
E	Bush mallow, Santa Cruz Island (*Malacothamnus fasciculatus* var. *nesioticus*)	E	Pentachaeta, white-rayed (*Pentachaeta bellidiflora*)
E	Malacothrix, Santa Cruz Island (*Malacothrix indecora*)	E	Pentachaeta, Lyon's (*Pentachaeta lyonii*)
E	Malacothrix, island (*Malacothrix squalida*)	E	Peperomia, Wheeler's (*Peperomia wheeleri*)
E	Manioc, Walker's (*Manihot walkerae*)	T	Makou (*Peucedanum sandwicense*)
E	*Mariscus fauriei* (No common name)	E	Phacelia, clay (*Phacelia argillacea*)
E	*Mariscus pennatiformis* (No common name)	E	Phacelia, North Park (*Phacelia formosula*)
T	Button, Mohr's Barbara (*Marshallia mohrii*)	E	Phacelia, island (*Phacelia insularis* ssp. *insularis*)
E	Alani (*Melicope adscendens*)	E	Phlox, Yreka (*Phlox hirsuta*)
E	Alani (*Melicope balloui*)	E	Phlox, Texas trailing (*Phlox nivalis* ssp. *texensis*)
E	Alani (*Melicope haupuensis*)	E	*Phyllostegia glabra* var. *lanaiensis* (No common name)
E	Alani (*Melicope knudsenii*)	E	*Phyllostegia hirsuta* (No common name)
E	Alani (*Melicope lydgatei*)	E	*Phyllostegia kaalaensis* (No common name)
E	Alani (*Melicope mucronulata*)	E	*Phyllostegia knudsenii* (No common name)
E	Alani (*Melicope munroi*)	E	*Phyllostegia mannii* (No common name)
E	Alani (*Melicope ovalis*)	E	*Phyllostegia mollis* (No common name)
E	Alani (*Melicope pallida*)	E	*Phyllostegia parviflora* (No common name)
E	Alani (*Melicope quadrangularis*)	E	Kiponapona (*Phyllostegia racemosa*)
E	Alani (*Melicope reflexa*)	E	*Phyllostegia velutina* (No common name)
E	Alani (*Melicope saint-johnii*)	E	*Phyllostegia waimeae* (No common name)
E	Alani (*Melicope zahlbruckneri*)	E	*Phyllostegia warshaueri* (No common name)
T	Blazingstar, Ash Meadows (*Mentzelia leucophylla*)	E	*Phyllostegia wawrana* (No common name)
E	Monkey flower, Michigan (*Mimulus glabratus* var. *michiganensis*)	T	Twinpod, Dudley Bluffs (*Physaria obcordata*)
T	Four o'clock, MacFarlane's (*Mirabilis macfarlanei*)	E	Cactus, Key tree (*Pilosocereus robinii*)
E	*Mitracarpus maxwelliae* (No common name)	T	Butterwort, Godfrey's (*Pinguicula ionantha*)
E	*Mitracarpus polycladus* (No common name)	E	Piperia, Yadon's (*Piperia yadonii*)
E	Monardella, willowy (*Monardella linoides* ssp. *viminea*)	E	Aster, Ruth's golden (*Pityopsis ruthii*)
E	Wooly threads, San Joaquin (*Monolopia* (= *Lembertia*) *congdonii*)	E	Popcornflower, rough (*Plagiobothrys hirtus*)
E	*Munroidendron racemosum* (No common name)	E	Allocarya, Calistoga (*Plagiobothrys strictus*)
E	*Myrcia paganii* (No common name)	E	Kuahiwi laukahi (*Plantago hawaiensis*)
E	Kolea (*Myrsine juddii*)	E	Kuahiwi laukahi (*Plantago princeps*)
T	Kolea (*Myrsine linearifolia*)	E	*Platanthera holochila* (No common name)
T	Navarretia, spreading (*Navarretia fossalis*)	T	Orchid, eastern prairie fringed (*Platanthera leucophaea*)
E	Navarretia, few-flowered (*Navarretia leucocephala* ssp. *pauciflora* (= *N. pauciflora*))	T	Orchid, western prairie fringed (*Platanthera praeclara*)
E	Navarretia, many-flowered (*Navarretia leucocephala* ssp. *plieantha*)	E	Chupacallos (*Pleodendron macranthum*)
E	Navarretia, many-flowered (*Navarretia leucocephala* ssp. *plieantha*)	E	Hala pepe (*Pleomele hawaiiensis*)
T	Grass, Colusa (*Neostapfia colusana*)	E	Bluegrass, San Bernardino (*Poa atropurpurea*)
E	*Neraudia angulata* (No common name)	E	Bluegrass, Mann's (*Poa mannii*)
E	*Neraudia ovata* (No common name)	E	Bluegrass, Napa (*Poa napensis*)
E	*Neraudia sericea* (No common name)	E	Bluegrass, Hawaiian (*Poa sandvicensis*)
E	Niterwort, Amargosa (*Nitrophila mohavensis*)	E	*Poa siphonoglossa* (No common name)
E	Beargrass, Britton's (*Nolina brittoniana*)	E	Mesa mint, San Diego (*Pogogyne abramsii*)
E	'Aiea (*Nothocestrum breviflorum*)	E	Mesa mint, Otay (*Pogogyne nudiuscula*)
E	'Aiea (*Nothocestrum peltatum*)	E	Polygala, Lewton's (*Polygala lewtonii*)
E	Kulu'i (*Nototrichium humile*)	E	Polygala, tiny (*Polygala smallii*)
E	Holei (*Ochrosia kilaueaensis*)	E	Wireweed (*Polygonella basiramia*)
E	Evening primrose, Eureka Valley (*Oenothera avita* ssp. *eurekensis*)	E	Sandlace (*Polygonella myriophylla*)
E	Evening primrose, Antioch Dunes (*Oenothera deltoides* ssp. *howellii*)	E	Polygonum, Scotts Valley (*Polygonum hickmanii*)
E	Cactus, Bakersfield (*Opuntia treleasei*)	E	Po'e (*Portulaca sclerocarpa*)
E	Orcutt grass, California (*Orcuttia californica*)	E	Pondweed, Little Aguja (= Creek) (*Potamogeton clystocarpus*)
T	Orcutt grass, San Joaquin (*Orcuttia inaequalis*)	E	Potentilla, Hickman's (*Potentilla hickmanii*)
		T	Primrose, Maguire (*Primula maguirei*)

species have been studied in sufficient detail to assess their status, and the actual number of threatened species is likely to be very much higher.

The majority of IUCN-listed species are flowering plants, a diverse and well-studied group. In 2003 the IUCN reported that 6,279 of 8,526—or 74 percent of—

TABLE 4.1

Endangered and threatened species of flowering plants, February 2004 [CONTINUED]

Status	Species name	Status	Species name
E	Loʻulu (*Pritchardia affinis*)	E	Checkermallow, pedate (*Sidalcea pedata*)
E	Wahane (*Pritchardia aylmer-robinsonii*)	E	*Silene alexandri* (No common name)
E	Loʻulu (*Pritchardia kaalae*)	T	*Silene hawaiiensis* (No common name)
E	Loʻulu (*Pritchardia munroi*)	E	*Silene lanceolata* (No common name)
E	Loʻulu (*Pritchardia napaliensis*)	E	*Silene perlmanii* (No common name)
E	Loʻulu (*Pritchardia remota*)	E	Campion, fringed (*Silene polypetala*)
E	Loʻulu (*Pritchardia schattaueri*)	T	Catchfly, Spalding's (*Silene spaldingii*)
E	Loʻulu (*Pritchardia viscosa*)	E	Irisette, white (*Sisyrinchium dichotomum*)
E	Plum, scrub (*Prunus geniculata*)	E	Erubia (*Solanum drymophilum*)
E	Sunburst, Hartweg's golden (*Pseudobahia bahiifolia*)	E	Popolo ku mai (*Solanum incompletum*)
T	Sunburst, San Joaquin adobe (*Pseudobahia peirsonii*)	E	ʻAiakeakua, popolo (*Solanum sandwicense*)
E	Kaulu (*Pteralyxia kauaiensis*)	T	Goldenrod, white-haired (*Solidago albopilosa*)
E	Harperella (*Ptilimnium nodosum*)	T	Goldenrod, Houghton's (*Solidago houghtonii*)
E	Cliff rose, Arizona (*Purshia* (= *Cowania*) *subintegra*)	E	Goldenrod, Short's (*Solidago shortii*)
T	Oak, Hinckley (*Quercus hinckleyi*)	T	Goldenrod, Blue Ridge (*Solidago spithamaea*)
E	Buttercup, autumn (*Ranunculus aestivalis* (= *acriformis*))	E	*Spermolepis hawaiiensis* (No common name)
E	*Remya kauaiensis* (No common name)	E	Pinkroot, gentian (*Spigelia gentianoides*)
E	Remya, Maui (*Remya mauiensis*)	T	Spiraea, Virginia (*Spiraea virginiana*)
E	*Remya montgomeryi* (No common name)	E	Ladies' tresses, Canelo Hills (*Spiranthes delitescens*)
E	Rhododendron, Chapman (*Rhododendron chapmanii*)	T	Ladies' tresses, Ute (*Spiranthes diluvialis*)
E	Sumac, Michaux's (*Rhus michauxii*)	E	Ladies' tresses, Navasota (*Spiranthes parksii*)
T	Beaked rush, Knieskern's (*Rhynchospora knieskernii*)	T	Cobana negra (*Stahlia monosperma*)
T	Gooseberry, Miccosukee (*Ribes echinellum*)	E	*Stenogyne angustifolia* var. *angustifolia* (No common name)
E	Watercress, Gambel's (*Rorippa gambellii*)	E	*Stenogyne bifida* (No common name)
E	Arrowhead, bunched (*Sagittaria fasciculata*)	E	*Stenogyne campanulata* (No common name)
T	Water plantain, Kral's (*Sagittaria secundifolia*)	E	*Stenogyne kanehoana* (No common name)
E	*Sanicula mariversa* (No common name)	E	Wire lettuce, Malheur (*Stephanomeria malheurensis*)
E	*Sanicula purpurea* (No common name)	E	Jewelflower, Metcalf Canyon (*Streptanthus albidus* ssp. *albidus*)
E	Sandalwood, Lanai (= ʻiliahi) (*Santalum freycinetianum* var. *lanaiense*)	E	Jewelflower, Tiburon (*Streptanthus niger*)
E	Pitcher plant, green (*Sarracenia oreophila*)	E	Palo de jazmin (*Styrax portoricensis*)
E	Pitcher plant, Alabama canebrake (*Sarracenia rubra alabamensis*)	E	Snowbells, Texas (*Styrax texanus*)
E	Pitcher plant, mountain sweet (*Sarracenia rubra* ssp. *jonesii*)	E	Seablite, California (*Suaeda californica*)
E	Naupaka, dwarf (*Scaevola coriacea*)	E	Grass, Eureka dune (*Swallenia alexandrae*)
E	Schiedea, Diamond Head (*Schiedea adamantis*)	E	Taraxacum, California (*Taraxacum californicum*)
E	Maʻoliʻoli (*Schiedea apokremnos*)	E	Palo colorado (*Ternstroemia luquillensis*)
E	*Schiedea haleakalensis* (No common name)	E	*Ternstroemia subsessilis* (No common name)
E	*Schiedea helleri* (No common name)	E	*Tetramolopium arenarium* (No common name)
E	*Schiedea hookeri* (No common name)	E	Pamakani (*Tetramolopium capillare*)
E	*Schiedea kaalae* (No common name)	E	*Tetramolopium filiforme* (No common name)
E	Maʻoliʻoli (*Schiedea kealiae*)	E	*Tetramolopium lepidotum* ssp. *lepidotum* (No common name)
E	*Schiedea lydgatei* (No common name)	E	*Tetramolopium remyi* (No common name)
E	*Schiedea membranacea* (No common name)	T	*Tetramolopium rockii* (No common name)
E	*Schiedea nuttallii* (No common name)	E	ʻOheʻohe (*Tetraplasandra gymnocarpa*)
E	*Schiedea sarmentosa* (No common name)	E	Meadowrue, Cooley's (*Thalictrum cooleyi*)
E	*Schiedea spergulina* var. *leiopoda* (No common name)	T	Thelypody, Howell's spectacular (*Thelypodium howellii spectabilis*)
T	*Schiedea spergulina* var. *spergulina* (No common name)	E	Mustard, slender-petaled (*Thelypodium stenopetalum*)
E	Laulihilihi (*Schiedea stellarioides*)	E	Penny cress, Kneeland Prairie (*Thlaspi californicum*)
E	*Schiedea verticillata* (No common name)	E	Dogweed, ashy (*Thymophylla tephroleuca*)
T	Reed mustard, clay (*Schoenocrambe argillacea*)	E	Fringepod, Santa Cruz Island (*Thysanocarpus conchuliferus*)
E	Reed mustard, Barneby (*Schoenocrambe barnebyi*)	T	Townsendia, Last Chance (*Townsendia aprica*)
E	Reed mustard, shrubby (*Schoenocrambe suffrutescens*)	E	*Trematolobelia singularis* (No common name)
T	*Schoepfia arenaria* (No common name)	E	Bariaco (*Trichilia triacantha*)
E	Chaffseed, American (*Schwalbea americana*)	T	Bluecurls, Hidden Lake (*Trichostema austromontanum* ssp. *compactum*)
E	Bulrush, northeastern (*Scirpus ancistrochaetus*)	E	Clover, showy Indian (*Trifolium amoenum*)
T	Cactus, Uinta Basin hookless (*Sclerocactus glaucus*)	E	Clover, running buffalo (*Trifolium stoloniferum*)
T	Cactus, Mesa Verde (*Sclerocactus mesae-verdae*)	E	Clover, Monterey (*Trifolium trichocalyx*)
E	Cactus, Wright fishhook (*Sclerocactus wrightiae*)	E	Trillium, persistent (*Trillium persistens*)
T	Skullcap, Florida (*Scutellaria floridana*)	E	Trillium, relict (*Trillium reliquum*)
T	Skullcap, large-flowered (*Scutellaria montana*)	E	Tuctoria, Greene's (*Tuctoria greenei*)
T	Roseroot, Leedy's (*Sedum integrifolium* ssp. *leedyi*)	E	Grass, Solano (*Tuctoria mucronata*)
T	Groundsel, San Francisco Peaks (*Senecio franciscanus*)	E	Opuhe (*Urera kaalae*)
T	Butterweed, Layne's (*Senecio layneae*)	T	Vervain, Red Hills (*Verbena californica*)
E	Iagu, Hayun (= [Guam], Tronkon guafi [Rota]) (*Serianthes nelsonii*)	T	Crownbeard, big-leaved (*Verbesina dissita*)
E	Ohai (*Sesbania tomentosa*)	E	*Vernonia proctorii* (No common name)
E	Rockcress, Santa Cruz Island (*Sibara filifolia*)	E	Vetch, Hawaiian (*Vicia menziesii*)
E	ʻAnunu (*Sicyos alba*)	E	*Vigna o-wahuensis* (No common name)
E	Checkermallow, Keck's (*Sidalcea keckii*)	E	Pamakani (*Viola chamissoniana* ssp. *chamissoniana*)
T	Checkermallow, Nelson's (*Sidalcea nelsoniana*)	E	*Viola helenae* (No common name)
E	Checkermallow, Kenwood Marsh (*Sidalcea oregana* ssp. *valida*)	E	Nani waiʻaleʻale (*Viola kauaiensis* var. *wahiawaensis*)
E	Checkermallow, Wenatchee Mountains (*Sidalcea oregana* var. *calva*)	E	*Viola lanaiensis* (No common name)
		E	*Viola oahuensis* (No common name)

flowering plants were threatened. Among coniferous plants, 152 species, or 25 percent of the total, are threatened. Other IUCN-listed species include 36 true mosses (92 percent of species studied), 11 club mosses (85 percent of species studied), 42 liverworts (81 percent of species studied), 98 true ferns (60 percent of

TABLE 4.1

Endangered and threatened species of flowering plants, February 2004 [CONTINUED]

Status	Species name	Status	Species name
E	Warea, wide-leaf *(Warea amplexifolia)*	E	A'e *(Zanthoxylum dipetalum* var. *tomentosum)*
E	Mustard, Carter's *(Warea carteri)*	E	A'e *(Zanthoxylum hawaiiense)*
E	Iliau, dwarf *(Wilkesia hobdyi)*	E	Prickly-ash, St. Thomas *(Zanthoxylum thomasianum)*
E	*Xylosma crenatum* (No common name)	E	Wild-rice, Texas *(Zizania texana)*
E	Grass, Tennessee yellow-eyed *(Xyris tennesseensis)*	E	Ziziphus, Florida *(Ziziphus celata)*
T	Yellowhead, desert *(Yermo xanthocephalus)*		

E = endangered
T = threatened

SOURCE: "U.S. Listed Flowering Plant Species Report by Taxonomic Group as of 02/12/2004," in *Threatened and Endangered Species System (TESS)*, U.S. Fish and Wildlife Service, Washington, DC, 2004 [Online] http://ecos.fws.gov/tess_public/TESSWebpageVipListed?code=F&listings=0#Q [accessed February 12, 2004]

species studied), and 151 cycads (52 percent of species studied).

Habitat loss accounts at least in part for the threatened status of 91 percent of IUCN-listed plants. The greatest number of threatened species are found in Central and South America, Central and West Africa, and Southeast Asia. Countries with the largest number of listed plants include Malaysia (681 species), Indonesia (384 species), Brazil (338 species), and Sri Lanka (280 species). Many of the threatened species from these countries represent tropical timber trees.

THE AMERICAN LANDSCAPE

Although North America has less plant diversity than the tropics, it is nonetheless amazingly rich. The diverse environmental conditions found on the continent allow representatives of most of the world's major plant groups to flourish in one region or another. For example, North America is home to more than 211 flowering plant families alone. The richest assemblages of flowering plants are found in Florida and Texas.

Botanists have divided North America into a series of ecosystems based on the underlying vegetation. Northern coniferous forests make up 28 percent of the North American continent; grasslands, 21–25 percent; arctic ecosystems, 19 percent; eastern deciduous forests, 11 percent; coastal plain ecosystems, 3 percent; desert ecosystems, 5 percent; western mountain coniferous forests, 7 percent; tidal wetlands, 1 percent; Mediterranean scrublands and woodlands, 1 percent; and beach vegetation, less than 1 percent.

Endangered U.S. Ecosystems

In 1995 the first full review of the health of the American landscape, "Endangered Ecosystems of the United States—A Preliminary Assessment of Loss and Degradation," was compiled by the National Biological Service (NBS) and published by the U.S. Geological Survey. It is still considered the definitive study of U.S. ecosystem health. Although individual species had been studied pre-

TABLE 4.2

Endangered and threatened species of nonflowering plants, February 2004

Status	Species name
Conifers and Cycads	
E	Cypress, Santa Cruz *(Cupressus abramsiana)*
T	Cypress, Gowen *(Cupressus goveniana* ssp. *goveniana)*
E	Torreya, Florida *(Torreya taxifolia)*
Ferns and Allies	
E	Fern, pendant kihi *(Adenophorus periens)*
E	*Adiantum vivesii* (No common name)
E	*Asplenium fragile* var. *insulare* (No common name)
T	Fern, American hart's-tongue *(Asplenium scolopendrium* var. *mericanum)*
E	Pauoa *(Ctenitis squamigera)*
E	Fern, elfin tree *(Cyathea dryopteroides)*
E	Diellia, asplenium-leaved *(Diellia erecta)*
E	*Diellia falcata* (No common name)
E	*Diellia pallida* (No common name)
E	*Diellia unisora* (No common name)
E	*Diplazium molokaiense* (No common name)
E	*Elaphoglossum serpens* (No common name)
E	Wawae'iole *(Huperzia mannii)*
E	Quillwort, Louisiana *(Isoetes louisianensis)*
E	Quillwort, black spored *(Isoetes melanospora)*
E	Quillwort, mat-forming *(Isoetes tegetiformans)*
E	Wawae'iole *(Lycopodium (=Phlegmariurus) nutans)*
E	Ihi'ihi *(Marsilea villosa)*
E	Fern, Aleutian shield *(Polystichum aleuticum)*
E	*Polystichum calderonense* (No common name)
E	*Pteris lidgatei* (No common name)
E	*Tectaria estremerana* (No common name)
E	*Thelypteris inabonensis* (No common name)
T	Fern, Alabama streak-sorus *(Thelypteris pilosa* var. *alabamensis)*
E	*Thelypteris verecunda* (No common name)
E	*Thelypteris yaucoensis* (No common name)
Lichens	
E	Cladonia, Florida perforate *(Cladonia perforata)*
E	Lichen, rock gnome *(Gymnoderma lineare)*

E = endangerd
T = threatened

SOURCE: "U.S. Listed Nonflowering Plant Species Report by Taxonomic Group as of 02/12/2004," in *Threatened and Endangered Species System (TESS)*, U.S. Fish and Wildlife Service, Washington, DC, 2004 [Online] http://ecos.fws.gov/tess_public/TESSWebpageVipListed?code=N&listings=0#R [accessed February 12, 2004]

viously, the health of the larger ecosystems had never before been considered. The study was based on surveys of state databases and the scientific literature. The report concluded that vast stretches of natural habitat, totaling

FIGURE 4.1

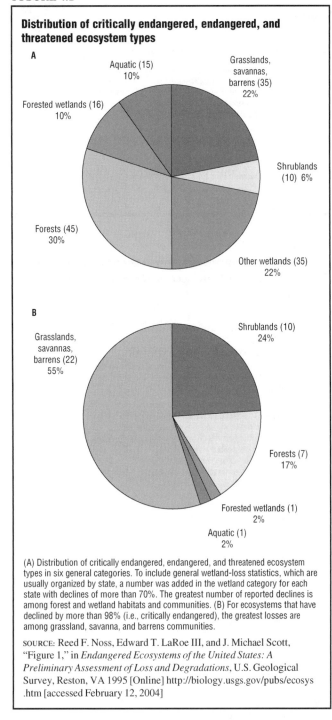

Distribution of critically endangered, endangered, and threatened ecosystem types

A

Aquatic (15) 10%

Grasslands, savannas, barrens (35) 22%

Forested wetlands (16) 10%

Shrublands (10) 6%

Forests (45) 30%

Other wetlands (35) 22%

B

Grasslands, savannas, barrens (22) 55%

Shrublands (10) 24%

Forests (7) 17%

Forested wetlands (1) 2%

Aquatic (1) 2%

(A) Distribution of critically endangered, endangered, and threatened ecosystem types in six general categories. To include general wetland-loss statistics, which are usually organized by state, a number was added in the wetland category for each state with declines of more than 70%. The greatest number of reported declines is among forest and wetland habitats and communities. (B) For ecosystems that have declined by more than 98% (i.e., critically endangered), the greatest losses are among grassland, savanna, and barrens communities.

SOURCE: Reed F. Noss, Edward T. LaRoe III, and J. Michael Scott, "Figure 1," in *Endangered Ecosystems of the United States: A Preliminary Assessment of Loss and Degradations*, U.S. Geological Survey, Reston, VA 1995 [Online] http://biology.usgs.gov/pubs/ecosys .htm [accessed February 12, 2004]

FIGURE 4.2

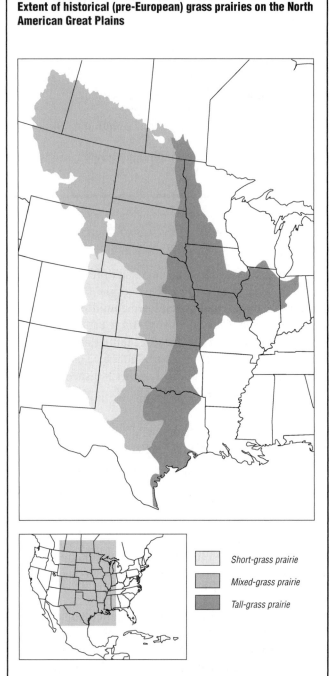

Extent of historical (pre-European) grass prairies on the North American Great Plains

Short-grass prairie

Mixed-grass prairie

Tall-grass prairie

SOURCE: M. J. Mac, P. A. Opler, C. E. Puckett Haecker, and P. D. Doran, "Figure 10: Extent of Historical (Pre-European) Tall-Grass, Mixed-Grass, and Short-Grass Prairies on the North American Great Plains," in *The Status and Trends of Our Nation's Biological Resources*, U.S. Geological Survey, Reston, VA, 1998

nearly half the area of the 48 contiguous states, had declined to the point of endangerment. Ecosystems suffered in two ways. Quantitative losses were measured by a decline in the area of an ecosystem. Qualitative losses involved degradation in the structure, function, or composition of an ecosystem.

Of the ecosystems that had declined by over 70 percent, 58 percent were terrestrial, 32 percent were wetland areas, and 10 percent were aquatic. Forests, grasslands, barrens, and savannas dominated the list. (See Figure 4.1.) American ecosystems identified by the NBS as suffering the greatest

overall decline include tall-grass prairies and oak savannas of the Midwest, deciduous forests of the East, and longleaf pine forests of the southern coastal plains. The midwestern prairies have been all but destroyed through conversion to agriculture—the original extent of these prairies is shown in Figure 4.2. As ecosystems shrink, the species that live in them become imperiled as well. The longleaf pine ecosystem of the southern coastal plain, for instance, is home to 27

TABLE 4.3

Critically endangered, endangered, and threatened ecosystems

Decline refers to destruction, conversion to other land uses, or significant degradation of ecological structure, function, or composition since European settlement. Estimates are from quantitative studies and qualitative assessments.

Critically endangered (>98% decline) ecosystems

Old-growth and other virgin stands in the eastern deciduous forest biome.

Spruce-fir (*Picea rubens-Abies fraseri*) forest in the southern Appalachians.

Red pine (*Pinus resinosaa*) and white pine (*Pinus strobus*) forests (mature and old-growth) in Michigan

Longleaf pine (*Pinus palustris*) forests and savannas in the southeastern coastal plain.

Slash pine (*Pinus elliottii*) rockland habitat in South Florida.

Loblolly pine-shortleaf pine (*Pinus taeda-Pinus echinata*) hardwood forests in the West Gulf Coastal Plain.

Arundinaria gigantea canebrakes in the Southeast.

Tallgrass prairie east of the Missouri River and on mesic sites across range.

Bluegrass savanna-woodland and prairies in Kentucky.

Black Belt prairies in Alabama and Mississippi and in the Jackson Prairie in Mississippi.

Ungrazed dry prairie in Florida.

Oak (*Quercus* spp.) savanna in the Midwest.

Wet and mesic coastal prairies in Louisiana.

Lakeplain wet prairie in Michigan.

Sedge (*Carex* spp. and others) meadows in Wisconsin.

Hempstead Plains grasslands on Long Island, New York.

Lake sand beaches in Vermont.

Serpentine barrens, maritime heathland, and pitch pine (*Pinus rigida*)-heath barrens in New York.

Prairies (all types) and oak savannas in the Willamette Valley and in the foothills of the Coast Range, Oregon.

Palouse prairie (Idaho, Oregon, and Washington and in similar communities in Montana).

Native grasslands (all types) in California.

Alkali sink scrub in southern California.

Coastal strand in southern California.

Ungrazed sagebrush steppe in the Intermourtain West.

Basin big sagebrush (*Artenisia tridentata*) in the Snake River Plain of Idaho.

Atlantic white-cedar (*Chamaecyparis thyoides*) stands in the Great Dismal Swamp of Virginia and in North Carolina and possibly across the entire range.

Streams in the Mississippi Alluvial Plain.

Endangered (85-98% decline)

Old-growth and other virgin forests in regions and in states other than in those already listed, except in Alaska.

Mesic limestone forest and barrier island beaches in Maryland.

Coastal plain Atlantic white-cedar swamp, maritime oak-holly (*Quercus* spp.-*Ilex* spp.) forest, maritime redcedar (*Juniperus virginiana*) forest, marl fen, marl pond shore, and oak openings in New York.

Coastal heathland in southern New England and on Long Island.

Pine-oak-heath sandplain woods and lake sand beach in Vermont.

Floodplain forests in New Hampshire.

Red spruce (*Picea rubens*) forests in the central Appalachians (West Virginia).

Upland hardwoods in the Coastal Plain of Tennessee.

Lowland forest in southeastern Missouri.

High-quality oak-hickory (*Quercus* spp.-*Carya* spp.) forest on the Cumberland Plateau and on the Highland Rim of Tennessee.

Limestone redcedar (*Juniperus virginianus*) glades in Tennessee.

Wet longleaf pine savanna and eastern upland longleaf pine forest in Louisiana.

Calcareous prairie, Fleming glade, shortleaf pine/oak-hickory forest, mixed hardwood-loblolly pine forest, eastern xeric sandhill woodland, and stream terrace sandy woodland/savanna in Louisiana.

Slash pine (*Pinus elliottii*) forests in southwestern Florida.

Red pine and white pine forest in Minnesota.

Coastal redwood (*Sequoia semper virens*) forests in California.

Old-growth ponderosa pine (*Pinus ponderosa*) forests in the northern Rocky Mountains, Intermountain West, and eastside Cascades Mountains.

Riparian forests in California, Arizona, and New Mexico.

Coastal sage scrub (especially maritime) and coastal mixed chaparral in southern California.

Dry forest on main islands of Hawaii.

All types of native habitats in the lower delta of the Rio Grande River, Texas.

Tallgrass prairie (all types combined).

Native shrub and grassland steppe in Oregon and in Washington.

Low elevation grasslands in Montana.

Gulf Coast pitcher plant (*Sarracenia* spp.) bogs.

Pocosins (evergreen shrub bogs) and ultramafic soligenous wetlands in Virginia.

Mountain bogs (southern Appalachian bogs and swamp forest-bog complex) in Tennessee and in North Carolina.

Upland wetlands on the Highland Rim of Tennessee.

Saline wetlands in eastern Nebraska.

Wetlands (all types combined) in south-central California, Illinois, Indiana, Iowa, Missouri, Nebraska, and Ohio.

Marshes in the Carson-Truckee area of western Nevada.

Low-elevation wetlands in Idaho.

Woody hardwood draws, glacial pothole ponds, and peatlands in Montana.

Vernal pools in the Central Valley and in southern California.

Marshes in the Coos Bay area of Oregon.

Freshwater marsh and coastal salt marsh in Southern California.

Seasonal wetlands of the San Francisco Bay, California.

Large streams and rivers in all major regions.

Aquatic mussel (Unionidae) beds in Tennessee.

Submersed aquatic vegetation in the Chesapeake Bay, in Maryland, and in Virginia.

Mangrove swamps and salt marsh along the Indian River lagoon, Florida.

Seagrass meadows in Galveston Bay, Texas.

Threatened (70-84% decline)

Nationwide riparian forests (other than in already listed regions), including southern bottomland hardwood forests.

Xeric habitats (scrub, scrubby flatwoods, sandhills) on the Lake Wales Ridge, Florida.

Tropical hardwood hammocks on the central Florida keys.

Northern hardwood forest, aspen (*Populus* spp.) parkland, and jack pine (*Pinus banksiana*) forests in Minnesota.

Saline prairie, western upland longleaf pine forest, live oak-pine-magnolia (*Quercus virginiana-Pinus* spp.-*Magnolia* spp.) forest, western xeric sandhill woodland, slash pine-pond baldcypress-hardwood (*Pinus elliottii-Taxodium ascendens*) forest, wet and mesic spruce-pine (*P. glabra*)-hardwood flatwoods, wet mixed hardwood-loblolly pine (*Pinus taeda*) flatwoods, and flatwoods ponds in Louisiana.

Alvar grassland, calcareous pavement barrens, dwarf pine ridges, mountain spruce-fir forest, inland Atlantic whitecedar swamp, freshwater tidal swamp, inland salt marsh, patterned peatland, perched bog, pitch pine-blueberry (*Pinus rigida-Vaccinium* spp.) peat swamp, coastal plain poor fens, rich graminoid fen, rich sloping fen, and riverside ice meadow in New York.

Maritime-like forests in the Clearwater Basin of Idaho.

Woodland and chaparral on Santa Catalina Inland.

Southern tamarack (*Lark laricina*) swamp in Michigan.

Wetlands (all kinds) in Arkansas, Connecticut, Kentucky, and Maryland.

Marshes in the Puget Sound region, Washington.

Cienegas (marshes) in Arizona.

Coastal wetlands in California.

SOURCE: Reed F. Noss, Edward T. LaRoe III, and J. Michael Scott, "Appendix B," in *Endangered Ecosystems of the United States: A Preliminary Assessment of Loss and Degradations*, U.S. Geological Survey, Reston, VA, 1995 [Online] http://biology.usgs.gov/pubs/ecosys.htm [accessed February 12, 2004]

TABLE 4.4

TABLE 4.5

Human-caused reductions in westside California plant communities and formations

Community/formation	Vegetation reduced (percent)
Native grasslands	99
Needlegrass steppe	99.9
Southern San Joaquin Valley alkali sink scrub	99
Southern California coastal sage-scrub	70–90
Vernal pools	91
Wetlands	91
Riparian woodlands	89
Coast redwood forest	85

SOURCE: M. J. Mac, P. A. Opler, C. E. Puckett Haecker, and P. D. Doran, "Table 1. Human-Caused Reductions in Westside California Plant Communities and Formations (after Noss and Peters, 1995)," in *The Status and Trends of Our Nation's Biological Resources,* U.S. Geological Survey, Reston, VA, 1998

At-risk species living in late-successional forests in western Oregon, Washington, and northwestern California

Listed species

Resident Fishes
　Oregon chub *(Oregonichthys crameri)* E

Birds
　Marbled murrelet *(Brachyramphus marmoratus)* T
　Bald eagle *(Haliaeetus leucocephalus)* E
　Northern spotted owl *(Strix occidentalis caurina)* T

Candidate and proposed species

Plants
　Wayside aster *(Aster vialis)* 2
　Bensonia *(Bensoniella oregana)* 2
　Mt. Mazama collomia *(Collomia mazama)* 2
　Cold-water corydalis *(Corydalis aquae-gelidae)* 2

Mollusks
　California floater mussel *(Anodonta californiensis)*
　Columbia pebblesnail or great Columbia river spire snail *(Fluminicola [= Lithoglyphu columbiana)* 2
　Snail *(Monadenia fidelis minor)* 2
　Trinity bristlesnail or California northern river snail *(Monadenia setosa)* 2
　Columbia pebblesnail or spire snail *(Monadenia troglodytes troglodytes)* 2

Resident Fishes
　Olympic mudminnow *(Novumbra hubbsi)* 2
　McCloud redband trout *(Oncorhynchus mykiss* ssp. *)* 2
　Bull trout *(Salvelinus confluentus)* 2

Amphibians
　Shasta salamander *(Hydromantes shastae)* 2
　Del Norte salamander *(Plethodon elongatus)* 2
　Larch mountain salamander *(Plethodon larselli)* 2
　Siskiyou mountain salamander *(Plethodon stormi)* 2

Birds
　Harlequin duck *(Histrionicus histrionicus)* 2
　Northern goshawk *(Accipiter gentilis)* 2

Mammals
　White-footed vole *(Arborimus albipes)* 2
　Lynx *(Felis lynx canadensis)* 2
　Pacific fisher *(Martes pennanti pacifica)* 2
　Pacific western big-eared bat *(Plecotus townsendii townsendii)* 2

E = Listed Endangered
T = Listed Threatened
2 = Candidate Category 2 (taxa that existing information indicates may warrant listing but for which substantial biological data in support of a proposed rule are lacking).

SOURCE: Reed F. Noss, Edward T. LaRoe III, and J. Michael Scott, "Appendix C," in *Endangered Ecosystems of the United States: A Preliminary Assessment of Loss and Degradations,* U.S. Geological Survey, Reston, VA, 1995 [Online] http://biology.usgs.gov/pubs/ecosys.htm [accessed February 12, 2004]

species on the Endangered Species List and another 99 species that have been proposed for listing.

The full NBS list of the most endangered ecosystems of the United States appears in Table 4.3. Thirty-two American ecosystems had declined by more than 98 percent and were classified as "critically endangered." Fifty-eight had declined by 85 to 98 percent and were classified as "endangered." Thirty-eight others declined by 70 to 84 percent and were listed as "threatened."

Endangered ecosystems were found in all major regions of the United States except Alaska. The greatest losses occurred in the Northeast, the South, and the Midwest, as well as in California. A list of some Californian plant communities, most of which are unique to the state, and percentage reductions in these community types appear in Table 4.4. Native grasslands, needlegrass steppes, and alkali sink scrubs are among the communities that have declined most precipitously in California.

Endangered ecosystems are linked to many federally listed threatened and endangered species. Table 4.5 shows the endangered, threatened, proposed, and candidate species that are found in old-growth forests in the Pacific Northwest. Although the northern spotted owl has become linked to this region in the minds of many, these forest habitats are essential to numerous other endangered species. Table 4.6 provides a similar list for the endangered coastal sage scrub ecosystem in California. Table 4.7 lists species associated with the critically endangered longleaf pine and wiregrass communities of the southern coastal plain (which includes parts of North and South Carolina, Georgia, Florida, Alabama, Mississippi, and Louisiana).

Hawaiian Plants

Because of its isolation from continental land masses, many of the species found in Hawaii exist nowhere else in the world. An estimated 90 percent of Hawaiian plant species are in fact endemic. Because of large-scale deforestation and habitat destruction on the Hawaiian islands, Hawaii is home to more endangered plants than any other state in the nation, with 312 listed species in 2004. Hawaiian plants have suffered from the introduction of invasive predators such as cows, pigs, and insects, as well as the loss of critical pollinators with the decline of numerous species of native birds and insects. Over 10 percent of Hawaiian plant species have gone extinct in the last few hundred years, and nearly 30 percent are currently believed to be imperiled.

In April 2002, a major step in protecting Hawaii's endemic flora was taken when the Fish and Wildlife Ser-

TABLE 4.6

At-risk species living in coastal sage scrub habitats in southern California

Listed species

Birds

California gnatcatcher *(Polioptila californica californica)* T

Mammals

Stephens' kangaroo rat *(Dipodomys stephensi)* E

Candidate species

Plants

San Diego thorn mint *(Acanthomintha ilicifolia)* 1
Munz's onion *(Allium fimbriatum var. munzii)* 1
Aphanisma *(Aphanisma blitoides)* 2
San Diego ambrosia *(Ambrosia pumila)* 2
Braunton's milk vetch *(Astragalus brauntonii)* 2
Dean's milk vetch *(Astragalus deani)* 2
Payson's jewelflower *(Caulanthus simulans)* 2
Orcutt's spineflower *(Chorizanthe orcuttiana)* 1
San Fernando Valley spineflower *(Chorizanthe parryi var. fernandina)* 1
Parry's spineflower *(Chorizanthe parryi var. parryi)* 2
Orcutt's bird's-beak *(Cordylanthus orcuttianus)* 2
Del Mar Mesa sand aster *(Corethrogyne filaginifolia var. linifolia)* 2
Western dichondra *(Dichondra occidentalis)* 2
Orcutt's dudleya *(Dudleya attenuata ssp. orcuttii)* 2
Short-leaved dudleya *(Dudleya brevifolia)* 1
Many-stemmed dudleya *(Dudleya multicaulis)* 2
Conejo dudleya *(Dudleya parva)* 2
Laguna Beach dudleya *(Dudleya stolonifera)* 1
Variegated dudleya *(Dudleya variegata)* 2
Verity's dudleya *(Dudleya verityi)* 2
Bright green dudleya *(Dudleya virens)* 2
Sticky dudleya *(Dudleya viscida)* 1
Conejo buckwheat *(Eriogonum crocatum)* 2
San Diego barrel cactus *(Ferocactus viridescens)* 2
Palmer's haplopappus *(Haplopappus palmeri ssp. palmeri)* 2
Orcutt's hazardia *(Hazardia orcuttii)* 2

Otay tarplant *(Hemizonia conjugens)* 2
Santa Susana Mountains tarplant *(Hemizonia minthornii)* 2
Nevin's barberry *(Mahonia nevinii)* 1
Davidson's bush mallow *(Malacothamnus davidsonii)* 2
San Diego goldenstar *(Muilla clevelandii)* 2
Willowy monardella *(Monardella linoides ssp. viminea)* 2
Pringle's monardella *(Monardella pringlei)* 1
Short-lobed broomrape *(Orobanche parishii ssp. brachyloba)* 2
Pringle's yampah *(Perideridia pringlei)* 3

Insects

Quino checkerspot butterfly *(Euphydryas editha quino)* 1
Hermes copper butterfly *(Lycaena hermes)* 2

Reptiles

Orange-throated whiptail *(Cnemidophorus hyperythrus)* 2
Coastal western whiptail *(Cnemidophorus tigris multiscutatus)* 2
San Diego banded gecko *(Coleonyx variegatus abbotti)* 2
Red diamond rattlesnake *(Crotalus ruber)* 2
Coastal rosy boa *(Lichanura trivirgata rosafusca)* 2
San Diego horned lizard *(Phrynosoma coronatum blainvillei)* 2
Coast patch-nosed snake *(Salvadora hexalepis virgultea)* 2

Birds

Southern California rufous-crowned sparrow *(Aimophila ruficeps canescens)* 2
Bell's sage sparrow *(Amphispiza belli belli)* 2
San Diego cactus wren *(Campylorhynchus brunnecapillus sandiegoensis)* 2

Mammals

Dulzura California pocket mouse *(Chaetodipus californicus femoralis)* 2
San Bernardino kangaroo rat *(Dipodomys merriami parvus)* 2
San Diego black-tailed jack rabbit *(Lepus californicus bennettii)* 2
Southern grasshopper mouse *(Onychomys torridus ramona)* 2
Los Angeles pocket mouse *(Perognathus longimembris brevinasus)* 2
Pacific pocket mouse *(Perognathus longimembris pacificus)* 2

E = Listed Endangered
T = Listed Threatened
1 = Candidate Category 1 (taxa for which the U.S. Fish and Wildlife Service has sufficient biological information in support of a listing proposal.
2 = Candidate category 2 (taxa for which existing information indicates listing but for which substantial biological data in support of a proposed rule are lacking).

SOURCE: Reed F. Noss, Edward T. LaRoe III, and J. Michael Scott, "Appendix D," in *Endangered Ecosystems of the United States: A Preliminary Assessment of Loss and Degradations,* U.S. Geological Survey, Reston, VA 1995 [Online] http://biology.usgs.gov/pubs/ecosys.htm [accessed February 12, 2004]

vice proposed critical habitat for native plant species on the islands of Maui and Kahoolawe. The proposal includes fifteen habitat areas covering approximately 128,000 acres. Protection of these areas would benefit at least 61 threatened and endangered species by preserving current habitat, as well as allowing for natural range expansion and the reintroduction of endangered species into portions of their historic ranges. The areas proposed for critical habitat include Hawaii state lands (45 percent), federal lands (17 percent), and privately owned land (37 percent). Only activity on federal lands is legally affected by critical habitat designation.

In July 2003 the Fish and Wildlife Service designated over 208,000 acres of critical habitat on the island of Hawaii (Big Island) as habitat for forty-one listed plant species. The area designated was 52 percent smaller than originally anticipated because it excluded a large tract of U.S. Army land as well as private land held by the Queen Liliuokalani Trust and others. The U.S. Army land was excluded because of national security concerns and

because the Army agreed to voluntarily cooperate with the Fish and Wildlife Service regarding activity that affects endangered species. The Queen Liliuokalani Trust land was excluded because the trust vowed to discontinue its current efforts on behalf of endangered species if its lands were included in the critical habitat designation. Finally, land near the cities of Kailua and Kona, for which housing development was planned, was excluded from critical habitat designation because the economic and social costs of inclusion were too great.

Designation of critical habitat in Hawaii was completed after a successful lawsuit brought against the Fish and Wildlife Service by Earthjustice, the Conservation Council for Hawaii, the Sierra Club, and the Hawaii Botanical Society.

Profiles of Some Endangered North American Plants

ENDANGERED CACTI. Over thirty cactus species are currently listed with the U.S. Fish and Wildlife Service as either threatened or endangered. Most of these species are found in arid habitats in the Southwest, particularly Texas,

TABLE 4.7

At-risk species living in longleaf pine or wiregrass habitats in the southern coastal plain

Listed species

Plants

Apalachicola rosemary *(Conradina glabra)* E
Pigeon-wing *(Clitoria fragrans)* T
Beautiful pawpaw *(Deeringothamnus pulchellus)* E
Rugel's pawpaw *(Deeringothamnus rugellii)* E
Scrub mint *(Dicerandra frutescens)* E
Scrub buckwheat *(Eriogonum longifolium var. gnaphalifolium)* T
Harper's beauty *(Harperocallis flava)* E
Rough-leaf loosestrife *(Lysimachia asperulifolia)* E
Britton's bear grass *(Nolina brittonia)* E
Godfrey's butterwort *(Pinguicula ionantha)* T
Chapman's rhododendron *(Rhododendron chapmanii)* E
Michaux's sumac *(Rhus michauxii)* E
Green pitcherplant *(Sarracenia oreophila)* E
Chaffseed *(Schwalbea americana)* E
Gentian pinkroot *(Spigelia gentianoides)* E
Cooley's meadowrue *(Thalictrum cooleyi)* E
Clasping warea *(Warea amplexifolia)* E
Carter's warea *(Warea carteri)* E

Reptiles

Gopher tortoise *(Gopherus polyphemus)* T
Sand skink *(Neoceps reynoldsi)* T
Indigo snake *(Drymarchon corais couperi)* T
Blue-tailed mole skink *(Eumeces egregius lividus)* T

Birds

Mississippi sandhill crane *(Grus canadensis pulla)* E
Bald eagle *(Haliaeetus leucocephalus)* E
Florida scrub jay *(Aphelocoma coerulescens coerulescens)* T
Red-cockaded woodpecker *(Picoides borealis)* E

Mammals

Florida panther *(Felis concolor coryi)* E

Candidate and proposed species

Plants

Incised groovebur *(Agrimonia incisa)* 2
Carolina lead plant *(Amorpha georgiana var. confusa)* 2
Georgia lead plant *(Amorpha georgiana var. georgiana)* 2
Southern three-awned grass *(Aristida simpliciflora)* 2
Southern milkweed *(Asclepias viridula)* 2
Chapman's aster *(Aster chapmani)* 2
Coyote-thistle aster *(Aster eryngiifolius)* 2
Pine woods aster *(Aster spinulosus)* 2
Sandhills milk vetch *(Astragalus michauxii)* 2
Purple balduina *(Balduina atropurpurea)* 2
Hairy wild indigo *(Baptisia calycosa var. villosa)* 2
Scare weed *(Baptisia simplicifolia)* 2
Ashe's savory *(Calamintha ashei)* 2
Sand grass *(Calamovilfa curtissii)* 2
Piedmont jointgrass *(Coelorachis tuberculosa)* 2
Large-flowered rosemary *(Conradina grandiflora)* 2
Tropical waxweed *(Cuphia aspera)* 2
Umbrella sedge *(Cyperus grayoides)* 2
Dwarf burhead *(Echinodorus parvulus)* 2
Telephus spurge *(Euphorbia telephioides)* PT
Wiregrass gentian *(Gentiana pennelliana)* 2
Florida beardgrass *(Gymnopogon floridanus)* 2
Hartwrightia *(Hartwrightia floridana)* 2
Mock pennyroyal *(Hedeoma graveolens)* 2
Spider lily *(Hymenocallis henryae)* 2
Thick-leaved water willow *(Justicia crassifolia)* 2
White wicky *(Kalmia cuneata)* 2
Tiny bog buttons *(Lachnocaulon digynum)* 2
Pine pinweed *(Lechea divaricata)* 2
Godfrey's blazing star *(Liatris provincialis)* 2
Slender gay feather *(Liatris tenuis)* 2
Panhandle lily *(Lilium iridollae)* 2

Listed species

Plants

Large-fruited flax *(Linum macrocarpum)* 2
Harper's grooved yellow flax *(Linum sulcatum var. harperi)* 2
West's flax *(Linum westii)* 2
Boykin's lobelia *(Lobelia boykinii)* 2
White birds-in-a-nest *(Macbridea alba)* PT
Carolina bogmint *(Macbridea caroliniana)* 2
Southern marshallia *(Marshallia ramosa)* 2
Bog asphodel *(Narthecium americanum)* 1
Fall-flowering ixia *(Nemastylis floridana)* 2
Florida bear grass *(Nolina atopocarpa)* 2
Savanna cowbane *(Oxypolis ternata)* 2
Naked-stemmed panic grass *(Panicum nudicaule)* 2
Carolina grass-of-parnassus *(Parnassia caroliniana)* 2
Wavyleaf wild quinine *(Parthenium radfordii)* 2
Chapman's butterwort *(Pinguicula planifolia)* 2
Bent golden aster *(Pityopsis flexuosa)* 2
Pineland plantain *(Plantago sparsiflora)* 2
Wild coco, eulophia *(Pteroglossaspis ecristata)* 2
Sandhills pixie moss *(Pyxidanthera barbulata var. brevifolia)* 2
St. John's Susan, yellow coneflower *(Rudbeckia nitida var. nitida)* 2
Bog coneflower *(Rudbeckia scabrifolia)* 2
White-top pitcherplant *(Sarracenia leucophylla)* 2
Wherry's pitcherplant *(Sarracenia rubra ssp. wherryi)* 2
Florida skullcap *(Scutellaria floridana)* PT
Scarlet catchfly *(Silene subciliata)* 2
Carolina goldenrod *(Solidago pulchra)* 2
Spring-flowering goldenrod *(Solidago verna)* 2
Wireleaf dropseed *(Sporobolus teretifolius)* 2
Pickering's morning glory *(Stylisma pickeringii)* 2
Pineland hoary pea *(Tephrosia mohrii)* 2
Smooth bog-asphodel *(Tofieldia glabra)* 2
Shinner's false-foxglove *(Tomanthera (Agalinis) pseudaphylla)* 2
Least trillium *(Trillium pusillum [5 varieties])* 2
Chapman's crownbeard *(Verbesina chapmanii)* 2
Variable-leaf crownbeard *(Verbesina heterophylla)* 2
Drummond's yellow-eyed grass *(Xyris drummondii)* 2
Harper's yellow-eyed grass *(Xyris scabrifolia)* 2

Insects

Buchholz's dart moth *(Agrotis buchholzi)* 2
Aphodius tortoise commensal scarab beetle *(Aphodius troglodytes)* 2
Arogos skipper *(Atrytone arogos arogos)* 2
Copris tortoise commensal scarab beetle *(Copris gopheri)* 2
Sandhills clubtail dragonfly *(Gomphus parvidens carolinus)* 2
Spiny Florida sandhill scarab beetle *(Gronocarus multispinosus)* 2
Prairie mole cricket *(Gryllotalpa major)* 2
Mitchell's satyr *(Neonympha mitchellii francisci)* 2
Onthophagus tortoise commensal scarab beetle *(Onthophagus polyphemi)* 2
Carter's noctuid moth *(Spartiniphaga carterae)* 2

Amphibians

Flatwoods salamander *(Ambystoma cingulatum)* 2
Gopher frog *(Rana areolata)* 2
Carolina gopher frog *(Rana capito capito)* 2
Dusky gopher frog *(Rana capito sevosa)* 1

Reptiles

Gopher tortoise *(Gopherus polyphemus)* 2
Florida scrub lizard *(Sceloporus woodi)* 2
Southern hognose snake *(Heterodon simus)* 2
Black pine snake *(Pituophis melanoleucus lodingi)* 2
Northern pine snake *(Pituophis melanoleucus melanoleucus)* 2
Florida pine snake *(Pituophis melanoleucus mugitus)* 2
Short-tailed snake *(Stilosoma extenuatum)* 2

Birds

Southeastern American kestrel *(Falco sparverius paulus)* 2
Loggerhead shrike *(Lanius ludovicianus)* 2
Bachman's sparrow *(Aimophila aestivalis)* 2
Henslow's sparrow *(Ammodramus henslowii)* 2

New Mexico, Arizona, and Utah. In addition to habitat loss and degradation, a prime reason for the endangerment of cactus species in general is over-collection by enthusiasts.

The star cactus is a spineless species found in Texas and parts of Mexico, and was listed as endangered across its entire range in 1993. In Texas, it is found only along a

TABLE 4.7

At-risk species living in longleaf pine or wiregrass habitats in the southern coastal plain [CONTINUED]

Listed species

Mammals
Florida weasel *(Mustela frenata peninsulae)* 2
Florida black bear *(Ursus americanus floridanus)* 2
Florida mouse *(Podomys floridanus)* 2
Sherman's fox squirrel *(Sciurus niger shermani)* 2

E = endangered
PT = proposd threatened
T = threatened
1 = candidate category 1 (taxa for which the U.S. Fish and Wildlife Service has sufficient biological information in support of a listing proposal).
2 = candidate category 2 (taxa for which existing information indicates listing but for which substantial biological data in support of a proposed rule are lacking).

SOURCE: Reed F. Noss, Edward T. LaRoe III, and J. Michael Scott, "Appendix E," in *Endangered Ecosystems of the United States: A Preliminary Assessment of Loss and Degradations,* U.S. Geological Survey, Reston, VA, 1995 [Online] http://biology.usgs.gov/pubs/ecosys.htm [accessed February 12, 2004]

single creek system in Starr County. The star cactus is several inches in diameter and only a few inches tall. The flowers have large yellow petals that form a deep bowl. Endangerment of this species resulted partly from over-collection in the wild by cactus enthusiasts, who greatly prize it. The star cactus has also suffered from habitat loss due to urban and agricultural development. The San Antonio Botanical Garden has attempted to aid conservation efforts by developing methods for propagating this species from seed.

The bunched cory cactus was first listed as threatened in 1979. It is a small species, reaching heights of up to four inches. The bunched cory cactus has rounded, single stems and occupies ledges and flats on limestone outcrops. Populations occur in Big Bend National Park in Texas, as well as on some private ranches—a total of approximately 25 different sites are known. Despite strict regulations against collection and monitoring in park sites, cactus poachers nonetheless continue to collect the plant illegally.

SHOWY STICKSEED. Showy stickseed is one of the most recent plants to be added to the Endangered Species List. It was officially listed in February 2002 as endangered throughout its habitat—a single site in the Wenatchee National Forest in Chelan County in the state of Washington. Showy stickseed was once observed at a second site in Chelan County but is now believed to be extinct there. Approximately 1,000 showy stickseed plants existed in the early 1980s, but only 500 plants were found in a 2001 survey. Critical habitat was not designated for showy stickseed by the Fish and Wildlife Service because it was believed to be imprudent to reveal the location of the sole population for fear of illegal collection.

Showy stickseed is an herb eight to sixteen inches tall. When in bloom, it has large, white flowers. Endangerment

is believed to have resulted from competition with invasive species such as weeds, woody shrubs, and trees. Showy stickseed requires large amounts of sunlight, which has become increasingly blocked by the larger invasive species. A long history of fire suppression has also contributed to the shading problem. The other major factor contributing to endangerment of this species is collection from the wild. Now that the species is listed under the Endangered Species Act, collection is considered a federal crime. The Fish and Wildlife Service is cooperating with the Wenatchee National Forest and the Washington Department of Transportation to help improve habitat areas for the showy stickseed. This includes thinning of invasive tree species and control of weeds. In addition, experimental propagation of the stickseed is being pursued.

DESERT YELLOWHEAD. In March 2002, the desert yellowhead was listed as threatened in its only known habitat, 50 acres of federal land in Wyoming. There were about 12,000 plants found in a survey conducted in 2001. The desert yellowhead is related to sunflowers, and has twenty-five to eighty flowers crowded atop each twelve-inch stem. The species was first discovered in 1990. The desert yellowhead is threatened due to human activity. Portions of its current habitat are being considered for oil and gas drilling. The Fish and Wildlife Service is working with the Bureau of Land Management, which manages desert yellowhead habitat, on a conservation plan.

ROBBINS' CINQUEFOIL. The Robbins' cinquefoil was officially listed as endangered in 1980. This plant species is related to roses, and is found in the alpine zone of the White Mountain National Forest in New Hampshire. It is a small species that bears a yellow flower. At the time of listing, there were approximately 3,700 plants surveyed. After concerted conservation efforts involving the Fish and Wildlife Service, the U.S. Forest Service, and the Appalachian Mountain Club, the population of the Robbins' cinquefoil increased to over 14,000 plants in 2001. In June 2001, the species was proposed for delisting. Critical actions that helped the population recover included a rerouting of the Appalachian Trail around the critical habitat areas of the species, as well as the building of an enclosure to protect the population from disturbance. In addition, two populations of Robbins' cinquefoil were introduced in new National Forest habitats.

LOS ANGELES BASIN MOUNTAIN PLANTS. Numerous species of threatened and endangered plants have reached their precarious state due to urbanization and other human activity. Figure 4.3 shows the species distribution of six threatened and endangered plant species found in the mountains surrounding the Los Angeles basin. The recovery plan for these species lists current threats to species survival as including: "urban development, recreational activities, alteration of fire cycles, fire suppression and pre-suppression (fuel modification) activities, over-

FIGURE 4.3

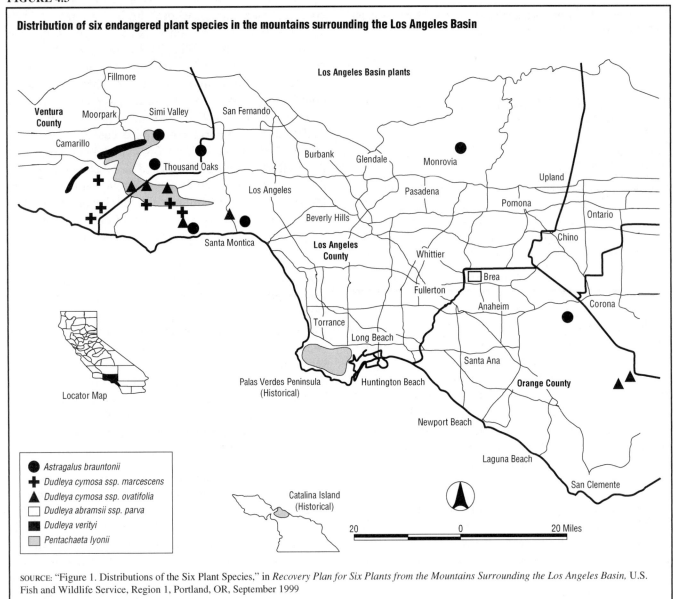

Distribution of six endangered plant species in the mountains surrounding the Los Angeles Basin

Legend:
- ● *Astragalus brauntonii*
- ✚ *Dudleya cymosa ssp. marcescens*
- ▲ *Dudleya cymosa ssp. ovatifolia*
- ☐ *Dudleya abramsii ssp. parva*
- ■ *Dudleya veritiyi*
- ▨ *Pentachaeta lyonii*

SOURCE: "Figure 1. Distributions of the Six Plant Species," in *Recovery Plan for Six Plants from the Mountains Surrounding the Los Angeles Basin,* U.S. Fish and Wildlife Service, Region 1, Portland, OR, September 1999

collecting, habitat fragmentation and degradation, and competition from invasive weeds." Some species are currently so reduced in number that extinction due to random events is also a threat.

MEAD'S MILKWEED. Mead's milkweed is a federally listed threatened species with populations in Kansas, Missouri, Iowa, and Illinois. The species has already gone extinct in Wisconsin and Indiana. Most population loss is attributed to agriculture. Figure 4.4 shows the counties where Mead's milkweed currently persists, counties where it once existed but is now extinct, and counties where reintroductions into suitable habitat are taking place. Table 4.8 lists the summary of threats to Mead's milkweed as well as the recommended recovery actions that appeared in the species recovery plan, published in September 2003 by the Fish and Wildlife Service.

ENDANGERED FORESTS

Forests perform a wide variety of social and ecological functions. They provide homes and sustenance for forest dwellers, protect and enrich soils, affect local and regional climate through the evaporation and storage of water, and help stabilize the global climate by processing carbon dioxide.

Forests are broadly classified by latitude as either tropical, temperate, or boreal. Tropical forests, or rainforests, are predominantly evergreen and occur close to the equator, in areas with plentiful rain and little temperature variation year-round. There are tropical forests in Central and South America, Africa, South and Southeast Asia, and Australia. Tropical forests are characterized by the greatest diversity of biological species. For example, as many as one hundred distinct tree species may inhabit a square kilometer. Vegetation is often so dense in tropical forests that very little light

FIGURE 4.4

Present and historic distribution of Mead's milkweed by county

O = Counties with extant populations

▲ = Counties in which restorations are taking place

x = Counties with historic records but without extant populations

SOURCE: "Figure 2. Present and Historic Distribution of Mead's Milkweed by County," in *Mead's Milkweed (Asclepias meadii) Recovery Plan*, U.S. Fish and Wildlife Service, Great Lakes-Big Rivers Region (Region 3), Fort Snelling, MN, September 2003

FIGURE 4.5

Coast redwood trees in Redwood National Park, California. Redwoods are found only on the West Coast of North America and are the tallest trees on earth. *(National Park Service)*

penetrates to the ground. Temperate forests are found in areas with distinct warm and cold seasons, including North America, northern Asia, and western and central Europe. Many temperate forests are made up of deciduous trees—species that shed their leaves during winter. Plant diversity is not as great in temperate forests as in rainforests. There are perhaps three or four tree species per square kilometer. Boreal forests, also known as taiga, are found at high latitudes in extremely cold climates where the growing season is short. Precipitation generally falls as snow rather than rain. Boreal forest flora includes evergreen trees and lichen ground cover. Boreal forests are present in Siberia, Scandinavia, Alaska, and Canada.

Deforestation

Deforestation refers to the destruction of forests through the removal of trees, most often by clear-cutting or burning. It results in habitat loss for countless species of plants as well as animals. Deforestation is occurring globally, but is proceeding at a particularly alarming rate in the world's tropical rainforests, which comprise the most diverse ecosystems in the world. Deforestation is one of the most pressing environmental issues today.

In addition to destruction of habitat for numerous plant and animal species, the loss of forests has other effects as well. For example, forests play a crucial role in the global cycling of carbon—vegetation stores two trillion tons of carbon worldwide, roughly triple the amount stored in the atmosphere. When forest trees are cleared, the carbon they contain

is oxidized and released to the air, adding to the carbon dioxide in the atmosphere. The burning of the Amazon rainforests and other forests thus has a two-fold effect—the release of large amounts of carbon dioxide into the atmosphere and the loss of the trees that help absorb carbon dioxide.

Furthermore, deforestation also results in forest fragmentation, which is itself detrimental for several reasons. First, forest fragmentation creates more "edge" habitats and destroys habitat for deep-forest creatures. Second, fragmentation isolates plant and animal populations, making them more vulnerable to local extinction. Third, some non-native species thrive in edge habitats, and are able to invade and displace native species in a fragmented habitat. In North America, for example, songbirds like the wood thrush and the promontory warbler are declining due to increasing numbers of blue jays and parasitic brown-headed cowbirds, both of which flourish at forest edges. Finally, most trees are more susceptible to weather at forest edges.

Rainforests

Tropical forests are the world's most biologically rich habitats. These storehouses of biological diversity cover less

TABLE 4.8

Mead's milkweed: Threats and recommended recovery actions

Listing factor	Threat	Recovery criteria	Task
A	Elimination of tallgrass prairie habitat due to urban development, agricultural expansion and detrimental agricultural practices	1, 2, 3	Identify and control threats to extant populations and available habitat, seek legal protection of sites, encourage landowners and agencies to manage habitat, survey for new populations or available habitat, and promote public understanding
C	Infestation of beetle larvae (Curculionidae) and other pathogens	1, 2, 3	Conduct research on management of herbivores and pathogens that may reduce reproduction and maintain conservation populations
D	The state of Kansas does not have specific legislation or rules to protect rare plants	1, 2	Protect habitat by landowner participation, seek legal dedication of habitat, acquirement of land by conservation organizations, maintain conservation populations, and promote public understanding
D	The majority of known populations are on private property and are unprotected.	2	Protect habitat by landowner participation, seek legal dedication of habitat, acquirement of land by conservation organizations, and promote public understanding
E	Lack of pollinators	1, 2, 3	Determine what species are pollinators
E	Fluctuation of flowering plants and population numbers	3	Increase number of sites managed or owned by conservation organizations, manage habitat and conduct research on restoration, management and introduction techniques

Listing factors:
A = The present or threatened destruction, modification, curtailment of its habitat or range
B = Overutilization for commercial, recreational, scientific, educational purposes (not a factor)
C = Disease or predation
D = The inadequacy of existing regulatory mechanisms;
E = Other natural or manmade factors affecting its continued existence
Recovery criteria:
1. Twenty-one populations are distributed across plant communities and physiographic regions within the historic range of the species.
2. Each of these 21 populations is highly viable. A highly viable population is defined as follows: more than 50 mature plants; seed production is occurring and the population is increasing in size and maturity; the population is genetically diverse with more than 50 genotypes; the available habitat size is at least 125 acres (50 hectares); the habitat is in a late-successional stage; the site is protected through long-term conservation easements, legal dedication as nature preserves, or other means; and the site is managed by fire in order to maintain a late-successional graminoid-vegetation structure free of woody vegetation.
3. Monitoring data indicates that these populations have had a stable or increasing trend for 15 years.

SOURCE: "Appendix 7. Summary of Threats and Recommended Recovery Actions," in *Mead's Milkweed (Asclepias meadii) Recovery Plan,* U.S. Fish and Wildlife Service, Great Lakes-Big Rivers Region (Region 3), Fort Snelling, MN, September 2003

than 1 percent of the earth, but are home to 50 to 90 percent of the world's species. Many rainforest species have yet to be discovered and described by humans. In May 2002 for example, ornithologists announced the discovery of a new species of parrot, described as possessing green feathers, a hooked neck like a vulture, and a bald orange head. If new discoveries are being made even among well-studied groups such as birds, one can only imagine the untold number of insects or plants that remain to be studied.

Tropical forests are also the most critically endangered of habitats and are shrinking faster than ever—about 42 million acres a year are lost, or 80 acres each minute. The primary threats to rainforests are logging and clearing for farms and ranches. Satellite photographs show that as much as 10 percent of the Amazon rainforest has been destroyed, mainly through "slash and burn" clearing for agricultural use. Conservative estimates suggest rates of decline as high as 6.5 percent per year for rainforests in the Cote d'Ivoire in Africa, and an average of 0.6 percent per year for all tropical forests. At this pace, all rainforests will be cleared within 177 years. Given the growth in human population and economic activity in developing countries, the rate of deforestation is more likely to increase than to stabilize. Losses have been greatest so far in West Africa, Brazil, Central America, Mexico, Southeast Asia, and Madagascar.

The major underlying causes of tropical deforestation are underdevelopment, unemployment, and poverty among the growing populations of tropical countries. Unrestricted by enforceable regulations, farmers clear forests to create meager cropland that is often useless three years after its conversion—this is because tropical forest soils are poor, because almost all available nutrients are locked up in the trees and other biomatter. Logging and the conversion of forestland to unsustainable, short-term agricultural use have resulted in the destruction of habitats, declining fisheries, erosion, and flooding. Forest loss also disrupts regional weather patterns and contributes to global climate change. Finally, it eliminates plant and animal species that may serve important medical, industrial, and agricultural purposes. However, arguments for protective measures that might not pay off for many decades are often of little interest to farmers with families to feed. Developing countries frequently voice resentment over what they see as the hypocrisy of industrialized nations, which invariably engaged in similarly destructive practices to build their own economies.

Conservation of tropical forests presents a considerable challenge. The creation of "protected areas" alone has often proven ineffectual, mostly because the people who exploit forests are given no other options for meeting their economic needs. Many conservationists have started

TABLE 4.9

Change in wetland area for selected wetland and deepwater categories, 1986–97

The coefficient of variation (CV) for each entry (expressed as a percentage) is given in parentheses.

Wetland/Deepwater Category	Area in thousands of acres			
	Estimated area, 1986	Estimated area, 1997	Change, 1986–97	Change (in percent)
Marine Intertidal	133.1 (19.6)	130.9 (19.9)	−2.2 (88.5)	−1.7
Estuarine Intertidal Non-vegetated[1]	580.4 (10.7)	580.1 (10.6)	−0.3 (*)	−0.1
Estuarine Intertidal Vegetated[2]	4,623.1 (4.0)	4,615.2 (4.0)	−7.9 (75.1)	−0.2
All Intertidal Wetlands	5,336.6 (3.8)	5,326.2 (3.8)	−10.4 (73.0)	−0.2
Freshwater Non-vegetated[3]	5,251.0 (4.1)	5,914.3 (3.9)	663.3 (13.4)	12.6
Freshwater Vegetated[4]	95,548.1 (3.0)	94,251.2 (3.0)	−1,296.9 (17.1)	−1.4
Freshwater Emergent	26,383.3 (8.1)	25,157.1 (8.4)	−1,226.2 (18.2)	−4.6
Freshwater Forested	51,929.6 (2.8)	50,728.5 (2.8)	−1,201.1 (23.8)	−2.3
Freshwater Shrub	17,235.2 (4.2)	18,365.6 (4.1)	1,130.4 (25.7)	6.6
All Freshwater Wetlands	100,799.1 (2.9)	100,165.5 (2.9)	−633.6 (36.5)	−0.6
All Wetlands	106,135.7 (2.8)	105,491.7 (2.8)	−644.0 (36.0)	0.6
Deepwater Habitats				
Lacustrine[5]	14,608.9 (10.6)	14,725.3 (10.5)	116.4 (*)	0.8
Riverine	6,291.1 (9.6)	6,255.9 (9.4)	−35.2 (*)	−0.6
Estuarine Subtidal	17,637.6 (2.2)	17,663.9 (2.2)	26.3 (95.6)	0.1
All Deepwater Habitats	38,537.6 (4.4)	38,645.1 (4.4)	107.5 (*)	0.3
All Wetlands and Deepwater Habitats[1,2]	144,673.3 (2.4)	144,136.8 (2.4)	−536.5 (30.7)	−0.4

*Statistically unreliable
[1]Includes the categories: Estuarine Intertidal Aquatic Bed and Estuarine Intertidal Unconsolidated Shore.
[2]Includes the categories: Estuarine Intertidal Emergent and Estuarine Intertidal Shrub.
[3]Includes the categories: Paustrine Aquatic Bed, Palustrine Unconsolidated Bottom and Palustrine Unconsolidated Shore.
[4]Includes the categories: Palustrine Emergent, Palustrine Forested and Palustrine Shrub.
[5]Does not include the Great Lakes.
SOURCE: Thomas E. Dahl, "Table 2. Change in Wetland Area for Selected Wetland and Deepwater Categories, 1986 to 1997," in *Status and Trends of Wetlands in the Conterminous United States 1986 to 1997*, U.S. Fish and Wildlife Service, Washington, DC, 2000

to focus on the promotion of sustainable development within rainforests. Agroforestry describes an agricultural strategy that involves the maintenance of diversity within developed tropical forest areas. This includes planting many different types of crops in patches that are mixed in among grazing lands and intact forest. Agroforestry often focuses on crops that produce goods for an indefinite period of time, including citrus fruits, bananas, cacao, coffee, and rubber.

Agroforestry can help to maintain soil quality as well as tropical biodiversity, allowing for a sustained productivity that makes it unnecessary to clear more and more areas of forest. In addition, rainforest conservationists have promoted the harvest of sustainable rainforest products, rather than unsustainable products such as timber. Sustainable harvests include those of medicines, food, and rubber.

Finally, a recent trend is certification of tropical timber. It is estimated that as much as 70 percent of tropical timber available for sale in the United States represents "stolen timber" obtained through illegal logging. The Forest Stewardship Council, based in Oaxaca, Mexico, runs a program that certifies timber obtained from forests managed as sustainable environments. Large wood suppliers, such as Home Depot in 1999, opted to give preference to certified wood by 2002 following extensive picketing by protesters at several stores.

North American Forests

In 2003, the U.S. Forest Service reported that the United States has a total of 747 million acres of forestland. Of these, 20 percent belong to the National Forests, 13 percent are controlled by other federal agencies, 8 percent are owned by states, 49 percent are held by nonindustrial landowners, and 10 percent are held by industrial landowners.

FIGURE 4.6

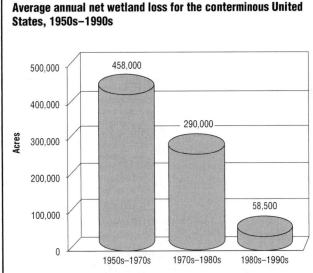

Average annual net wetland loss for the conterminous United States, 1950s–1990s

SOURCE: Thomas E. Dahl, "Figure 13. Average Annual Net Wetland Loss over Time for the Conterminous United States," in *Status and Trends of Wetlands in the Conterminous United States 1986 to 1997*, U.S. Fish and Wildlife Service, Washington, DC, 2000

FIGURE 4.7

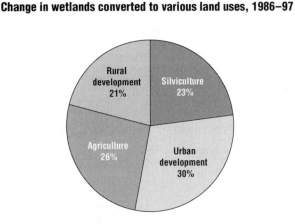

Change in wetlands converted to various land uses, 1986–97

SOURCE: Thomas E. Dahl, "Figure 23. Change in Wetlands Converted to Various Land Uses between 1986 and 1997," in *Status and Trends of Wetlands in the Conterminous United States 1986 to 1997*, U.S. Fish and Wildlife Service, Washington, DC, 2000

Many U.S. forests are highly imperiled. One of the greatest threats to forests is deforestation via clear cutting, a method of logging in which all the trees in an area are cut. Serious damage to the old-growth forests of the Pacific Northwest, for example, is visible from National Aeronautics and Space Administration (NASA) satellite photos. Old-growth forests harbor many unique species, including numerous species that are threatened or endangered. An alternative to clear-cutting is selective management, in which only some trees are removed from an area. Even selective management practices, however, frequently deplete forests more quickly than they are able to recover. The lumber industry continues to battle with environmentalists and the U.S. Forest Service over the right to log National Forest lands, including the unique redwood forests of the West Coast. (See Figure 4.5.)

Huge forest fires raged through the western United States in 2000 and 2002. The Forest Service reported that these were two of the worst fire seasons in over fifty years. In 2002 forest fires scorched over 7 million acres and caused over $1.7 billion in damages. The fires were partly the result of long decades of fire suppression. In response, President Bush announced the "Healthy Forest Initiative" in 2002. This initiative was immediately attacked by conservationists, who claimed that its only aim was to roll back federal regulations on logging, and that it was intended to benefit logging companies rather than to protect people or wildlife. Conservationists further argued that the Bush Administration was merely using the forest fires as an excuse for forwarding its pro-business/anti-environment agenda.

In addition to logging and fire risk, the Forest Service highlighted several other major threats to forests in its 2003 forest health update. These include:

• Invasive insects and pathogens. Sudden Oak Death, caused by a new, unidentified pathogen, has killed thousands of oak and other species in coastal forests, mixed evergreen forests, and urban-wildland interfaces in California and southern Oregon. White Pine Blister Rust is a non-native fungus from Asia that has killed white pine trees in the western United States and Canada. The gypsy moth, first introduced from native habitats in Europe and Asia in the 1800s, continues to damage eastern U.S. forests. The hemlock woolly adelgid, native to Asia and introduced in the 1920s, continues to kill hemlock trees in the eastern United States.

• Invasive plants. About 1,400 species of non-native plants are recognized as pest species that threaten forests and grasslands. Invasive plant species currently affect over 100 million acres of U.S. forestland. The Forest Service spends about $16 million annually in preventing the spread of invasive plants such as the "mile a minute" weed, which infests northeastern forests, and leafy spurge, which affects ecosystems in southern Canada and the northern United States.

• Outbreaks of native insects. Certain native insects, including bark beetles, mountain pine beetles, and southern pine beetles, can also lay waste to native forests when they occur in large outbreaks.

TONGASS NATIONAL FOREST. During the first millennium A.D., an expanse of ancient forest flourished along the entire western coast of the United States and Canada. Today, a portion of this habitat, a 500-mile expanse along the southeastern coast of Alaska, has been preserved as

FIGURE 4.8

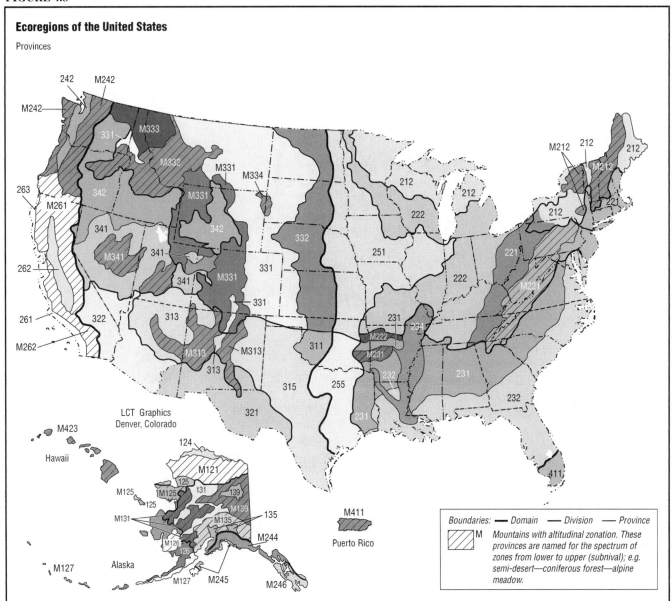

Ecoregions of the United States

Provinces

Boundaries: —— Domain —— Division —— Province

M Mountains with altitudinal zonation. These provinces are named for the spectrum of zones from lower to upper (subnival); e.g. semi-desert—coniferous forest—alpine meadow.

LCT Graphics
Denver, Colorado

Hawaii

Alaska

Puerto Rico

SOURCE: R. G. Bailey, "Ecoregions of the United States," in *Ecological Subregions of the United States*, U.S. Department of Agriculture Forest Service, Washington, DC, October 30, 1996 [Online] http://www.fs.fed.us/land/pubs/ecoregions/index.html [accessed February 12, 2004]

Tongass National Forest. Tongass National Forest represents an unblemished stretch of trees and other wildlife that has existed as a completely intact ecosystem for over a thousand years. It includes 17 million acres of pristine woodland and has never experienced an extinction in modern times. The Tongass preserve comprises 26 percent of the world's temperate rainforest and is the largest on earth.

In the mid-twentieth century, however, the federal government began to negotiate with logging companies to open small portions of the ancient forest for clear-cutting. This has generated ongoing debate in Congress. In the 1990s loggers appealed to the government to open more access roads to facilitate logging, whereas environmentalists fought to preserve the area from human tampering altogether. In May 2000 the National Forest Service drafted a proposal urging renewed protection of roadless areas. A lawsuit brought by the Natural Resources Defense Council in 2003 succeeded in protecting Tongass and other roadless national forests from logging. The Bush Administration exempted Tongass from these protections and is attempting to open 2.5 million acres of the forest to logging.

WETLANDS

Wetlands are transitional areas between land and water bodies where water periodically floods the land or saturates the soil. The term wetland includes environments such as marshes, swamps, bogs, and estuaries. Wetlands may be covered in shallow water most of the year or be wet only seasonally. Plants and animals found in wetlands are uniquely adapted to these conditions.

FIGURE 4.9

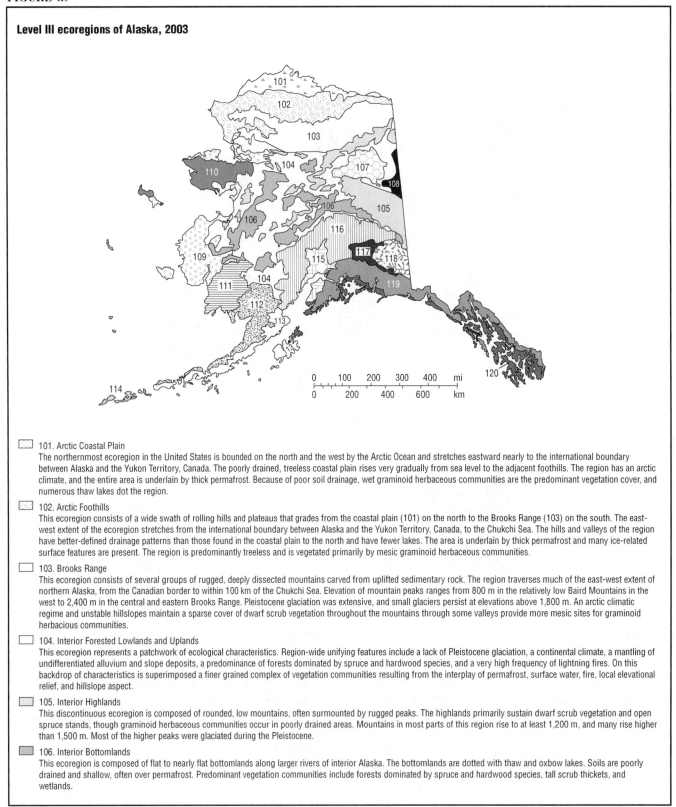

Level III ecoregions of Alaska, 2003

101. Arctic Coastal Plain
The northernmost ecoregion in the United States is bounded on the north and the west by the Arctic Ocean and stretches eastward nearly to the international boundary between Alaska and the Yukon Territory, Canada. The poorly drained, treeless coastal plain rises very gradually from sea level to the adjacent foothills. The region has an arctic climate, and the entire area is underlain by thick permafrost. Because of poor soil drainage, wet graminoid herbaceous communities are the predominant vegetation cover, and numerous thaw lakes dot the region.

102. Arctic Foothills
This ecoregion consists of a wide swath of rolling hills and plateaus that grades from the coastal plain (101) on the north to the Brooks Range (103) on the south. The east-west extent of the ecoregion stretches from the international boundary between Alaska and the Yukon Territory, Canada, to the Chukchi Sea. The hills and valleys of the region have better-defined drainage patterns than those found in the coastal plain to the north and have fewer lakes. The area is underlain by thick permafrost and many ice-related surface features are present. The region is predominantly treeless and is vegetated primarily by mesic graminoid herbaceous communities.

103. Brooks Range
This ecoregion consists of several groups of rugged, deeply dissected mountains carved from uplifted sedimentary rock. The region traverses much of the east-west extent of northern Alaska, from the Canadian border to within 100 km of the Chukchi Sea. Elevation of mountain peaks ranges from 800 m in the relatively low Baird Mountains in the west to 2,400 m in the central and eastern Brooks Range. Pleistocene glaciation was extensive, and small glaciers persist at elevations above 1,800 m. An arctic climatic regime and unstable hillslopes maintain a sparse cover of dwarf scrub vegetation throughout the mountains through some valleys provide more mesic sites for graminoid herbacious communities.

104. Interior Forested Lowlands and Uplands
This ecoregion represents a patchwork of ecological characteristics. Region-wide unifying features include a lack of Pleistocene glaciation, a continental climate, a mantling of undifferentiated alluvium and slope deposits, a predominance of forests dominated by spruce and hardwood species, and a very high frequency of lightning fires. On this backdrop of characteristics is superimposed a finer grained complex of vegetation communities resulting from the interplay of permafrost, surface water, fire, local elevational relief, and hillslope aspect.

105. Interior Highlands
This discontinuous ecoregion is composed of rounded, low mountains, often surmounted by rugged peaks. The highlands primarily sustain dwarf scrub vegetation and open spruce stands, though graminoid herbaceous communities occur in poorly drained areas. Mountains in most parts of this region rise to at least 1,200 m, and many rise higher than 1,500 m. Most of the higher peaks were glaciated during the Pleistocene.

106. Interior Bottomlands
This ecoregion is composed of flat to nearly flat bottomlands along larger rivers of interior Alaska. The bottomlands are dotted with thaw and oxbow lakes. Soils are poorly drained and shallow, often over permafrost. Predominant vegetation communities include forests dominated by spruce and hardwood species, tall scrub thickets, and wetlands.

Wetlands in the United States are highly diverse because of regional differences in climate, geology, soils, and vegetation. There are approximately 105.5 million acres of wetlands in the country. The majority of this is freshwater wetland (95 percent, or 100.5 million acres). The rest is tidal, or saltwater, wetland and is found along the coasts.

Wetlands are found in nearly all states—there are arctic tundra wetlands in Alaska, peat bogs in the Appalachians, and riparian (riverbank) wetlands in the arid west. Table 4.9 lists some of the different types of wetlands and their acreage in the forty-eight contiguous United States, as well as how acreage has changed in the decade from 1986 to1997.

FIGURE 4.9

Level III ecoregions of Alaska, 2003 [CONTINUED]

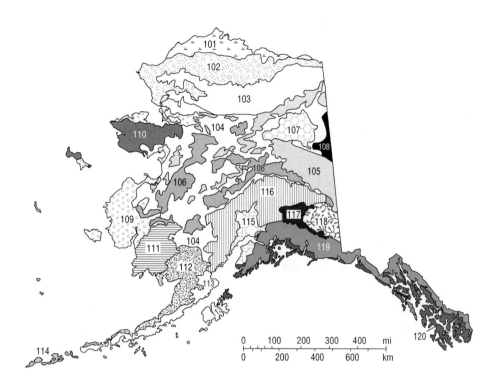

107. Yukon Flats
The Yukon Flats is a relatively flat, marshy basin floor in east central Alaska that is patterned with braided and meandering streams, numerous thaw and oxbow lakes, and meander scars. Surrounding the basin floor is a variable band of more undulating topography with fewer water bodies. In many respects the ecoregion is similar to the Interior Bottomlands Ecoregion (106), but differs in climatic characteristics. Temperatures tend to be more extreme; summers are warmer and winters are colder than in other areas of comparable latitude. The ecoregion also receives less annual precipitation than the Interior Bottomlands. Forests dominated by spruce and hardwood species, tall scrub communities, and wet graminoid herbaceous communities are the predominant vegetation types.

108. Ogilvie Mountains
This ecoregion, along the eastern edge of Alaska, consists of flat-topped hills eroded from a former plain and broad pediment slopes built up from mountains that are much subdued from their former stature. Karst topography is common. Mesic graminoid herbaceous communities and tall scrub communities are widespread throughout the region. Forest communities occupy lower hillslopes and valleys.

109. Subarctic Coastal Plains
This ecoregion mainly includes coastal plains of the Kotzebue Sound area and the Yukon and Kuskokwim River delta area. Flat, lake-dotted coastal plains and river deltas are characteristic of the region. Streams have very wide and serpentine meanders. Soils are wet and the permafrost table is shallow, providing conditions for wet graminoid herbaceous communities, the predominant vegetation type. The region is affected by both marine and continental climatic influences.

110. Seward Peninsula
Some of the oldest geologic formations in Alaska provide a backdrop for this predominantly treeless ecoregion. Mesic graminoid herbaceous and low scrub communities occupy extensive areas. The ecoregion is surrounded on three sides by water, yet this has little ameliorating effect on the climate. Winters tend to be long and harsh and summers short and cool.

111. Ahklun and Kilbuck Mountains
Located in southwestern Alaska off Bristol and Kuskokwim Bays, this ecoregion is composed of steep, sharp, often ringlike groupings of rugged mountains separated by broad, flat valleys and lowlands. The mountains were glaciated during the Pleistocene epoch, but only a few small glaciers persist. Dwarf scrub communities are the predominant vegetation cover in the mountains. Tall scrub and graminoid herbaceous communities are common in valleys and on lower mountain slopes. Valley bottoms may support stands of spruce and hardwood species.

112. Bristol Bay-Nushagak Lowlands
This lowland ecoregion is located in southwestern Alaska off Bristol Bay. The region has rolling terrain, formed from morainal deposits. Soils of the lowlands are somewhat better drained than soils of the Subarctic Coastal Plains Ecoregion (109). Dwarf scrub communities are widespread, but large areas of wetland communities occur. Lakes are scattered throughout the lowlands, but are not nearly as numerous as in the Subarctic Coastal Plains.

113. Alaska Peninsula Mountains
This ecoregion is composed of rounded, folded and faulted sedimentary ridges intermittently surmounted by volcanoes. The mountains were heavily glaciated during the Pleistocene epoch. A marine climate prevails, and the region is generally free of permafrost. Many soils formed in deposits of volcanic ash and cinder over glacial deposits and are highly erodible. Vegetation cover commonly consists of dwarf scrub communities at higher elevations and on sites exposed to wind, and low scrub communities at lower elevations and in more protected sites.

As of 2004, well over half the original North American wetlands have vanished. A few states have lost nearly all their original wetlands. With the recognition of the importance of wetlands and the institution of protective measures, the pace of wetland loss has slowed in recent decades. About 58,500 wetland acres were lost each year between 1986 and 1997, with forested wetlands suffering the most damage. Although this represents an 80 percent

FIGURE 4.9

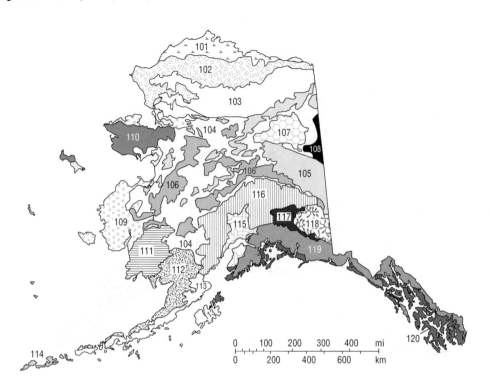

Level III ecoregions of Alaska, 2003 [CONTINUED]

▢ 114. Aleutian Islands (Western portion not shown)
This ecoregion in southwestern Alaska is composed of a chain of sedimentary islands (eroded from older volcanic formations) that are crowned by steep volcanoes. Maritime climate prevails. The region is south of the winter sea ice pack and is generally free from permafrost. Vegetation cover mainly consists of dwarf scrub communities at higher elevations and on sites exposed to wind, and of graminoid herbaceous communities in more protected sites.

▢ 115. Cook Inlet
Located in the south central part of Alaska adjacent to the Cook Inlet, the ecoregion has one of the mildest climates in the State. The climate, the level to rolling topography, and the coastal proximity have attracted most of the settlement and development in Alaska. The region has a variety of vegetation communities but is dominated by stands of spruce and hardwood species. The area is generally free from permafrost. Unlike many of the other nonmontane ecoregions, the Cook Inlet Ecoregion was intensely glaciated during the Pleistocene.

▥ 116. Alaska Range
The mountains of south central Alaska, the Alaska Range, are very high and steep. This ecoregion is covered by rocky slopes, icefields, and glaciers. Much of the area is barren of vegetation. Dwarf scrub communities are common at higher elevations and on windswept sites where vegetation does exist. The Alaska Range has a continental climatic regime, but because of the extreme height of many of the ridges and peaks, annual precipitation at higher elevations is similar to that measured for some ecoregions having maritime climate.

■ 117. Copper Plateau
This ecoregion in south central Alaska occupies the site of a large lake that existed during glacial times. The nearly level to rolling plain has many lakes and wetlands. Soils are predominantly silty or clayey, formed from glaciolacustrine sediments. Much of the region has a shallow permafrost table, and soils are poorly drained. Black spruce forests and tall scrub, interspersed with wetlands, are the major types of vegetation communities.

▨ 118. Wrangell Mountains
This ecoregion consists of steep, rugged mountains of volcanic origin that are extensively covered by ice fields and glaciers. Most slopes are barren of vegetation. Dwarf scrub tundra communities, consisting of mats of low shrubs, fobs, grasses, and lichens, predominate where vegetation does occur. The climate has harsh winters and short summers.

▨ 119. Pacific Coastal Mountains
The steep and rugged mountains along the southeastern and south central coast of Alaska receive more precipitation annually than either the Alaska Range (116) or Wrangell Mountains (118) Ecoregions. Glaciated during the Pleistocene, most of the ecoregion is still covered by glaciers and ice fields. Most of the area is barren of vegetation, but where plants do occur, dwarf and low scrub communities dominate.

▨ 120. Coastal Western Hemlock-Sitka Spruce Forests
Located along the southeastern and south central shores of Alaska, the terrain of this ecoregion is a result of intense glaciation during late advances of the Pleistocene. The deep, narrow bays, steep valley walls that expose much bedrock, thin moraine deposits on hills and in valleys, very irregular coastline, high sea cliffs, and deeply dissected glacial moraine deposits covering the lower slopes of valley walls are all evidence of the effects of glaciation. The region has the mildest winter temperatures in Alaska, accompanied by large amounts of precipitation. Forests of western hemlock and Sitka spruce are widespread.

SOURCE: Adapted from "Level III Ecoregions of the Continental United States," National Health and Environmental Effects Research Laboratory, U.S. Environmental Protection Agency, Corvallis, OR, May 2003 [Online] http://www.epa.gov/wed/pages/ecoregions/level_iii.htm [accessed February 12, 2004]

drop from the previous decade, wetland loss is still significant. (See Figure 4.6.) The new land uses of these converted wetlands are shown in Figure 4.7. Wetlands provide critical habitats for fish and wildlife. They also purify polluted water and check the destructive power of floods and storms. Finally, wetlands provide recreational

FIGURE 4.10

Ecosystem boundaries

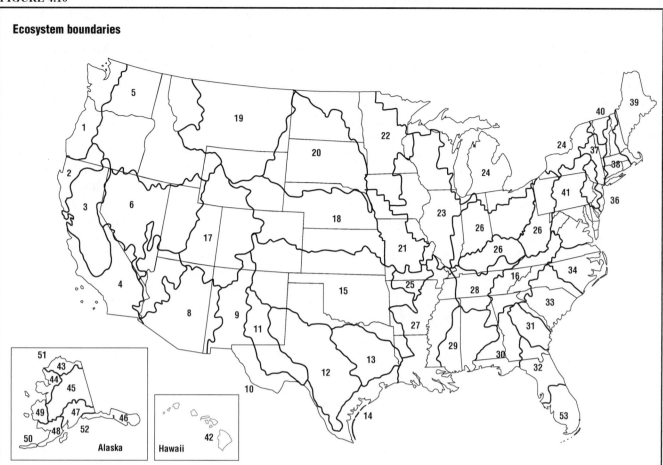

Unit #	Unit Name	Unit #	Unit Name
1	North Pacific Coast	27	Lower Mississippi River
2	Klamath/Central Pacific Coast	28	Tennessee/Cumberland River
3	Central Valley of California/San Francisco Bay	29	Central Gulf Watersheds
		30	Florida Panhandle Watersheds
4	Southern California	31	Altamaha Watershed
5	Columbia Basin	32	Peninsular Florida
6	Interior Basin	33	Savannah/Santee/Pee Dee Rivers
7	Lower Colorado River	34	Roanoke/Tar/Neuse/Cape Fear Rivers
8	Gila/Salt/Verde River	35	Caribbean
9	Middle and Upper Rio Grande	36	Deleware River/Delmarva Coastal Area
10	Lower Rio Grande	37	Hudson River/New York Bight
11	Pecos River	38	Connecticut River/Long Island Sound
12	Edwards Plateau	39	Gulf of Maine Rivers
13	East Texas	40	Lake Champlain
14	Texas Gulf Coast	41	Chesapeake Bay/Susquehanna River
15	Arkansas/Red Rivers	42	Pacific Islands
16	Southern Appalachians	43	Arctic Alaska
17	Upper Colorado River	44	Northwest Alaska
18	Platte/Kansas Rivers	45	Interior Alaska
19	Upper Missouri, Yellowstone and Upper Columbia River	46	Southeast Alaska
		47	South Central Alaska
20	Missouri Main Stem	48	Bristol Bay/Kodiak
21	Lower Missouri River	49	Yukon - Kuskokwim Delta
22	Mississippi Headwaters/Tallgrass Prarie	50	Bering Sea/Aleutian Islands
23	Upper Mississippi River/Tallgrass Prarie	51	Beaufort/Chukchi Seas
24	Great Lakes	52	North Pacific/Gulf of Alaska
25	Ozark Watersheds	53	South Florida
26	Ohio River Valley		

SOURCE: "U.S. Fish and Wildlife Service Ecosystem Approach: Watershed Based Units," in *An Ecosystem Approach to Fish and Wildlife Conservation,* U.S. Fish and Wildlife Service, Washington, DC 2004 [Online] http://training.fws.gov/library/pubs9/habitatmgmt/concept.html [accessed February 12, 2004]

opportunities such as fishing, hunting, photography, and wildlife observation.

Endangered Bog Plants

Bogs are non-tidal wetland ecosystems that form where poor drainage and low oxygen levels combine with a low mineral content to retard the decay of organic material. Over time, peat, partially decayed organic substances, begins to solidify, forming layers over the surface of ponds. Migrating birds and amphibians, including some salamanders, are among the animals most commonly found in bog habitats. Bog flora includes coarse, grasslike plants called sedges and unusual carnivorous plants such as sundew and pitcher plants. Carnivorous plants capture and digest small insects in order to obtain nutrients unavailable in their unique environments, most often minerals such as nitrogen and phosphorus. The leaves of the sundew are covered with hundreds of tiny "tentacles" that are used to trap insects. The sundew traps an average of five insects per month. Pitcher plants maintain a pool of acidic fluid at the bottom of their "pitchers." Hairs on the inside of the pitchers point downward, preventing insects from exiting once they enter. Insects are attracted to the pitchers by the enticing red color inside.

Bog plants are threatened primarily by encroaching urbanization. Boggy wetlands are either drained or filled for use as dumping grounds. In addition, the suppression of naturally occurring fires discourages the formation of bog ecosystems. One bog species, the funnel-shaped green pitcher plant, first appeared on the Endangered Species List in 1979. Found in Alabama, North Carolina, and Georgia, it has declined largely due to collection by humans, who find these insect-eating plants both interesting and exotic. The collection of carnivorous plant species has also disrupted bog ecosystems by allowing mosquitoes and flies to proliferate.

The Florida Everglades

The Everglades covers approximately 5,000 square miles of southern Florida. It includes a wide diversity of both temperate and tropical habitat types, including sawgrass prairies, mangrove swamps, pine forests, cypress forests, marshes, and estuaries, and represents one of the wildest and most inaccessible areas in the United States. The area was formed by centuries of water flow from Lake Okeechobee in south-central Florida to Florida Bay, and is often described as a shallow "river of grass." The highest land in the Everglades is a mere seven feet above sea level. Everglades National Park is the largest remaining subtropical wilderness in the United States, and is home to endangered species such as the American crocodile, Florida panther, wood stork, and West Indian manatee. The Everglades became a National Park in 1947, and the region has also been designated an International Biosphere Reserve, a World Heritage Site, and a Wetland of International Importance.

Everglades habitats are now threatened by many factors. First, water control through an extensive system of canals and levees has brought both droughts and floods to Everglades lands. Much of the Everglades' water has traditionally been diverted for irrigation or to supply metropolitan areas. In fact, the portion of the Everglades inundated by water has been reduced drastically over the twentieth century, destroying numerous habitat areas. Occasional releases of large amounts of water, on the other hand, flood habitats, harming species such as alligators, whose nests may be washed away. Pollution is a second factor in Everglades deterioration. Harmful pollutants now found in the Everglades include fertilizers and pesticides from agricultural runoff, as well as mercury. Fertilizers encourage the rampant growth of vegetation that chokes wetlands, while pesticides and mercury poison species. One plant species that is affected is Garber's spurge, a beach herb that thrives in sandy peripheral soil. With its decline, parts of the Everglades have been more prone to soil erosion. Invasive species have also altered Everglades habitats. Alien species such as Brazilian pepper and Australian pine have reduced native plant populations. Finally, fire suppression related to human encroachment has caused habitat alteration. Park officials now adhere to a prescribed burn schedule, setting fires in three- to ten-year intervals as necessary.

Multiple efforts were made in the 1990s and early 2000s to help restore the Everglades. Florida's Everglades Forever Act, passed in 1994, attempted to limit agricultural runoff as well as set water quality standards. The Comprehensive Everglades Restoration Plan, passed by Congress in 2000, is a 38-year project drawn up by the U.S. Army Corps of Engineers. It aims to restore natural water flow patterns in the Everglades and to redirect water to the marshes. In December 2000, President Bill Clinton signed the Water Resources Development Act of 2000, which committed over $4 billion to Everglades restoration.

Tidal Wetlands—The Mangroves

Mangrove forests are among the most biodiverse wetland ecosystems on earth. They are found in tropical coastal waters, often near river mouths. The tree species found in mangrove forests possess special roots that allow them to survive in brackish water. Mangrove forests harbor numerous unique species worldwide, such as crab-eating monkeys, fishing cats, and diverse species of birds and fish. They also provide food and wood for local communities, stabilize coastlines, and provide barriers from the sea during storms. Mangrove forests once lined three-quarters of the world's tropical coasts. Now, according to the World Resources Institute, an environmental advocacy group, less than half these forests remain. Indonesia, a country of more than 13,000 islands, possesses the most mangrove forestland of any country. Brazil and Australia also have extensive mangrove habitats.

Mangroves are disappearing in part because they have traditionally been regarded as sinister, malarial wastelands. In Florida, for example, mangroves were flooded every year to control mosquito populations. Mangrove forests have also been sold to logging companies for paper pulp, pest-proof timber, and chipboard for coastal development. Many mangrove forests have also been replaced with saltwater ponds for commercial shrimp farming. The shrimp industry is perhaps the most immediate threat to mangrove forests today.

During the Vietnam War, herbicides were dumped on an estimated 124,000 hectares (approximately 306,410 acres) of mangrove forests in South Vietnam. These areas remain, for the most part, entirely barren—a true wasteland.

PLANT CONSERVATION

Protection under the Endangered Species Act

The Endangered Species Act of 1973 protects listed plants from deliberate destruction or vandalism. Plants also receive protection under the consultation requirements of the act—that is, all federal agencies must consult with the Fish and Wildlife Service to determine how best to conserve species as well as to ensure that no issued permits will jeopardize listed species or harm their habitats.

However, many conservationists believe that plants receive less protection than animals under the Endangered Species Act. First, the Endangered Species Act only protects plants that are found on federal lands. It imposes no restrictions on private landowners whose property is home to endangered plants. Critics also complain that the Fish and Wildlife Service has been slow to list plant species. Hundreds of plant species first proposed for listing in 1976 are still awaiting action. Critics also charge that damage to plant habitats is not addressed with the same seriousness as for animal species. The Fish and Wildlife Service only rarely designates critical habitat for plant species, and only rarely acquires national wildlife refuges to protect plants. Finally, of all Fish and Wildlife Service funds spent on threatened and endangered species, about half goes to a handful of listed animal species. Plants typically receive less than 3 percent of the total, and about 15 percent of plant species receive no funding at all—twice the proportion of animals that receive no funding.

In June 2000, in an effort to bolster conservation efforts for plants, the Fish and Wildlife Service announced an agreement with the Center for Plant Conservation, a national association of botanical gardens and arboreta. The two groups will cooperate in developing conservation measures to help save North American plant species, particularly those listed as threatened or endangered. Central to the effort will be the creation of educational programs aimed at informing the public about the importance of plant species for aesthetic, economic, bio-logical, and medical reasons. The Center for Plant Conservation will also aid in developing recovery plans for listed species.

Wildcrafting

Wildcrafting describes the harvest of forest resources for profit or recreation without damaging habitat. Wildcrafting has enjoyed a resurgence since the government and courts curtailed logging on public land in the early 1990s. The wildcrafting industry brings in hundreds of millions of dollars annually.

In 1995 American exports of commercial moss and lichen alone amounted to $14 million, according to U.S. Forest Service scientists. Mushrooms—matsutakes, chanterelles, and morels—also bring good prices. Burls, hard woody growths on trees, which become unusually attractive when sanded and polished, can be used for furniture, cabinets, and trims. Ferns and shrubs for floral arrangements, Christmas greens, and more than 100 medicinal herbs are also collected.

The U.S. Forest Service, which issues permits to wildcrafters on public lands, is still examining how much wildcrafters can harvest without causing damage. Some rangers and environmentalists worry that forest products may be over-harvested, causing habitat damage, or that trampling will damage the forest floor.

Plant-Derived Medications

Numerous plant species have medicinal uses—in fact, the global market in plant-derived medications is worth $40 billion annually. Unfortunately, less than 1 percent of plant species have been evaluated for potential medical use. With as many as 50 plant species disappearing daily, botanists calculate that the planet's diversity could be reduced by 10 percent by the year 2015. Extinction will deprive future generations of potentially powerful medications. The rapid destruction of tropical rainforests is particularly alarming, as 60 percent of higher plant species occupy those ecosystems.

Between 25 and 40 percent of all prescription drugs in the United States contain active ingredients derived from plants. For example, *Cinchona ledgeriana* is the source of quinine, the oldest malaria medicine. The Madagascar periwinkle, found in a country that has lost 80 percent of its vegetation, provides two potent compounds used in the treatment of cancer. Vinblastine is used to treat Hodgkin's disease, and vincristine is used to treat leukemia. Sales of these two drugs exceed $180 million a year. Wild yam is the source of diosgenin (a key ingredient in some oral contraceptives), steroids, and muscle relaxants used in anesthesia. Morphine, a powerful pain medication, comes from the opium poppy. Scopolamine, a drug used for motion sickness, is derived from a plant called *Hyocyamus niger*. Taxol, a drug used to treat ovarian cancer, comes from the Pacific yew.

Numerous plants are also found on the non-prescription medicinal herb market. In the United States, some 175 North American species alone are available on the non-prescription market. In North America and Europe, herbal medicine markets have increased by 10 percent per year for over a decade. Examples of medicinal herbs include mullein, which is said to relieve asthma, and ginseng, which is claimed to boost vitality.

The use of medicinal plants is even greater in non-industrial societies, where large segments of the population rely on traditional medicine. Traditional healers in South Asia use nearly 2,000 plant species. Over 5,000 species are used by traditional healers in China. Over 1,300 species are used by healers in Amazonia. Furthermore, nearly 100 commercial drugs derived from plants were originally discovered by traditional healers.

Medicinal plants are declining in many areas as a result of habitat degradation and non-sustainable use. In fact, a report from the *New Scientist* ("Herbal medicine boom threatens plants," 8 January 2004) suggests that, of the 50,000 medicinal plants in use, two-thirds are harvested from the wild, and 4,000–10,000 of these are now endangered. Because health fads change constantly, causing demand for certain plants to change to over time, herbal remedy companies have little incentive to harvest in a sustainable way.

The African cherry, used by traditional healers in Cameroon, has declined so much due to overexploitation that the market has now collapsed. Much of the African cherry harvested had been exported to Western Europe, where the plant is used to treat prostate disease. In North America, medically valuable species such as the Pacific yew, a "trash" evergreen found in old-growth forests of the Pacific Northwest, have been cleared to make way for tree species profitable to the timber industry. The cessation of logging in the Pacific Northwest—in order to protect northern spotted owl habitat as required by the Endangered Species Act—has protected the Pacific yew as well.

In 1990 the National Institute for Biodiversity in Costa Rica entered into a landmark deal with Merck, a pharmaceutical company, in which the institute would provide rights to drug exploration, while Merck would fund tropical forest conservation and research. Tropical forests have produced at least forty-seven major pharmaceutical drugs, and scientists estimate that several hundred more plants with medicinal properties have yet to be discovered. This agreement became a model for other such arrangements. However, no deals were attempted in the United States until 1996, when the idea caught the attention of U.S. conservationists. That year Dr. James Tiedje, director of the National Science Foundation's Center for

Microbial Ecology at Michigan State University, reported that a single gram of temperate forest soil could harbor as many as 10,000 species of bacteria. By 2000 a group of drug manufacturers had agreed to support a 270-acre pharmaceutical preserve in upstate New York, the first preserve outside the tropics set aside specifically for chemical prospecting. Scientists already have discovered a mold that produces a substance called cyclosporin, which is used to prevent the rejection of transplanted organs.

ECOSYSTEMS APPROACHES TO CONSERVATION

Many environmentalists are now calling for the protection of entire ecosystems, which they believe will be more effective in preserving biodiversity than focusing on individual endangered species. Ecosystem approaches consider entire communities of species as well as their interactions with the physical environment, and aim to develop integrated plans involving wildlife, physical resources, and sustainable use.

Several federal agencies have produced ecosystem-level analyses of U.S. land areas. The U.S. Forest Service has divided the U.S. into different ecoregions based on vegetation patterns. (See Figure 4.8.) The U.S. Environmental Protection Agency's National Health and Environmental Effects Research Laboratory has identified Level III ecoregions based on various factors including climate and vegetation. Figure 4.9 illustrates the Level III ecoregions for the state of Alaska. The most prominent environmental challenges in each ecoregion have also been identified. The Fish and Wildlife Service has divided the country into a series of fifty-three ecosystem units based on the location of watershed areas. (See Figure 4.10.) Each unit is associated with a team that develops a comprehensive strategy for conservation. Central to ecosystem conservation strategies is the preservation of large, intact areas of habitat.

Ecosystem approaches to conservation sometime require compromise with developers as well. This is the case for several Habitat Conservation Plans developed in recent years. In Southern California developers and environmentalists had long battled over hundreds of thousands of biologically rich acres lying between Los Angeles and Mexico that were home to uncounted species of plants and animals. Developers wanted to build there, while federal regulators wanted to protect the habitat for wildlife. Haggling over small parcels of land had already cost significant time and money and caused frustration on both sides. A compromise resolution permitted developers to develop some large parcels of land while setting aside other large, intact regions as conservation areas. A similar agreement between developers and environmentalists was reached in the Texas Hill Country. The Balcones Canyonlands Conservation Plan set aside 111,428 acres for ecosystem enhancement while allowing uncontested development of many thousands of acres of land in the central Texas corridor.

CHAPTER 5
AQUATIC SPECIES AND THEIR ENVIRONMENTS

Approximately 1.4 pentillion tons (1,400,000,000, 000,000,000) of water cover the surface of the earth—466 billion tons for each of the six billion people on the planet. Amazing as it may seem, most of this water has been affected by human activity. Numerous aquatic species are in decline because of degraded water quality, development or alteration of aquatic habitats, and overhunting or overfishing. Figure 5.1 shows the number of aquatic and wetlands species at risk by watershed.

WATER POLLUTION—MANY, MANY CAUSES

Humans burn fuels, produce wastes, and use large amounts of fertilizers, pesticides, and other chemicals. These by-products of industrialization end up in the environment and are often harmful to living organisms. The condition of water-dwelling animals is in fact often a good measure of the condition of the environment; their demise suggests that something may be wrong in their habitat. Figure 5.2 illustrates the overall condition of U.S. watersheds based on data collected by the U.S. Environmental Protection Agency (EPA). Large portions of the country suffer from serious water quality problems.

Pesticides

Pesticides are chemicals used to kill insects that feed on crops and vegetation. The first documented use of pesticides was by the ancient Greeks. Pliny the Elder (23–79 A.D.) reported using common compounds such as arsenic, sulfur, caustic soda, and olive oil to protect crops. The Chinese later used similar substances to retard infestation by insects and fungi. In the 1800s Europeans used heavy metal salts such as copper sulfate and iron sulfate as weed killers.

The invention of DDT (dichloro-diphenyl-trichloroethane) in 1939 marked a revolution in the war against pests. DDT was effective, relatively cheap, and apparently safe for people—on the face of it, a miracle chemical that promised a world with unprecedented crop yields. Its dis-

coverer, Paul Muller, received a Nobel Prize for discovering the high efficiency of DDT as a contact poison against pests. In the United States, pesticide use in agriculture nearly tripled after 1965, as farmers began to use DDT and other pesticides, herbicides, and fungicides intensively and began to accept these chemicals as essential to agriculture.

For many years, it was thought that if pesticides were properly used, the risk of harm to humans and wildlife was slight. As the boom in pesticide use continued, however, it eventually became apparent that pesticides were not safe after all. The fundamental reason that pesticides are dangerous is that they are poisons purposely designed to kill living organisms. Part of the problem is biomagnification—a predator that eats organisms with pesticides in their bodies ends up concentrating all those pesticides in its own tissues. Eventually, the concentration of pesticides causes serious problems. DDT was eventually shown to have harmed numerous bird species, particularly those high in the food chain, such as bald eagles and peregrine falcons. DDT caused the production of eggs with shells so thin they could not protect the developing chick.

As the dangers of pesticides became more apparent in the 1960s and 1970s, some of the most dangerous, like DDT, were banned in the United States. However, the use of other chemical pesticides increased until the 1980s. Use levels have generally held steady since then. Farmers continue to apply about one pound of pesticide per year for every person on Earth. The majority of pesticide use—75 percent—occurs in industrialized countries. Unfortunately, the primary reason that pesticide use has leveled off in recent decades is not concern regarding its safety, but declines in its effectiveness. This is due to the fact that pest species quickly evolve resistance to pesticides. Worldwide, the number of resistant pests continues to climb. Unfortunately, increased resistance has only created a demand for more, and more powerful, chemicals.

FIGURE 5.1

Aquatic/wetland species at risk, 1996

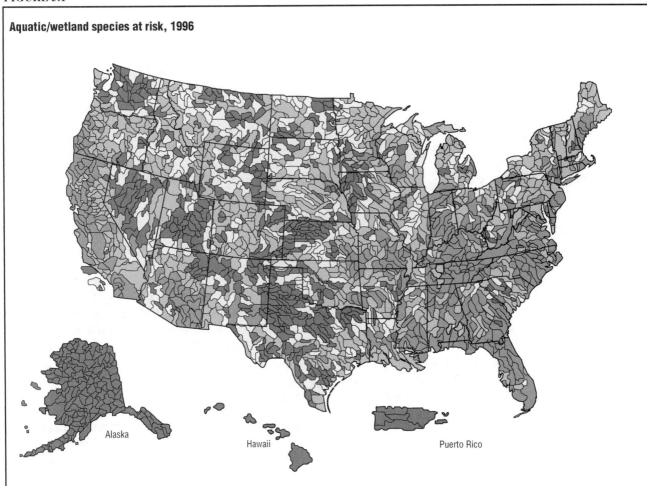

Category	Number of watersheds
1 Species known to be at risk	403
2–5 Species at risk	745
>5 Species known to be at risk	422
No recorded data	665

Importance of aquatic/wetland species at risk

The state agency-based Natural Heritage Network and the Nature Conservancy (TNC) assess the conservation status of plants and animals and map out the population occurrences of those species at greatest risk of extinction. This map shows the number of aquatic or wetland-dependent species documented in a watershed that are classified by the Heritage Network as critically imperiled (identified by TNC as G1), imperiled (G2), or vulnerable (G3), or that are listed under the federal Endangered Species Act (ESA) as threatened or endangered.

The presence of rare or endangered species in a watershed is not necessarily an indication of poor watershed conditions. Indeed, it more likely indicates the opposite: in many instances these species persist only in areas of exceptionally high quality habitat. The presence of species at risk in a watershed indicates, however, that these watersheds are especially vulnerable to future water quality or habitat degradation, which could jeopardize the maintenance or recovery of these organisms. Watersheds considered vulnerable because of the presence of species at risk may require special attention to protect or restore water quality in order to maintain these biological values.

The presence of an individual species in a watershed is based on the existence in the heritage databases of at least one documented occurrence in that watershed since 1970.

Notes on interpreting this information

State Natural Heritage data centers process data according to consistent inventory and data management standards, producing information that is comparable from state to state. Aquatic inventory efforts and data processing backlogs, however, vary from state to state. Thus while available data is comparable, level of data completeness is inconsistent. Heritage species occurrence data are not based on comprehensive inventories of each watershed and major inventory gaps remain, especially for aquatic species. For this reason, some watersheds may actually have more species at risk than indicated. Similarly, lack of data for a watershed cannot be construed to mean that no species at risk are present. It is not currently possible using this data set to distinguish between lack of inventory data for a watershed and the absence of species at risk in that watershed.

SOURCE: Adapted from "Aquatic/Wetland Species at Risk: 1996," in *Watershed Information Network*, U.S. Environmental Protection Agency, Washington, DC, September 4, 2003 [Online] http://www.epa.gov/iwi/1999sept/iv8_usmap.html [accessed February 17, 2004]

FIGURE 5.2

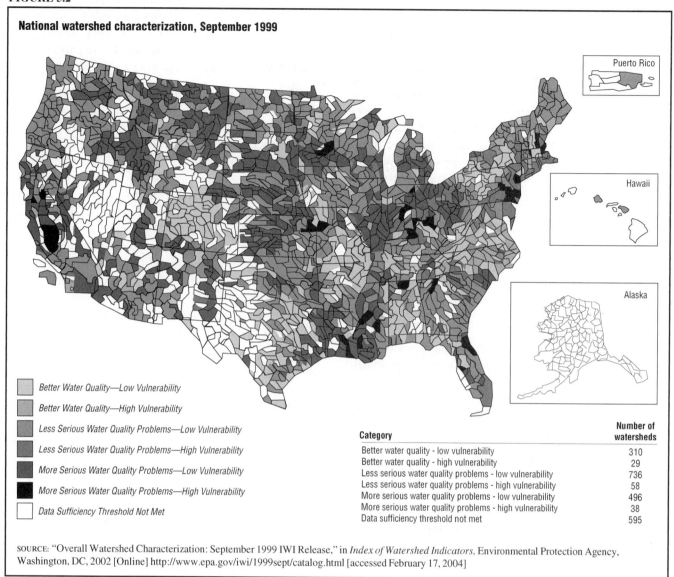

National watershed characterization, September 1999

Better Water Quality—Low Vulnerability

Better Water Quality—High Vulnerability

Less Serious Water Quality Problems—Low Vulnerability

Less Serious Water Quality Problems—High Vulnerability

More Serious Water Quality Problems—Low Vulnerability

More Serious Water Quality Problems—High Vulnerability

Data Sufficiency Threshold Not Met

Category	Number of watersheds
Better water quality - low vulnerability	310
Better water quality - high vulnerability	29
Less serious water quality problems - low vulnerability	736
Less serious water quality problems - high vulnerability	58
More serious water quality problems - low vulnerability	496
More serious water quality problems - high vulnerability	38
Data sufficiency threshold not met	595

SOURCE: "Overall Watershed Characterization: September 1999 IWI Release," in *Index of Watershed Indicators,* Environmental Protection Agency, Washington, DC, 2002 [Online] http://www.epa.gov/iwi/1999sept/catalog.html [accessed February 17, 2004]

Pesticides degrade numerous aquatic ecosystems after seeping into the ground as runoff from watering or rain. The U.S. Fish and Wildlife Service reports that pesticides harm about 20 percent of the country's threatened and endangered animal and plant species.

Fertilizers

For decades, farmers have tried to increase the productivity of their land by using ever-increasing amounts of fertilizers. Fertilizers are biological products or chemicals applied to increase crop growth. Fertilizers may seep into water and collect in lakes, streams, and groundwater. While fertilizers are not poisonous by nature, large quantities of fertilizers can cause serious health problems in aquatic animals. Fertilizers also encourage the growth of aquatic plant life, disrupting food webs and biological communities. Aquatic plants and algae may grow so rapidly that they block off sunshine or deplete nutrients essential to other species.

Oil Spills and Runoff

Oil spills represent regular and devastating accidents to aquatic life. Oil spilled into the ocean floats on the water surface, cutting off oxygen to the sea life below and killing mammals, birds, fish, and other animals. The dangers presented by oil spills have grown worse over the years. In 1945 the largest tanker held 16,500 tons of oil. Now, supertankers the length of several football fields regularly carry more than 550,000 tons.

In 1989 the tanker *Exxon Valdez* ran aground on the pristine Alaskan coastline, spilling 11 million gallons of oil into the bay and killing millions of animals. In 1994 a federal jury assessed $5 billion in punitive damages and $3.5 billion in criminal fines and cleanup costs against Exxon. The *Valdez* spill led to additional safety requirements for tankers, including double hulls. Larger oil spills than the *Valdez* have occurred both before and since, but the incident alerted many people to the damage that can be done to marine habitats. Many species impacted by the spill, particularly seabird species, have yet to recover more than a decade later.

In January 2001 the tanker *Jessica* released 150,000 gallons of fuel near the Galapagos Islands, a biologically rich area harboring numerous unique species including Darwin's famous finches, marine iguanas, and a tropical penguin population. There was widespread relief when winds blew the oil slick seaward rather than towards the islands. Sea bird and sea lion deaths numbered in the dozens, and it was believed that a true catastrophe had been avoided. Ongoing studies of the Galapagos' unique marine iguanas, however, revealed in June 2002 that numerous iguanas likely died due to oil-related injuries after the spill. In particular, 60 percent of the marine iguanas on Santa Fe Island died in 2001, despite the fact that oil contamination was relatively low, with only about one quart of oil per yard of shoreline. Similar deaths were not found on another island where there was no contamination. Scientists believe that the deaths occurred when oil contamination killed the iguanas' gut bacteria, making them unable to digest seaweed and causing them to starve. Marine iguanas have no natural predators and generally die either of starvation or old age.

The U.S. National Research Council warns that, even without large catastrophic oil spills, many marine habitats are regularly exposed to oil pollution. Harbors and aquatic habitats near developed areas are in particular jeopardy. The U.S. National Research Council estimates that approximately 8.4 billion gallons of oil enter marine waters each year from street runoff, industrial liquid wastes, and intentional discharge from ships flushing their oil tanks. As little as one part of oil per million parts of water can be detrimental to the reproduction and growth of fish, crustaceans, and plankton.

Ocean Dumping and Debris

Ocean debris comes from many sources and affects diverse marine species. Waterborne litter entangles wildlife, masquerades as a food source, smothers beach and bottom-dwelling plants, provides a means for small organisms to invade non-native areas, and contributes to toxic water pollution. Records of interactions between ocean debris and wildlife date back to the first half of the twentieth century. Northern fur seals entangled in debris were spotted as early as the 1930s. In the 1960s, various seabirds were found to have plastic in their stomachs. By the early twenty-first century, a total of 255 species were documented to have become entangled in marine debris or to have ingested it.

Some scientists once thought it was safe to dump garbage into the oceans, believing the oceans were large enough to absorb sludge without harmful effects. Other scientists argued dumping would eventually lead to the pollution of the oceans. Metropolitan centers such as New York City once loaded their sludge and debris onto barges, took the vessels out to sea, and dumped the refuse, in a practice called ocean dumping. Problems with ocean dumping were not fully recognized until floating plastic particles were found throughout the Atlantic and Pacific Oceans.

The perils of ocean dumping and debris struck home both literally and figuratively in the summer of 1988, when debris from the ocean, including sewage, garbage, and biohazards from medical waste, washed up on the Atlantic seaboard, forcing an unprecedented 803 beach closures. In some cases authorities were alerted to beach wash-ups when children turned up hypodermic needles in the sand. Aquatic species also faced serious dangers from these materials, including absorbing or ingesting hazardous waste substances, and ingesting needles, forceps, and other dangerous solid debris. In 1994 hundreds of dead dolphins washed up on Mediterranean beaches, killed by a virus linked to water pollution. Scientists pointed to this event as an indication of what may happen to other marine animals (and humans) if pollution continues.

At the urging of the Environmental Protection Agency (EPA), the dumping of potentially infectious medical waste into ocean waters from public vessels was prohibited in 1988. In 1992 the federal government banned ocean dumping. In 1995 the EPA stepped up efforts to educate people about the dangers of polluting coastal waters through improper disposal of trash on land, sewer overflows to rivers and streams, and dumping by ships and other vessels. The EPA further warned that marine debris poses not only a serious threat to wildlife, but remains in the environment for many years. (See Table 5.1.)

Mercury and Other Toxic Pollutants

Mercury poisoning is a problem in many lakes and oceans. Mercury can cause brain damage and other serious health problems in wild species and in humans. During the 1990s scientists began to report widespread mercury contamination in fish, including those inhabiting remote lakes that were assumed pristine. As a result, many states now warn people against eating certain types of fish.

The Environmental Protection Agency's National Fish and Wildlife Contamination Program reported that in 2002 mercury was the cause of 2,140 fish and wildlife consumption advisories. This represented an 11 percent increase from mercury consumption advisories in 2001. Scientists believe that the main source of mercury pollution is rainwater that carries mercury from coal-burning power plants, incinerators that burn garbage, and smelters that make metals. Because mercury becomes concentrated in organic tissues like DDT, even small concentrations of mercury in the water can be harmful to health. (See Figure 5.3.)

While it is not the only pollutant causing fish and wildlife consumption advisories, mercury is the fastest-

TABLE 5.1

How long does marine debris stay in the environment?

Cardboard box	2 weeks
Paper towels	2-4 weeks
Newspaper	6 weeks
Cotton glove	1-5 months
Apple core	2 months
Waxed milk carton	3 months
Cotton rope	3-14 months
Photodegredable 6-pack ring	6 months
Biodegradable diaper	1 year
Wool glove	1 year
Plywood	1-3 years
Painted wooden stick	13 years
Foam cup	50 years
Tin can	50 years
Styrofoam buoy	80 years
Aluminum Can	200 years
Plastic 6-pack ring	400 years
Disposable diapers	450 years
Plastic bottles	450 years
Microfilament fishing line	600 years
Glass bottles/jars	Undetermined

SOURCE: Adapted from "Marine Debris Timeline," U.S. Environmental Protection Agency, Gulf of Mexico Program, Stennis Space Center, MS, October 9, 2003 [Online] http://www.epa.gov/gmpo/edresources/debris_t .html [accessed February 17, 2004]

growing contaminant. Figure 5.4 lists the pollutants for which advisories were published between 1993 and 2002. The number of lake acres affected by advisories issued due to DDT, chlordane, and PCBs remained relatively stable during the ten-year tracking period, while those affected by mercury increased dramatically.

Figure 5.5 shows the total number of fish consumption advisories in each state in 2002, from mercury as well as other pollutants. The percentage of lake acres and river miles under advisory between 1993 and 2002 are shown in Figure 5.6. Pollution in aquatic environments has increased steadily in the past decade.

DAMS

Some 100,000 dams regulate America's rivers and creeks. Of the major rivers in the lower 48 states (those more than 600 miles in length), only the Yellowstone River still flows freely. In fact, University of Alabama ecologist Arthur Benke notes that it is difficult to find any river in the United States that hasn't been dammed or channeled.

Dams epitomized progress, American ingenuity, and humankind's mastery of nature. In North America, more than 200 major dams were completed each year between 1962 and 1968. Dams were promoted for their role in water storage, energy generation, flood control, irrigation, and recreation. Worldwide, dams now collectively store 15 percent of Earth's annual renewable water supply. Figure 5.7 illustrates the primary uses of U.S. dams.

The very success of the dam-building endeavor accounted, in part, for its decline. By 1980 nearly all the

FIGURE 5.3

Biomagnification of mercury in the food chain

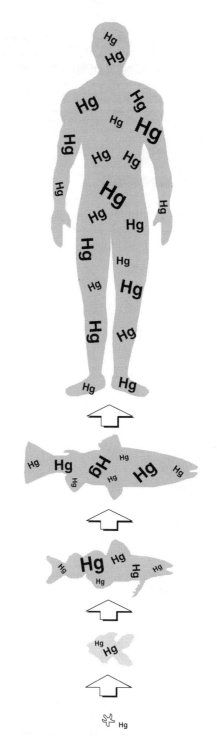

Note: Even at very low input rates to aquatic ecosystems that are remote from point sources, biomagnification effects can result in mercury levels of toxicological concern.

SOURCE: David P. Krabbenhoft and David A. Rickert, "Figure 4: Mercury (Hg) biomagnifies from the bottom to the top of the food chain," in *Mercury Contamination of Aquatic Ecosystems*, U.S. Geological Survey, Reston, VA, 1995

FIGURE 5.4

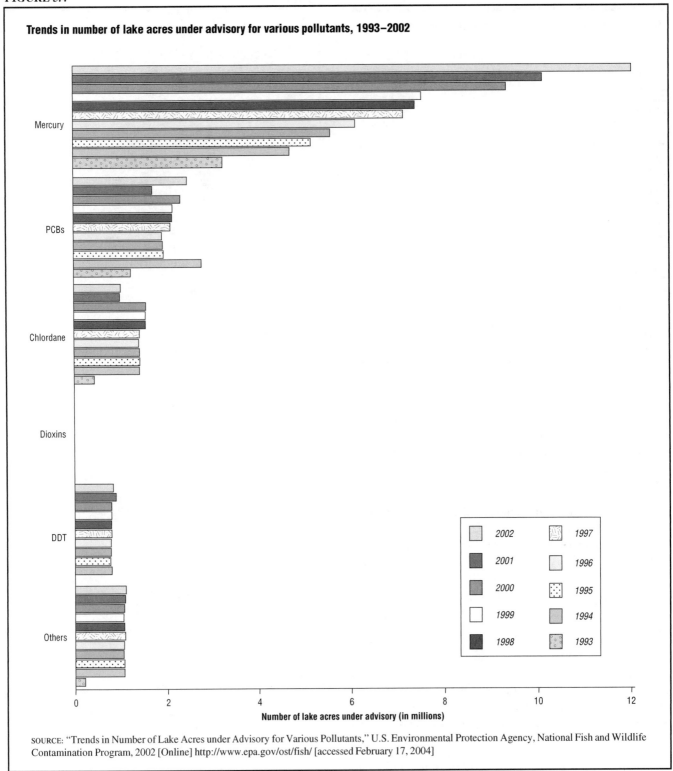

Trends in number of lake acres under advisory for various pollutants, 1993–2002

Number of lake acres under advisory (in millions)

SOURCE: "Trends in Number of Lake Acres under Advisory for Various Pollutants," U.S. Environmental Protection Agency, National Fish and Wildlife Contamination Program, 2002 [Online] http://www.epa.gov/ost/fish/ [accessed February 17, 2004]

nation's best-suited sites—and many dubious ones—had been dammed. Three other factors, however, also contributed to the decline in dam construction: public resistance to the enormous costs, a growing belief that dams were unnecessary "pork-barrel" projects being used by politicians to boost their own popularity, and a developing awareness of the profound environmental degradation caused by dams. In 1986 Congress passed a law requiring the U.S. Bureau of Reclamation to balance issues of power generation and environmental protection when it licenses dams.

Where Have All the Rivers Gone?

Dams have affected rivers, the lands abutting them, the water bodies they join, and aquatic wildlife throughout the United States. Water flow is reduced or stopped altogether downstream of dams, altering aquatic habitats

FIGURE 5.5

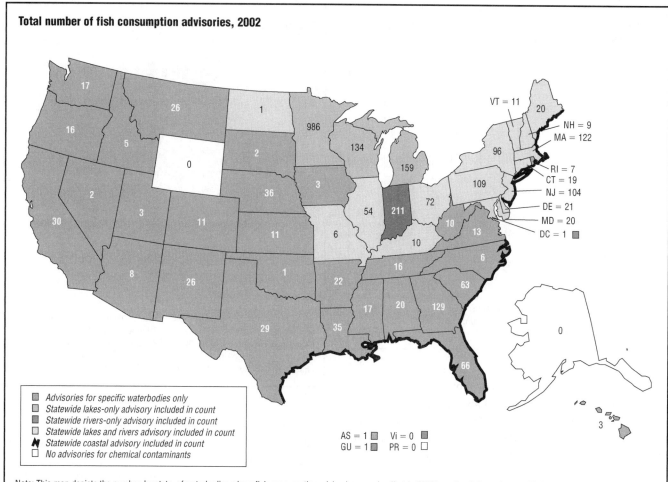

Total number of fish consumption advisories, 2002

Advisories for specific waterbodies only
Statewide lakes-only advisory included in count
Statewide rivers-only advisory included in count
Statewide lakes and rivers advisory included in count
Statewide coastal advisory included in count
No advisories for chemical contaminants

AS = 1   Vi = 0
GU = 1   PR = 0

Note: This map depicts the number, by state, of waterbodies where fish consumption advisories were in effect in 2002 based on information provided to the U.S. Environmental Protection Agency (USEPA) by the states in December 2002 and by the Canadian provinces in December 1997. Because only selected waterbodies are monitored, this map does not reflect the full extent of chemical contamination of fish tissues in each state or province.

SOURCE: "Total Number of Fish Consumption Advisories—2002," U.S. Environmental Protection Agency, National Fish and Wildlife Contamination Program, 2002 [Online] http://www.epa.gov/ost/fish/ [accessed February 17, 2004]

and drying wetlands. Some rivers, including the large Colorado River, no longer reach the sea at all, except in years of unusually high precipitation. Keeping enough water in rivers is especially difficult in the arid West.

Numerous species of salmon are in decline, at least partly due to the effects of dams. In the Pacific Northwest in particular, most experts estimate that native salmon will be gone in 25 years. Salmon have an unusual life cycle that involves a migration from freshwater habitats to oceans and back. Hatching and the juvenile period occur in rivers, followed by a long downstream migration to the ocean, where individuals mature. Adult salmon eventually make an arduous, upstream return to freshwater habitats, where they spawn (lay their eggs, burying them in gravel nests) and then die. Dams are associated with high salmon mortality during both downstream and upstream migrations.

There are ongoing debates regarding dam management throughout the Pacific Northwest. In April 2002, for example, American Rivers, the National Wildlife Federation, and other fisheries and conservation groups initiated a lawsuit

against the Grant County Public Utility District (PUD) in eastern Washington State over the management of two dams on the Columbia River. The NWF is charging that dam mismanagement is responsible for the continued decline of chinook and steelhead salmon, both of which are protected under the Endangered Species Act. Some 32 percent of juvenile salmon migrating downstream towards the ocean are killed at the dam. Many adult salmon are also dying as they swim upstream to spawning grounds. Fishermen are particularly outraged at the collapse of salmon runs, since they have been required to limit their catch in the hope of population recovery. There are a total of eight dams on the Columbia River, all of which must be surmounted successfully for salmon to complete their migrations.

Tearing Down Dams?

In November 1997, for the first time in U.S. history, the Federal Energy Regulatory Commission ordered the Edwards Dam removed from the Kennebec River in Augusta, Maine, to restore habitats for sea-run fish. The dam's owner, Edwards Manufacturing, appealed the decision, but the federal govern-

FIGURE 5.6

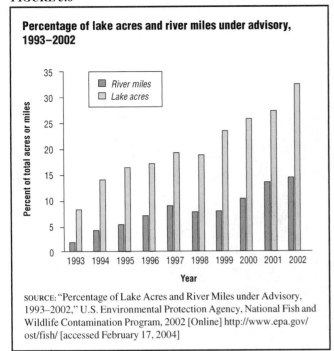

Percentage of lake acres and river miles under advisory, 1993–2002

SOURCE: "Percentage of Lake Acres and River Miles under Advisory, 1993–2002," U.S. Environmental Protection Agency, National Fish and Wildlife Contamination Program, 2002 [Online] http://www.epa.gov/ost/fish/ [accessed February 17, 2004]

FIGURE 5.7

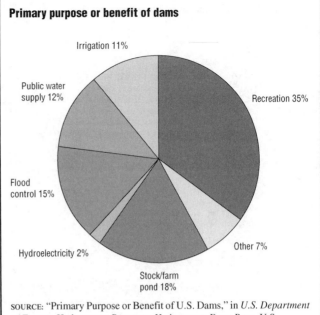

Primary purpose or benefit of dams

SOURCE: "Primary Purpose or Benefit of U.S. Dams," in *U.S. Department of Energy, Hydropower Program: Hydropower Facts Page*, U.S. Department of Energy, Washington, DC, 2002 [Online] http://hydropower.inel.gov/facts/benefit.htm [accessed February 17, 2004]. Data from U.S. Army Corps of Engineers, National Inventory of Dams

ment prevailed. The 160-year old dam produced 1 percent of Maine's electricity. Normal river conditions were achieved at the site within days of water release. Environmentalists viewed the removal of the dam as a boon to both aquatic species and the terrestrial species that feed on them.

Conservation and fisheries interests have also argued for the removal of four dams on the Snake River in the Pacific Northwest, to allow salmon runs to recover. The issue was extremely contentious, with over 8,700 people attending public hearings on the debate and over 230,000 written comments submitted. The Army Corps of Engineers announced in February 2002 that the dams would not be removed, citing the fact that they produce $324 million in electricity and water with operating costs of only $36.5 million. The Corps will, however, budget $390 million over the next ten years to improve salmon survival, including trucking juvenile salmon around the dams. This decision represented the culmination of nearly ten years of debate regarding the Snake River dams.

Foreign Dams

As the era of big dams faded in North America, construction increased in Asia, fueled by growing demand for electricity and irrigation water. China now accounts for more than one-fourth of the big dams under construction, and China, Japan, South Korea, and India together account for more than half.

The Three Gorges Dam on the Yangtze River in China (see Figure 5.8) will be the largest dam in the world when it is completed in 2009. It will be 6,600 feet—over a mile—wide and over 600 feet high. The creation of a

water reservoir upstream of the dam will flood 13 cities and countless villages, and displace well over a million people. In addition, the dam will disrupt water flow and increase water pollution, threatening unique species such as the Yangtze River dolphin, one of only five freshwater dolphin species in the world.

The Yangtze River dolphin was placed on the Endangered Species List in 1989 and is at extreme risk of extinction, with only 150 individuals remaining. Other species likely to be threatened or wiped out altogether include the Chinese sturgeon, the Chinese tiger, the Chinese alligator, the Siberian crane, the giant panda, and countless species of fish, freshwater invertebrates, and plants. Several U.S. agencies provided much technical assistance in planning the Three Gorges Dam. However, U.S. government involvement ceased due to a challenge under the Endangered Species Act, which prohibits government activity detrimental to listed species. The main part of dam construction has been completed, and filling of the Three Gorges Dam began in June 2003.

Although the long controversy surrounding the Three Gorges dam did not prevent its erection, it has perhaps raised awareness within China regarding some of the destructive impacts of other proposed dams. In 2003 China's Environmental Protection Agency and the Chinese Academy of Sciences announced their opposition to plans to dam the Nu River, a World Heritage Site that has been described as the "Grand Canyon of the Orient." The proposed series of 13 dams would affect over 7,000 plant

FIGURE 5.8

The Three Gorges Dam, currently under construction on the Yangtze River in China, will be the largest dam in the world when it is completed. This dam will likely result in the extinction of numerous unique species, including the Yangtze River dolphin. *(AP/Wide World Photos)*

species and 80 rare and endangered animals, in addition to requiring over 50,000 people to be relocated. Many of these are farmers and herders from ethnic minorities in China.

WATER DIVERSION—THE ARAL SEA

The Aral Sea is bounded by Uzbekistan and Kazakhstan, and was once the fourth-largest lake in the world. However, over the past 30 years, the lake has lost 60 percent of its water and shrunk to half its original area. This is due to the long practice of diverting water from the Amu-Darya and the Syr-Darya, two rivers that feed the lake, for irrigation and agriculture. With water loss, the lake has also increased in salinity—from 10 percent salt content to 23 percent salt content in 1999. Aral Sea habitats have been utterly destroyed. The Aral Sea was once a thriving fishery, with a total catch of 26,000 tons in 1957. Thousands of fishermen were once employed at the sea, and commercial species included carp, pike-perch, and roach. Commercial fishing in the Aral had ceased entirely by 1982.

The destruction of the Aral Sea has had numerous other consequences as well. Exposure of the lakebed has resulted in dust storms and air pollution, which affect much of the human population living around the Aral Sea. In the last 15 years, liver disease, kidney disease, and chronic bronchitis have increased 30-fold, and incidence of arthritic disease

has increased by a factor of 60. The loss of the lake has also affected regional climate patterns, so that summers are now hotter and drier and winters are longer and colder. Agriculture in the region has also been severely impaired, both by the shortening of the growing season and the degradation of soil, which is prone to high salinity and erosion.

OVERFISHING—TOO MANY BOATS, NOT ENOUGH FISH

Worldwide, humans obtain 16 percent of their animal protein from fish. As the human population explodes, the fishing industry has tried to keep up with demand. Up to a certain point, fishermen are able to catch more fish without damaging the ecological balance. This is known as the maximum sustainable yield. Catches beyond the maximum sustainable yield represent overfishing. Overfishing removes fish faster than they can reproduce and causes serious population declines. Furthermore, once fishermen deplete all the large fish of a species, they often begin to target smaller, younger individuals. Targeting young fish undermines future breeding populations and guarantees a smaller biological return in future years. Swordfish have been seriously depleted in this way. In the early 1900s, the average weight of a swordfish when caught was around 300 pounds. By 1960, it was 266 pounds, and at the close of the twentieth century it was 90 pounds.

Technological advances have enabled numerous marine fisheries to be depleted in a short amount of time. In addition, the eight regional councils that regulate commercial fishing, all of which are dominated by the fishing industry, have been either unable or unwilling to set limits for themselves. As a result, most fishing areas are free-for-alls.

The U.S. government attempted to eliminate overfishing in U.S. coastal waters by passing the Magnuson Act in 1976. The Magnuson Act expanded the coastal economic zone claimed by the United States from three miles offshore to 200 miles offshore, preventing foreign fishing fleets from exploiting these waters. However, with foreign fleets gone, American fishermen built up their own fleets, buying large, well-equipped vessels with low-interest loans from the federal government. For several years U.S. fishermen reported record catches. Then these declined. Government officials now report that most of the major commercial fishing areas in the United States are in trouble. According to the National Marine Fisheries Service (NMFS), about 40 percent of the nation's saltwater species have been overfished.

From Drift Nets to Longlines

Drift nets are the world's largest fishing nets, reaching lengths of up to 30 miles. Conservationists refer to them as "walls of death" because they indiscriminately catch and kill marine species. Over 100 species—including whales, sea turtles, dolphins, seabirds, sharks, salmon, and numerous other fish species—have been killed in drift nets. Drift nets were eventually banned because of their destructiveness to wildlife.

After the banning of drift nets, many fishermen turned to longlines. Longlines are fishing lines with a single main line attached to many shorter lines that terminate in baited hooks. They are used to catch wide-ranging oceanic species such as tuna, swordfish, and sharks, as well as bottom dwellers such as cod and halibut. A single boat can trail thousands of hooks from lines stretching 20 to 80 miles.

Longline fishing kills fewer marine mammals than drift nets but captures more surface-feeding sea birds, particularly the rare albatrosses. Longline fishing has in fact resulted in the decline of numerous albatross species, almost all of which are now listed by the World Conservation Union (IUCN) as endangered. Australian scientists estimate that longline fishing kills more than 40,000 albatrosses each year. Longline fishing has also caused rapid declines in some fish species. Longlining is an old practice, but modern technology has vastly increased its efficiency and ecological impact.

Fish Declines and Deep-Sea Harvesting

As catches of shallow water fishes decline, trawlers have increasingly been used to scour the deep seas for new varieties of fish, such as the nine-inch long royal red shrimp, rattails, skates, squid, red crabs, orange roughy, oreos, hoki, blue ling, southern blue whiting, and spiny dogfish. Although limited commercial deep-sea fishing has occurred for decades, new technologies are making it considerably more practical and efficient. As stocks of better-known fish shrink and international quotas tighten, experts say deep ocean waters will increasingly be targeted as a source of seafood.

UNWELCOME GUESTS—AQUATIC INVASIVE SPECIES

Numerous aquatic ecosystems have been degraded by invasive species. The primary source of aquatic invasive species has traditionally been ship ballast water, which is generally picked up in one location and released in another. In San Francisco Bay alone, it is estimated that a new invasive species becomes established every 14 weeks through ballast water. Invasive species are also established through transfer from recreational boating vessels; intentional release, usually in attempts to establish new populations for fishing; dumping of live bait; release of aquarium species; and accidental escapes from research facilities. The Nonindigenous Aquatic Nuisance Prevention and Control Act of 1990 and the National Invasive Species Act of 1996 are intended to help prevent unintentional introductions of aquatic nuisance species.

The zebra mussel is an invasive species that both degrades aquatic resources and threatens native species, particularly native freshwater mussels. Zebra mussels first appeared in the United States in 1988. Figure 5.9 illustrates the spread of zebra mussels throughout the Great Lakes and beyond during the following ten years. According to the U.S. Geological Survey, zebra mussels were found in Virginia in 2002, and in a lake in Kansas in 2003; signs of juvenile zebra mussels were detected in Nebraska, as well, in early 2004. This pest species reproduces rapidly and threatens aquatic habitats by clogging water passages and starving out native species. U.S. freshwater mussel species are in fact disappearing at an alarming rate. Figure 5.10 shows the decline in the number of pearly mussel species in the Mississippi River.

In the state of Georgia, invasive Asian eels have increased in number in many habitats. These species were brought over from Southeast Asia or Australia, where they are considered delicacies. The three-foot-long, flesh-eating eel preys on species such as largemouth bass and crawfish in and around the Chattahoochee River. The eels have gills but can also breathe air—this enables them to worm their way across dry ground to get from one body of water to another. Asian eels have few predators in their new habitat, and humans have found no effective way to control them. In March 2000 an Asian eel was reported near Florida's Everglades National Park, confirming fears that the eel would spread beyond Georgia.

FIGURE 5.9

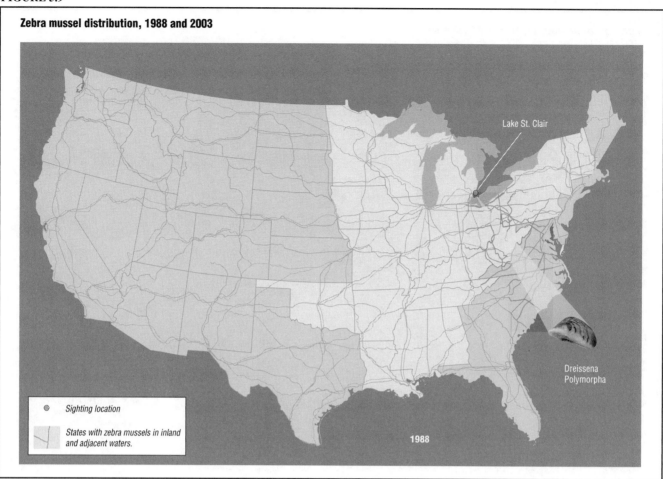

Zebra mussel distribution, 1988 and 2003

Lake St. Clair

Dreissena Polymorpha

● Sighting location

▱ States with zebra mussels in inland and adjacent waters.

1988

Striking at the Base of the Food Chain

Phytoplankton (planktonic plant life) are microscopic photosynthesizing species that form the basis of nearly all marine food chains. (See Figure 5.11.) In many parts of the world, phytoplankton seems to be declining. The most severe damage appears to be in the waters off Antarctica, where phytoplankton are severely depleted. The depletion of phytoplankton has implications all the way up the food chain, affecting not only the zooplankton that consume them but larger species such as penguins, seals, and whales. Scientists believe that phytoplankton declines are a result of the thinning atmospheric ozone layer (caused by industrial pollutants such as chlorofluorocarbons, or CFCs), which allows increasing amounts of ultraviolet radiation to penetrate the Earth's surface. Ultraviolet radiation decreases the ability of phytoplankton to photosynthesize and also damages their genetic material.

IMPERILED AQUATIC SPECIES

Numerous aquatic species are endangered in the United States. In fact, Figure 5.12 shows that the biological groups with the greatest proportion of endangered species—freshwater mussels, crayfishes, amphibians, and freshwater fishes—are all aquatic. The U.S. also possess-

es some of the most diverse freshwater fauna in the world, including 29 percent of the world's freshwater mussels, 61 percent of crayfish, 17 percent of freshwater snails, and 10 percent of freshwater fish.

In 2004 there were a total of 125 listed fish species—82 of these were endangered (71 U.S. and 11 foreign) and 43 were threatened (all U.S.). Table 5.2 shows the listed fish species found in the United States. There are also 72 threatened and endangered clams and other bivalves (70 U.S. and 2 foreign), 33 threatened and endangered snails (32 U.S. and 1 foreign), and 21 threatened and endangered crustaceans (all U.S.). Table 5.3 lists the threatened and endangered U.S. bivalve, snail, and crustacean species as of 2004.

Freshwater Mussels

The United States has the greatest diversity of freshwater mussels in the world. Figure 5.13 illustrates Higgins eye, a species of pearly mussel. Unfortunately, many freshwater mussels are in decline. In 2002, of the 297 native mussel species in the United States, 12 percent were believed extinct and 23 percent were listed as threatened or endangered. Furthermore, numerous additional mussel species are being considered for listing. The

FIGURE 5.9

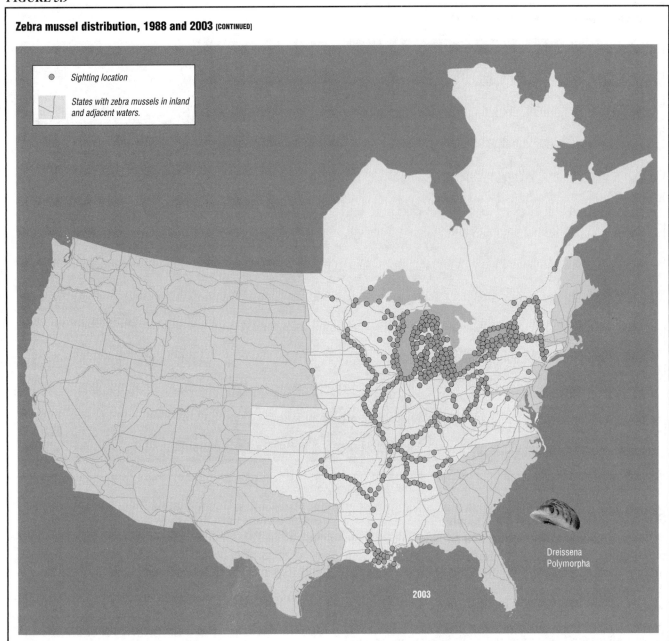

Zebra mussel distribution, 1988 and 2003 [CONTINUED]

Sighting location

States with zebra mussels in inland and adjacent waters.

Dreissena Polymorpha

2003

SOURCE: "Zebra Mussel Sightings Distribution," U.S. Geological Survey, Gainesville, FL, October 2003 [Online] http://nas.er.usgs.gov/mollusks/maps/current_zm_map.jpg [accessed February 17, 2004]

Nature Conservancy and the American Fisheries Society estimate that about 70 percent of freshwater mussels will require protection. The decline of freshwater mussels, which began in the 1800s, has resulted largely from habitat disturbance, especially water pollution and the modification of aquatic habitats by dams. Dams have single-handedly caused the loss of 30 to 60 percent of native mussels in U.S. rivers. The invasive zebra mussel has also harmed native freshwater mussel species by competing with them for food and other resources.

The decline of freshwater mussels, scientists fear, is a sign of serious problems in freshwater ecosystems. Mussels perform many essential functions in these ecosys-

tems, providing food for many species and improving water quality by filtering particles and excess nutrients. Other freshwater mollusks, particularly snails, may also be declining. Conservation efforts for freshwater mussels include the captive breeding and reintroduction of some species, as well as measures to restore damaged habitats.

Fish

Fish occur in nearly all permanent water environments, from deep oceans to remote alpine lakes and desert springs. They are the most diverse vertebrate group—scientists have officially catalogued nearly 24,000 fish species, about as many as all other vertebrates combined.

FIGURE 5.10

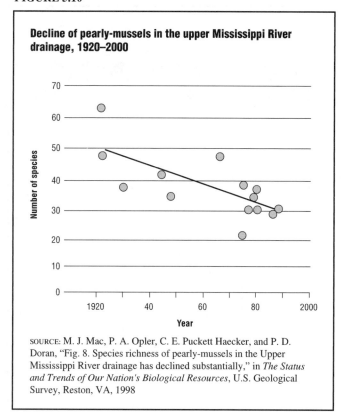

Decline of pearly-mussels in the upper Mississippi River drainage, 1920–2000

SOURCE: M. J. Mac, P. A. Opler, C. E. Puckett Haecker, and P. D. Doran, "Fig. 8. Species richness of pearly-mussels in the Upper Mississippi River drainage has declined substantially," in *The Status and Trends of Our Nation's Biological Resources*, U.S. Geological Survey, Reston, VA, 1998

FIGURE 5.11

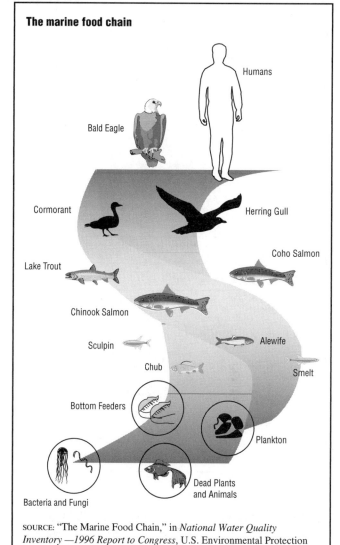

The marine food chain

SOURCE: "The Marine Food Chain," in *National Water Quality Inventory —1996 Report to Congress*, U.S. Environmental Protection Agency, Washington, DC, 1998

Less than 10 percent of these species have been assessed for their conservation status.

The IUCN listed 750 species of fish as threatened in its *2003 Red List of Threatened Species*, approximately half of the species examined. However, the IUCN reports that many more, perhaps as many as a third of all fish species, are likely to be listed once surveys are complete. The IUCN also reported that at least 60 percent of threatened freshwater fish species are in decline because of habitat alteration, whereas 34 percent face pressure from introduced species. The U.S. Fish and Wildlife Service listed a total of 82 endangered and 43 threatened fish species in 2004.

CICHLIDS. The cichlids are a large family of fish that evolved over a period of 750,000 years in African rift lakes including Lake Malawi, Lake Tanganyika, and Lake Victoria. Lake Malawi probably has more fish species than any other lake in the world, with over 1,000 identified—95 percent of these are cichlids. Many cichlid fishes, however, are now facing extinction. British colonialists introduced the Nile perch into Lake Victoria in 1954 because it is significantly larger (up to 300 pounds) than native fish species and can more easily be caught with nets. The aggressive Nile perch have since eaten about half the native cichlid species in Lake Victoria to extinction. With the loss of cichlid species, which feed on algae and insects, algae has grown out of control, damaging all lake habitats. Insects have also flourished.

SALMON. In recent decades, many salmon species, particularly those that inhabit the Columbia and Snake Rivers in the Pacific Northwest, have declined. Salmon are of significant economic and social importance for the commercial food harvest as well as for sport fishing. Salmon are also important to Pacific Northwest Native American tribes for economic as well as cultural and religious reasons. Species in danger of extinction include the coho, sockeye, chinook, and steelhead. Two major causes of salmon endangerment are overfishing and dams, which interfere with salmon runs.

During the 1800s annual salmon runs were estimated to include some 10 to 16 million individuals. At present, total salmon runs have declined to an estimated 2.5 million annually. Declines prior to 1930 resulted largely from overfishing. Since then, however, the major causes of salmon declines have been dam construction in the Columbia River Basin and water pollution, including nitrogen saturation below dam spillways. In 1992 the National Marine Fisheries Service began to designate critical habitat for salmon

FIGURE 5.12

Proportion of species at risk of extinction, 1997

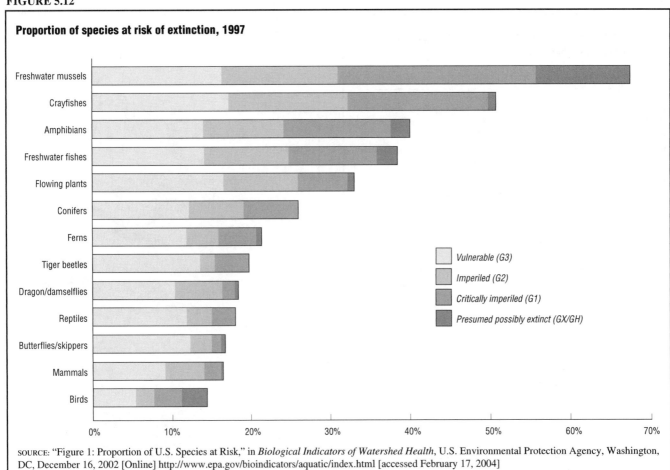

Freshwater mussels
Crayfishes
Amphibians
Freshwater fishes
Flowing plants
Conifers
Ferns
Tiger beetles
Dragon/damselflies
Reptiles
Butterflies/skippers
Mammals
Birds

Vulnerable (G3)
Imperiled (G2)
Critically imperiled (G1)
Presumed possibly extinct (GX/GH)

0%   10%   20%   30%   40%   50%   60%   70%

SOURCE: "Figure 1: Proportion of U.S. Species at Risk," in *Biological Indicators of Watershed Health*, U.S. Environmental Protection Agency, Washington, DC, December 16, 2002 [Online] http://www.epa.gov/bioindicators/aquatic/index.html [accessed February 17, 2004]

species and to develop recovery plans. In 1994 the Pacific Fisheries Management Council issued strict regulations limiting salmon catches. Soon after that, the government announced that Pacific salmon were nearly extinct and began to list species for protection under the Endangered Species Act. Listed species now include the chum salmon (threatened in Oregon and Washington), the coho salmon (threatened, California and Oregon), the sockeye salmon (endangered in Idaho and Oregon, and threatened or endangered in Washington), the chinook salmon (threatened or endangered in California, Oregon, Washington, and Idaho), and the Atlantic salmon (endangered in Maine). Figure 5.14 shows the locations of existing populations of chinook salmon, and Figure 5.15 shows population trends over various periods of time in the last two decades of the twentieth century. Some populations have increased in number since listing, while others have not. Listing of salmon species came after nearly ten years of study, and marked the first time vast urban areas saw land and water use restricted under the Endangered Species Act.

THE KLAMATH BASIN—AN ONGOING CONFLICT. The Klamath Basin in southern Oregon and northern California is the site of a heated battle pitting farmers against a coalition of fishermen and environmentalists who wish to

FIGURE 5.13

Higgins eye, a species of pearly mussel, is listed as endangered throughout its range in the Great Lakes-Big Rivers region. While the United States harbors the greatest diversity of freshwater mussel species in the world, many of them are now in danger of extinction. *(U.S. Fish and Wildlife Service)*

protect three listed species, the coho salmon, shortnose sucker fish, and Lost River sucker fish. Opponents are battling over water, which has been in particularly short supply due to recent droughts in the Pacific Northwest.

TABLE 5.2

Endangered or threatened fish species, February 2004

Status	Species name	Status	Species name
Fishes			
T	Catfish, Yaqui *(Ictalurus pricei)*	T	Minnow, loach *(Tiaroga cobitis)*
E	Cavefish, Alabama *(Speoplatyrhinus poulsoni)*	E	Minnow, Rio Grande silvery *(Hybognathus amarus)*
T	Cavefish, Ozark *(Amblyopsis rosae)*	E, XN	Pikeminnow (=squawfish), Colorado *(Ptychocheilus lucius)*
E	Chub, bonytail *(Gila elegans)*	E	Poolfish, Pahrump *(Empetrichthys latos)*
E	Chub, Borax Lake *(Gila boraxobius)*	E	Pupfish, Ash Meadows Amargosa *(Cyprinodon nevadensis mionectes)*
T	Chub, Chihuahua *(Gila nigrescens)*	E	Pupfish, Comanche Springs *(Cyprinodon elegans)*
E	Chub, humpback *(Gila cypha)*	E	Pupfish, desert *(Cyprinodon macularius)*
T	Chub, Hutton tui *(Gila bicolor* ssp.*)*	E	Pupfish, Devils Hole *(Cyprinodon diabolis)*
E	Chub, Mohave tui *(Gila bicolor mohavensis)*	E	Pupfish, Leon Springs *(Cyprinodon bovinus)*
E	Chub, Oregon *(Oregonichthys crameri)*	E	Pupfish, Owens *(Cyprinodon radiosus)*
E	Chub, Owens tui *(Gila bicolor snyderi)*	E	Pupfish, Warm Springs *(Cyprinodon nevadensis pectoralis)*
E	Chub, Pahranagat roundtail *(Gila robusta jordani)*	E	Salmon, Atlantic *(Salmo salar)*
T	Chub, slender *(Erimystax cahni)*	E, T	Salmon, chinook *(Oncorhynchus [=Salmo] tshawytscha)*
T	Chub, Sonora *(Gila ditaenia)*	T	Salmon, chum *(Oncorhynchus [=Salmo] keta)*
XN, T	Chub, spotfin *(Cyprinella monacha)*	T	Salmon, coho *(Oncorhynchus [=Salmo] kisutch)*
E	Chub, Virgin River *(Gila seminuda [= robusta])*	E, T	Salmon, sockeye *(Oncorhynchus [=Salmo] nerka)*
E	Chub, Yaqui *(Gila purpurea)*	T	Sculpin, pygmy *(Cottus paulus [=pygmaeus])*
E	Cui-ui *(Chasmistes cujus)*	T	Shiner, Arkansas River *(Notropis girardi)*
E	Dace, Ash Meadows speckled *(Rhinichthys osculus nevadensis)*	T	Shiner, beautiful *(Cyprinella formosa)*
T	Dace, blackside *(Phoxinus cumberlandensis)*	T	Shiner, blue *(Cyprinella caerulea)*
E	Dace, Clover Valley speckled *(Rhinichthys osculus oligoporus)*	E	Shiner, Cahaba *(Notropis cahabae)*
T	Dace, desert *(Eremichthys acros)*	E	Shiner, Cape Fear *(Notropis mekistocholas)*
T	Dace, Foskett speckled *(Rhinichthys osculus* ssp.*)*	E	Shiner, palezone *(Notropis albizonatus)*
E	Dace, Independence Valley speckled *(Rhinichthys osculus lethoporus)*	T	Shiner, Pecos bluntnose *(Notropis simus pecosensis)*
E	Dace, Kendall Warm Springs *(Rhinichthys osculus thermalis)*	E	Shiner, Topeka *(Notropis topeka [=tristis])*
E	Dace, Moapa *(Moapa coriacea)*	T	Silverside, Waccamaw *(Menidia extensa)*
E	Darter, amber *(Percina antesella)*	T	Smelt, delta *(Hypomesus transpacificus)*
T	Darter, bayou *(Etheostoma rubrum)*	T	Spikedace *(Meda fulgida)*
E	Darter, bluemask (=jewel) *(Etheostoma)*	T	Spinedace, Big Spring *(Lepidomeda mollispinis pratensis)*
E	Darter, boulder *(Etheostoma wapiti)*	T	Spinedace, Little Colorado *(Lepidomeda vittata)*
T	Darter, Cherokee *(Etheostoma scotti)*	E	Spinedace, White River *(Lepidomeda albivallis)*
E, XN	Darter, duskytail *(Etheostoma percnurum)*	E	Springfish, Hiko White River *(Crenichthys baileyi grandis)*
E	Darter, Etowah *(Etheostoma etowahae)*	T	Springfish, Railroad Valley *(Crenichthys nevadae)*
E	Darter, fountain *(Etheostoma fonticola)*	E	Springfish, White River *(Crenichthys baileyi baileyi)*
T	Darter, goldline *(Percina aurolineata)*	E, T	Steelhead *(Oncorhynchus [=Salmo] mykiss)*
T	Darter, leopard *(Percina pantherina)*	E	Stickleback, unarmored threespine *(Gasterosteus aculeatus williamsoni)*
E	Darter, Maryland *(Etheostoma sellare)*	E	Sturgeon, Alabama *(Scaphirhynchus suttkusi)*
E	Darter, Niangua *(Etheostoma nianguae)*	T	Sturgeon, gulf *(Acipenser oxyrinchus desotoi)*
E	Darter, Okaloosa *(Etheostoma okaloosae)*	E	Sturgeon, pallid *(Scaphirhynchus albus)*
E	Darter, relict *(Etheostoma chienense)*	E	Sturgeon, shortnose *(Acipenser brevirostrum)*
T	Darter, slackwater *(Etheostoma boschungi)*	E	Sturgeon, white *(Acipenser transmontanus)*
T	Darter, snail *(Percina tanasi)*	E	Sucker, June *(Chasmistes liorus)*
E	Darter, vermilion *(Etheostoma chermocki)*	E	Sucker, Lost River *(Deltistes luxatus)*
E	Darter, watercress *(Etheostoma nuchale)*	E	Sucker, Modoc *(Catostomus microps)*
E	Gambusia, Big Bend *(Gambusia gaigei)*	E	Sucker, razorback *(Xyrauchen texanus)*
E	Gambusia, Clear Creek *(Gambusia heterochir)*	T	Sucker, Santa Ana *(Catostomus santaanae)*
E	Gambusia, Pecos *(Gambusia nobilis)*	E	Sucker, shortnose *(Chasmistes brevirostris)*
E	Gambusia, San Marcos *(Gambusia georgei)*	T	Sucker, Warner *(Catostomus warnerensis)*
E	Goby, tidewater *(Eucyclogobius newberryi)*	E	Topminnow, Gila (including Yaqui) *(Poeciliopsis occidentalis)*
E	Logperch, Conasauga *(Percina jenkinsi)*	T	Trout, Apache *(Oncorhynchus apache)*
E	Logperch, Roanoke *(Percina rex)*	T	Trout, bull *(Salvelinus confluentus)*
T	Madtom, Neosho *(Noturus placidus)*	E	Trout, Gila *(Oncorhynchus gilae)*
E	Madtom, pygmy *(Noturus stanauli)*	T	Trout, greenback cutthroat *(Oncorhynchus clarki stomias)*
E	Madtom, Scioto *(Noturus trautmani)*	T	Trout, Lahontan cutthroat *(Oncorhynchus clarki henshawi)*
E, XN	Madtom, smoky *(Noturus baileyi)*	T	Trout, Little Kern golden *(Oncorhynchus aguabonita whitei)*
XN, T	Madtom, yellowfin *(Noturus flavipinnis)*	T	Trout, Paiute cutthroat *(Oncorhynchus clarki seleniris)*
T	Minnow, Devils River *(Dionda diaboli)*	E, XN	Woundfin *(Plagopterus argentissimus)*

E = Endangered
T = Threatened
XN = Experimental population, non-essential

SOURCE: Adapted from "U.S. Listed Vertebrate Animal Species Report by Taxonomic Group as of 02/17/2004," Threatened and Endangered Species System (TESS), U.S. Fish and Wildlife Service, Washington, DC, 2004 [Online] http://ecos.fws.gov/tess_public TESSWebpageVipListed?code=V&listings=0#E [accessed February 17, 2004]

The Klamath River once supported the third-largest salmon run in the country. However, in recent years, water diversion has caused river water levels to be too low to maintain healthy stream conditions and temperatures.

Over 7,000 fishing jobs have been lost due to salmon declines. Water diversion practices also violate agreements with Native American tribes to avoid harming healthy salmon runs. Water diversion in the Klamath Basin has

TABLE 5.3

Endangered species of clams, snails, and crustaceans, February 2004

Status	Species name	Status	Species name
Clams		E	Ring pink (mussel) *(Obovaria retusa)*
E	Acornshell, southern *(Epioblasma othcaloogensis)*	T	Slabshell, Chipola *(Elliptio chipolaensis)*
T	Bankclimber, purple (mussel) *(Elliptoideus sloatianus)*	E	Spinymussel, James *(Pleurobema collina)*
E, XN	Bean, Cumberland (pearlymussel) *(Villosa trabalis)*	E	Spinymussel, Tar River *(Elliptio steinstansana)*
E	Bean, purple *(Villosa perpurpurea)*	E	Stirrupshell *(Quadrula stapes)*
E	Blossom, green (pearlymussel) *(Epioblasma torulosa gubernaculum)*	E	Three-ridge, fat (mussel) *(Amblema neislerii)*
E, XN	Blossom, tubercled (pearlymussel) *(Epioblasma torulosa torulosa)*	E	Wartyback, white (pearlymussel) *(Plethobasus cicatricosus)*
E, XN	Blossom, turgid (pearlymussel) *(Epioblasma turgidula)*	E	Wedgemussel, dwarf *(Alasmidonta heterodon)*
E, XN	Blossom, yellow (pearlymussel) *(Epioblasma florentina florentina)*	**Snails**	
E, XN	Catspaw (=purple cat's paw pearlymussel) *(Epioblasma obliqua obliqua)*		
E	Catspaw, white (pearlymussel) *(Epioblasma obliqua perobliqua)*	E	Ambersnail, Kanab *(Oxyloma haydeni kanabensis)*
E, XN	Clubshell *(Pleurobema clava)*	E	Campeloma, slender *(Campeloma decampi)*
E	Clubshell, black *(Pleurobema curtum)*	E	Cavesnail, Tumbling Creek *(Antrobia culveri)*
E	Clubshell, ovate *(Pleurobema perovatum)*	T	Elimia, lacy (snail) *(Elimia crenatella)*
E	Clubshell, southern *(Pleurobema decisum)*	E	Limpet, Banbury Springs *(Lanx sp.)*
E, XN	Combshell, Cumberlandian *(Epioblasma brevidens)*	E	Lioplax, cylindrical (snail) *(Lioplax cyclostomaformis)*
E	Combshell, southern *(Epioblasma penita)*	E	Marstonia, royal (snail) *(Pyrgulopsis ogmorhaphe)*
E	Combshell, upland *(Epioblasma metastriata)*	E	Pebblesnail, flat *(Lepyrium showalteri)*
E	Elktoe, Appalachian *(Alasmidonta raveneliana)*	E, XN	Riversnail, Anthony's *(Athearnia anthonyi)*
E	Elktoe, Cumberland *(Alasmidonta atropurpurea)*	T	Rocksnail, painted *(Leptoxis taeniata)*
E	Fanshell *(Cyprogenia stegaria)*	E	Rocksnail, plicate *(Leptoxis plicata)*
T	Fatmucket, Arkansas *(Lampsilis powelli)*	T	Rocksnail, round *(Leptoxis ampla)*
T	Heelsplitter, Alabama (=inflated) *(Potamilus inflatus)*	T	Shagreen, Magazine Mountain *(Mesodon magazinensis)*
E	Heelsplitter, Carolina *(Lasmigona decorata)*	E	Snail, armored *(Pyrgulopsis (=Marstonia) pachyta)*
E	Higgins eye (pearlymussel) *(Lampsilis higginsii)*	T	Snail, Bliss Rapids *(Taylorconcha serpenticola)*
E	Kidneyshell, triangular *(Ptychobranchus greeni)*	T	Snail, Chittenango ovate amber *(Succinea chittenangoensis)*
E, XN	Lampmussel, Alabama *(Lampsilis virescens)*	T	Snail, flat-spired three-toothed *(Triodopsis platysayoides)*
E	Lilliput, pale (pearlymussel) *(Toxolasma cylindrellus)*	E	Snail, Iowa Pleistocene *(Discus macclintocki)*
E, XN	Mapleleaf, winged (mussel) *(Quadrula fragosa)*	E	Snail, Morro shoulderband (=Banded dune) *(Helminthoglypta walkeriana)*
T	Moccasinshell, Alabama *(Medionidus acutissimus)*	T	Snail, Newcomb's *(Erinna newcombi)*
E	Moccasinshell, Coosa *(Medionidus parvulus)*	T	Snail, noonday *(Mesodon clarki nantahala)*
E	Moccasinshell, Gulf *(Medionidus penicillatus)*	T	Snail, painted snake coiled forest *(Anguispira picta)*
E	Moccasinshell, Ochlockonee *(Medionidus simpsonianus)*	E	Snail, Snake River physa *(Physa natricina)*
E	Monkeyface, Appalachian (pearlymussel) *(Quadrula sparsa)*	T	Snail, Stock Island tree *(Orthalicus reses [not including nesodryas])*
E, XN	Monkeyface, Cumberland (pearlymussel) *(Quadrula intermedia)*	E	Snail, tulotoma *(Tulotoma magnifica)*
T	Mucket, orangenacre *(Lampsilis perovalis)*	E	Snail, Utah valvata *(Valvata utahensis)*
E	Mucket, pink (pearlymussel) *(Lampsilis abrupta)*	E	Snail, Virginia fringed mountain *(Polygyriscus virginianus)*
E, XN	Mussel, oyster *(Epioblasma capsaeformis)*	E	Snails, Oahu tree *(Achatinella ssp.)*
E	Mussel, scaleshell *(Leptodea leptodon)*	E	Springsnail, Alamosa *(Tryonia alamosae)*
T	Pearlshell, Louisiana *(Margaritifera hembeli)*	E	Springsnail, Bruneau Hot *(Pyrgulopsis bruneauensis)*
E, XN	Pearlymussel, birdwing *(Conradilla caelata)*	E	Springsnail, Idaho *(Fontelicella idahoensis)*
E, XN	Pearlymussel, cracking *(Hemistena lata)*	**Crustaceans**	
E	Pearlymussel, Curtis *(Epioblasma florentina curtisii)*		
E, XN	Pearlymussel, dromedary *(Dromus dromas)*	E	Amphipod, Hay's Spring *(Stygobromus hayi)*
E	Pearlymussel, littlewing *(Pegias fabula)*	E	Amphipod, Illinois cave *(Gammarus acherondytes)*
E	Pigtoe, Cumberland *(Pleurobema gibberum)*	E	Amphipod, Kauai cave *(Spelaeorchestia koloana)*
E	Pigtoe, dark *(Pleurobema furvum)*	E	Amphipod, Peck's cave *(Stygobromus [= Stygonectes] pecki)*
E, XN	Pigtoe, finerayed *(Fusconaia cuneolus)*	E	Crayfish, cave *(Cambarus aculabrum)*
E	Pigtoe, flat *(Pleurobema marshalli)*	E	Crayfish, cave *(Cambarus zophonastes)*
E	Pigtoe, heavy *(Pleurobema taitianum)*	E	Crayfish, Nashville *(Orconectes shoupi)*
E	Pigtoe, oval *(Pleurobema pyriforme)*	E	Crayfish, Shasta *(Pacifastacus fortis)*
E	Pigtoe, rough *(Pleurobema plenum)*	E	Fairy shrimp, Conservancy *(Branchinecta conservatio)*
E, XN	Pigtoe, shiny *(Fusconaia cor)*	E	Fairy shrimp, longhorn *(Branchinecta longiantenna)*
E	Pigtoe, southern *(Pleurobema georgianum)*	E	Fairy shrimp, Riverside *(Streptocephalus woottoni)*
E	Pimpleback, orangefoot (pearlymussel) *(Plethobasus cooperianus)*	E	Fairy shrimp, San Diego *(Branchinecta sandiegonensis)*
E	Pocketbook, fat *(Potamilus capax)*	T	Fairy shrimp, vernal pool *(Branchinecta lynchi)*
T	Pocketbook, finelined *(Lampsilis altilis)*	E	Isopod, Lee County cave *(Lirceus usdagalun)*
E	Pocketbook, Ouachita rock *(Arkansia wheeleri)*	T	Isopod, Madison Cave *(Antrolana lira)*
E	Pocketbook, shiny-rayed *(Lampsilis subangulata)*	E	Isopod, Socorro *(Thermosphaeroma thermophilus)*
E	Pocketbook, speckled *(Lampsilis streckeri)*	E	Shrimp, Alabama cave *(Palaemonias alabamae)*
E	Rabbitsfoot, rough *(Quadrula cylindrica strigillata)*	E	Shrimp, California freshwater *(Syncaris pacifica)*
E	Riffleshell, northern *(Epioblasma torulosa rangiana)*	E	Shrimp, Kentucky cave *(Palaemonias ganteri)*
E	Riffleshell, tan *(Epioblasma florentina walkeri (=E. walkeri))*	T	Shrimp, Squirrel Chimney Cave *(Palaemonetes cummingi)*
		E	Tadpole shrimp, vernal pool *(Lepidurus packardi)*

E = Endangered
T = Threatened
XN = Experimental population, non-essential

SOURCE: Adapted from "U.S. Listed Invertebrate Animal Species Report by Taxonomic Group as of 02/17/2004," Threatened and Endangered Species System (TESS), U.S. Fish and Wildlife Service, Washington, DC, 2004 [Online] http://ecos.fws.gov/tess_public/TESSWebpageVipListed?code=I&listings=0#F [accessed February 17, 2004]

FIGURE 5.14

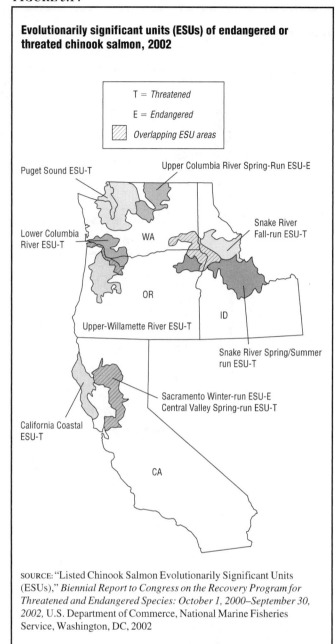

Evolutionarily significant units (ESUs) of endangered or threated chinook salmon, 2002

T = *Threatened*

E = *Endangered*

▨ *Overlapping ESU areas*

Puget Sound ESU-T

Upper Columbia River Spring-Run ESU-E

Lower Columbia River ESU-T

WA

Snake River Fall-run ESU-T

OR

ID

Upper-Willamette River ESU-T

Snake River Spring/Summer run ESU-T

Sacramento Winter-run ESU-E
Central Valley Spring-run ESU-T

California Coastal ESU-T

CA

SOURCE: "Listed Chinook Salmon Evolutionarily Significant Units (ESUs)," *Biennial Report to Congress on the Recovery Program for Threatened and Endangered Species: October 1, 2000–September 30, 2002,* U.S. Department of Commerce, National Marine Fisheries Service, Washington, DC, 2002

also caused the loss of over 75 percent of area wetlands, including portions of the Klamath Marsh National Wildlife Refuge in southern Oregon, at the headwaters of the Klamath River. This habitat supports the shortnose sucker and the Lost River sucker, which were listed as endangered in their entire ranges in California and Oregon in 1988. Both were once highly abundant in the Upper Klamath Lake, but populations have declined due to alteration of water flow patterns, habitat degradation, and water pollution. Suckerfish species live in the lake most of the year, but migrate downstream to spawn. Habitat alteration has particularly affected the survival of juvenile suckers. The Klamath Marsh National Wildlife Refuge also supports other listed species such as the bald eagle, northern spotted owl, and several species of endangered coastal dune plants.

A lawsuit regarding the distribution of Klamath Basin waters was brought against the U.S. Bureau of Reclamation by the Pacific Coast Federation of Fishermen's Associations, the Klamath Forest Alliance, the Institute for Fisheries Resources, the Oregon Natural Resources Council, and other groups. The plaintiffs argued that the Bureau of Reclamation had met farmers' demands for water, but left Klamath River flows much lower than that required for survival of the coho salmon, shortnose sucker fish, and Lost River sucker fish. Furthermore, the Bureau was charged with violating the Endangered Species Act in not consulting with the National Marine Fisheries Service regarding endangered species conservation. Farmers were also accused of wasting water.

In April 2001 the U.S. Bureau of Reclamation was found by a Federal District Court to have knowingly violated the Endangered Species Act when it allowed delivery of irrigation water required to maintain habitat of the three listed species. As a result of the court decision, federal agencies cut water to irrigation canals in order to preserve water levels in the Upper Klamath Lake for the two species of sucker fish and to increase water flow in the Klamath River for coho salmon. In April 2002, a lawsuit was filed on behalf of the farmers to remove all three species from the Endangered Species List. Water flow was an issue again in 2002. After a federal judge decided not to force the Bureau of Reclamation to provide water to listed species in 2002, there was a massive fish-kill involving approximately 33,000 salmon.

THE MISSOURI "SPRING RISE" ISSUE. A similarly heated debate addresses the issue of water flow on the Missouri River. The U.S. Fish and Wildlife Service determined in 2000 that existing water flow patterns—managed to create a steady depth for barge traffic—were endangering three listed species: the pallid sturgeon, piping plover, and least tern. The U.S. Fish and Wildlife Service argued that increased water flow in the spring—a "spring rise"—was necessary for sturgeon spawning. In addition, it called for less water flow in the summer, which is necessary for exposing the sandbars used by the bird species as nesting grounds. The Fish and Wildlife Service gave the Army Corps of Engineers, which controls Missouri water flow, until 2003 to implement these changes. However, the Bush administration delayed decision on a final plan in 2002. The *Washington Post* reported that the administration had "begun an 'informal consultation' on possible changes to the wildlife service's demands." ("Bush Delays Action on Missouri River: Agencies Order to Consult on 'Spring Rise,'" *Washington Post,* 14 June 2002.) The issue has been extremely controversial in the Midwest, with environmentalists, recreation interests, and upper-basin officials favoring a spring rise, and farmers, barge interests, and Missouri leaders opposed. There have been 55,000 submitted comments on the issue, with 54,000 favoring a spring rise.

FIGURE 5.15

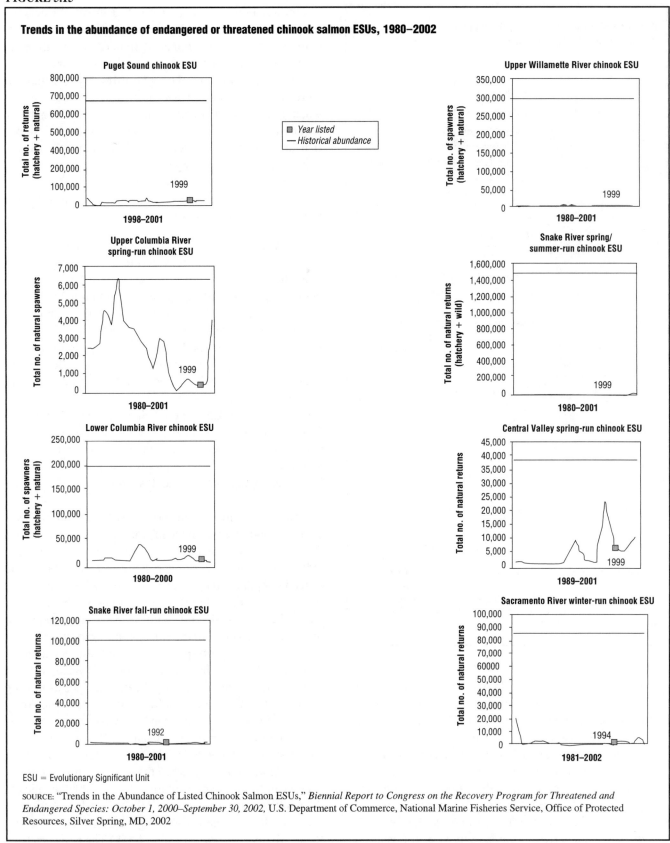

Trends in the abundance of endangered or threatened chinook salmon ESUs, 1980–2002

ESU = Evolutionary Significant Unit

SOURCE: "Trends in the Abundance of Listed Chinook Salmon ESUs," *Biennial Report to Congress on the Recovery Program for Threatened and Endangered Species: October 1, 2000–September 30, 2002,* U.S. Department of Commerce, National Marine Fisheries Service, Office of Protected Resources, Silver Spring, MD, 2002

RAZORBACK SUCKER. The razorback sucker is an endangered fish species found in the lower Colorado River. It is named for the razor-like ridge on its back that helps it swim in rapid waters. The razorback sucker is in danger of extinction due to habitat loss, competition with introduced species, and predation by non-native species such as carp. Habitat destruction is largely the result of dam-building, which has affected water temperature and

TABLE 5.4

Paiute cutthroat trout recovery plan overview

Recovery objectives: Improve the status and habitat of Paiute cutthroat trout and eliminate competition from nonnative salmonid species.

Recovery criteria: Paiute cutthroat trout will be considered for delisting when the following objectives are met:

1) All nonnative salmonids are removed in Silver King Creek and its tributaries downstream of Llewellyn Falls to fish barriers in Silver King Canyon;
2) A viable population occupies all historic habitat in Silver King Creek and its tributaries downstream of Llewellyn Falls to fish barriers in Silver King Canyon;
3) Paiute cutthroat trout habitat is maintained in all occupied streams;
4) The refuge populations in Corral and Coyote Creeks, Silver King Creek, and tributaries above Llewellyn Falls as well as out-of-basin populations are maintained as refugia and are secured from the introduction of other salmonid species; and
5) A long-term conservation plan and conservation agreement are developed, which will be the guiding management documents once Paiute cutthroat trout are delisted.

Recovery actions:

1. Remove nonnative trout from historic Paiute cutthroat trout habitat.
2. Reintroduce Paiute cutthroat trout into historic habitat.
3. Protect and enhance all occupied Paiute cutthroat trout habitat.
4. Continue to monitor and manage existing and reintroduced populations.
5 Develop a long-term conservation plan and conservation agreement.
6. Provide public information.

Total estimated cost of recovery ($1,000's):

Year	Action 1	Action 2	Action 3	Action 4	Action 5	Action 6
2004	38	—	2	19.73	—	2.9
2005	31	—	49.5	31.23	—	2.9
2006	31	—	51.1	38.31	—	2.9
2007	—	8	37	20.73	—	2.9
2008	—	8	4.08	20.73	—	0.4
2009	—	8	3.6	23.81	—	—
2010	—	8	2	20.73	6	—
2011	—	8	2	20.73	6	—
2012	—	—	3.6	20.81	—	—
2013	—	—	4.08	18.73	—	—
Total	**100**	**40**	**158.95**	**235.5**	**12**	**12**

The total estimated cost of recovering Paiute cutthroat trout is $558,450, plus additional costs that cannot be estimated at this time.

Date of recovery: Delisting of the Paiute cutthroat trout could be initiated in 2013, if tasks are implemented as recommended and recovery criteria are met.

SOURCE: Adapted from "Executive Summary," in *Draft Revised Recovery Plan for the Paiute Cutthroat Trout (Oncorhynchus clarki seleniris),* Department of the Interior, U.S. Fish & Wildlife Service, Region 1, Portland, OR, November 2003

flooded habitat areas. Razorback suckers can live up to 45 years, and the fish that remain are generally old individuals. Over 90 percent of existing razorback suckers inhabit a single site, Lake Mojave in Arizona.

In an attempt to help razorback sucker populations recover, mature fish are collected and transported to the Willow Beach National Fish Hatchery each spring, where they spawn. In spring 2000, for example, 80 adult fish were collected from Lake Mojave and laid a total of over 300,000 eggs. Juveniles are then returned to various Colorado River habitats when they are larger and have a better chance of survival (usually when they reach 10 inches in size and 18 months of age). It is estimated that about 9,000 razorback sucker adults remain in the population, as well as some 3,000 to 4,000 younger individuals that have been reintroduced from captivity.

THE PAIUTE CUTTHROAT TROUT. The Paiute cutthroat trout is found in the Silver King drainage on the eastern slope of the Sierra Nevada Mountains in California. The species was listed as endangered in 1970 and reclassified as threatened in 1975. Table 5.4 shows the recovery objectives, recovery criteria, actions needed, estimated cost of

recovery, and date of recovery for the species from the recovery plan released by the Fish and Wildlife Service in November 2003. The Paiute cutthroat trout is threatened primarily by introduced trout species and is considered to have a high potential for recovery. Figure 5.16 shows adult and juvenile population size in one habitat from 1964 to 2001. Some years in which few or no fish were found correspond to treatment with the chemical rotenone, a naturally occurring compound used for fish control. Table 5.5 summarizes the threats and recovery recommendations for the species.

THE SNAIL DARTER. The snail darter, a small fish species related to perch, was the object of perhaps the largest controversy regarding endangered species conservation prior to the conflict surrounding the northern spotted owl. The snail darter was originally listed as endangered by the U.S. Fish and Wildlife Service in 1975. At the time, it was believed only to exist in the Little Tennessee River, and this area was designated as critical habitat for the species. That same year, the Tellico Dam was near completion on the Little Tennessee River, and the filling of the Tellico Reservoir would have destroyed the entire habitat of the snail darter. A lawsuit was filed to pre-

FIGURE 5.16

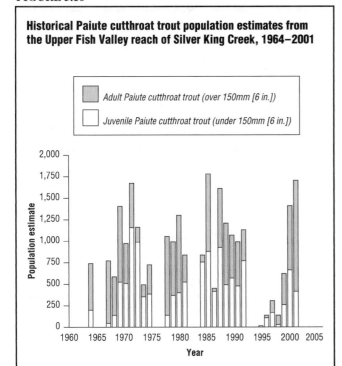

Historical Paiute cutthroat trout population estimates from the Upper Fish Valley reach of Silver King Creek, 1964–2001

☐ Adult Paiute cutthroat trout (over 150mm [6 in.])

☐ Juvenile Paiute cutthroat trout (under 150mm [6 in.])

SOURCE: "Figure 4. Historical Population Estimates (1964 to 2001) from the Upper Fish Valley Reach of Silver King Creek," in *Draft Revised Recovery Plan for the Paiute Cutthroat Trout (Oncorhynchus clarki seleniris),* Department of the Interior, U.S. Fish & Wildlife Service, Region 1, Portland, OR, November 2003

TABLE 5.5

Summary of threats and recommended recovery actions for the Paiute cutthroat trout

Listing factor	Threat
A	Streambank degradation from recreational activities
A	Streambank degradation from cattle grazing
A	Degradation of water quality and spawning substrates by beavers
B	Unregulated angling
C	Natural predators [not currently significant]
C	Fungal infections
D	Potential budgetary constraints on agency commitment to recovery actions
E	Hybridization and competition with introduced trout
E	Need for fish barriers to prevent upstream migration of introduced trout
E	Human introduction of trout
E	Vulnerability to catastrophic events due to limited distribution

Listing factors:

A. The present or threatened destruction, modification, or curtailment of its habitat or range

B. Overutilization for commercial, recreational, scientific, educational purposes (not a factor)

C. Disease or predation

D. The inadequacy of existing regulatory mechanisms

E. Other natural or manmade factors affecting its continued existence

SOURCE: Adapted from "Appendix B. Summary of Threats and Recommended Recovery Actions," in *Draft Revised Recovery Plan for the Paiute Cutthroat Trout (Oncorhynchus clarki seleniris),* Department of the Interior, U.S. Fish & Wildlife Service, Region 1, Portland, OR, November 2003

vent this from happening. The case went all the way to the Supreme Court, which ruled in 1978 that under the Endangered Species Act, species protection must take priority over economic and developmental concerns. One month after this court decision, Congress amended the Endangered Species Act to allow for exemptions under certain circumstances. In late 1979, the Tellico Dam received an exemption and the Tellico Reservoir was filled. The snail darter is now extinct in that habitat. Fortuitously, however, snail darter populations were later discovered in other river systems. In addition, the species has been introduced into several other habitats. Due to an increase in numbers, the snail darter was reclassified as threatened in 1984. Currently, it is found in Alabama, Georgia, and Tennessee.

SHARKS. Sharks have been predators of the seas for nearly 400 million years. There are more than 350 species of sharks, ranging in size from the tiny pygmy shark to the giant whale shark.

Shark populations are being decimated because of the growing demand for shark meat and shark fins. Fins and tails sell for as much as $100 a pound. In the United States, some shark populations have already declined 70 to 80 percent from levels in the 1980s and 1990s due to overfishing. Overfishing is particularly harmful to sharks because they reproduce slowly. In 1997 the Fisheries Service cut quotas on commercial harvests of some shark

species by half and completely banned harvest of the most vulnerable species—whale sharks, white sharks, basking sharks, sand tiger sharks, and bigeye sand tiger sharks. The annual U.S. commercial shark quota for the Caribbean, the Gulf of Mexico, and the Atlantic coast is 150,000 large coastal sharks. However, many biologists consider that number too high to be sustainable.

Fishermen in Costa Rica, where several manufacturers process shark cartilage for medicinal purposes, claim that the real cause of shark declines is trolling by large fleets from China, Japan, and other countries. A few shark species, including whale sharks and basking sharks, were given protection by CITES for the first time in 2002. This was considered a landmark decision because CITES had never before addressed fisheries.

A study published in 2003 by biologists Julia Baum and Ransom Myers of Dalhousie University in Canada showed that many shark populations in the Gulf of Mexico have plummeted since the 1950s. ("Collapse and Conservation of Shark Populations in the Northwest Atlantic," *Science,* vol. 299, 17 January 2003.) In particular, whitetip shark populations have declined by 90 percent. The researchers blamed the decline on overfishing due to demand for sharkfin soup, which is considered a luxury. Professor Myers said, "Researchers in the 1960s suggested that oceanic whitetip sharks were the most common large species on Earth. What we have shown is akin to the herds of buffalo disappearing from the Great Plains and no one noticing." Other species which have been affected include the silk shark, whose populations have dropped by 90 percent, and the mako shark, which has declined 79 percent.

Coral Reefs

Coral reefs are found in coastal, tropical waters and are the largest living structures on Earth. Biologically, the richness of coral reef ecosystems is comparable to that of tropical rainforests. The reefs themselves are formed from calcium carbonate skeletons secreted by corals. Corals maintain a close relationship with certain species of photosynthetic algae, providing shelter to them and receiving nutrients in exchange.

The IUCN reports that 30 percent of coral reefs worldwide are in critical condition—10 percent have already been destroyed. In 1997 researchers at the Florida Keys National Marine Sanctuary reported that unidentified diseases affected coral at 94 of 160 monitoring stations in the 2,800-square-mile coral reef sanctuary. Coral reefs are also threatened by coastal development that spurs the growth of unfriendly algae. Coastal development increases the danger of the reefs being trampled by divers and boat anchors. Other serious threats to reef ecosystems include marine pollution, blast fishing, and cyanide fishing. Collection of tropical reef specimens for the aquarium trade has also damaged a number of species. Perhaps the greatest immediate threat to coral reefs is rising water temperature due to global climate change. This has caused extensive coral bleaching in recent years.

Marine Mammals

Dolphins, whales, and numerous other marine mammals are threatened with extinction. Some species have declined due to centuries of hunting, while others have been harmed as a result of habitat decline or other forms of human activity.

GREAT WHALES. Whales are the largest animals on Earth. The blue whale, the largest whale species, can reach a length of 80 feet and weigh 150 tons. Its heart alone weighs 1,000 pounds and is the size of a small car. Whales are found throughout the world's oceans and are highly intelligent. Some species communicate via haunting "songs." In 2004 eight whale species had been listed for protection under the Endangered Species Act: humpback whales, sperm whales, bowhead whales, right whales, sei whales, finback whales, blue whales, and gray whales.

Whale populations have declined due to a long history of hunting by humans. As early as the eighth century, humans hunted whales for meat and whalebone. In the nineteenth century, large numbers of whales were killed for whale oil, which was used to light lamps, as well as for baleen—the large horny plates that some species use to filter food. Baleen or "whalebone" was particularly valued for making fans and corsets. Today whales are hunted

FIGURE 5.17

Manatees, also known as "sea cows," are endangered throughout their range in Florida and the southeastern United States. *(Corbis/Brandon D. Cole)*

primarily for meat and for whale oil used in the manufacture of cosmetics and industrial lubricants. The Marine Mammal Protection Act, passed in 1972, made it illegal to import goods containing ingredients from whales. The International Whaling Commission (IWC) has imposed a moratorium on whale hunting since 1986, but animals continue to be killed by countries that flout its regulations or claim that the hunts are for "research."

The northern right whale is the most endangered of the great whales, with fewer than 300 individuals in existence. Once the "right" whale to hunt because it swims slowly and floats upon death, the species has been protected for several decades. However, northern right whale populations are not increasing. The primary threat to the species is continued mortality from collisions with ships. Entanglement in fishing gear and habitat decline in right whale feeding areas are additional causes of population decline. Research has also revealed that the northern right whale's huge fat reserves store an array of toxic substances, possibly affecting whales' health. The situation is so dire, says Dr. Scott Kraus, chief scientist at the New England Aquarium in Boston, that the right whale may become extinct in our lifetime. The National Marine Fisheries Service has declared an area off the coast of Georgia and northern Florida coast as critical right whale habitat.

MANATEES. The last remaining West Indian manatees, also known as Florida manatees, swim in the rivers, bays, and estuaries of Florida and surrounding states. (See Figure 5.17.) These mammals are often called "sea cows" and can reach weights of up to 2,000 pounds. Manatees swim just below the surface of the water and feed on vegetation. Females bear a single offspring every three to five years. West Indian manatees migrate north in the summer, though generally no farther than the North Carolina coast. In 1995 a manatee nicknamed "Chessie" made headlines by swimming all the way to Chesapeake Bay. Eventually biologists, concerned about his health in cooler waters, had him airlifted back to Florida.

Unlike most animals, manatees have no natural predators. The primary dangers to this species come from humans. Motorboats are the major cause of manatee mortalities—because of their large size, manatees often cannot move away from boats quickly enough to avoid being hit. Environmentalists have tried to protect manatees from boat collisions, and have successfully had several Florida waterways declared boat-free zones. There are also areas where boaters are required to lower their speeds. Because manatees do not produce young very often, their population is decreasing due to high death rates.

The manatee population has suffered severe losses in the last decade. In 1995 approximately 10 percent of Florida's manatees died suddenly, most likely from an unidentified virus. The following year 20 percent of the remaining population—a total of 415 manatees—died. Researchers attributed mortality to a variety of causes, including red tide, which occurs when toxin-producing aquatic organisms called dinoflagellates bloom in large quantities, and motorboat collisions. In 2001 the Florida Fish and Wildlife Conservation Commission and Florida Marine Research Institute reported 325 manatee deaths. Eighty-one were due to collisions with watercraft, and another 110 were due to unknown causes. The Florida Marine Research Institute reported that human-related activity accounted for 44 percent of all manatee deaths between 1976 and 2001, most from watercraft collisions.

A lawsuit by the Save the Manatee Club and other environmental and conservation organizations in 2000 successfully required the state to implement new boat speed zones and establish areas for manatee "safe havens." However, new rules were immediately challenged by individual boaters and boating organizations. The restrictions were upheld by Florida courts in 2002.

Biologists estimate that between 2,000 and 3,000 manatees remain in the wild. An aerial survey in 2004 counted 2,568 individuals. Most of these manatees have scars on their backs from motorboat propellers—these allow individual manatees to be recognized. The National Biological Service has catalogued about 1,000 manatees using scar patterns, and maintains manatee sighting histories in a computer-based system.

DOLPHINS. Large numbers of dolphins have been killed by the tuna fishing industry. These marine mammals are often found swimming over tuna schools—in fact, tuna fishers have learned to locate tuna by looking for dolphin pods. Dolphins die when they become trapped in commercial tuna nets and drown. Many millions of dolphins have been killed this way since tuna netting began in 1958.

In 1972 more than 360,000 dolphins were killed by U.S. tuna fishermen. Congress passed the Marine Mammal Protection Act the same year, partly to reduce dolphin deaths. Amendments to the law in 1982 and 1985 theoretically halted U.S. tuna purchases from countries whose fishing methods endangered dolphins. In the years after passage, however, these laws were often ignored. Public awareness of dolphin killings was critical in bringing more interest and attention to the issue. In 1988 a reauthorization of marine mammal laws required observers to be present on all tuna boats. Even this measure, however, had only limited impact. In 1990 StarKist, the biggest tuna canner in the world, declared that it would no longer purchase tuna caught in ways that harmed dolphins. Within hours of StarKist's press conference, the next two largest tuna canners followed suit. In 1991 the government established standards for tuna canners that wished to label their products "Dolphin Safe." The International Dolphin Conservation Act, passed in 1992, reduced the number of legally permitted dolphin deaths. This act also made the United States a dolphin-safe zone in 1994, when it became illegal to sell, buy, or ship tuna products obtained using methods that kill dolphins. Reputable tuna canners now label their canned tuna "Dolphin Safe."

SEALS AND SEA LIONS. In 2004 six species of pinnipeds—seals and sea lions—were considered endangered worldwide. These were the Caribbean monk seal, Hawaiian monk seal, Guadalupe fur seal, Mediterranean monk seal, Saimaa seal, and Steller sea lion. However, the Caribbean monk seal has not been sighted since 1952 and is believed extinct. The species was widely hunted for both blubber and meat.

Hawaiian monk seals are the only pinnipeds found on Hawaii and are endemic to those islands—that is, they occur nowhere else on Earth. Because Hawaiian monk seals have no natural terrestrial enemies, they are not afraid of humans and were once easily hunted for blubber and fur. Hunting was the primary cause of population decline. Hawaiian monk seals are also extremely sensitive to human activity and disturbance and now breed exclusively on the remote northwestern Hawaiian islands, which are not inhabited by humans. Most females give birth to a single pup every two years, a reproductive rate lower than other pinniped species. Hawaiian monk seals feed on fish, octopuses, eels, and lobsters. This species was officially listed as endangered in 1976. In 2002 seal populations were estimated at between 1,200 and 1,500 individuals.

The Guadalupe fur seal breeds on the Isla de Guadalupe and the Isla Benito del Este near Baja California in Mexico. Although populations once included as many as 20,000 to 100,000 individuals, decline and endangerment resulted from extensive fur hunting in the 1700s and 1800s. The species was believed extinct in the early twentieth century, but a small population was discovered in 1954. The species was listed as threatened in 1967. Protection of the Guadalupe fur seal under both Mexican and U.S. law has resulted in population increases, and there are

TABLE 5.6

Marine Mammal Authorization Program mortality/injury report, 2000

Species	Fisheries	Injured	Killed
Gray whale	trap/crab	0	1
Pilot whale	Atlantic Ocean, Caribbean, Gulf of Mexico large pelagics longline	3	0
Bottlenose dolphin	U.S. Mid-Atlantic coastal gillnet	0	2
	Gulf of Mexico menhaden purse seine	1	4
Common dolphin	CA/OR thresher shark/swordfish drift gillnet	3	15
	Gulf of Mexico menhaden purse seine	0	1
	Atlantic squid, mackerel, butterfish trawl fishery	0	5
Harbor porpoise	AK Peninsula/Aleutian Islands salmon set gillnet	1	0
	Northeast sink gillnet	0	3
Humpback whale	Northeast sink gillnet	0	1
	CA/OR thresher shark/swordfish drift gillnet	1	0
	Prince William Sound salmon drift gillnet	1	0
Pacific white-sided dolphin	CA/OR thresher shark/swordfish drift gillnet	0	11
Risso's dolphin	CA/OR thresher shark/swordfish drift gillnet	0	2
	Northeast sink gillnet	0	1
Unidentified small cetacean	CA/OR thresher shark/swordfish drift gillnet	4	1
	Atlantic Ocean, Caribbean, Gulf of Mexico large pelagics longline	1	0
California sea lion	CA/OR thresher shark/swordfish drift gillnet	0	23
	CA angel shark/halibut & other species large mesh (3.5 inch) set gillnet	0	25
Steller sea lion	AK Bering Sea & Aleutian Islands groundfish trawl	0	5
Harbor seal	CA angel shark/halibut & other species large mesh (3.5 inch) set gillnet	0	3
	Northeast sink gillnet	0	3
Northern elephant seal	CA angel shark/halibut & other species large mesh (3.5 inch) set gillnet	0	1
	CA/OR thresher shark/swordfish drift gillnet	1	1
Grey seal	Northeast sink gillnet	0	4
Unidentified seal	AK Bering Sea & Aleutian Islands groundfish trawl	0	1
	CA/OR thresher shark/swordfish drift gillnet	0	1
Walrus	AK Bering Sea & Aleutian Islands groundfish trawl	0	1
Total		**16**	**115**

SOURCE: "Table 4. 2000 Marine Mammal Authorization Program Mortality/Injury Report," *Administration of the Marine Mammal Protection Act of 1972 Annual Report 1999–2000,* U.S. Department of Commerce, National Marine Fisheries Service, Office of Protected Resources, Silver Spring, MD, 2004

now an estimated 7,000 individuals in the wild. However, some individuals continue to be killed by driftnets.

Steller sea lions are large animals, with males reaching lengths of 11 feet and weights of 2,500 pounds. Females are significantly smaller. Steller sea lions are found in Pacific waters from Japan to central California, but most populations breed near Alaska and the Aleutian Islands. Populations have declined by 80 percent in the last three decades, most likely due to the decline of fish that provide food for the species. In February 2004 the North Pacific Universities Marine Mammal Consortium reported that population declines may be explained by the fact that Steller sea lions had switched from eating fatty fish to fish with low fat content. In particular, their diet now consists primarily of pollock and flatfish, rather than herring. The low fat content of the new diet prevents Steller sea lions from building up enough blubber to survive and reproduce in their cold aquatic habitat. In addition, many sea lions are also killed in driftnets. In 1990 the Steller sea lion was listed as endangered in Alaska and Russia and threatened in other habitats. There are currently about 30,000 individuals in the wild.

LAWS PROTECTING AQUATIC SPECIES

The Lacey Act

The Lacey Act was originally passed in 1900 and is the oldest wildlife conservation law in the United States.

The Lacey Act prohibits interstate and international trade in wildlife that has been collected or exported illegally. In 1999 the U.S. Fish and Wildlife Service processed 1,476 cases under the Lacey Act. These included illegal commerce in endangered species, illegal hunting, and illegal harvest of shellfish from closed areas.

The Magnuson Act

The Magnuson Fishery Conservation and Management Act of 1976 established a system for fisheries management within U.S. waters. Examples of Magnuson Act violations include fishing without a permit, possessing out-of-season fish, or retaining undersized fish.

The Marine Mammal Protection Act

The Marine Mammal Protection Act (MMPA), passed in 1972, recognized that many marine mammals are either endangered or have suffered declines as a result of human activity. The MMPA prohibits the taking (hunting, killing, capturing, and harassing) of marine mammals. The act also bars importation of most marine mammals or their products. Exceptions are occasionally granted for scientific research, public display in aquariums, subsistence hunting (by Alaskan natives), and some incidental take during commercial fishing operations. The goal of the MMPA is to maintain marine populations at or above "optimum sustainable" levels. Under the MMPA, the National Marine Fisheries Service manages all cetaceans (whales and dolphins) and pinnipeds (seals and sea lions) except walruses. The National Marine Fisheries Service relies on the U.S. Coast Guard and other federal and state agencies to assist with the detection of violations. Table 5.6 shows the list of marine mammal injuries and mortalities that resulted from interactions with commercial fisheries in 2000. This is a standard part of the *Administration of the Marine Mammal Protection Act of 1972* report that the National Marine Fisheries Service submits to Congress every two years.

The U.S. Fish and Wildlife Service manages polar bears, walruses, sea otters, manatees, and dugongs (manatee relatives).

CHAPTER 6
IMPERILED AMPHIBIANS AND REPTILES

Amphibians and reptiles are collectively known by biologists as herpetofauna. At present, there are over 5,000 described amphibian species and over 6,000 reptiles. New species in both these groups are being discovered every day, particularly in remote tropical regions that are only now being explored.

Amphibians and reptiles are also among the world's most threatened groups. The World Conservation Union (IUCN) reported in its *2003 Red List of Threatened Species* that some 39 percent of surveyed reptiles and 62 percent of surveyed amphibians are imperiled. However, conservation status has yet to be assessed for numerous species—only one-fifth of reptiles and one-eighth of amphibians have been examined. The IUCN list currently includes 293 threatened reptiles and 157 threatened amphibians, up from 253 and 63 respectively in 1996. The increase in the number of listed reptiles reflects, in part, more complete examination of freshwater turtle species. Many of these are highly imperiled, particularly in Asia, where they are hunted for both food and medicine (see Figure 6.1). Recent amphibian declines—part of a global pattern—have been particularly alarming to researchers and conservationists.

AMPHIBIANS

Amphibians represent the most ancient group of terrestrial vertebrates. The earliest amphibians are known from fossils and date from the early Devonian era, some 400 million years ago. The three groups of amphibians that have survived to the present day are salamanders, frogs and toads, and caecilians. Table 6.1 describes some of the major amphibian groups in North America.

"Amphi-" means "both," and amphibians get their name from the fact that many species occupy both aquatic and terrestrial habitats. In particular, a large number of amphibian species undergo a dramatic change called

TABLE 6.1

Major amphibian groups

A. Completely aquatic
  1. Salamanders (for example, hellbender, mudpuppy, siren, amphiuma, neotenic[1] ambystomatid salamanders).
  2. Frogs (for example, African clawed frog; introduced)

B. Lentic (still water) breeding/semi-terrestrial adults
  1. Salamanders (for example, ambystomatid salamanders, newts[2])
  2. Frogs (for example, spotted frogs, wood frogs, treefrogs, toads)

C. Lotic (running water) breeding/semi-terrestrial adults
  1. Salamanders (for example, red and spring salamanders)
  2. Frogs (for example, foothill yellow-legged frog, tailed frog)

D. Completely terrestrial
  1. Salamanders (for example, red-backed salamander, slender salamanders)

[1]Animals reach sexual maturity but retain the larval form.
[2]The eastern red-spotted newt (*Notophthalmus viridescens*) has an aquatic larval form that metamorphoses into a terrestrial subadult form (red eft). When the newt reaches sexual maturity (3-7 years) it makes a few more changes (morphological and physiological) and returns to the water for the rest of its life.

SOURCE: J. K. Reaser, "Major Amphibian Groups of North America," in *Amphibian Declines: An Issue Overview*, Federal Task Force on Amphibian Declines and Deformities, Washington, DC, 2000

metamorphosis, in which individuals move from an aquatic larval stage to a terrestrial adult stage. In many frog species, for example, aquatic, swimming tadpoles metamorphose into terrestrial jumping frogs. In the process, they lose their muscular swimming tails and acquire forelimbs and hind limbs. Many amphibian species occupy terrestrial habitats through most of the year, but migrate to ponds to breed. However, there are also species that are either entirely aquatic or entirely terrestrial. Whatever their habitat, amphibians generally require some moisture to survive. This is because amphibians pass some oxygen and other chemicals in and out of their body directly through their living skin, using processes that require water to function.

A large number of amphibian species are in serious decline due to factors such as habitat loss, pollution, and

FIGURE 6.1

This Asian box turtle, native to China, is seriously threatened due to demand for trade. *(Photograph by David Northcott. Reproduced by permission of the Corbis Corporation.)*

climate change. Amphibians are particularly vulnerable to pollution because their skin readily absorbs water and other substances from the environment. For this reason, amphibians are frequently considered biological indicator species. There are currently 30 amphibian species listed with the Fish and Wildlife Service as either threatened or endangered. The 21 U.S. species listed—11 salamanders and 10 frogs and toads—appear in Table 6.2.

Sudden Disappearances

At the end of the twentieth century, biologists uncovered growing evidence of an unexplained global decline in amphibian populations. AmphibiaWeb, a conservation organization that monitors amphibian species worldwide, reported in 2004 that at least 200 amphibian species had experienced serious population declines in the last few decades. In addition, no fewer than 32 amphibian species have gone extinct. Amphibian declines have been documented worldwide, though the degree of decline varies across regions. Areas that have been hardest hit include Central America and Australia. In the U.S., amphibian declines have been concentrated in California, the Rocky Mountains, the Southwest, and Puerto Rico. Particularly disturbing is the loss of numerous populations within protected and relatively pristine wildlife refuges.

The golden toad, named for its unusual and striking orange color, is a prime example of the global amphibian decline. Over a three-year period, golden toads disappeared inexplicably from their only known habitat in the Monteverde Cloud Forest Reserve in Costa Rica. In 1987 herpetologists observed an apparently healthy golden toad population estimated at 1,500 adults along with a new generation of tadpoles. The following year, in 1988, there were only 11 toads. In 1989 only a single surviving toad was found. It was the last individual on record for the species.

Concern regarding declining amphibian populations led then-U.S. Secretary of the Interior Bruce Babbitt to meet with amphibian biologists in 1998. These scientists reported that a large number of amphibian species—particularly frogs—had become extinct over a very short period of time. They also noted that numerous other species were either declining or showing high levels of gross deformities, such as extra limbs, and that amphibians were dying out in unexpected places, such as protected national parks in the western United States. Secretary Babbitt commented:

Many of these frogs and amphibian species have been in an evolutionary relationship with our landscape for millions of years, and when all of a sudden they start to

TABLE 6.2

Endangered or threatened amphibians, February 2004

Status	Species name
T	Coqui, golden *(Eleutherodactylus jasperi)*
T	Frog, California red-legged *(Rana aurora draytonii)*
T	Frog, Chiricahua leopard *(Rana chiricahuensis)*
E	Frog, Mississippi gopher *(Rana capito sevosa)*
E	Frog, mountain yellow-legged *(Rana muscosa)*
T	Guajon *(Eleutherodactylus cooki)*
E	Salamander, Barton Springs *(Eurycea sosorum)*
E	Salamander, California tiger *(Ambystoma californiense)*
T	Salamander, Cheat Mountain *(Plethodon nettingi)*
E	Salamander, desert slender *(Batrachoseps aridus)*
T	Salamander, flatwoods *(Ambystoma cingulatum)*
T	Salamander, Red Hills *(Phaeognathus hubrichti)*
T	Salamander, San Marcos *(Eurycea nana)*
E	Salamander, Santa Cruz long-toed *(Ambystoma macrodactylum croceum)*
E	Salamander, Shenandoah *(Plethodon shenandoah)*
E	Salamander, Sonora tiger *(Ambystoma tigrinum stebbinsi)*
E	Salamander, Texas blind *(Typhlomolge rathbuni)*
E	Toad, arroyo (=arroyo southwesten) *(Bufo californicus [=microscaphus])*
E	Toad, Houston *(Bufo houstonensis)*
T	Toad, Puerto Rican crested *(Peltophryne lemur)*
E	Toad, Wyoming *(Bufo baxteri [=hemiophrys])*

E = Endangered
T = Threatened

SOURCE: Adapted from "U.S. Listed Vertebrate Animal Species Report by Taxonomic Group as of 02/17/2004," Threatened and Endangered Species System (TESS), U.S. Fish and Wildlife Service, Washington, DC, 2004 [Online] http://ecos.fws.gov/tess_public/TESSWebpageVipListed?code=V&listings=0#E [accessed February 17, 2004]

just, in the blink of an eye, disappear, there's clearly some external cause that's probably related to something that we are doing across the broader landscape. The deformities are particularly ominous because of the potential human implications as well.

Recent amphibian declines and deformities appear to result from a combination of causes.

HABITAT DESTRUCTION. Loss of habitat is a major factor in the decline of numerous amphibian species, as it is for many endangered species. The destruction of tropical forests and wetlands, ecosystems that are rich with amphibians, has done particular damage to populations. In the U.S., deforestation has caused the loss or decline of at least seven salamander species in the Pacific Northwest and 16 salamander species in Appalachian hardwood forests. Global climate change has also destroyed unique habitats such as cloud forests (forests containing large amounts of water mists), resulting in the loss of cloud forest amphibian species. In addition, some amphibians have lost appropriate aquatic breeding habitats, particularly small bodies of water such as ponds. These aquatic habitats are often developed or filled in by humans, because they appear to be less biologically valuable than larger aquatic habitats.

Finally, habitat fragmentation may be particularly harmful to amphibian species that migrate during the breeding season. These species require not only that both breeding and non-breeding habitats remain undisturbed, but also that there be intact habitat along migration routes.

POLLUTION. Pollution is a second major factor in global amphibian declines. Because amphibians absorb water directly through skin and into their bodies, they are particularly vulnerable to water pollution from pesticides or fertilizer runoff.

Air pollution by substances such as chlorofluorocarbons (CFCs) has reduced the amount of protective ozone in the Earth's atmosphere. This has resulted in increased levels of UV radiation striking the Earth's surface. Exposure to UV radiation causes genetic mutations that can prevent normal development or kill eggs. Increased UV levels particularly affect the many frog species whose eggs float on the exposed surfaces of ponds.

INVASIVE SPECIES. Many amphibian species have also been affected by the introduction of non-native species that either compete with them or prey on them. These include fish, crayfish, and other amphibians. The bullfrog, the cane toad (a very large frog species), and the African clawed frog (a species used in much biological research) are some of the invasive species believed to have affected amphibian populations. In addition, introduced trout are blamed for the extinction of several species of harlequin frogs in Costa Rica. It is hypothesized that trout consume tadpoles. Similarly, introduced salmon have affected native frog populations in California.

EPIDEMICS. Amphibian diseases caused variously by bacteria, viruses, and fungi have devastated certain populations. Of particular importance in recent years is the chytrid fungus. This fungus attacks skin, and was first identified in 1998 in diseased amphibians. There are often no symptoms initially, but eventually individuals begin to shed skin and die. The precise cause of death is not known, though damage to the skin can interfere with respiration. The chytrid fungus is believed to be responsible for the demise of numerous species in Australia and Panama. In 2000, it was also documented in populations of the Chiricahua leopard frog in Arizona and the boreal toad in the Rocky Mountains.

HUMAN COLLECTION. Many amphibian species are vigorously hunted for food, the pet trade, or as medical research specimens.

Amphibian Deformities

Amphibian deformities (see Figure 6.2) first hit the spotlight in 1995, when middle-school students discovered large numbers of deformed frogs in a pond in Minnesota. Deformed frogs have since been found in 44 states in the United States. These include representatives of 38 different frog species and 19 different toad species. In some populations, over 60 percent of individuals are deformed.

FIGURE 6.2

A frog showing deformed and extra limbs. The high incidence of amphibian deformities in the United States is cause for concern. (*JLM Visuals*)

FIGURE 6.3

The Texas blind salamander has been listed by the Fish and Wildlife Service as endangered since 1967. Because it lives in underground caves, the salamander has only vestigial eyes, found below the skin. (*U.S. Fish and Wildlife Service*)

The high incidence of amphibian deformities in U.S. species appears to have multiple causes, as no single hypothesis accounts for all the different types of deformities seen. The most common deformities include missing hind limbs and toes, missing feet, misshapen feet, missing eyes, deformed front legs, and extra legs. Some of these malformations are believed to be related to a parasitic trematode, or flatworm, which in experiments causes the development of additional limbs. Aquatic trematodes have increased in number due to human activity, via a complicated chain of events. First, fertilizer runoff increases nutrient levels in ponds, allowing more algae to grow. More algae results in more algae-eating snails, and snails host juvenile parasitic trematodes. Trematodes move on to frogs when they mature, forming cysts in the vicinity of developing frog legs. Chemical pollution and UV radiation may account for some of the other observed deformities.

Salamanders

Salamanders are tailed amphibians. The group contains over 500 described species, including the newts. The majority of salamanders are fairly small in size, most often six inches long or less. The Chinese and Japanese giant salamanders, which grow to as large as five feet long, are the largest of all amphibians. In 2004, salamanders comprised 11 of the 21 U.S. amphibians on the Endangered Species List. Some endangered salamanders, including many cave species (see Figure 6.3), have highly restricted habitats. The Barton Springs salamander, for example, is only found in a single locale in and around the Barton Springs pool in Austin, Texas. The Barton Springs salamander has been the subject of contentious debate between conservationists and those who wish to guarantee free recreational use of the pool.

GIANT SALAMANDERS. There are two species of giant salamanders, the Chinese giant salamander and the Japanese giant salamander. These are by far the largest currently living amphibian species, reaching lengths of up to five feet. Both are listed with the Fish and Wildlife Service and

are highly endangered. Giant salamanders are aquatic, and have folded and wrinkled skin that allows them to absorb oxygen from their watery habitats. The Chinese giant salamander is found in fast mountain streams in western China. Despite official protection, the species is endangered partly because of hunting for food or medicine. The Chinese giant salamander is also harmed by loss of habitat and aquatic pollution. Its close relative, the Japanese giant salamander, is also endangered and protected. This species inhabits cold, fast mountain streams in northern Kyushu Island and western Honshu in Japan. Japanese giant salamanders have been successfully bred in captivity.

Caecilians

Very little is known about most species of legless, worm-like amphibians called caecilians. Some caecilians are aquatic, but most of these elusive animals are underground burrowers that are difficult to locate and to study. Caecilians generally have very poor eyesight because of their underground habitat—some have no eyes at all or are nearly blind. There are 160 described species of caecilians. All live in tropical climates. Because so little is known about this group, it is difficult for environmentalists to assess the level of endangerment of these animals. Although there are no currently listed species, the loss of tropical habitats worldwide suggests that many caecilians are likely imperiled.

Frogs and Toads

Over 5,000 species of frogs and toads have been described worldwide, making this by far the most diverse group of living amphibians. Most occupy tropical habitats, though two species are found within the Arctic Circle. Many frog species go through a swimming tadpole stage before metamorphosing into a tailless, jumping, adult frog. However, in some species, eggs hatch directly as juvenile froglets, which are miniature versions of the adults. Tadpoles are most often herbivorous, although there are some carnivorous tadpoles, including cannibalistic species. Adult frogs are carnivorous and catch prey with their sticky tongues. Altogether, ten frogs and toads were listed by the Fish and Wildlife Service as threatened or endangered in 2004.

GASTRIC-BROODING FROGS. There are two species of gastric-brooding frogs, both found in Australia. Gastric-brooding frogs are described as timid and are often found hiding under rocks in water. These species were only discovered in the 1970s, and, unfortunately, went extinct only a decade after their discovery. One species was last seen in the wild in September 1982; the other was last seen in March 1985. Gastric-brooding frogs get their name from their unusual reproductive strategy—females brood their young in their stomachs! During brooding, the mother does not eat and does not produce stomach acids. The gestation period lasts about eight weeks, and as many as 30 tadpoles may be in the brood. Juveniles eventually emerge as miniature froglets from the mother's mouth. Although it is not certain what led to the extinction of gastric-brooding frogs, one hypothesis is that populations were killed off by the chytrid fungus, which is also responsible for the decline of other frog species.

CALIFORNIA RED-LEGGED FROG. The California red-legged frog, made famous by Mark Twain's short story "The Celebrated Jumping Frog of Calaveras County," experienced a significant decline during the mid-twentieth century. By 1960 California red-legged frogs had disappeared altogether from California's Central Valley, probably due to the loss of 70 percent of their habitat. The California red-legged frog, the largest native frog in the western United States, was officially listed as a threatened species by the Fish and Wildlife Service in 1996.

California red-legged frogs require riverside habitats covered by vegetation and close to deep water pools. They are extremely sensitive to habitat disturbance and water pollution—tadpoles are particularly sensitive to varying oxygen levels and siltation (mud and other natural impurities) during metamorphosis. California red-legged frogs require three to four years to reach maturity and have a normal life span of eight to ten years.

Water reservoir construction and agricultural or residential development are the primary factors in this species' decline. Biologists have shown that California red-legged frogs generally disappear from habitats within five years of a reservoir or water diversion project. The removal of vegetation associated with flood control, combined with the use of herbicides and restructuring of landscapes, further degrade remaining habitat. Finally, non-native species have also attacked red-legged frog populations. These include alien fish predators as well as competing species such as bullfrogs.

In 2004 California red-legged frogs were known to occupy approximately 238 streams or drainages, primari-ly in central and southern California. Only four localities are known to support substantial populations (over 350 individuals) of adult frogs. The recovery plan for the California red-legged frog includes eliminating threats in current habitats, restoring damaged habitats, and re-introducing populations into the historic range of the species. The U.S. National Park Service helped to preserve one current frog habitat by altering water flow in the Piru Creek connection between Lake Piru and Pyramid Lake, located in the Los Angeles and Los Padres National Forests about 60 miles northwest of Los Angeles. This also benefited another threatened species, the arroyo southwestern toad.

The Fish and Wildlife Service has taken measures to preserve habitat in the foothills of the Sierra Nevada, in the central coastal mountains near San Francisco, along the Pacific coast near Los Angeles, and in the Tehachapi Mountains. Protected frog habitats have also been established in Marin and Sonoma Counties. The Contra Costa Water District east of San Francisco Bay has established protected habitat areas in an attempt to compensate for habitat destruction caused at the Los Vaqueros watershed and reservoir. Finally, captive breeding of California red-legged frogs is being considered for feasibility at the Los Angeles Zoo, in a coordinated effort with The Nature Conservancy.

GUAJÓN. The threatened web-footed guajón is a Puerto Rican cave-dwelling frog species. Its decline has resulted largely from introductions of alien species such as mongooses, rats, and cats, all of which eat unhatched guajón eggs. In addition the species has experienced habitat loss from garbage dumping in caves and deforestation for agriculture, roads, and dams. Deforestation also creates the potential for future environmental disasters such as flash floods, which drown adult frogs and destroy nests. Encroaching agriculture causes pollution from fertilizer runoff. Finally, the guajón, with its large white-rimmed eyes and phantom-like appearance, is frequently killed by superstitious local residents who believe the mere sight of the animal can bring disaster.

REPTILES

Approximately 6,300 species of reptiles have been described. These include turtles, snakes, lizards, and crocodilians. Birds are also technically reptiles (birds and crocodiles are actually close relatives), but have historically been treated separately. Reptiles differ from amphibians in that their skin is cornified—that is, made of dead cells. All reptiles obtain oxygen from the air using lungs. Most reptiles lay shelled eggs, although many species, particularly lizards and snakes, give birth to live young.

Many reptiles are in serious decline. Numerous species are endangered due to habitat loss or degradation. In addition, humans hunt some reptiles for their skins, shells, or meat. Global climate change has affected some reptile species, particularly turtles, in ominous ways—this is because in some reptiles, ambient temperatures determine whether males or females are produced, in some cases resulting in few or no males being born. Natural disasters may also affect reptiles, as in 1999, when tens of thousands of turtle hatchlings were lost to the fury of Hurricane Floyd.

There are 78 reptiles listed as endangered, including 14 U.S. species and 64 foreign species. An additional 37 species are listed as threatened, including 22 U.S. species and 15 foreign species. Threatened and endangered U.S. reptiles are listed in Table 6.3.

Sea Turtles

Sea turtles are excellent swimmers and spend nearly their entire lives in water. They feed on a wide array of food items, including mollusks, vegetation, and crustaceans. Some sea turtles are migratory, swimming thousands of miles between feeding and nesting areas. Individuals are exposed to a variety of both natural and human threats. Because of these, only an estimated one in 10,000 sea turtles survives to adulthood.

Of the seven species of sea turtles that exist worldwide, six spend part or all of their lives in U.S. territorial waters—the loggerhead turtle, green turtle, leatherback turtle, hawksbill turtle, olive ridley turtle, and Kemp's ridley turtle. (The seventh species, the flatback turtle, occurs near Australia.) All are listed by the Fish and Wildlife Service as either threatened or endangered. Figure 6.4 shows leatherback turtle population trends at nesting grounds in St. Croix, Virgin Islands, over the last several decades. Conservation efforts for this species have met with some success.

THREATS TO NESTING TURTLES. Sea turtles bury their eggs in nests on sandy beaches. The building of beachfront resorts and homes has destroyed a large proportion of nesting habitat. Artificial lighting associated with coastal development also poses a problem—lights discourage females from nesting and also cause hatchlings to become disoriented and wander inland instead of out to sea. Finally, beach nourishment, the practice of rebuilding eroded beach soil, creates unusually compacted sand on which turtles are unable to nest. The sands of Tortuguero National Park in Costa Rica are believed to be the last remaining nesting ground for one species, the endangered green turtle.

SHRIMP-NET CASUALTIES. Large numbers of sea turtles are killed in shrimp nets in the Gulf of Mexico and the Caribbean. In 1990 the National Academy of Sciences reported that shrimp trawling was the greatest cause of sea turtle deaths in U.S. waters, killing 55,000 turtles every year. In 1981 the turtle excluder device (TED), which allows sea turtles to escape from shrimp nets, was invent-

TABLE 6.3

Endangered or threatened reptiles, February 2004

Status	Species name
T(S/A)	Alligator, American (*Alligator mississippiensis*)
E	Anole, Culebra Island giant (*Anolis roosevelti*)
T	Boa, Mona (*Epicrates monensis monensis*)
E	Boa, Puerto Rican (*Epicrates inornatus*)
E	Boa, Virgin Islands tree (*Epicrates monensis granti*)
E	Cooter (=turtle), northern redbelly (=Plymouth) (*Pseudemys rubriventris bangsi*)
E	Crocodile, American (*Crocodylus acutus*)
E	Gecko, Monito (*Sphaerodactylus micropithecus*)
T	Iguana, Mona ground (*Cyclura stejnegeri*)
E	Lizard, blunt-nosed leopard (*Gambelia silus*)
T	Lizard, Coachella Valley fringe-toed (*Uma inornata*)
T	Lizard, island night (*Xantusia riversiana*)
E	Lizard, St. Croix ground (*Ameiva polops*)
T	Rattlesnake, New Mexican ridge-nosed (*Crotalus willardi obscurus*)
E, T	Sea turtle, green (*Chelonia mydas*)
E	Sea turtle, hawksbill (*Eretmochelys imbricata*)
E	Sea turtle, Kemp's ridley (*Lepidochelys kempii*)
E	Sea turtle, leatherback (*Dermochelys coriacea*)
T	Sea turtle, loggerhead (*Caretta caretta*)
T	Sea turtle, olive ridley (*Lepidochelys olivacea*)
T	Skink, bluetail mole (*Eumeces egregius lividus*)
T	Skink, sand (*Neoseps reynoldsi*)
T	Snake, Atlantic salt marsh (*Nerodia clarkii taeniata*)
T	Snake, Concho water (*Nerodia paucimaculata*)
T	Snake, copperbelly water (*Nerodia erythrogaster neglecta*)
T	Snake, eastern indigo (*Drymarchon corais couperi*)
T	Snake, giant garter (*Thamnophis gigas*)
T	Snake, Lake Erie water (*Nerodia sipedon insularum*)
E	Snake, San Francisco garter (*Thamnophis sirtalis tetrataenia*)
T(S/A), T	Tortoise, desert (*Gopherus agassizii*)
T	Tortoise, gopher (*Gopherus polyphemus*)
E	Turtle, Alabama redbelly (*Pseudemys alabamensis*)
T(S/A), T	Turtle, bog (=Muhlenberg) (*Clemmys muhlenbergii*)
T	Turtle, flattened musk (*Sternotherus depressus*)
T	Turtle, ringed map (*Graptemys oculifera*)
T	Turtle, yellow-blotched map (*Graptemys flavimaculata*)
T	Whipsnake (=striped racer), Alameda (*Masticophis lateralis euryxanthus*)

E = Endangered
T = Threatened
T(SA) = Similarity of appearance to a threatened taxon

SOURCE: Adapted from "U.S. Listed Vertebrate Animal Species Report by Taxonomic Group as of 02/17/2004," Threatened and Endangered Species System (TESS), U.S. Fish and Wildlife Service, Washington, DC, 2004 [Online] http://ecos.fws.gov/tess_public/TESSWebpageVipListed?code=V&listings=0#E [accessed February 17, 2004]

ed. The use of TEDs became a requirement under the Endangered Species Act. Biologists attribute the gradual increase in some turtle species in the 1990s to the use of TEDs. In January 1996 federal courts ruled that, under provisions of the Endangered Species Act, the Commerce Department must require all nations that export shrimp to the United States to use TEDs as well.

In April 1998 the World Trade Organization (WTO), an international trade body, ruled that the United States could not prohibit shrimp imports from countries that do not use turtle excluder devices. Experts fear that when free trade conflicts with environmental protection, the WTO is likely to favor trade over environmental protection. In addition, the law requiring TEDs be used by countries that export shrimp to the United States has been

FIGURE 6.4

Number of leatherback turtles and leatherback remigrants returning to nesting grounds at Sandy Point, St. Croix, U.S. Virgin Islands, 1981–97

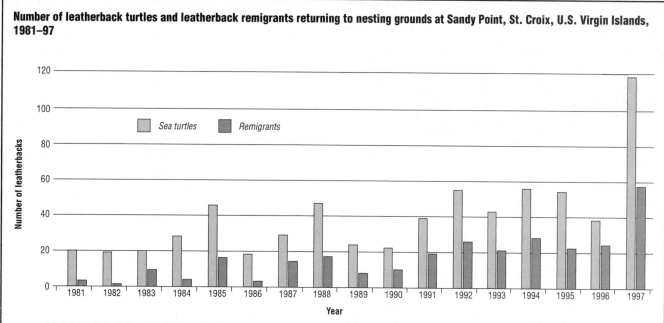

SOURCE: M. J. Mac, P.A. Opler, C.E. Puckett Haecker, and P.D. Doran, "Fig. 7: The number of leatherback turtles and leatherback remigrants (that is, a nesting female who returns to nest at a particular site in subsequent nesting seasons) returning to nesting grounds at Sandy Point, St. Croix, U.S. Virgin Islands, 1981–1997," in *The Status and Trends of Our Nation's Biological Resources*, U.S. Geological Survey, Reston, VA, 1998

suspended by the Bush administration, under the assumption that it would hurt commerce

KEMP'S RIDLEY TURTLE. Kemp's ridley turtle is the smallest sea turtle, with individuals measuring some three feet in length and weighing less than 100 pounds. Kemp's ridley is also the most endangered of the sea turtle species. It has only one major nesting site, located in Rancho Nuevo, Mexico, where it faces increasing threats from human activity. In particular, eggs and hatched juveniles are collected by people or eaten by coyotes. At Rancho Nuevo, numerous female Kemp's ridley turtles nest at the same time—this is referred to as an "arribada." Female ridleys nest in daylight, unlike other sea turtle species. Kemp's ridley populations have declined drastically over the past several decades—in 1947, approximately 42,000 females nested in one day. In 1990, only 300 females were observed. Since then, Kemp's ridley numbers have improved a little, with approximately 900 females tallied in Mexico in 1999.

The decline of the Kemp's ridley turtle is due primarily to human activities such as egg collecting, fishing for juveniles and adults, and killing of adults for meat or other products. In addition, Kemp's ridleys have been subject to high levels of incidental take by shrimp trawlers. They are also affected by pollution from oil wells, and by floating debris in the Gulf of Mexico, which can choke or entangle turtles. Now under strict protection, the population appears to be in the earliest stages of recovery, with numbers having increased annually for several years. Population increase can be attributed to two primary factors—full protection of nest-

ing females and their nests in Rancho Nuevo, and TED requirements for shrimp trawlers in the U.S. and Mexican waters. Prior to TED requirements, shrimp boats killed 500 to 5,000 Kemp's ridleys each year. Responsibility for conservation of the Kemp's ridley turtle is shared by the Fish and Wildlife Service and the National Marine Fisheries Service because turtles nest on land but otherwise live in the ocean.

In the late 1970s, biologists attempted to establish a second nesting site for Kemp's ridleys on the Padre Island National Seashore in Texas. In 2001, eight Kemp's ridley nests were found there. Padre Island is also the site of a captive breeding program for Kemp's ridleys—eggs are collected from nests and raised in a protected environment. After hatching, baby turtles are returned to the sea. This allows turtle hatchlings to bypass one of the most dangerous parts of the life cycle—approximately 85 percent of hatchlings survive incubation at the station, whereas only 17 percent survive in unprotected nests. In 2001, 656 eggs were incubated at the Padre Island Station, and several hundred turtles released. In 2002, a record 23 nests were found, and about 1,887 hatchlings were ultimately released in the fall of 2002.

However, in 2002, the National Park Service issued permits to BNP Petroleum for drilling gas wells in Padre Island's seaside dunes. The Sierra Club filed a lawsuit against the Fish and Wildlife Service, the National Park Service, and Secretary of the Interior Gale Norton for failing to adequately assess the impact of drilling on Kemp's ridley.

FIGURE 6.5

The desert tortoise is threatened due to habitat destruction, livestock grazing, invasion of non-native plant species, collection, and predation by ravens. *(U.S. Fish and Wildlife Service)*

Desert Tortoise

The desert tortoise (see Figure 6.5) was listed in 1990 as threatened in most of its range in the Mojave and Sonoran Deserts in California, Arizona, Nevada, and Utah. Decline of this species has resulted from collection by humans, predation of young turtles by ravens, off-road vehicles, invasive plant species, and habitat destruction due to development for agriculture, mining, and livestock grazing. Livestock grazing is particularly harmful to tortoises because it results in competition for food, as well as the trampling of young tortoises, eggs, or tortoise burrows. Invasive plant species have caused declines in the native plants that serve as food for tortoises. Off-road vehicles destroy vegetation and sometimes hit tortoises.

Desert tortoise populations are constrained by the fact that females do not reproduce until they are 15 to 20 years of age (individuals can live 80–100 years), and by small clutch sizes, with only 3–14 eggs per clutch. Juvenile mortality is also extremely high, with only 2 to 3 percent surviving to adulthood. About half this mortality is due to predation by ravens, whose populations in the desert tortoise's habitat have increased with increasing urbanization of desert areas—human garbage provides food for ravens and power lines provide perches.

Protected habitat for the desert tortoise includes areas within Joshua Tree National Park and Lake Mead National Recreation Area in Nevada and Arizona. There is also a Desert Tortoise Research Natural Area on a Bureau of Land Management habitat in California. A Habitat Conservation Plan for the area around Las Vegas requires developers to pay fees for tortoise conservation.

Snakes and Lizards

There are approximately 2,400 species of snakes and 3,800 species of lizards. Although they represent the largest group of reptiles, snakes and lizards are also among the least studied. There are numerous groups of lizards, including iguanas, chameleons, geckos, and horned lizards, among many others. There are even "flying" lizards found in the tropical forests of Southeast Asia—these are not capable of true flight, like birds and bats, but actually glide with "wings" formed by skin stretched over mobile and elongated ribs. Most lizards are carnivorous, although there are some herbivorous species as well, including the iguanas. Snakes are elongate reptiles that have, during the course of evolution, lost their limbs. All species are carnivorous. Most snakes are adapted to eating relatively large prey items, and have highly mobile jaws that allow them to swallow large prey. In some species, the jaw can be unhinged to accommodate prey. Several groups of snakes are also characterized by a poisonous venom which they use to kill prey.

In 2004 there were 12 U.S. snakes and 9 U.S. lizards listed as threatened or endangered.

SAN FRANCISCO GARTER SNAKE. The San Francisco garter snake is one of the most endangered reptiles in the United States. It was one of the first species to be listed under the Endangered Species Act. The decline of this species can be attributed primarily to habitat loss resulting from urbanization. Most of the snake's habitat was lost when the Skyline Ponds, located along Skyline Boulevard south of San Francisco County along the San Andreas Fault, were drained in 1966 for development. In addition, the building of the San Francisco International Airport and the Bay Area Rapid Transit regional commuter network destroyed additional snake habitat. Pollution and illegal collection have also contributed to the species' decline. Most San Francisco garter snakes today inhabit areas in San Mateo County, south of San Francisco. The species lives close to streams or ponds and feeds mainly on frogs, including Pacific tree frogs, small bullfrogs, and California red-legged frogs, which are also endangered.

LAKE ERIE WATERSNAKE. The Lake Erie watersnake inhabits portions of the Ohio mainland, as well as several small islands in Lake Erie. Its population has declined due primarily to habitat loss and human persecution, among other factors. Table 6.4 summarizes the sources of stress on Lake Erie watersnake populations, as well as the severity of stress and restoration feasibility. Historical and current ranges for the species are described in Figure 6.6. The Lake Erie watersnake is now extinct on three islands that it previously inhabited. The species was listed as threatened in 1999, and a recovery plan was completed by the Fish and Wildlife Service in September 2003.

MONITO GECKO. The endangered Monito gecko is a small lizard less than two inches long. This species exists only on the 38-acre Monito Island off the Puerto Rican coast. Endangerment of the Monito gecko has resulted from human activity and habitat destruction. After World War II the U.S. military used Monito Island as a site for bombing exercises, causing large-scale habitat destruction. The military also introduced predatory rats, which

TABLE 6.4

Threats to the Lake Erie watersnake

Stress	Source of stress	Severity	Restoration feasibility	Score
Mortality	intentional human-induced killing	high	medium	5
Hibernation habitat alteration	interior island development—homes, roads, commercial development	medium	low	5
Summer habitat alteration	shoreline development—construction of docks, marinas, erosion protection, etc.	low	low	4
Summer habitat degradation	incompatible shoreline management practices	low	medium	3
Habitat loss	weather events	low	low	4
Mortality	weather events	low	low	4
Mortality	roadkill	low	medium	3

Note: Threats were scored based on level of severity and feasibility of restoration. The score of the stress increases as severity increases and restoration feasibility decreases. Scores for secerity are as follows: low = 1; medium = 2; high = 3. Scores for restoration feasibility are as follows: low = 3; medium = 2; high = 1. Scores are achieved by adding the value of the severity and restoration feasibility columns. A score of 6 represents the most severe threat, while 2 represents the least severe threat.

SOURCE: "Table 2. Assessment of Threats to the Lake Erie Watersnake," in *Lake Erie Watersnake Recovery Plan (Nerodia sipedon insularum)*, U.S. Fish & Wildlife Service, Great Lakes-Big Rivers Region (Region 3), Fort Snelling, MN, September 2003

FIGURE 6.6

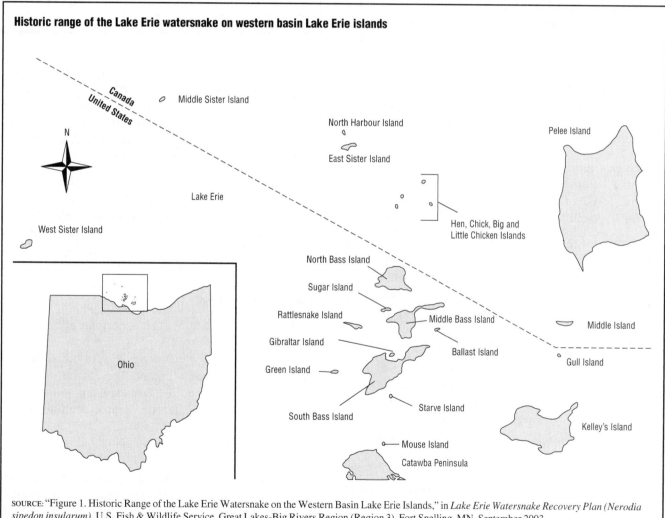

Historic range of the Lake Erie watersnake on western basin Lake Erie islands

SOURCE: "Figure 1. Historic Range of the Lake Erie Watersnake on the Western Basin Lake Erie Islands," in *Lake Erie Watersnake Recovery Plan (Nerodia sipedon insularum)*, U.S. Fish & Wildlife Service, Great Lakes-Big Rivers Region (Region 3), Fort Snelling, MN, September 2003

eat gecko eggs. In 1982 the FWS observed only 24 Monito geckos on Monito Island. In 1985 Monito Island was designated critical habitat for the species. The Commonwealth of Puerto Rico is now managing the island for the gecko and as a refuge for seabirds; unauthorized human visitation is prohibited.

FIGURE 6.7

Once abundant across Texas, the Texas horned lizard has disappeared from much of its habitat. *(Corbis Corporation. Reproduced by permission.)*

FIGURE 6.8

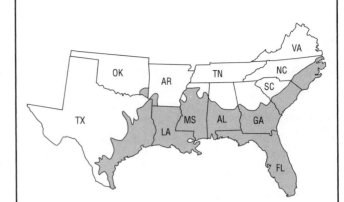

Range of the American alligator *(alligator mississippiensis)*

SOURCE: H. C. Percival, S. R. Howarter, K. G. Rice, C. R. Morea, C. L. Abercrombie, K. Portier, A. G. Finger, "Range of the American Alligator *(Alligator mississippiensis)*," in *Thermoregulation of the American Alligator in the Everglades,* U.S. Department of the Interior, U.S. Geological Survey, Center for Coastal Geology, Miami, FL, December 2000 [Online] http://sofia.usgs.gov/geer/2000/posters/ thermoreg_gator/ [accessed February 17, 2004]

MONITOR LIZARDS. In contrast to the Monito gecko, monitor lizards are among the largest lizard species in existence. The Komodo dragon, native to only a few islands in Indonesia, is the world's largest lizard. It reaches lengths of as much as ten feet and weighs as much as 300 pounds. Despite the fact that the Komodo dragon is protected under Appendix I of the CITES treaty, one of the greatest threats to this species is illegal trade. The price on delivery is approximately $30,000 for one Komodo dragon specimen.

Gray's monitor, a species found in forested low mountain habitats on the Philippine Islands, is also prized in illegal trade. Gray's monitor is also protected under CITES Appendix I.

HORNED LIZARDS (HORNY TOADS). Horned lizards, sometimes called "horny toads," are native to the deserts of North America. There are 14 species of horned lizards. All species have flat, broad torsos and spiny scales and feed largely on ants. Although all horned lizards are reptiles, they are often referred to as horny toads because they bear some resemblance to toads in size and shape.

The Texas horned lizard (see Figure 6.7) was once abundant in the state of Texas and was designated the official state reptile in 1992. It has declined largely as a result of pesticide pollution, the spread of invasive fire ants across the state, and habitat loss. It is protected by state law in Texas.

Crocodilians

There are 22 existing species of crocodilians, a group that includes crocodiles, alligators, caimans, and gavials. Crocodilians play a crucial role in their habitats. They control fish populations and also dig water holes, which are important to many species in times of drought. The disappearance of alligators and crocodiles has a profound effect on the biological communities these animals occupy.

Worldwide, 17 species of crocodilians are in serious danger of extinction. Illegal trade poses one of the greatest threats to crocodilians, despite CITES restrictions. Conservation efforts include enforcement of trade restrictions and habitat restoration. Captive breeding programs are also underway for several species.

The Chinese alligator is one of many species listed in CITES Appendix I. Unfortunately, this species is among those most prized by collectors, commanding a black market price of as much as $15,000. The false gavial, a crocodilian that grows to 13 feet in length and is native to Indonesia, sells for an estimated $5,000 per specimen. Like the Chinese alligator, the false gavial is protected under CITES Appendix I.

In the United States, the American alligator was once a threatened species but has now recovered enough to qualify for delisting. Figure 6.8 shows the range of the American alligator. The elusive and reclusive American crocodile, however, remains highly endangered. Less than 500 American crocodiles remain in Florida swamps.

Tuatara

The two-foot-long, lizard-like tuatara is sometimes called a living fossil, being the sole existing representative of a once diverse group. Tuataras are native to New Zealand and the Cook Strait. Like many other reptiles, tuataras are valued by collectors. They are protected by CITES under Appendix I.

CHAPTER 7
ENDANGERED MAMMALS

The majority of threatened and endangered mammals are imperiled for the same reasons as other biological species—habitat destruction, pollution, competition with invasive species, and so on. However, some mammals have also been intentionally killed-off by humans. For example, in the nineteenth century, the quagga of southern Africa was hunted to extinction because it competed with sheep for grazing land. Similarly, in the late nineteenth and early twentieth centuries, the thylacine, or Tasmanian tiger, was driven to extinction through hunting, in response to its attacks on domestic sheep.

Other mammal species have been driven to endangerment or extinction because they are seen as dangerous. Large predators such as grizzly bears, wolves, and mountain lions are endangered at least partly for this reason. Changing attitudes have led to interest in preserving all species, and conservation measures have allowed several predatory mammals to recover. As their populations increase, however, encounters with humans are also becoming more common.

- In California, following a ban on mountain lion hunting, reports of mountain lions rose through the 1990s. In January 2004 a mountain lion killed one bicyclist and severely injured a second in southern California. The mountain lion was later found and shot. In 114 years, California has reported a total of fourteen mountain lion attacks, of which six were fatal.

- In Yosemite National Park in California, black bears have increasingly confronted park visitors, causing significant damage and occasional injury. However, biologists attribute the incidents not to aggressive bears but to careless park visitors. In 2001 park officials killed a female bear, the mother of two cubs, because she was allegedly teaching her cubs to raid cars, campsites, and picnic areas for food.

- In 2000 biathlete Mary Beth Miller was mauled to death by a black bear as she ran along a wooded path

during her training routine in Quebec, Canada. The tragedy ignited controversy over attempts by Canadian officials to protect the species, including the cancellation of an annual bear hunt.

LEVELS OF ENDANGERMENT

In 2004 there were a total of 342 threatened and endangered mammals listed under the Endangered Species Act. Of the endangered mammals, 65 are found in the U.S. and 251 are foreign. Of the threatened species, 9 are found in the U.S. and 17 are foreign. U.S. threatened and endangered mammals are shown in Table 7.1. Some mammalian groups that are particularly well-represented on the U.S. list include bats (9 species), bears (3 species), kangaroo rats (6 species), mice (10 species), and whales (7 species).

The 2003 *Red List* report of the World Conservation Union (IUCN) reports that 1,130 mammals, or 24 percent of species examined, are threatened globally. Nearly all are imperiled because of human activity. The last major IUCN assessment of the Red List, in 2000, revealed that a large majority—83 percent—are endangered due to loss of habitat. This was significantly worse than in the 1996 assessment, when 478 species were listed. The IUCN Director-General, Maritta con Bieberstein Koch-Weser, described the 2000 results as "a jolting surprise, even to those already familiar with today's increasing threats to biodiversity." The habitat types occupied by the largest numbers of threatened mammal species are lowland and tropical rainforests, both of which are being rapidly degraded. In 2003, the countries that harbored the largest number of threatened mammals included Indonesia (147), India (86), China (81), Brazil (74), Mexico (72), Australia (63), Papua New Guinea (58), Kenya (50), the Philippines (50), Madagascar (50), Malaysia (50), Peru (46), Russia (45), Vietnam (42), Tanzania (41), the Democratic Republic of the Congo (40), Myanmar (39), the United States

TABLE 7.1

Endangered or threatened mammals, February 2004

Status	Species name	Status	Species name
E	Bat, gray *(Myotis grisescens)*	E	Mouse, St. Andrew beach *(Peromyscus polionotus peninsularis)*
E	Bat, Hawaiian hoary *(Lasiurus cinereus semotus)*	E	Ocelot *(Leopardus [=Felis] pardalis)*
E	Bat, Indiana *(Myotis sodalis)*	XN, T	Otter, southern sea *(Enhydra lutris nereis)*
E	Bat, lesser long-nosed *(Leptonycteris curasoae yerbabuenae)*	E	Panther, Florida *(Puma [=Felis] concolor coryi)*
E	Bat, little Mariana fruit *(Pteropus tokudae)*	T	Prairie dog, Utah *(Cynomys parvidens)*
E	Bat, Mariana fruit (=Mariana flying fox) *(Pteropus mariannus mariannus)*	E	Pronghorn, Sonoran *(Antilocapra americana sonoriensis)*
E	Bat, Mexican long-nosed *(Leptonycteris nivalis)*	E	Puma (=cougar), eastern *(Puma [=Felis] concolor couguar)*
E	Bat, Ozark big-eared *(Corynorhinus [=Plecotus] townsendii ingens)*	T(S/A)	Puma (=mountain lion) *(Puma [=Felis] concolor* [all subsp. except *coryi*]*)*
E	Bat, Virginia big-eared *(Corynorhinus [=Plecotus] townsendii virginianus)*	E	Rabbit, Lower Keys marsh *(Sylvilagus palustris hefneri)*
T(S/A)	Bear, American black *(Ursus americanus)*	E	Rabbit, pygmy *(Brachylagus idahoensis)*
XN, T	Bear, grizzly *(Ursus arctos horribilis)*	E	Rabbit, riparian brush *(Sylvilagus bachmani riparius)*
T	Bear, Louisiana black *(Ursus americanus luteolus)*	E	Rice rat *(Oryzomys palustris natator)*
E	Caribou, woodland *(Rangifer tarandus caribou)*	E	Seal, Caribbean monk *(Monachus tropicalis)*
E	Deer, Columbian white-tailed *(Odocoileus virginianus leucurus)*	T	Seal, Guadalupe fur *(Arctocephalus townsendi)*
E	Deer, key *(Odocoileus virginianus clavium)*	E	Seal, Hawaiian monk *(Monachus schauinslandi)*
E, XN	Ferret, black-footed *(Mustela nigripes)*	E, T	Sea-lion, Steller *(Eumetopias jubatus)*
E	Fox, San Joaquin kit *(Vulpes macrotis mutica)*	E	Sheep, bighorn *(Ovis canadensis)*
E	Jaguar *(Panthera onca)*	E	Sheep, bighorn *(Ovis canadensis californiana)*
E	Jaguarundi, Gulf Coast *(Herpailurus [=Felis] yagouaroundi cacomitli)*	E	Shrew, Buena Vista Lake ornate *(Sorex ornatus relictus)*
E	Jaguarundi, Sinaloan *(Herpailurus [=Felis] yagouaroundi tolteca)*	E	Squirrel, Carolina northern flying *(Glaucomys sabrinus coloratus)*
E	Kangaroo rat, Fresno *(Dipodomys nitratoides exilis)*	E, XN	Squirrel, Delmarva Peninsula fox *(Sciurus niger cinereus)*
E	Kangaroo rat, giant *(Dipodomys ingens)*	E	Squirrel, Mount Graham red *(Tamiasciurus hudsonicus grahamensis)*
E	Kangaroo rat, Morro Bay *(Dipodomys heermanni morroensis)*	T	Squirrel, northern Idaho ground *(Spermophilus brunneus brunneus)*
E	Kangaroo rat, San Bernardino Merriam's *(Dipodomys merriami parvus)*	E	Squirrel, Virginia northern flying *(Glaucomys sabrinus fuscus)*
E	Kangaroo rat, Stephens' *(Dipodomys stephensi* [including *D. cascus*]*)*	E	Vole, Amargosa *(Microtus californicus scirpensis)*
E	Kangaroo rat, Tipton *(Dipodomys nitratoides nitratoides)*	E	Vole, Florida salt marsh *(Microtus pennsylvanicus dukecampbelli)*
T	Lynx, Canada *(Lynx canadensis)*	E	Vole, Hualapai Mexican *(Microtus mexicanus hualpaiensis)*
E	Manatee, West Indian *(Trichechus manatus)*	E	Whale, blue *(Balaenoptera musculus)*
E	Mountain beaver, Point Arena *(Aplodontia rufa nigra)*	E	Whale, bowhead *(Balaena mysticetus)*
E	Mouse, Alabama beach *(Peromyscus polionotus ammobates)*	E	Whale, finback *(Balaenoptera physalus)*
E	Mouse, Anastasia Island beach *(Peromyscus polionotus phasma)*	E	Whale, humpback *(Megaptera novaeangliae)*
E	Mouse, Choctawhatchee beach *(Peromyscus polionotus allophrys)*	E	Whale, right *(Balaena glacialis* [including *australis*]*)*
E	Mouse, Key Largo cotton *(Peromyscus gossypinus allapaticola)*	E	Whale, Sei *(Balaenoptera borealis)*
E	Mouse, Pacific pocket *(Perognathus longimembris pacificus)*	E	Whale, sperm *(Physeter catodon [=macrocephalus])*
E	Mouse, Perdido Key beach *(Peromyscus polionotus trissyllepsis)*	E, XN, T	Wolf, gray *(Canis lupus)*
T	Mouse, Preble's meadow jumping *(Zapus hudsonius preblei)*	E, XN	Wolf, red *(Canis rufus)*
E	Mouse, salt marsh harvest *(Reithrodontomys raviventris)*	E	Woodrat, Key Largo *(Neotoma floridana smalli)*
T	Mouse, southeastern beach *(Peromyscus polionotus niveiventris)*	E	Woodrat, riparian (=San Joaquin Valley) *(Neotoma fuscipes riparia)*

E = Endangered
T = Threatened
T(SA) = Similarity of appearance to a threatened taxon
XN = experimental population, non-essential

SOURCE: Adapted from "U.S. Listed Vertebrate Animal Species Report by Taxonomic Group as of 02/17/2004," Threatened and Endangered Species System (TESS), U.S. Fish and Wildlife Service, Washington, DC, 2004 [Online] http://ecos.fws.gov/tess_public/TESSWebpageVipListed?code=V&listings=0#E [accessed February 17, 2004]

(39), Columbia (39), Cameroon (38), Thailand (37), and Japan (37).

The biggest cause of mammalian decline and extinction in the twentieth century is habitat loss and degradation. As humans convert forests, grasslands, rivers, and wetlands for various uses, they relegate many species to precarious existences in small, fragmented habitat patches. Primates, for example, are highly threatened partly because they are dependent on large expanses of tropical forests, a habitat under siege worldwide. In regions where tropical forest degradation and conversion have been most intense, such as South and Southeast Asia, Madagascar, and Brazil, as many as 70 percent of native primate species face extinction.

The introduction of invasive species by humans has also taken a toll on mammalian wildlife. Australia is overrun with domestic cats whose ancestors were brought by settlers to the island continent two hundred years ago. Stray domestic cats have driven indigenous species such as bandicoots, bettongs, numbats, wallabies, and dozens of other bird and mammal species, most of which are found nowhere else on Earth, towards extinction. Richard Evans, a member of the Australian Parliament, claims the feral cats are responsible for the extinction of at least thirty-nine species in Australia. He has called for total eradication of cats from the island by 2020, to be achieved by neutering pets and spreading feline diseases in the wild. The Australian National Parks and Wildlife Service reports that each house cats kills twenty-five native animals each year on average, and feral domestic cats kill as many as 1,000 per year.

THE BLACK-FOOTED FERRET

The black-footed ferret (see Figure 7.1) is a small furrow-digging mammal and member of the weasel fami-

FIGURE 7.1

Black-footed ferrets, once thought extinct, are now being successfully bred in captivity. A few reintroduced ferret populations are doing well. *(U.S. Fish and Wildlife Service)*

ly. Nocturnal creatures, ferrets help to control populations of snakes and rodents, including their primary prey, black-tailed prairie dogs. Black-footed ferrets once ranged over eleven Rocky Mountain states as well as parts of Canada. They have declined drastically because of the large-scale conversion of prairie habitats to farmland, and because their primary prey, prairie dogs, have been nearly exterminated by humans. Prairie dogs are considered pests because they dig holes and tunnels just beneath the ground surface. These can cause serious injury to horses or other large animals that step into them. (Some municipalities also poison prairie dogs in city parks, where burrow holes can trip and injure humans.) Poisons used to kill prairie dogs may also kill some ferrets.

Black-footed ferret populations had declined so greatly that the species was put on the Endangered Species List in 1973. However, prairie dog poisonings continued, and by 1979 it was believed that the black-footed ferret was extinct. In 1981 a ferret was sighted in Wyoming and discovered to be part of a remnant population. Rewards were offered for more sightings, and by the end of the year a few black-footed ferret populations had been located. These typically existed in close proximity to prairie dog popula-

tions in sagebrush-heavy areas. In 1985 ferret populations were struck by disease, and by 1987, only eighteen black-footed ferrets were in existence. These individuals were captured and entered into a captive breeding program.

The captive breeding of ferrets has been reasonably successful. There are now core populations of 269 breeding-age individuals in five zoos in the U.S. and Canada as well as one Fish and Wildlife Service facility. In 1999 a total of 133 kits were born. The Fish and Wildlife Service has also tried to reintroduce black-footed ferrets in several states. Studies suggest that each population of black-footed ferret requires approximately 10,000 acres of black-tailed prairie dog habitat to survive. Unfortunately, prairie dogs are also in decline due to habitat loss and episodes of sylvatic plague, which have decimated many populations. Although some reintroductions have failed, two are doing well—one in National Forest habitat in Conata Basin/Badlands, South Dakota, and another in the Charles M. Russell National Wildlife Refuge in Montana. In 2000 there were already many more wild-born than captive-born ferrets at those sites. The Fish and Wildlife Service recovery plan for black-footed ferrets hopes to move the species from endangered to threatened status by 2010. This would require that 1,500 breeding adults exist in the wild in a minimum of ten separate locations, with a minimum of 30 breeding adults included in each population. Captive breeding and reintroductions of black-footed ferrets were organized by the Black-Footed Ferret Recovery Implementation Team, and involved twenty-six separate state and federal organizations, conservation groups, and Native American tribes.

NORTHERN IDAHO GROUND SQUIRREL

The Northern Idaho ground squirrel was listed as a threatened species in April 2000. It occurs only in two counties in Idaho. The species was initially listed after the population dropped from 5,000 individuals in 1985 to less than 1,000 in 1998. In 2002, an estimated 450–500 ground squirrels were believed to exist. Figure 7.2 shows the historical range of the species as well as current primary and secondary populations.

The Northern Idaho ground squirrel is threatened primarily by habitat loss. It occupies dry rocky meadows at moderate elevation which have been increasingly lost to forest encroachment. Other factors leading to its threatened status include shooting by humans, poisoning, natural events, and competition from the Columbian ground squirrel, a larger species. The listing factors and recovery action recommendations, from the recovery plan completed in July 2003, appear in Table 7.2.

WOLVES

Wolves were once among the most widely distributed mammals on Earth. Prior to European settlement, wolves

FIGURE 7.2

Northern Idaho ground squirrel probable historical distribution and primary/secondary metapopulation sites, 2003

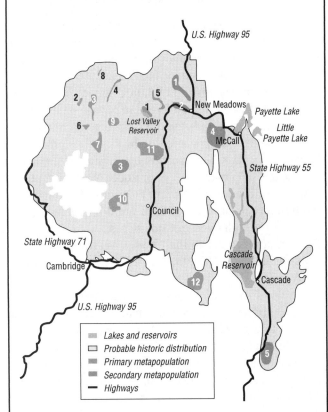

Legend:
- Lakes and reservoirs
- Probable historic distribution
- Primary metapopulation
- Secondary metapopulation
- Highways

Primary metapopulation sites

1. Lost Valley—Slaughter Gulch
2. Tree Farm—Calf Pen—Summit
3. Bear Meadows Complex—Rocky Comfort Flat
4. Lick Creek Canyon (Fawn Creek to upper Lick Creek)
5. Price Valley
6. Paradise Flat—Ditch Creek Road
7. Cottonwood—Halfway—Mill Creek
8. Huckleberry—Mesa
9. Chipmunk Springs
10. Johnson Creek—Pole Creek
11. Warm Springs—Fruitvale
12. West Mountain

Secondary metapopulation sites

1. Mud Creek
2. New Meadows
3. North Hornet area
4. Ecks Flat—Rock Flat—Big Creek
5. Round Valley

Note: Primary metapopulation sites are predominantly on lands administered by the Forest Service, but there are some state and private lands included. Secondary metapopulation sites are predominantly on private lands that could be useful in the recovery of the subspecies if landowners are willing to participate in this conservation effort.

SOURCE: Adapted from "Figure 3. Northern Idaho Ground Squirrel Probable Historical Distribution Map and Primary and Secondary Metapopulation Sites" and "Table 3. Northern Idaho Ground Squirrel Primary and Secondary Metapopulation Sites and Land Ownership," in *Recovery Plan for the Northern Idaho Ground Squirrel (Spermophilus brunneus brunneus)*, U.S. Fish and Wildlife Service, Region 1, Portland, OR, July 2003

TABLE 7.2

Listing factors and threats for the northern Idaho ground squirrel

Listing factor	Threat	Still a threat?
A	Forest encroachment into grassland meadows/fire suppression	Yes
A	Conversion of meadows to agriculture	Yes
A	Grazing practices	Unknown/ needs evaluation
A	Residential construction	Yes
A	Development of recreational facilities, *e.g.*, golf courses	Yes
A	Dam expansion for irrigation	Yes
A	Road construction and maintenance	Yes
B	Recreational shooting	Yes
C	Predation, primarily by badgers	Yes
C	Disease, plague	Potential only
D	Inadequate local land use ordinances relating to housing developments	Yes
E	Land ownership patterns	Yes
E	Winter mortality	Yes

Listing factors:
A. The present of threatened destruction, modification, or entailment of its habitat or range
B. Overutilization for commercial, recreational, scientific, educational purposes (not a factor)
C. Disease or predation
D. The inadequacy of existing regulatory mechanisms
E. Other natural or man made factors affecting its continued existence

SOURCE: Adapted from "Table 4. Cross-Reference of Recovery Actions and Listing Factors for the Northern Idaho Ground Squirrel," in *Recovery Plan for the Northern Idaho Ground Squirrel (Spermophilus brunneus brunneus)*, U.S. Fish and Wildlife Service, Region 1, Portland, OR, July 2003

the removal of all large predators, including wolves, from federal lands. By the 1940s wolves had been eliminated from most of the contiguous United States. In 1973 the wolf, which had all but disappeared, became the first animal listed as endangered under the Endangered Species Act. Two species of wolves exist in North America today, the red wolf and the gray wolf. Both are imperiled.

The Gray Wolf Reintroduction Program

In 1991 Congress instructed the Fish and Wildlife Service to prepare an environmental impact report on the possibility of reintroducing wolves to habitats in Yellowstone National Park and central Idaho. Reintroductions began in 1995, when fourteen Canadian gray wolves were released in Yellowstone National Park.

Wolf reintroductions were not greeted with universal enthusiasm. Ranchers, in particular, were concerned that wolves would attack livestock. They were also worried that their land would be open to government restrictions as a result of the wolves' presence. Some ranchers said openly that they would shoot wolves they found on their land. Several measures were adopted to address ranchers' concerns. The most significant was that ranchers would be reimbursed for livestock losses from a compensation fund maintained by the Defenders of Wildlife, a private conservation group based in Washington, D.C. As of 2004 the

ranged over most of North America, from central Mexico to the Arctic Ocean. Their decline has largely resulted from hunting. In 1914 Congress authorized funding for

FIGURE 7.3

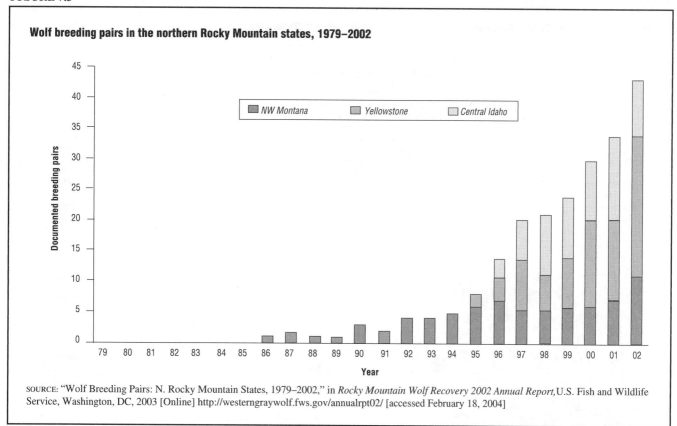

Wolf breeding pairs in the northern Rocky Mountain states, 1979–2002

SOURCE: "Wolf Breeding Pairs: N. Rocky Mountain States, 1979–2002," in *Rocky Mountain Wolf Recovery 2002 Annual Report,* U.S. Fish and Wildlife Service, Washington, DC, 2003 [Online] http://westerngraywolf.fws.gov/annualrpt02/ [accessed February 18, 2004]

fund had paid out $359,124 to 295 ranchers, covering the losses of 399 cattle, 1001 sheep, and 49 other animals killed by wolves.

Nonetheless, wolf introductions were legally challenged in 1997, when the American Farm Bureau Federation initiated a lawsuit calling for the removal of wolves from Yellowstone. The farm coalition scored an initial victory, but in January 2000 the 10th Circuit Court of Appeals in Denver overturned the decision upon appeal by the United States Department of the Interior, the World Wildlife Fund, and other conservation groups.

As of 2002 the FWS had reintroduced forty-one wolves into Yellowstone and thirty-five wolves into central Idaho. Wolf packs in both Yellowstone and Idaho have thrived. Figure 7.3 shows the number of breeding pairs in northwest Montana, Yellowstone, and Central Idaho from 1979 to 2002. A map of the wolf recovery area is shown in Figure 7.4.

Despite the concern of ranchers and livestock owners, a recovered wolf population in the Yellowstone Park area has only slightly reduced populations of cattle, sheep, elk, moose, bison, and deer. In fact, wolves weed out sick and weak animals, thus improving the overall health of prey populations. Wolf predation on herbivorous species also takes pressure off vegetation and produces carrion for an array of scavengers including eagles, ravens, cougars, and foxes. Finally, wolves have increased visitor attendance to

Yellowstone National Park, generating an estimated $7–10 million in additional net income each year.

In 2002 the wolf population in the continental United States was estimated at 3,500 individuals. The gray wolf was officially reclassified by the Fish and Wildlife Service from endangered to threatened in March 2003, and delisted in areas outside the western and eastern recovery regions.

The Mexican Gray Wolf

In 1998 the Fish and Wildlife Service began to reintroduce rare Mexican gray wolves, the smallest of North America's gray wolves, into federal lands in the Southwest. This distinct subspecies once occupied habitats in central and southern Arizona, central New Mexico, western Texas, and northern Mexico. The Mexican gray wolf had been hunted to near extinction in the late 1800s and early 1900s in the United States. By 1960 only seven individuals survived in captivity. Captive breeding programs in the U.S. and Mexico have helped to increase population numbers. Released Mexican gray wolves are being tracked using radio collars. Subsequent releases are expected to create a viable population of one hundred individuals by 2005.

The Red Wolf

The red wolf (see Figure 7.5) was once found throughout the eastern United States, but declined as a

FIGURE 7.4

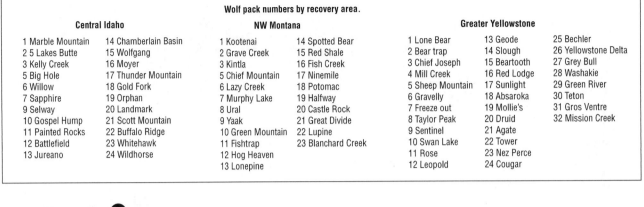

Central Idaho, northwest Montana, and Greater Yellowstone wolf recovery areas, 2002

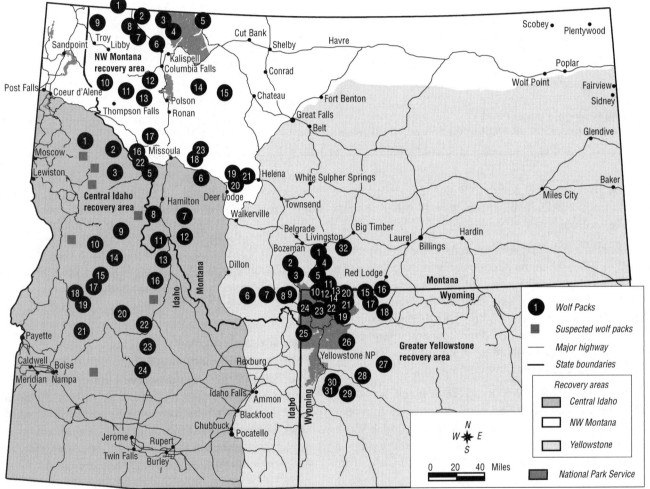

SOURCE: "Figure 1. Central Idaho, Northwest Montana, and Greater Yellowstone Wolf Recovery Areas," in *Rocky Mountain Wolf Recovery 2002 Annual Report*, U.S. Fish and Wildlife Service, Washington, DC, 2003 [Online] http://westerngraywolf.fws.gov/annualrpt02/ [accessed February 18, 2004]

result of habitat loss and aggressive hunting by humans. It has been considered endangered since 1967. The red wolf is a smaller species than its relative, the gray wolf, and, despite its name, may have any of several coat colors including black, brown, gray, and yellow. In 1975, to prevent the immediate extinction of this species, the Fish and

Wildlife Service captured the twenty-some remaining individuals and began a captive breeding program. The red wolf reintroduction program began in 1987, marking the first reintroduction of a species extinct in the wild. Red wolves now reside over about one million acres in North Carolina and Tennessee, including three National

FIGURE 7.5

The red wolf is one of the most endangered animals in the world, with an estimated population of less than 300. *(U.S. Fish and Wildlife Service)*

FIGURE 7.6

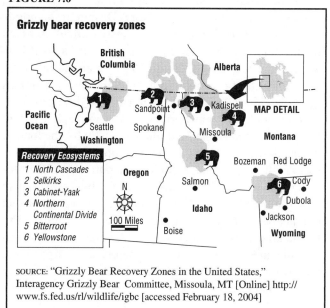

SOURCE: "Grizzly Bear Recovery Zones in the United States," Interagency Grizzly Bear Committee, Missoula, MT [Online] http://www.fs.fed.us/rl/wildlife/igbc [accessed February 18, 2004]

Wildlife Refuges, a Department of Defense bombing range, some state-owned lands, and private property (with the permission and cooperation of landowners). As of 2002 there are nearly one hundred red wolves in these populations, with about 90 percent of these born in the wild. There are also approximately two hundred red wolves managed among captive-breeding facilities around the lower forty-eight states.

BEARS AND PANDAS

Bears and pandas are imperiled worldwide. In 2002 seven species were listed as in immediate danger of extinction under Appendix I of the Convention on International Trade in Endangered Species (CITES): the giant panda (China), red panda (Himalayas), Asiatic black bear, sloth bear (Asia), sun bear (Asia), spectacled bear (South America), and grizzly bear (North America). U.S. bear species listed by the Fish and Wildlife Service in 2004 included the American black bear, the Louisiana black bear, and the grizzly bear.

Many bears are endangered due to habitat loss. According to the Fish and Wildlife Service, bears have been eliminated from about 50 to 75 percent of their natural ranges. Some bears have traditionally been hunted because they are considered predatory or threatening. Others are hunted for sport. In addition, bears are killed in large numbers by poachers, who sell bear organs and body parts in the illegal wildlife trade. These organs usually end up in Asia, where they are valued as ingredients in treatments for ailments or illnesses, or to delay the effects of aging—although there is no evidence that such treatments are effective.

Grizzly Bears

The grizzly bear was originally found throughout the continental United States, but has now been eliminated from every state except Colorado, Idaho, Montana, Washington, and Wyoming. In 2004, there were an estimated 1,000 individuals in the wild, down from some 50,000 to 100,000

before human interference. The grizzly bear has declined due primarily to aggressive hunting and habitat loss. It is listed as threatened under the Endangered Species Act.

Grizzly bears are large animals, standing four feet high at the shoulder when on four paws, and as tall as seven feet when upright. Males weigh 500 pounds on average but are sometimes as large as 900 pounds. Females weigh 350 pounds on average. Grizzlies have a distinctive shoulder hump, which actually represents a massive digging muscle. Their claws are two to four inches long. They are more aggressive than black bears.

The federal government has established recovery zones for the grizzly bear in Yellowstone National Park, the North Continental Divide, the Selkirk and Bitterroot Mountains in Idaho, the North Cascades, the San Juan Mountains in Colorado, and the Cabinet/Yaak area on the Canadian border. (See Figure 7.6.) Recovery plans for this species are coordinated under the Interagency Grizzly Bear Committee, which was created in 1983.

Giant Pandas

Few creatures have engendered more human affection than the giant panda, with its roly-poly character, small ears, and black eye patches on a snow-white face. Giant pandas are highly endangered, with only approximately 1,000 pandas in the wild and some one hundred individuals in captivity. Pandas are found only in portions of southwestern China, where they inhabit a few fragmentary areas of high altitude bamboo forest. Unlike other bear species, to which they are closely related, pandas have a vegetarian diet that consists entirely of bamboo. Pandas also have a "sixth digit" which functions like a thumb, and which they use to peel tender bamboo leaves from their stalks.

Pandas have become star attractions at many zoos, where they draw scores of visitors. Despite tremendous efforts, pandas have proven notoriously difficult to breed in captivity. The birth of a giant panda cub, named Hua Mei, at the San Diego Zoo in 1999 was a major event, with millions of people following the cub's progress online and in the papers through her first days of life. A second panda cub was born at the zoo in 2003. The San Diego Zoo pays China $1 million annually for the loan of the pandas. These funds are used to support panda conservation efforts in China, including the purchase of land for refuges as well as the development of habitat corridors to link protected areas. The agreement also requires that pandas born at the San Diego Zoo will be returned to China after they are three years old. Hua Mei was flown to China in February 2004 to join nearly seventy pandas at the Wolong Giant Panda Protection Research Centre in the Sichuan Province of China.

Red Pandas

The red panda is also called the lesser panda because it is significantly smaller than the giant panda. Red pandas are not, like giant pandas, related to bears—they are actually raccoon relatives. Red pandas are virtually extinct in the wild, mostly because of habitat loss and degradation. Red pandas occupy temperate forests in the foothills of the Himalayas in Nepal, Burma, and southwestern China at altitudes between 5,000 and 13,000 feet. They are solitary creatures, occupying non-overlapping home ranges of approximately one square mile for females and two square miles for males. Like giant pandas, red pandas eat bamboo, focusing on the most tender leaves. Because bamboo is not very nutritious, red pandas spend as much as thirteen hours each day eating in order to acquire the nutrients they need. Red pandas have difficulty recovering from population declines because of a slow rate of reproduction. A captive breeding effort for red pandas is underway at zoos across the world to prevent the complete extinction of this species. Over three hundred red pandas are found in captivity.

BIG CATS

Of the nearly forty feline, or cat, species, only one—the domestic cat—is believed to be secure. As undeveloped land becomes harder to find, large cats, such as lions, panthers, tigers, jaguars, and cheetahs, are left with less and less natural habitat in which to live.

Mountain Lions—America's Large Cat

The mountain lion is a seven-foot-long cat that can weigh between 70 and 170 pounds. It was once found throughout North America from southern Argentina to northern British Columbia, making it one of the most widely distributed terrestrial species on the continent. It is also known as the panther, puma, or cougar, and preys on large animals, particularly deer. Mountain lions may also eat wild hogs, rabbits, and rodents. They require large home ranges for securing food—a single individual may have a home range spanning 85 square kilometers. By 1900 the species was nearly extinct due to habitat loss and hunting. Until the 1960s, many states offered monetary rewards for the killing of mountain lions. Mountain lions are now found primarily in mountainous, unpopulated areas.

Conservation efforts have met with success in some portions of the country. In fact, there are now so many encounters between humans and mountain lions in California that hikers and park officials are given instruction in how to react to these large cats. Scientists attribute the increased encounter rate to more wilderness ventures by humans as well as a larger mountain lion population—an estimated 6,000 individuals. Because of these events, some people are demanding that hunting be reinstituted.

In most of the eastern United States, however, mountain lions have long been presumed extinct. If they are present, they are still extremely rare. In 1997 several sightings were reported in the Appalachian Mountains, but these have not been confirmed.

THE FLORIDA PANTHER. The Florida panther is one of twenty-seven subspecies of the mountain lion. It has been considered endangered since 1967, and there are only thirty to fifty individuals surviving in the wild. The Florida panther has declined due to loss of habitat to urbanization and development, water contamination, and highway traffic. Its population is now so small that many individuals suffer from genetic disorders due to inbreeding. Ninety percent of male Florida panthers suffer from sperm abnormality, sterility, congenital heart defects, and possible immune deficiencies due to long-term inbreeding. Experts fear the species may die out in less than 20 years without aggressive intervention.

In 1994 and 1995 scientists and wildlife managers introduced Texas cougars, the Florida panthers' closest relatives, into habitats in Florida. Eight female Texas cougars were released. Biologists hoped that interbreeding would strengthen and diversify the Florida panther gene pool. "This is a very drastic measure and not one we ordinarily undertake," reported Dr. John Fay of the U.S. Department of the Interior. Dr. Fay noted that the strategy had helped save woodland caribou in Idaho and Washington in the 1980s, when individuals were interbred with Canadian caribou. In fact, Florida panthers and Texas cougars once formed a single, interbreeding population that ranged freely throughout the southeastern United States. They were eventually isolated from each other by human encroachment a little more than a hundred years ago.

Other efforts are also underway to help maintain the existing Florida panther gene pool. A captive breeding program was initiated in 1991 with ten panther cubs that had been removed from the wild. It is hoped that captive breeding will allow for the establishment of two additional populations of 50 individuals each. Scientists are also hopeful that the habitat destruction that threatens the Florida panther has slowed. The primary issue in panther conservation today is providing large enough expanses of protected habitat for the species. This is particularly challenging not simply because the carnivores need large home ranges to feed, but because male panthers are territorial and will not tolerate the presence of other males. About half the area occupied by Florida panthers is private land, including farms, ranches, and citrus groves adjacent to protected reserves. Efforts are being made to secure the cooperation of landowners in conservation efforts.

As a result of the Florida panther's plight and public affection for the animal, in 1982 Florida declared the panther its state animal. Florida businessman Wayne Huizenga named his National Hockey League (NHL) team the Florida Panthers and has pledged many thousands of dollars to panther recovery efforts.

Jaguars

The jaguar is the largest cat in the Americas, measuring five to six feet long and weighing some two hundred pounds. Jaguars once ranged from Arizona to Argentina, but are now quite rare in the United States, where they may still occur in low numbers in Arizona, New Mexico, and Texas. Jaguars are listed as endangered throughout their range, which also includes Mexico and Central and South America. An estimated 15,000 individuals remain in the wild. Jaguars occupy a wide variety of habitats, from dense jungle and scrubland to reed thickets, forests, and even open country. They prey on wild pigs, rodents, deer, sloths, tapirs, and a variety of smaller species. They are endangered primarily due to habitat destruction and habitat fragmentation. Because they are so rare, much of what is known about the species comes from studying zoo populations.

Tigers

Wild tigers are found exclusively in Asia, from India to Siberia. Although the world tiger population surpassed 100,000 in the nineteenth century, experts fear that as few as 7,000 tigers remained in 2004. Approximately 2,000 of these are found in captivity. In addition to habitat loss, countless tigers fall victim to the illegal wildlife trade every year. Many tiger body parts are used as ingredients in traditional Chinese medicine, and the big cats are also prized in the exotic pet industry.

In 1999 the Wildlife Conservation Society reported a rebound in the world tiger population, in part because of a worldwide moratorium on tiger hunting imposed by CITES listing. However, ecologists warn that tigers, which hunt deer, wild pigs, cattle, antelope, and other large mammals, are threatened seriously by loss of prey, much of which consists of non-protected species being eliminated by hunters.

In January 2004 Indian officials announced that the endangered Bengal tiger population might be increasing in the Sunderbans Forest, a World Heritage Site and one of the last protected wild habitat areas for tigers. The census was completed by locating, plaster-casting, and studying tiger paw prints, or pugmarks, in the forest. Tiger pugmarks are unique the same way human fingerprints are unique. Most encouraging was the fact that the number of cub prints had increased in 2004.

On the other hand, the World Conservation Union (IUCN) declared that the Sumatran tiger was on the verge of extinction in March 2004, with only four hundred to five hundred individuals remaining in the wild. The IUCN also called on the Indonesian government to stop habitat destruction and poaching. Approximately fifty Sumatran tigers were killed each year by poachers between 1998 and 2002.

THE SIBERIAN TIGER. The Siberian tiger (see Figure 7.7) is the largest cat in the world and one of the world's most endangered species, with only five hundred individuals estimated to exist in the wild. There are also several hundred Siberian tigers in captivity. The Siberian tiger, also known as the Amur tiger, once occupied mixed deciduous and coniferous forest habitats in the Amur-Ussuri area in Siberia, as well as in northern China and Korea. It is now believed to be extinct, or nearly extinct, in China and Korea. Individuals reach lengths of eight to ten feet and weigh up to 800 pounds. They eat wild boars, Sika deer, and elk. Siberian tigers are territorial and require large home ranges of some 500 to 600 square miles.

Populations have suffered greatly from habitat loss caused by logging and deforestation, as well as illegal trade. The Siberian tiger is sought for its skin, bones, eyes, whiskers, teeth, internal organs, and genitals. These are used for everything from skin cures to tooth medicine. In Russia, where unemployment is high, poachers have flooded nearby Asian markets with tiger parts. In 1995 alone, poachers killed more than sixty-five Siberian tigers. The financially strapped Russian government can devote neither money nor time to protecting the tigers. Like the Florida panther, the Siberian tiger has also been weakened by inbreeding, which increases the possibility of reproductive problems and birth defects.

Cheetahs

The cheetah is the fastest land animal on Earth, able to sprint at speeds up to 70 mph. Cheetahs occupy grassland, shrubland, and woodland habitats. Their range once extended through most of Africa as well as southwestern Asia. Currently, cheetahs are found only in a few areas in

FIGURE 7.7

The Siberian tiger is one of the most endangered species in the world. It now occupies forest habitats in the Amur-Ussuri region of Siberia. *(Field Mark Publications)*

Iran, North Africa, and sub-Saharan Africa. Cheetahs hunt small prey, particularly Thomson's gazelle. The cheetah has been listed in CITES Appendix I since 1975. In 2004 there were an estimated 10,000 cheetahs in the wild.

Cheetah populations have declined for many reasons. Much of the species' habitat has been developed for agricultural or ranching use, and many of the cats are shot by farmers who wish to protect their livestock. In addition, cheetahs are badly inbred, and many individuals are infertile. In addition, cheetahs are smaller and less aggressive than other predators that share their environment (including lions and leopards) and often have their food kills stolen or their cubs killed. Conservation biologists have determined that in order to save the cheetah, human assistance in the form of habitat protection, protection from competitor species, and measures to improve the genetic diversity of the species are required.

RHINOCEROS

Rhinoceros are among the largest land mammals. They weigh up to 8,000 pounds—as much as fifty average-sized men—and are herbivorous grazers. The name rhinoceros is made up of two Greek words meaning "nose" and "horn," and rhinos are in fact the only animals on Earth that have horns on their noses. Figure 7.8 shows an African white rhinoceros with two horns. The female may be identified by her longer, more slender primary horn.

Rhinoceros have roamed the land for more than 40 million years, but in less than a century, humans—their only predators—have reduced populations to dangerously low levels. There are five species of rhinoceros—the black rhino (African), white rhino (African), Sumatran rhino (found in Borneo, Malaysia, and Sumatra), Javan rhino (found in Indonesia and Vietnam), and Indian rhino (found in both India and Nepal). Certain rhino species can be divided into distinct subspecies. For example, the Javan rhino has two subspecies, one found in Vietnam, the

other in Indonesia. The Vietnamese subspecies consists of only one tiny population of five to seven individuals, and was thought extinct until this tiny population was discovered in 1999. All rhinos are close to extinction. In 2004 the International Rhino Foundation (IRF) estimated populations of 11,670 for the white rhino, 3,100 for the black rhino, 2,400 for the Indian rhino, 300 for the Sumatran rhino, and 60 for the Javan rhino. Some individuals are also found in captivity.

Hunting has been the primary cause of rhinoceros decline. Rhinoceros horn is highly prized as an aphrodisiac, as well as an ingredient in Chinese medicine (although its potency has never been shown). Rhinos were first listed by CITES in 1976. This banned international trade in the species and their products. In 1992 CITES also started requiring the destruction of horn caches confiscated from poachers. Nonetheless, people continue to buy and consume rhinoceros horn, and many poachers are willing to risk death to acquire it.

Indian Rhinos

Conservation efforts have improved the status of some rhino species. The Indian rhinoceros, which was reduced to fewer than one hundred individuals in the mid-1970s, has experienced significant population growth in the past twenty-five years. In 2004 the IRF reported some 2,400 Indian rhinos in the wild. Population increase resulted from habitat protection, including the designation of several national parks, as well as measures that curbed poaching.

The Royal Chitwan National Park was established in Nepal in 1973 and includes over 1,000 square kilometers of protected habitat. At the time of establishment, fewer than 80 Indian rhinos were found in the park. Troops from the Royal Nepalese Army were dispatched to help prevent poaching. Indian rhinos flourished at Royal Chitwan, and individuals were later transported to a second rhino conservation area at Royal Bardia National Park, a few hundred miles from Royal Chitwan. In April 2002 the Department of National Parks and Wildlife Conservation in Nepal reported 529 rhinos at Royal Chitwan and 63 at Royal Bardia, a substantial increase from when conservation efforts began.

However, in April 2002 the Department of National Parks and Wildlife Conservation reported that thirty-nine rhinos had died in the past twelve months at Royal Chitwan. Of these, only nine were believed to have died from natural causes. Twenty-five were almost certainly killed by poachers. Horns and other body parts had been removed from the carcasses. Two other rhinos were found electrocuted and three had been poisoned. These were found intact by park officials, who believe that they were killed by villagers whose crops were damaged by rhinos in areas adjacent to the park. The 2002 numbers represent the continuation of a disturbing pattern—forty-two rhinos died in 1999 and twenty-three were killed in 1997–1998.

FIGURE 7.8

The white rhinoceros is native to Africa and can weigh up to 8,000 pounds. *(U.S. Fish and Wildlife Service)*

African Rhinos

Africa is home to two species of highly imperiled rhinoceros, the black rhino and the white rhino. Both species have a second, smaller horn situated slightly behind the larger main horn. They are threatened primarily by poaching. Wildlife officials in Zimbabwe, Swaziland, and Namibia have gone so far as to sever rhino horns in an effort to curtail poaching. Most experts, however, discourage the practice, as animals use their horns for both digging and defense. In 2004 the IRF reported 3,100 black rhinos in the wild. Of the black rhinoceros subspecies, the northwestern variety is the most severely endangered, with only ten currently found in the wild. Approximately 11,000 white rhinos were reported in 2004. African rhino numbers have risen in recent years, primarily due to improved management as well as private sector and community involvement. Captive breeding efforts for the African rhino species have also met with some success, particularly at the San Diego Wild Animal Park, and may aid in the conservation of these species.

ELEPHANTS

Elephants are the largest land animals on Earth. They are frequently described as the "architects" of the savanna habitats in which they live. Elephants dig water holes, keep forest growth in check, and open up grasslands that support other species, including the livestock of African herders. Elephants are highly intelligent, emotional animals and form socially complex herds. There are two species of elephants, African elephants and Asian elephants, both of which are highly endangered. The African elephant (see Figure 7.9), which sometimes weighs as much as six tons, is the larger species. In 2004 there were an estimated 500,000 African elephants and 50,000 Asian elephants in the wild.

Elephants have huge protruding teeth—tusks—made of ivory. Ivory is valued by humans for several reasons, particularly for use in making jewelry and figurines. Piano keys were also once made almost exclusively of ivory; however, that practice has ceased. The market for ivory has had tragic consequences for African elephants. Their numbers dropped from over 10 million individuals in 1900 to only 600,000 in 1989. As a result of this decline, the UN-administered CITES banned worldwide commerce in ivory and other elephant products in 1990. However, like rhinoceros horns, elephant tusks continue to be illegally traded. Numerous elephants are poached each year. The price of poached elephant ivory is reported to be as high as $90 per pound.

Despite continued poaching, elephant populations have recovered somewhat since receiving CITES protection. In 1997 Zimbabwe requested that CITES change the listing status of the African elephant in three South African nations—Zimbabwe, Botswana, and Namibia—

FIGURE 7.9

Elephants are highly intelligent and social animals. Once on the verge of extinction, elephants have recovered somewhat after a worldwide ban on the ivory trade. *(Field Mark Publications)*

movement to allow the culling of elephants, noting that its national conservation parks were overrun. At South Africa's Kruger Park, for example, 7,000 elephants occupied an area designated to support 5,000 individuals. Under the South African plan, the funding for elephant culling would be obtained through a legitimate, but limited, international trade in ivory and elephant skin. Kenya and India, on the other hand, renewed a request to relist the elephant under CITES Appendix I, as immediately endangered. In the end, the opposing factions reached a compromise in which both proposals were withdrawn—elephants remained listed under Appendix II, and the ban on ivory sales remained in effect.

At the 2002 CITES Conference, CITES conditionally accepted one-time sales by Botswana, Namibia, and South Africa of ivory collected from elephants that died a natural death. However, the sales can occur only after data is collected on poaching and population levels. CITES Secretary-General Willem Wijnstekers said:

> The African elephant is valued and admired by people all over the world. But it is significant that today's decision embodies an African solution to an African problem—the challenge of conserving the continent's wild herds of elephants in an age of growing human needs and population. While richer countries can often afford to promote conservation through strict protection, many poorer nations must do so in ways that benefit local communities and bring in much-needed cash for conservation. In the African context, a conservation strategy based on sustainable use may offer elephants the best possible long-term future. The key is finding solutions that benefit states that rely on tourism as well as those that seek income from elephant products.

Although the ivory trade has always been the largest threat to elephants, conflicts between humans and elephants are an increasing issue. The ranges of many elephant herds now extend outside protected refuges, and elephants frequently come into contact with farmers, eating or otherwise destroying crops. Increasing human settlement in areas inhabited by elephants will likely result in more conflicts over time.

PRIMATES

The World Conservation Union (IUCN), in its *2003 Red List of Threatened Species*, reported that the 295 examined species of primates (excluding humans) are among the most endangered mammals. Since the 1996 IUCN assessment, the number of "critically endangered" primates increased from thirteen to twenty species, and the number of "endangered" primates rose from twenty-nine to forty-seven. Another forty-seven primates are considered "vulnerable." Critically endangered primate species included the Roloway monkey (lowland tropical rainforest in Ghana and Cote d'Ivoire), Mentawai macaque (Indonesia), Sclater's black lemur (lowland trop-

from Appendix I status (a species in immediate danger of extinction) to Appendix II status (threatened in the absence of trade controls), and include a yearly quota for ivory trade. South Africa has requested a similar downlisting. Kenya, India, and other nations, along with many environmental organizations, opposed the downlisting, in part because they felt that a reopening of the ivory trade might cause a resurgence in demand and poaching. CITES responded by downlisting the elephant to Appendix II, while simultaneously initiating a program, the Monitoring of Illegal Killing of Elephants (MIKE) to better assess poaching. Although MIKE statistics would not be available until 2003, CITES did approve an experimental interim proposal allowing a one-time sale of stockpiled ivory from Namibia, Botswana, and Zimbabwe to Japan. This one-time ivory transaction was made in 1999 and grossed approximately $5 million.

At the 2000 CITES Conference, South Africa, Zimbabwe, Namibia, and Botswana again petitioned CITES to authorize ivory sales. South Africa also spearheaded a

ical rainforest, Madagascar), red-handed howling monkey (Brazil), and the black lion tamarin (lowland tropical rainforest, Brazil), among others. Much of the increased endangerment of primate species is due to loss of habitat and hunting.

Brazil is home to the largest number of primate species—seventy-seven at present—followed by Indonesia (33), Democratic Republic of Congo (33), and Madagascar (30). Many of the most endangered primate species are found on Madagascar, which has a diverse and unique primate fauna. The majority of Madagascar's primate species are endemic—that is, they are found nowhere else on earth.

Habitat loss, especially the fragmentation and conversion of tropical forests for road building and agriculture, contributes to the decline of nearly 90 percent of all IUCN-listed primates. In Indonesia and Borneo, for example, home to most of the world's 20,000 to 30,000 orangutans (see Figure 7.10), deforestation has shrunk orangutan habitat by over 90 percent. A 2004 census suggested that the total orangutan population has halved in the last fifteen years. Logging and extensive burning have caused many orangutans to flee the forests for villages, where they have been killed or captured by humans.

Thirty-six percent of threatened primates also face pressures from excessive hunting and poaching. Today, almost all countries have either banned or strictly regulated the trade of primates, but these laws are often hard to enforce. Large numbers of primates are also used in medical research because of their close biological relationship with humans.

Not all relationships between primates and humans are exploitative. People in some regions protect primates from harm by according them sacred status or by making it taboo to hunt or eat them. One of the rarest African monkeys, the Sclater's guenon, survives in three areas of Nigeria in part because residents regard the animal as sacred.

Good news arrived in January 2004 when it was announced that the highly endangered mountain gorilla had experienced a population rebound, with numbers increasing 17 percent since 1989 in the Virunga forest of Rwanda, Uganda, and The Democratic Republic of Congo. Gorilla populations had plummeted in the 1960s and 1970s due to civil unrest, habitat destruction, and poaching. A total of 380 mountain gorillas were counted in the Virunga Forest, and an additional 320 were identified in the Bwindi Impenetrable Forest National Park in Uganda.

BIGHORN SHEEP

A hundred years ago, desert bighorn sheep were commonly seen climbing the mountains of the American West. The species is named for its large, curved horns, which males use to battle for access to females, wrestling with horns interlocked. Overhunting and disease have decimated bighorn sheep populations across the U.S. In Texas, for

FIGURE 7.10

The orangutan is highly endangered, along with the majority of the world's primate species. *(Field Mark Publications)*

example, the number of bighorn sheep had fallen to 500 by 1903, when hunting was finally banned. In 1945 the state set aside 11,625 acres for bighorn sheep habitat in the Sierra Diablo Wildlife Management Area near Big Bend National Park. As populations continued to decline, Texas began to import desert bighorns from other states for captive breeding. Despite these efforts, the last native bighorn in Texas is believed to have died in the 1960s.

Since then, however, new management efforts have met with some success. Private landowners have donated the use of thousands of acres of mountainous terrain as breeding grounds for reintroduced bighorns. Unlike other subjects of restoration efforts, such as wolves, bighorns pose no threats to ranchers—they do not prey on livestock, and they graze in remote areas, where they do not compete with livestock. Bighorn sheep also offer landowners potential income through the sale of hunting permits—when biologists determine the sheep population has surplus rams, the state may issue a limited number of hunting permits. The permits are rare and are very expensive, frequently commanding five-figure prices. They are issued only to landowners participating in the restoration effort. The first Texas permit sold for $61,000. In 1993 a hunter paid more than $300,000 at auction for an Arizona permit. Money raised from hunting permits is put back into bighorn sheep conservation. In 1998 experts estimated the population of bighorn sheep in Texas at 320 and at almost 30,000 nationwide.

In 1998 the Fish and Wildlife Service proposed an emergency endangered listing for the California peninsular bighorn sheep, a subspecies of the common bighorn. In July 2000 the Fish and Wildlife Service proposed critical habitat for these sheep. Estimated at 1.5 million in the early 1800s, the population size had dwindled due to disease, overhunting, loss of habitat, fragmentation of habitat, and predation. A helicopter survey conducted in fall 2000 estimated that some the population of peninsular bighorn is around four hundred.

FIGURE 7.11

Bison are the largest terrestrial animals in North America. *(Field Mark Publications)*

BISON

Sixty million bison (see Figure 7.11)—or buffalo—once roamed the grasslands of America. Historical accounts describe herds stretching as far as the eye could see. Although Native Americans hunted bison, it was not until European settlers came with firearms that their numbers fell drastically. Many people shot the animals for fun, while others sold the hides. Bison numbers were eventually reduced to fewer than 1,000. Today they are found in the Great Plains from Mexico to Canada.

The bison is the largest terrestrial animal in North America. It has short, pointed horns and a hump over the front shoulders. The head, neck, and front parts of the body are covered by a thick, dark coat of long, curly hair; the rear has shorter, lighter hair. Adult males weigh as much as 1,800 to 2,400 pounds; females are smaller. Adult males also have black "beards" about a foot long. Bison are social animals and travel in herds. Considering their size and weight, bison are remarkably light on their hooves—unlike cattle, they love to run and are surprisingly fast. Bison were central to the existence of Plains Native Americans, who used them for food and made clothing from their hides and tools from

their bones. The dried dung, called buffalo chips, was used for fuel.

Bison first received protection from the U.S. government in 1872, with the establishment of Yellowstone National Park in Wyoming and Montana. However, the welfare of the small herd of bison in the park was largely ignored until 1901, when it was discovered that only twenty-five individuals remained. The herd was restored to 1,000 by 1930 with bison imported from the Great Plains. As the Yellowstone herd multiplied, the park service shot animals to keep the population under control. This practice was unnecessary, however, because harsh winters caused the herd to dwindle naturally. The park service stopped shooting bison in the 1960s, and by 1994 the population of the Yellowstone herd had reached a peak of 4,200 animals. Over 3,000 individuals were documented in April 2002.

However, conflict over bison management continues at the park. Half the Yellowstone bison are carriers of a cattle disease called brucellosis. In domestic cattle, it can cause miscarriage in pregnant cows. Although there is no evidence that the disease can be transmitted from bison to livestock, and the popular elk in the area also carry brucellosis, ranchers are nonetheless wary.

Today some populations of bison are managed as livestock because they have become a food source for humans. Bison are a source of high-protein, low-fat, low-cholesterol meat. The National Bison Association estimates that 150,000 bison are slaughtered for food each year, producing 7.5 million pounds of meat. Bison meat is not expected to replace beef, but some people think it might become an alternative red meat source. In *Bring Back the Buffalo!* (Washington, DC: Island Press, 1996), researcher and writer Ernest Callenbach argues that bison will gradually gain support as a food source, as it becomes evident that bison are better adapted to grasslands and require much less human management than cattle. There are even bison ranchers abroad, including in Canada, Southern France, Switzerland, and Belgium.

By the end of the twentieth century, the National Bison Association reported a total of over 350,000 bison in the 48 continental United States, Alaska, and Canada—344,000 bison were privately owned, and 13,000 lived in public herds. An additional 1,000 lived in zoos or outside of the United States and Canada.

REBIRTH OF THE QUAGGA

Why do zebras have stripes? Nobody knows for sure. Although scientists have proposed a variety of theories, none has proved conclusive. What is known is that among the varieties of African plains zebras, those that are native to southern Africa display less striping than zebras that inhabit the northern regions. Perhaps the most uniquely

FIGURE 7.12

Three quaggas now run at a national park in South Africa, the result of a program to rebreed this zebra subspecies from other subspecies. *(AP/Wide World Photos)*

striped variety of zebra was the quagga, or Burchell's zebra. The quagga, a lightly browned zebra, displayed virtually no striping on its hindquarters and legs (see Figure 7.12). In the nineteenth century, sheep and goat herders who settled within the quagga's grazing range hunted the odd-looking animal literally to extinction. When the last living quagga died at the Amsterdam Zoo on August 12, 1883, all that remained of the species were 23 preserved animal skins.

Approximately 100 years later, scientists analyzed tissue from an old quagga skin and discovered that, genetically, the quagga was nearly identical to other zebras—it was therefore likely to be a subspecies of zebra and not a separate species, as had originally been thought. A selective breeding project was undertaken in 1987 in an attempt to breed zebras that had the striping traits of the extinct quagga. South African taxidermist Reinhold Rau

spearheaded the project. He hypothesized that the genes that code for the distinctive color and striping patterns of quaggas existed recessively in South African zebras of the late twentieth century. Quagga project members assembled a collection of zebras that most closely resembled the extinct quagga in striping and coloring and began the slow process of breeding successive generations that increasingly resembled the quagga. By 2000 the project had produced a number of individuals that resembled the preserved quagga skins in pattern, and others that resembled the skins in color. However, no individuals resembled the extinct animal in both striping and coloring. The project received public funding for the first time in June 2000, as breeding attempts continued.

A similar project was underway to rebreed the endangered Mongolian Przewalski horse and another to rebreed the tarpan, a European wild horse.

CHAPTER 8
THE STATUS OF BIRD SPECIES

Birds have always been among the best-studied biological groups, in part because of the efforts of countless amateur birdwatchers. In 2003 the World Conservation Union (IUCN) reported that 129 bird species have gone extinct, with another four species extinct in the wild. The rate of extinction among birds has increased every fifty years. Bird species have died out because of habitat destruction, hunting and collection, pollution, and predation by non-native species. The extinction rate of bird species is alarming not only because of the irrevocable loss of each species but also because of implications for the health of entire ecosystems.

The United States government has long recognized the importance of bird biodiversity and promoted habitat conservation under the Migratory Bird Conservation Act, passed by Congress in 1929. This law established the Migratory Bird Conservation Commission, which works with the Secretary of the Interior to designate and fund avian wildlife refuge areas. The U.S. Fish and Wildlife Service is responsible for acquiring necessary lands through direct purchase, lease, or easement (agreement with landowners). The Fish and Wildlife Service has procured over 4 million acres of land for bird refuges.

Birds received considerable attention in the *2003 IUCN Red List of Threatened Species*. A total of 1,194 bird species were considered threatened—one of every eight described species. Another 727 bird species were considered "near threatened." There were 182 bird species categorized as "critically endangered," a significant increase from 168 listed species only seven years earlier. Of these critically endangered species, a large majority— 89 percent—have been harmed by loss of habitat. The number of "endangered" birds listed by the IUCN also increased dramatically, from 235 to 331 species.

Certain groups of birds have declined particularly. All twenty-one albatross species are considered threatened

under the 2003 *Red List*, due largely to deaths from long-line fishing. Prior to the rise of long-line fishing, most albatross populations were fairly stable. The number of threatened penguin species has also jumped, increasing to ten in 2003. Finally, rapid deforestation in Southeast Asian rainforests has increased the number of threatened doves, parrots, and perching birds.

Less than 5 percent of Earth's land area is home to 75 percent of the world's threatened bird species. The largest numbers of endangered birds are found in Indonesia, the Philippines, Brazil, Colombia, China, Peru, India, and Tanzania. New Zealand and the Philippines have the highest proportion of threatened species, with 42 percent and 35 percent respectively.

WHAT ARE THE MAJOR THREATS TO BIRDS?
Habitat Loss and Environmental Decline
The driving force behind current declines in many bird species is the destruction, degradation, and fragmentation of habitat due to increasing human population size and the wasteful consumption of resources. The leading cause of habitat destruction in the United States is agricultural development. Large corporate farms cause environmental damage by clearing out native plant species, planting only one or a few crops, and draining wetlands. Natural habitats are also lost to urban sprawl, logging, mining, and road building.

Tropical bird species are threatened by large-scale deforestation worldwide. In Asia, for example, a 2001 study by BirdLife International suggested that one in four bird species is threatened, the majority due to loss of forest habitat. Populations have declined especially sharply in the last two decades, coincident with what BirdLife International calls "habitat loss or degradation resulting from unsustainable and often illegal logging, and land or wetland clearance for agriculture or exotic timber plantations." Large species, such as the Philippine eagle, are most quickly harmed by deforestation—these require large areas of undisturbed forest to hunt and breed.

Many Arctic bird species are threatened by habitat loss due to global warming. In April 2000 the World Wildlife Fund released a report indicating that a world climate change as small as 1.7 degrees centigrade (about 3.3 degrees Fahrenheit) would significantly reduce tundra habitat—the frozen arctic plain that serves as a breeding ground for many bird species. Among the tundra species already threatened are the red-breasted goose, the tundra bean goose, and the spoon-billed sandpiper.

Island species are also particularly vulnerable to habitat destruction because their ranges are usually very small to begin with. In addition, because many island birds evolved in the absence of predators, there are a large number of flightless species—these are highly vulnerable to hunting or predation by introduced species, including humans, cats, dogs, and rats. At one time some 75 percent of all bird extinctions occurred on islands. It is estimated that two-thirds of Hawaii's original bird fauna is already extinct. Of the remaining one-third, a large majority are imperiled. Habitat destruction in Hawaii has been so extensive that all the lowland species now present are non-native species introduced by humans.

Pesticides

During the latter half of the twentieth century, pesticides and other toxic chemicals were recognized as a major cause of avian mortality and a primary factor in the endangerment of several species, including the bald eagle and peregrine falcon. While the U.S. Environmental Protection Agency regulates the manufacture and use of toxic chemicals nationwide, the Fish and Wildlife Service (under the Federal Insecticide, Fungicide, and Rodenticide Act [Amended 1988]) is responsible for preventing and punishing the misuse of chemicals that affect wildlife.

Many chemicals harmful to birds, such as DDT and toxaphene, have been banned. Other chemicals, such as endrin, the most toxic of the chlorinated hydrocarbon pesticides, are still legal for some uses. Endrin was responsible for the disappearance of the brown pelican from Louisiana, a population that once numbered 50,000 individuals.

Oil Spills

Oil spills constitute a major threat to birds. (See Figure 8.1.) One of the worst and most infamous spills in history occurred on March 24, 1989, when the *Exxon Valdez* tanker released 11 million tons of crude oil into Alaska's Prince William Sound. To many Americans, it still exemplifies the disastrous effects oil spills have on wildlife. Thousands of birds died immediately after coming in contact with the oil, either from losing the insulation of their feathers or by ingesting lethal amounts of oil when they tried to clean

themselves. Exxon personnel burned untold piles of birds; others were saved in cold storage under orders from the Fish and Wildlife Service. A complete count was never obtained, but Wildlife Service biologists estimated that between 250,000 and 400,000 sea birds died.

Approximately 40 percent of the region's entire population of common murres—estimated at 91,000—was eliminated. The yellow-billed loon population was also seriously depleted, as was the population of Kittlitz's murrelet, a species found almost exclusively in Prince William Sound. Other affected bird species included the bald eagle, black oystercatcher, common loon, harlequin duck, marbled murrelet, pigeon guillemot, and the pelagic, red-faced, and double-crested cormorants. Of these, the common loon, the harlequin duck, the pigeon guillemot, and the three species of cormorants have not increased in population size since the spill and were still considered "not recovered" in 2002. In addition, the Kittlitz's murrelet appears to be suffering from continued population decline, and its future prospects appear bleak.

The detergents used to clean up oil spills can also be deadly to waterfowl—detergents destroy feathers, which leads to fatal chills or trauma. Research has shown that even after careful rehabilitation, birds that have been returned to nature after a spill often die in a matter of months. In 1996 Dr. Daniel Anderson, a biologist at the University of California at Davis, found that only 12 to 15 percent of rehabilitated pelicans survived for two years, compared to the 80 to 90 percent of pelicans not exposed to oil. For many ornithologists, these dismal results raise the issue of whether avian rescue efforts are worthwhile. Could money spent on rehabilitation be better used for spill prevention and habitat restoration? Oregon ornithologist Dr. Brian Sharp argues that the cleanup effort might ease the conscience of the public and of politicians, but in reality, does very little to benefit birds. However, new methods of treating oiled birds and of controlling spills have increased the bird survival rate from 5 percent to between 60 and 80 percent for some species. Under the Clean Water Act, the oil industry pays a tax that helps fund cleanups after spills.

Domestic Cats

Studies in the United States and Britain have shown that house cats kill millions of small birds and mammals every year, a death toll that contributes to declines of rare species in some areas. The University of Wisconsin reported that in that state alone, cats killed 19 million songbirds and 140,000 game birds in a single year. The British study reported that Britain's 5 million house cats account for an annual prey toll of some 70 million animals, 20 million of which are birds. The study also found that cats were responsible for a third to half of all the sparrow deaths in England. Both studies determined that factors such as whether a cat was well-fed at home, wore a bell collar, or was declawed made no difference to its

FIGURE 8.1

A bird is cleaned of oil after the disastrous *Exxon Valdez* spill in Prince William Sound, Alaska, in 1989. An estimated 250,000–400,000 sea birds died in the spill. *(AP/Wide World Photos)*

hunting habits. Many cat victims are plentiful urban species, but Fish and Wildlife studies show that cats also kill hundreds of millions of migratory songbirds annually. In addition, cats have devastated bird fauna on some islands and are believed to have contributed to the declines of several grassland species in the U.S.

Trade in Exotic Birds

Birds are among the most popular pets in American homes. An estimated 6–10 percent of American households own pet birds. Many of these are common finches, canaries, or parakeets, all of which are raised in captivity in the United States. However, wild birds are owned and traded as well, including numerous species of passerines (song birds) and psittacines (parrots and their relatives).

Passerines include any of the approximately 4,800 species of song birds. The most commonly traded passerines include warblers, buntings, weavers, finches, starlings, flycatchers, and sparrows. Passerines are regarded as low-value birds, and few passerines are endangered due to trade.

The 333 species of psittacines, however, are generally rarer, and thus much more valuable, than passerines. They comprise about 15 percent of the pet bird market in the United States. The most commonly traded psittacines are macaws, Amazons, cockatoos, lovebirds, lories, and parakeets. In addition to their vivid colors and pleasant songs, many of these birds possess the ability to "talk," which makes them particularly appealing to some owners. Bird dealers have created demand for an ever-increasing variety of birds, including parrots, macaws, cockatoos, parakeets, mynahs, toucans, tanagers, and other tropical species.

Laws in Mexico, Guatemala, and Honduras ban trade in parrots, and U.S. law bars importation of birds taken illegally from other countries. Some countries still allow exports, however, and there is also a great deal of smug-

gling. Legislation passed in 1992 to halt the legal importation of parrots is, ironically, believed to have increased smuggling. In 1998 customs officials announced the arrest of more than forty people for smuggling hundreds of rare parrots and other wildlife across the Mexican border. The animals seized were believed to be worth hundreds of thousands of dollars in the pet trade, although some were considered nearly priceless because of their rarity in the wild.

The illegal bird trade has severely harmed many threatened species. New York Zoological Society bird curator Don Bruning believes that species such as the scarlet macaw are now practically extinct throughout Central America due to illegal trade. Over the past twenty years, smuggling has reduced red crown parrot populations by 80 percent and yellow-headed parrots by 90 percent in Mexico. In 2000 the World Wildlife Fund (WWF) identified the horned parakeet as one of the ten species most threatened by illegal trade.

Invasive Species—The Case of Guam

Invasive species have damaged bird populations in some parts of the world, particularly those that occupy islands. Guam's unique bird fauna has been all but wiped out by the brown tree snake, an invasive species. The brown tree snake was probably introduced from New Guinea via ship cargo in the 1950s, and had spread throughout the island by 1968. The snakes have no natural enemies on the island and plentiful prey in the form of forest birds. There are now believed to be as many as 13,000 snakes in a single square mile in some forest habitats. Twelve bird species have already gone extinct on Guam, including the Guam flycatcher, the Rufus fantail, the white-throated ground dove, and the cardinal honey-eater. Several other Guam bird species are close to extinction. Many of these birds are or were unique to Guam. Measures have been implemented to try to keep this destructive snake from invading other islands, including careful inspection of all cargo arriving from Guam. The removal of the brown tree snake in select habitat areas on Guam (which is a high effort project, requiring the constant trapping of snakes) allowed the reintroduction of one bird, the flightless Guam rail, in 1998. The Guam rail had gone extinct in the wild, but a population is maintained in captivity.

Other particularly destructive invasive species include several associated with humans, including cats, dogs, and rats, which often prey on birds and their eggs. In fact, the World Conservation Union (IUCN) reports that invasive species represent the single most frequent cause of bird extinctions since 1800. Invasive species are currently estimated to affect 350, or 30 percent, of all IUCN-listed threatened birds.

Salton Sea Deaths

The Salton Sea, located 150 miles southeast of Los Angeles in the Sonora Desert, is a 35-mile-long expanse of salt marsh and open water encompassing 35,484 acres and situated 227 feet below sea level. The sea formed from a salt-covered depression known as the Salton Sink in 1905, when a levee on the Colorado River broke, filling the depression with water. Subsequently, the area has received additional water, primarily from agricultural runoff. Because the Salton Sea has no outlet, water is lost only through evaporation, leaving dissolved salts behind. The salinity (the amount of salt in the water) in the Salton Sea has increased gradually over time, and is estimated at 25 percent greater than the ocean in 2004. The Salton Sea serves as habitat for migrating birds and provides winter habitat for waterfowl. The area is second only to the Texas coastline in the number of bird species sighted, and nearly 400 species had been reported by 2004. The Salton Sea National Wildlife Refuge was established in 1930 by presidential proclamation.

In the last decades of the twentieth century the Salton Sea entered a rapid and initially inexplicable decline that resulted in the deaths of countless birds and fish. The first unusual avian deaths were reported in 1987, and a task force was created by the California Department of Fish and Game in 1988 to study the problem. In 1992 a massive die-off occurred in which over 150,000 birds died. Some of the fatalities were attributed to avian cholera, but experts remained baffled by the majority of casualties. At that point, the Department of the Interior initiated a $10 million Salton Sea project aimed at combating rising salinity and other environmental problems. The Salton Sea Authority was established in 1993 to coordinate activity. In 1996 there was another mass epidemic in which over 20,000 birds from 64 species died, including 1,200 brown pelicans, an endangered species. This time, the cause was identified as avian botulism. The same year, thousands of tilapia fish were also killed by botulism. Authorities tentatively attributed the avian deaths to botulism from consuming tainted fish. Throughout 1997 a variety of initiatives were proposed in an effort to combat high salinity and other problems at the Salton Sea. Nonetheless, in May of that year another 10,000 birds from 51 species died, along with thousands of tilapia. Causes of death included avian botulism, Newcastle disease, avian cholera, and poisoning by toxic algae.

Scientists have so far failed to establish a precise link between water quality and bird die-offs, but suspect a combination of natural and man-made contaminants. Evaporation and agricultural runoff have increased the salinity of the Salton Sea to levels 25 percent higher than in the Pacific Ocean. Experts fear that high salt levels increase the susceptibility of fish to disease, and that birds are impacted when they consume affected fish. Another suspected cause of environmental deterioration is the defunct Salton Sea Test Base (SSTB), which served as a center for arms testing and weapons research during World War II. The U.S. Army Corps of Engineers initiated a clean-up project to decontaminate the SSTB, which occupied over 20,000 acres of land and water in the southwest corner of the Salton Sea. Environmentalists also believe that agricultural runoff from California's Imperial Valley, one of the most productive farming areas in the United States, encourages algae blooms that are deadly to fish. The Salton Sea is also polluted by additional agricultural runoff from Mexico and by untreated sewage from rivers that flow across the Mexican-U.S. border. Contamination from DDT, DDE (a byproduct of DDT), and selenium also were documented as contributing to the decline.

The Salton Sea Task Force, the U.S. Bureau of Reclamation, and the California State Legislature have combined forces to restore the Salton Sea to health. However, another outbreak of botulism was reported in 2000. The endangered brown pelican suffered greatly in this outbreak, with 717 individuals dying. Another six hundred brown pelicans were rehabilitated and released in December 2000. Avian botulism is not fatal if treatment is begun early, but birds do not show symptoms until the disease has progressed. In addition to the brown pelican, thirty-five other species were affected in the 2000 outbreak. All affected species eat tilapia. Fish and Wildlife Service employees, along with California Department of Fish and Game, helped to round up sick birds and transport them to an open-air bird hospital built in 1997 from funds raised by volunteers. Recovered birds were released near the Tijuana Slough and Seal Beach national wildlife refuges, both located in Southern California.

ENDANGERED BIRD SPECIES

In 2004 there were 273 birds on the Endangered Species List. Of these, 253 are endangered, including 78 U.S. species and 175 foreign species. In addition, twenty birds are threatened, including fourteen U.S. species and six foreign species. Threatened and endangered U.S. bird species are shown in Table 8.1. This list includes many types of birds, including sparrows, albatrosses, terns, plovers, hawks, and woodpeckers. There are also a disproportionate number of Hawaiian bird species listed. Several threatened and endangered species will be discussed below.

Migratory Songbirds

Every year, more than 120 songbird species migrate between North America and tropical areas in Central and South America. Although many are appreciated by humans for their beautiful songs and colorful plumage, migratory songbirds also play a vital role in many ecosystems. During spring migration in the Ozarks, for example, some forty to fifty migratory bird species arrive and feed on the insects that inhabit oak trees, thereby helping to control insect populations. Migratory species are particularly vulnerable because they are dependent on suitable habitat in both their winter and spring ranges. In North

TABLE 8.1

Endangered or threatened bird species, February 2004

Status	Species name	Status	Species name
E	Akepa, Hawaii (honeycreeper) (*Loxops coccineus coccineus*)	T	Murrelet, marbled (*Brachyramphus marmoratus marmoratus*)
E	Akepa, Maui (honeycreeper) (*Loxops coccineus ochraceus*)	E	Nightjar, Puerto Rican (*Caprimulgus noctitherus*)
E	Akialoa, Kauai (honeycreeper) (*Hemignathus procerus*)	E	Nukupu'u (honeycreeper) (*Hemignathus lucidus*)
E	Akiapola'au (honeycreeper) (*Hemignathus munroi*)	E	'O'o, Kauai (honeyeater) (*Moho braccatus*)
E	Albatross, short-tailed (*Phoebatria [=Diomedea] albatrus*)	E	'O'u (honeycreeper) (*Psittirostra psittacea*)
E	Blackbird, yellow-shouldered (*Agelaius xanthomus*)	T	Owl, Mexican spotted (*Strix occidentalis lucida*)
E	Bobwhite, masked (quail) (*Colinus virginianus ridgwayi*)	T	Owl, northern spotted (*Strix occidentalis caurina*)
E	Broadbill, Guam (*Myiagra freycineti*)	E	Palila (honeycreeper) (*Loxioides bailleui*)
E	Cahow (*Pterodroma cahow*)	E	Parrot, Puerto Rican (*Amazona vittata*)
T	Caracara, Audubon's crested (*Polyborus plancus audubonii*)	E	Parrotbill, Maui (honeycreeper) (*Pseudonestor xanthophrys*)
E, XN	Condor, California (*Gymnogyps californianus*)	E	Pelican, brown (*Pelecanus occidentalis*)
E	Coot, Hawaiian (*Fulica americana alai*)	E	Petrel, Hawaiian dark-rumped (*Pterodroma phaeopygia sandwichensis*)
E	Crane, Mississippi sandhill (*Grus canadensis pulla*)	E	Pigeon, Puerto Rican plain (*Columba inornata wetmorei*)
E, XN	Crane, whooping (*Grus americana*)	E, T	Plover, piping (*Charadrius melodus*)
E	Creeper, Hawaii (*Oreomystis mana*)	T	Plover, western snowy (*Charadrius alexandrinus nivosus*)
E	Creeper, Molokai (*Paroreomyza flammea*)	E	Po'ouli (honeycreeper) (*Melamprosops phaeosoma*)
E	Creeper, Oahu (*Paroreomyza maculata*)	E	Prairie chicken, Attwater's greater (*Tympanuchus cupido attwateri*)
E	Crow, Hawaiian (='alala) (*Corvus hawaiiensis*)	E	Pygmy owl, cactus ferruginous (*Glaucidium brasilianum cactorum*)
E	Crow, Mariana (=aga) (*Corvus kubaryi*)	E	Rail, California clapper (*Rallus longirostris obsoletus*)
E	Crow, white-necked (*Corvus leucognaphalus*)	E, XN	Rail, Guam (*Rallus owstoni*)
E	Curlew, Eskimo (*Numenius borealis*)	E	Rail, light-footed clapper (*Rallus longirostris levipes*)
E	Duck, Hawaiian (=koloa) (*Anas wyvilliana*)	E	Rail, Yuma clapper (*Rallus longirostris yumanensis*)
E	Duck, Laysan (*Anas laysanensis*)	T	Shearwater, Newell's Townsend's (*Puffinus auricularis newelli*)
T	Eagle, bald (*Haliaeetus leucocephalus*)	E	Shrike, San Clemente loggerhead (*Lanius ludovicianus mearnsi*)
T	Eider, spectacled (*Somateria fischeri*)	E	Sparrow, Cape Sable seaside (*Ammodramus maritimus mirabilis*)
T	Eider, Steller's (*Polysticta stelleri*)	E	Sparrow, Florida grasshopper (*Ammodramus savannarum floridanus*)
E	Elepaio, Oahu (*Chasiempis sandwichensis ibidis*)	T	Sparrow, San Clemente sage (*Amphispiza belli clementeae*)
E	Falcon, northern aplomado (*Falco femoralis septentrionalis*)	E	Stilt, Hawaiian (*Himantopus mexicanus knudseni*)
E	Finch, Laysan (honeycreeper) (*Telespyza cantans*)	E	Stork, wood (*Mycteria americana*)
E	Finch, Nihoa (honeycreeper) (*Telespyza ultima*)	E	Swiftlet, Mariana gray (*Aerodramus vanikorensis bartschi*)
E	Flycatcher, southwestern willow (*Empidonax traillii extimus*)	E	Tern, California least (*Sterna antillarum browni*)
T	Gnatcatcher, coastal California (*Polioptila californica californica*)	E	Tern, least (*Sterna antillarum*)
E	Goose, Hawaiian (*Branta [=Nesochen] sandvicensis*)	E, T	Tern, roseate (*Sterna dougallii dougallii*)
E	Hawk, Hawaiian (='Io) (*Buteo solitarius*)	E	Thrush, large Kauai (=kamao) (*Myadestes myadestinus*)
E	Hawk, Puerto Rican broad-winged (*Buteo platypterus brunnescens*)	E	Thrush, Molokai (*Myadestes lanaiensis rutha*)
E	Hawk, Puerto Rican sharp-shinned (*Accipiter striatus venator*)	E	Thrush, small Kauai (=puaiohi) (*Myadestes palmeri*)
E	Honeycreeper, crested (*Palmeria dolei*)	T	Towhee, Inyo California (*Pipilo crissalis eremophilus*)
T	Jay, Florida scrub (*Aphelocoma coerulescens*)	E	Vireo, black-capped (*Vireo atricapilla*)
E	Kingfisher, Guam Micronesian (*Halcyon cinnamomina cinnamomina*)	E	Vireo, least Bell's (*Vireo bellii pusillus*)
E	Kite, Everglade snail (*Rostrhamus sociabilis plumbeus*)	E	Warbler (=wood), Bachman's (*Vermivora bachmanii*)
E	Mallard, Mariana (*Anas oustaleti*)	E	Warbler (=wood), golden-cheeked (*Dendroica chrysoparia*)
E	Megapode, Micronesian (*Megapodius laperouse*)	E	Warbler (=wood), Kirtland's (*Dendroica kirtlandii*)
E	Millerbird, Nihoa (old world warbler) (*Acrocephalus familiaris kingi*)	E	Warbler, nightingale reed (old world warbler) (*Acrocephalus luscinia*)
T	Monarch, Tinian (old world flycatcher) (*Monarcha takatsukasae*)	E	White-eye, bridled (*Zosterops conspicillatus conspicillatus*)
E	Moorhen, Hawaiian common (*Gallinula chloropus sandvicensis*)	E	Woodpecker, ivory-billed (*Campephilus principalis*)
E	Moorhen, Mariana common (*Gallinula chloropus guami*)	E	Woodpecker, red-cockaded (*Picoides borealis*)

E = Endangered
T = Threatened
XN = Experimental population, non-essential

SOURCE: Adapted from "U.S. Listed Vertebrate Animal Species Report by Taxonomic Group as of 02/17/2004," Threatened and Endangered Species System (TESS), U.S. Fish and Wildlife Service, Washington, DC, 2004 [Online] http://ecos.fws.gov/tess_public/TESSWebpageVipListed?code=V&listings=0#E [accessed February 17, 2004]

America, real estate development has eliminated many forest habitats. Migratory songbird habitats are also jeopardized in Central and South America, where farmers and ranchers have been burning and clearing tropical forests to plant crops and graze livestock. Some countries, including Belize, Costa Rica, Guatemala, and Mexico, have set up preserves for songbirds, but improved forest management is needed to save them.

The North American Breeding Bird Survey

The *North American Breeding Bird Survey* is a continent-wide study begun in 1966 and carried on annu-

ally ever since. Each year, more than 3,500 routes are surveyed by experienced birders. Surveys occur primarily during the month of June, which represents the peak in the songbird nesting season. The results of this survey allow scientists to document changes in the distributions and populations of bird species throughout North America. The survey is conducted by the Biological Resource Division of the United States Geological Survey. Results compiled from 1966 to 2002 indicate that:

• 61 percent of 28 grassland-breeding species surveyed are declining, whereas 11 percent are increasing

- 14 percent of 87 wetland-breeding species surveyed are declining, whereas 39 percent are increasing

- 36 percent of 87 successional- or scrub-breeding species are declining, whereas 15 percent are increasing

- 23 percent of 131 woodland-breeding species are declining, whereas 30 percent are increasing

- 47 percent of 15 urban-breeding species are declining, whereas 27 percent are increasing

Results among birds with different migratory strategies include:

- among 107 short distance migrants, 37 percent are declining whereas 26 percent are increasing

- among 137 neotropical migrants, 31 percent are declining whereas 24 percent are increasing

- among 93 permanent residents, 22 percent are declining whereas 25 percent are increasing

The Black-Capped Vireo and Golden-Cheeked Warbler

The black-capped vireo and golden-cheeked warbler are among the threatened songbirds listed with the Fish and Wildlife Service. Both species nest in central Texas and other locations in the U.S. and winter in Mexico and Central America. Both species have declined largely due to loss of habitat caused by land clearing for development. Another factor in the decline of the black-capped vireo is harm from "brood parasites"—bird species that lay their eggs in the nests of other species. In certain areas, more than half the black-capped vireo nests contain eggs of brood parasites called brown-headed cowbirds. The black-capped vireo was placed on the Endangered Species List in 1987, the golden-cheeked warbler in 1990.

Much of the critical nesting habitat for black-capped vireos and golden-cheeked warblers lies in the Hill Country of central Texas. The Texas Hill Country is characterized by diverse habitats and a high concentration of rare bird species. In the last decade, however, increased water demand by metropolitan areas has caused the local Edwards Aquifer to drop by thirty feet, resulting in a 15 to 45 percent decrease in available bird habitat. In an effort to balance development with wildlife preservation, the city of Austin, Texas invited The Nature Conservancy to formulate a plan to protect Hill Country habitats while enabling some development. The result was the Balcones Canyonlands Conservation Plan, which includes a 75,000-acre preserve in the Texas Hill Country.

Fort Hood, Texas, a heavy artillery training site for the U.S. Army, was designated essential nesting habitat for the golden-cheeked warbler and black-capped vireo in 1993. With the help of The Nature Conservancy, the Army currently manages some 66,000 acres of habitat for these species. Control of brown-headed cowbird populations

has been a major part of the conservation efforts. Brown-headed cowbirds parasitize the nests of over two hundred species of songbirds, and have caused declines in many of these species. Nest parasitism rates for the black-capped vireo were as high as 90 percent before control measures were begun. They are now at less than 10 percent. In 2000, surveys at Fort Hood documented 236 male black-capped vireos and 229 vireo territories, which produced an average of 1.75 fledglings each. Many other bird species also use habitat at Fort Hood, including threatened and endangered species such as the bald eagle, peregrine falcon, and whooping crane.

The California Gnatcatcher

The California gnatcatcher is a small, gray and black songbird known for its "kitten-like" mewing call. Gnatcatchers are non-migratory, permanent residents of California coastal sage scrub communities, one of the most threatened vegetation types in the nation. Estimates of coastal scrub loss in the United States range from 70 to 90 percent of historic levels.

Fewer than 2,000 pairs of California gnatcatchers are estimated to remain in the United States. The plight of the species has emphasized the importance of preserving coastal sage scrub habitat, which supports many other distinctive species as well. The California gnatcatcher was listed as threatened across its entire range in California and Mexico in 1993.

Woodpeckers

Red-cockaded woodpeckers are named for the red patches, or cockades, of feathers found on the heads of males. This species is found in old pine forests in the southeastern United States, where family groups—consisting of a breeding male and female as well as several helpers—nest within self-dug cavities in pine trees. Tree cavities serve as nesting sites in addition to providing protection from predators. Because red-cockaded woodpeckers rarely nest in trees less than 80 years old, heavy logging has destroyed much of their former habitat. The red-cockaded woodpecker was first placed on the Endangered Species List in 1970. It is currently found in fragmented populations in the southeastern seaboard westward into Texas. The total population size is estimated at 10,000–14,000 individuals.

In March 2001 the U.S. Fish and Wildlife Service was forced to rescue several red-cockaded woodpeckers from habitat areas in Daniel Boone National Forest in Kentucky. Fifteen woodpeckers in six family groups were relocated to the Carolina Sandhills National Wildlife Refuge in South Carolina and the Ouachita National Forest in Arkansas. Daniel Boone National Forest had become uninhabitable for the woodpeckers after a 1999 infestation of southern pine beetles. The beetles quickly destroyed 90 percent of local woodpecker habitat despite valiant efforts by Forest Service officials and volunteers to control the insect's spread. The removal of this red-cockaded woodpecker population from Kentucky means that the species is now absent from the state.

The ivory-billed woodpecker, the largest woodpecker species, has long been thought extinct. A century ago, the species was found throughout the southeastern United States as well as in Cuba. The last confirmed sightings in the U.S. were reported in the 1970s. However, tantalizing hints that the ivory-billed woodpecker may yet survive in North America persist. Hunters occasionally report seeing it or, more often, hearing its characteristic double-rap sound deep in the Louisiana bayou. Several groups of ornithologists have devoted significant effort to relocating this species, particularly since a hunter reported seeing one on April Fool's Day in 1999. As of 2004 there have been no definitive sightings. The Cuban subspecies of the ivory-billed woodpecker was also rediscovered in 1986 after being presumed extinct. However, populations had reached such a low point by then that measures to help save the group were ineffectual.

Spotted Owls

The northern spotted owl occupies old-growth forests in the Pacific Northwest, where it nests in the cavities of trees two hundred years old or older. It does not seem afraid of humans and in fact appears to be curious about humans and human activity. Its primary prey includes the nocturnal northern flying squirrel, mice, and other rodents and reptiles. Owl pairs may forage across areas as large as 2,200 acres. There are about 2,000 breeding pairs in California, Oregon, and Washington, and another hundred pairs in British Columbia, Canada.

Northern spotted owl populations have declined primarily due to habitat loss. Most of the private lands in its range have been heavily logged, leaving only public lands, such as National Forests and National Parks, for habitat. Because logging has also been permitted in many old-growth National Forest areas, the species has lost approximately 90 percent of its original habitat. In 1990 the Fish and Wildlife Service placed the northern spotted owl on its list of threatened species. Court battles began over continued logging in National Forest habitats. In March 1991 U.S. Federal District Court Judge William Dwyer ruled in favor of the Seattle Audubon Society and against the U.S. Forest Service, declaring that the Forest Service was not meeting its obligation to "maintain viable populations." The Forest Service had argued that the Fish and Wildlife Service was responsible for the management and recovery of this species. However, Dwyer pointed out that the Forest Service had its own distinct obligations to protect species under the Endangered Species Act, and that courts had already reprimanded the Fish and Wildlife Service for failing to designate critical habitat for the northern spotted owl.

In 1992 the Fish and Wildlife Service set aside 7 million acres as "critical habitat" for the species. The Northwest Forest Plan was established in 1993. This plan reduced logging in thirteen National Forests by about 85 percent in order to protect northern spotted owl habitats. However, the northern spotted owl has continued to decline by 7 to 10 percent per year—this despite the unanticipated discovery of fifty pairs of nesting adults in California's Marin County, just north of the Golden Gate Bridge.

In 1993 the Mexican spotted owl, a species native to the Southwest, was also placed on the list of threatened species. As with the northern spotted owl, the prime threat to this group is poorly managed timber harvesting. The Mexican spotted owl has a wide range, and is found in Utah, Colorado, Arizona, New Mexico, and Texas, as well as in central Mexico. Both northern and Mexican spotted owls remained threatened in 2004.

The California Condor

California condors, whose wingspans exceed nine feet, are among the continent's most impressive birds. Ten thousand years ago, this species soared over most of North America. However, its range contracted at the end of the ice age, and eventually individuals were found only along the Pacific Coast. Like other vulture species, the California condor is a carrion eater, and feeds on the carcasses of deer, sheep, and smaller species such as rodents. Random shooting, egg collection, poisoning, and loss of habitat devastated the condor population. The species was listed as endangered in 1967.

An intense captive breeding program for the California condor was initiated in 1987. (See Figure 8.2.) The first chick hatched in 1988. In 1994, after a series of deaths in the wild in which seven condors perished in rapid succession, the eight remaining wild condors were also captured and entered into the captive breeding program. The breeding program was successful enough that California condors were released into the wild beginning in 1992. In April 2002, for the first time in eighteen years, a condor egg laid in the wild hatched in the wild. The parents of this chick had been captive-bred at the Los Angeles Zoo and the San Diego Wild Animal Park respectively and released into the wild in 1995 at the age of one. Wild condors now inhabit parts of California as well as Nevada, Utah, and Arizona, where a population was introduced in the vicinity of the Grand Canyon in 1996, providing spectacular opportunities to view the largest bird in North America.

In March 2004 the California Department of Fish and Game reported that there were a total of 215 California condors in existence, including 125 captive individuals and 90 in the wild population—20 in southern California, 24 in central California, 5 in Baja California, and 41 in Arizona. Total production in 2003 included 28 offspring in captivity and one wild fledgling.

FIGURE 8.2

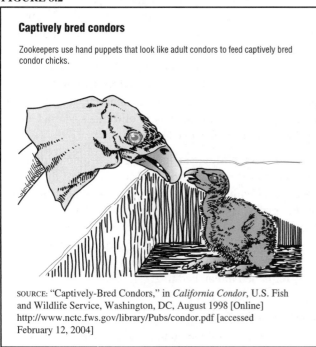

Captively bred condors

Zookeepers use hand puppets that look like adult condors to feed captively bred condor chicks.

SOURCE: "Captively-Bred Condors," in *California Condor*, U.S. Fish and Wildlife Service, Washington, DC, August 1998 [Online] http://www.nctc.fws.gov/library/Pubs/condor.pdf [accessed February 12, 2004]

FIGURE 8.3

The whooping crane is highly endangered. Each year, whooping cranes migrate from breeding grounds in Canada to wintering grounds in south Texas. The Fish and Wildlife Service has introduced captive-bred whooping cranes to new habitats in recent years. *(Field Mark Publications)*

The Great White Whooping Crane

Standing five feet, the whooping crane (see Figure 8.3) is North America's tallest bird and among the best known endangered species in the United States. Its name comes from its loud and distinctive call, which can be heard for miles. Each year, whooping cranes fly 2,500 miles from nesting grounds in Wood Buffalo, Canada to Aransas, south Texas for the winter before returning north in March to breed. Whooping cranes return to the same nesting site each year with the same mate. The birds were once heavily hunted, for meat as well as for their beautiful, long white feathers. In addition, the heavy loss of wetland areas in the U.S. deprived whooping cranes of much of their original habitat. In 1937 it was discovered that fewer than twenty whooping cranes were left in the wild. That same year, the Aransas Wildlife Refuge was established in south Texas to protect the species' wintering habitat. Conservation efforts for the whooping crane are coordinated with the Canadian government, which manages its breeding areas.

Captive breeding programs have helped to increase the worldwide whooping crane population. As of 2004, the International Whooping Crane Recovery Team reported that 194 whooping cranes inhabit the traditional territory, migrating from Wood Buffalo, Canada to Aransas yearly. In addition, an introduced population of captive-bred individuals has been established in the Kissimmee Prairie in Florida. This population contains 90 individuals, and has bred with success in its new habitat. A second introduced population breeds in Wisconsin on the Necedah National Wildlife Refuge and winters in Florida on the Chassahowitzka National Wildlife Refuge. This population numbered thirty-six in 2004. Introduced cranes were led to their Flori-

da wintering grounds along the migration route by ultra-light aircraft in 2001, and successfully made the return trip on their own in following years. Figure 8.4 illustrates the migration routes and locales of all three whooping crane populations. In addition to these wild populations, another 128 whooping cranes are found in captivity.

Hawaiian Honeycreepers

The Hawaiian honeycreepers are a group of songbirds endemic to Hawaii—that is, species in this group are found there and nowhere else on Earth. Hawaiian honeycreepers are believed to have radiated—formed many separate species, each adapted to a particular lifestyle—from a single species that colonized the Hawaiian Islands thousands of years ago. The honeycreepers are named for the characteristic "creeping" behavior some species exhibit as they search for nectar. The Hawaiian honeycreepers are extremely diverse in their diet—different species are seed-eaters, insect-eaters, or nectar-eaters. Species also differ in the shapes of the beaks and in plumage coloration. Hawaiian honeycreepers are found in forest habitats at high elevations. There were some fifty or sixty Hawaiian honeycreeper species originally, but a third of them are already extinct.

Twelve species of Hawaiian honeycreepers are currently listed with the Fish and Wildlife Service as endangered. Some honeycreeper species are among the most endangered animals on earth, with only a few individuals left. One of the primary factors involved in honeycreeper endangerment is loss of habitat. The Hawaiian Islands are estimated to retain a mere 20 to 30 percent of their original forest cover. In addition, the introduction of predators that hunt birds or eat their eggs, such as rats, cats, and mongooses, has contributed to the decline of numerous species. The introduction of bird diseases, particularly those spread by introduced mosquitoes, has also decimated honeycreeper populations. The success of mosquitoes in Hawaii has been dependent on another introduced species, pigs. The

FIGURE 8.4

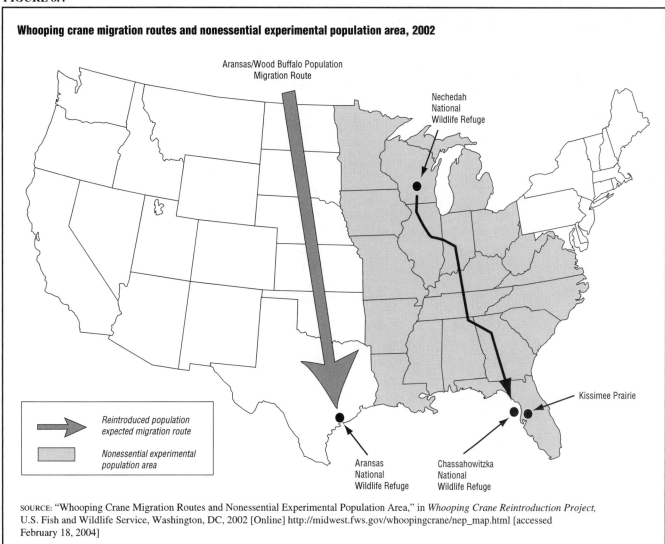

Whooping crane migration routes and nonessential experimental population area, 2002

Aransas/Wood Buffalo Population
Migration Route

Nechedah
National
Wildlife Refuge

Kissimee Prairie

Reintroduced population
expected migration route

Nonessential experimental
population area

Aransas
National
Wildlife Refuge

Chassahowitzka
National
Wildlife Refuge

SOURCE: "Whooping Crane Migration Routes and Nonessential Experimental Population Area," in *Whooping Crane Reintroduction Project,*
U.S. Fish and Wildlife Service, Washington, DC, 2002 [Online] http://midwest.fws.gov/whoopingcrane/nep_map.html [accessed
February 18, 2004]

rooting activity of pigs creates pools of water where mosquitoes lay their eggs. In fact, the greater the number of pigs in a habitat, the more bird disease will be prevalent. Finally, competition with introduced bird species for food and habitat has also been a significant cause of decline.

The Po'ouli is the most endangered Hawaiian honeycreeper and probably the most endangered bird species in the world. Along with many other endangered native species, it occupies the Hanawi Natural Reserve Area in Maui, which has been aggressively rehabilitated and cleared of invasive species. There are three Po'ouli individuals left, two females and one male. The Maui Forest Bird Recovery Project and the Fish and Wildlife Service worked together in May 2002 to mate one of the Po'ouli females with the single remaining male. Unfortunately, the attempts were unsuccessful, and in October 2003 scientists began efforts to capture the last remaining individuals in the hope that captive breeding may hold off extinction.

In August 2003, the Fish and Wildlife Service published a recovery plan for nineteen endangered Hawaiian

forest birds. (See Table 8.2.) The Fish and Wildlife Service reports that ten of these species have not been definitely observed in at least a decade and may well be extinct already. Two additional species are listed as either a candidate species or a species of concern. Most of these species are native to rain forests at elevations above 4,000 feet on the islands of Hawaii (Big Island), Maui, and Kauai. Major threats to endangered forest species listed by the Fish and Wildlife Service include habitat loss and modification, other human activity, disease, and predation. Of particular importance are non-native plants which have converted native plant communities to alien ecosystems unsuitable as habitat. Alien plant species known to threaten Hawaiian forest birds as well as the urgency of the need for control are shown in Table 8.3.

South Asian Vultures

In March 2004 BirdLife International warned that South Asian vulture populations were plummeting due to the drug diclofenac, which is used to treat cattle and other livestock. The three South Asian vulture species are the

TABLE 8.2

Federally listed endangered species of Hawaiian forest birds, 2003

Species (common name, scientific name, 4-letter acronym)	Total population estimate	Federal listing date and reference; state listing date	Federal status; recovery priority number	IUCN status listing
O'ahu 'elepaio, *Chasiempis sandwichensis ibidis*, OAEL	1,970	18 April 2000 (USFWS 2000); 18 April 2000	Endangered; 3	Vulnerable
Kāma'o (large Kaua'i thrush), *Myadestes myadestinus*, KAMO	Last detected in 1989	13 October 1970 (USFWS 1970, 1980, 1992); 22 March 1982	Endangered; 5	Critically endangered
Oloma'o (Moloka'i thrush), *Myadestes lanaiensis rutha*, OLOM	Last detected in 1988	13 October 1970 (USFWS 1970, 1980, 1992); 22 March 1982	Endangered; 5	Critically endangered
Puaiohi (small Kaua'i thrush), *Myadestes palmeri*, PUAI	300	11 March 1967 (USFWS 1967, 1980, 1992); 22 March 1982	Endangered; 2	Critically endangered
'Ō 'ō 'ā 'ā (Kaua'i 'ō 'ō), *Moho braccatus*, OO	Last detected 28 Apr 1987	11 March 1967 (USFWS 1967, 1980); 22 March 1982	Endangered; 4	Extinct
'Ō 'ū, *Psittirostra psittacea*, OU	Last detected in 1979	11 March 1967 (USFWS 1967, 1980); 22 March 1982	Endangered; 4	Criticall
Palila, *Loxioides bailleui*, PALI	3,390 (16-year average)	11 March 1967 (USFWS 1967, 1980); 22 March 1982	Endangered; 1	Endangered
Maui parrotbill, *Pseudonestor xanthophrys* MAPA	500	11 March 1967 (USFWS 1967, 1980); 22 March 1982	Endangered; 1	Vulnerable
Kaua'i 'akialoa, *Hemignathus procerus*, KAAK	Last detected in late 1960s 1982	11 March 1967 (USFWS 1967, 1980); 22 March	Endangered; 5	Extinct
Kaua'i nuku pu'u, *Hemignathus lucidus Hanapepe*, KANU	Last confirmed detection in 1960s	11 March 1967 (USFWS 1967, 1970, 1980); 22 March 1982	Endangered; 5	Critically endangered
Maui nuku pu'u, *Hemignathus lucidus affinis*, MANU	Last detected in 1979	11 March 1967 (USFWS 1967, 1970, 1980); 22 March 1982	Endangered; 5	Critically endangered
'Akiapōlā'au, *Hemignathus munroi*, AKIP	1,163	11 March 1967 (USFWS 1967, 1980, 1992); 22 March 1982	Endangered; 2	Endangered
Hawai'i creeper, *Oreomystis mana*, HCRE	12,500	25 September 1975 (USFWS 1975, 1980, 1992); 22 March 1982	Endangered; 8	Endangered
O'ahu 'alauahio (O'ahu creeper), *Paroreomyza maculata*, OAAL	Last confirmed detection in 1985	13 October 1970 (USFWS 1970, 1980, 1992); 22 March 1982	Endangered; 5	Critically endangered
Kākāwahie (Moloka'i creeper), *Paroreomyza flammea*, MOCR	Last detected in 1963	13 October 1970 (USFWS 1970, 1992); 22 March 1982	Endangered; 5	Extinct
Hawai'i 'ākepa, *Loxops coccineus coccineus*, AKEP	14,000	13 October 1970 (USFWS 1970, 1992); 22 March 1982	Endangered; 8	Endangered
Maui ' ākepa, *Loxops coccineus ochraceus*, MAAK	Last confirmed detection in 1970	13 October 1970 (USFWS 1970, 1992); 22 March 1982	Endangered; 6	Endangered
'Ākohekohe (crested honeycreeper), *Palmeria dolei*, AKOH	3,800	11 March 1967 (USFWS 1967); 22 March 1982	Endangered; 7	Vulnerable
Po'ouli, *Melamprosops phaeosoma*, POOU	3	25 September 1975 (USFWS 1975, 1992); 22 March 1982	Endangered; 4	Critically endangered

SOURCE: "Table 1. Federally Listed Endangered Species of Hawaiian Forest Birds Included in This Recovery Plan and the International Union for the Conservation of Nature Species Status Listing (IUCN 1994)," in *Draft Revised Recovery Plan for Hawaiian Forest Birds,* U.S. Fish and Wildlife Service, Region 1, Portland, OR, August 2003

white-rumped vulture, the slender-billed vulture, and the Indian vulture. Populations have declined 95 percent over the course of eight years. Diclofenac causes kidney failure and other problems in vultures that feed on the carcasses of deceased livestock. The problem is particularly severe in India, where dead cattle are often left to rot because

TABLE 8.3

Alien plants known or suspected to pose a significant threat to Hawaiian forest birds, 2003

Scientific name	Common name	Hawai'i	Maui Nui	O'ahu	Kaua'i
Acacia mearnsii	black wattle	3	1		3
Acacia melanoxylon	Australian blackwood		1		3
Cinchona pubescens	Quinine		1	3	
Cinnamomum burmannii	padang cassia		2		
Cinnamomum camphora	camphor tree		1		
Cortaderia jubata	Andean pampas grass	2	2		
Cortaderia selloana		2	2		
Delairea odorata	German ivy	2			
Ehrharta stipoides	meadow ricegrass	2			
Erigeron karvinskianus	daisy fleabane		3		1
Heliocarpus popayanensis	white moho	3	3	1	
Holcus lanatus	velvetgrass, yorkshire fog	3	3		
Ilex aquifolium	English or European holly	1	2		
Juncus effuses	Japanese mat rush	1	3		2
Juncus planifolius	Rush	3	3		
Lantana camara	lantana, lakana	3	3	1	
Leptospermum scoparium	New Zealand tea tree			2	
Lonicera japonica	Japanese honeysuckle	3	3		2
Melinis minutiflora	Molasses grass	3	3		3
Myrica faya	Firetree	1	2		1
Oplismenus hirtellus	basketgrass, honohono			3	
Panicum maximum	Guinea grass	3	2		
Paspalum conjugatum	Hilo grass, mau'u-hilo	3	3		3
Paspalum urvillei	Vasey grass	3	3		2
Pennisetum clandestinum	kikuyu grass	1			
Pennisetum setaceum	fountain grass	1			
Pyracantha angustifolia	firethorn, pyracantha	3	3		3
Rubus argutus	blackberry	1	1	1	1
Rubus discolor		3	2		
Rubus ellipticus var. obcordatus	yellow Himalayan raspberry	1	2		
Rubus niveus	hill or mysore raspberry	3	2		
Rubus rosifolius	Thimbleberry	3	3	2	2
Schinus terebinthifolius	Christmas berry	2	2	1	
Schizachyrium condensatum	beardgrass	3	3		2
Setaria palmifolia	palmgrass	2	2	2	
Sphaeropteris cooperi	Australian tree fern	2	2	2	2
Toona ciliata	Australian red cedar		3	1	
Ulex europaeus	Gorse	2	2		
Genera					
Eucalyptus spp. (90+ spp)	gum trees	2	1	1	3
Ficus (microcarpa, nota, platyphyllum, rubigenosa)	Figs	2	2	1	
Fraxinus (uhdei, griffithi)	Ashes	1	1	3	
Hedychium (coronarium, flavescens, gardnerianum)	Gingers	1	1	3	1
Psidium (cattleianum, guajava)	Guavas	1	1	1	1
Families					
Melastomataceae	Melastome family	1	1	1	3
Passifloraceae	passion fruit family	1	2	2	2
Pinaceae	pine family	2	2		
Proteaceae	Protea family	2	3	2	

At the species level, 39 taxa of alien grasses, shrubs, vines or trees pose a significant threat to forest bird recovery habit at. At higher taxonimic levels, all known naturalized taxa from five genera and four families pose significant threats to forest bird recovery habitat. Urgency of the need for management of each taxon is represented by a code:
1 = high
2 = moderate
3 = low

SOURCE: "Table 10. List of Alien Plant Taxa Known or Suspected to Pose a Significant Threat to Forest Bird Recovery Habitat on the Main Hawaiian Islands," in *Draft Revised Recovery Plan for Hawaiian Forest Birds,* U.S. Fish and Wildlife Service, Region 1, Portland, OR, August 2003

beef is taboo to the largely Hindu population. As many as two hundred vultures may feed on a single carcass.

BACK FROM THE BRINK—SUCCESS STORIES

The Peregrine Falcon

Many falcon species have declined with the spread of humans. Like other predatory species, falcons were often hunted, either for sport or because they were considered a threat to chickens or livestock.

The peregrine falcon is the fastest bird on Earth. It can achieve diving speeds of over 200 miles per hour. Like the bald eagle, much of the species' decline was due to the pesticide DDT. Populations sank to approximately 325 nesting pairs during the 1930s and 1940s. The recovery of this species was made possible by the banning of DDT as well as the establishment of special captive breeding centers on several continents. Between 1974 and 1999 more than 6,000 peregrine falcons were released into the wild. Federal and state agencies contributed to the conservation effort, as did private organizations such as the Peregrine Fund, Santa Cruz Predatory Bird Research Group, and Midwestern Peregrine Falcon Restoration Project.

In 1996 the Fish and Wildlife Service declared the peregrine falcon "officially recovered" and began the process to remove the species from the Endangered Species List. The American peregrine falcon was delisted in 1999 across its entire range, although it will be monitored for the next five years to assure that its recovery continues. By August 1999 about 1,650 breeding pairs of peregrine falcons inhabited the lower forty-eight states and Canada, with additional populations surviving in Mexico. The Arctic peregrine falcon, which recovered on its own after DDT was made illegal, was delisted in 1994. However, as of 2002 the Eurasian peregrine falcon, which occurs in Eurasia south to Africa and the Middle East, is still listed as endangered across its entire range.

The Bald Eagle

Almost everyone recognizes the bald eagle (see Figure 8.5). Symbol of honor, courage, nobility, and independence (eagles do not fly in flocks), the bald eagle is found only in North America, and its image is engraved on the official seal of the United States of America. There were an estimated 100,000 bald eagles in the Unites States in the late eighteenth century when the nation was founded.

The bald eagle nests over most of the United States and Canada, building its aerie, or nest, in mature conifer forests or on top of rocks or cliffs. Its nest is of such a grand size—sometimes as large as a small car—that a huge rock or tree is necessary to secure it. The birds use the same nest year after year, adding to it each nesting season. It is believed that eagles mate for life. Bald eagles prey primarily on fish, water birds, and turtles.

Bald eagles came dangerously close to extinction in the twentieth century, largely due to the pesticide DDT, which was introduced in 1947. Like other carnivorous species, bald eagles ingested large amounts of DDT from poisoned prey. DDT either prevents birds from laying eggs or causes the eggshells to be so thin they are unable to protect eggs until they hatch. The Bald Eagle Protection Act of 1940, which made it a federal offense to kill bald eagles, helped protect the species. However, numbers continued to dwindle and the bald eagle was listed as endangered in 1967.

Bald eagle populations started to recover with the banning of DDT in 1972. The species also benefited from habitat protection and attempts to clean up water pollution. In 1995 the bald eagle was moved from endangered to threatened sta-

FIGURE 8.5

The bald eagle was once endangered due to habitat destruction and pollution by pesticides such as DDT. Its populations have recovered with protection and a ban on DDT. *(Field Mark Publications)*

tus on the Endangered Species List. In 2000, surveys showed that there were about 5,800 breeding pairs in the forty-eight contiguous states. The species was proposed for delisting in 1999; that proposal was still awaiting action in 2004.

Aleutian Canada Goose

The Aleutian Canada goose was first placed on the Endangered Species List in 1966, when there were an estimated 800 individuals. The species had been thought extinct for several decades until a remnant population was discovered in 1962 by Fish and Wildlife biologists on a remote Aleutian island. Deterioration of habitat and the introduction of predators such as Arctic foxes and red foxes were blamed for the animal's decline. The goose population rebounded to 6,300 in 1991, and there were well over 35,000 geese by 2002. Conservation efforts included captive breeding, removal of foxes, and relocation and reintroduction of geese to unoccupied islands. The Aleutian Canada goose was officially delisted by the Fish and Wildlife Service in 2001. A graph of population growth over time for this recovered species is shown in Figure 8.6. Table 8.4 shows some of the important events contributing to the recovery of this species.

FIGURE 8.6

Peak counts of Aleutian Canada geese on wintering areas in California, 1975–2000

Year	Count
1975	790
1976	900
1977	1200
1978	1500
1979	1500
1980	1740
1981	2000
1982	2700
1983	3500
1984	3800
1985	4200
1986	4300
1987	4800
1988	5400
1989	5800
1990	6300
1991	7000
1992	7800
1993	11,680
1994	15,700
1995	19,150
1996	21,420
1997	22,815
1998	27,700
1999	32,281
2000	36,978

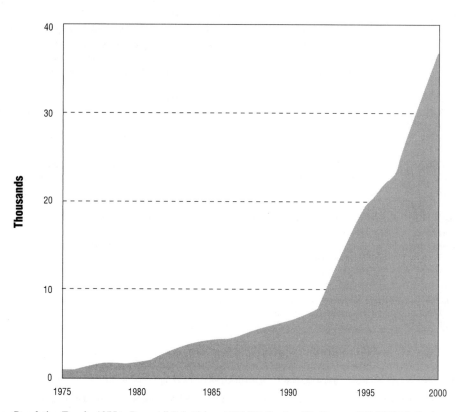

SOURCE: "Return of the Aleutian Canada Goose: Population Trends, 1975 to Present," U.S. Fish and Wildlife Service, Washington, DC, 2000 [Online] http://www.r7.fws.gov/media/acg.htm [Accessed June 5, 2002]

TABLE 8.4

Decline and recovery of the Aleutian Canada goose population

1750	First known introduction of foxes onto Aleutian Islands.
1750–1936	Arctic foxes and red foxes introduced to at least 190 islands within the breeding range of the Aleutian Canada goose in Alaska.
1811	First complaints from Aleut Natives that foxes had caused severe declines in birds that had once been numerous.
1938–1962	Aleutian Canada geese were not found on any of the islands where they historically nested; thought to be extinct.
1962	Fish and Wildlife Service biologist found remnant population on remote Buldir Island in the western Aleutian Islands. Population estimated at between 200 and 300 birds.
1963	Goslings captured to start first captive flock for propogation.
March 1967	The Aleutian Canada goose was officially declared an endangered species under the Endangered Species Protection Act of 1966 (law that preceded the Endangered Species Act).
1971–1991	Captive-reared and translocated wild Aleutian Canada geese released on fox-free islands.
1973	Passage of the Endangered Species Act.
1973–1984	Hunting closures implemented for Aleutian Canada geese on wintering and breeding grounds.
1975	Recovery team begins developing formal recovery program. Spring population estimate 790 birds.
	Recovery actions implemented including the removal of foxes from breeding grounds on the Aleutian Islands and translocation of geese to unpopulated islands.
1984	Geese began to breed successfully on the islands. Foxes removed from four islands.
1990	Populations reached 6,300 geese.
December 1990	The Aleutian Canada goose was reclassified from endangered to the less imperiled threatened status. Recovery plan was revised, establishing objectives for measuring recovery and indicating when delisting was appropriate.
1990–1998	Recovery plans continue to be implemented. Population averages 20% annual growth rate.
1999	Populations reach more than 30,000 geese, over four times the original goal for delisting.
July 1999	The U.S. Fish and Wildlife Service proposed to delist the species, opening a 90 day public comment period.
	Fish and Wildlife Service evaluates comments.
March 2001	Fish and Wildlife Service removes the Aleutian Canada Goose from the list of endangered and threatened species. The goose will be managed and protected by the Migratory Bird Treaty Act.
	The FWS will continue to monitor the Aleutian Canada goose with the help of the states for five years.
	If populations decline significantly, the species can be relisted.
2005	If the status remains stable or improves, monitoring is no longer required under the ESA.

SOURCE: "Aleutian Canada Goose Road to Recovery," U.S. Fish and Wildlife Service, Washington, DC, 2001 [Online] http://www.r7.fws.gov/media/acg.htm [accessed June 5, 2002]

CHAPTER 9

ENDANGERED INSECTS AND SPIDERS

Insects are the most diverse group in the animal kingdom, with close to a million named and described species and countless species yet to be discovered. Insects have not been nearly as thoroughly studied as the vertebrate groups, and so there are likely to be many endangered insects whose desperate state remains unrealized. In 2004 there were 39 endangered insects (35 U.S., four foreign) and nine threatened insects (all U.S.) listed with the U.S. Fish and Wildlife Service under the Endangered Species Act. There are also 12 endangered arachnids (all U.S. species), a group related to insects that includes spiders, ticks, and mites. Listed U.S. threatened and endangered insects and spiders are shown in Table 9.1.

There are also 553 threatened insect species and ten threatened arachnids listed in the *2003 IUCN Red List of Threatened Species* from the World Conservation Union. Most of the IUCN-listed species are butterflies, dragonflies, and damselflies, which are among the better examined insect groups.

BUTTERFLIES

Like amphibians, many butterflies and moths are considered by scientists to be "indicator species" because they are particularly sensitive to environmental degradation. The decline of these species serves as a warning to human beings about the condition of the environment. Part of the reason butterflies are sensitive to many aspects of the environment is that these species undergo a drastic metamorphosis, or change, from larva to adult as a natural part of their life cycles. Butterfly larvae are generally crawling, herbivorous caterpillars, whereas butterfly adults fly and are nectar-eating. Butterflies can thrive only when intact habitats are available for both caterpillars and adults. Consequently, healthy butterfly populations tend to occur in areas with healthy ecosystems. Because many species are extremely sensitive to changing environmental conditions, the 20,000 known species of moths and butterflies are carefully monitored by scientists and conservationists around the world.

Butterflies and moths have alerted scientists to numerous habitat changes. In southern Florida, for example, the sharp decline of swallowtail butterflies alerted biologists to the harm caused by mosquito sprays, as well as to the fact that pesticides had contaminated the water. In 1996 scientists in Michigan and England reported in the *Journal of Heredity* (September/October 1996), that during the 1960s, darker-colored moths began to predominate over light, white-and-black-flecked moths in polluted areas. This was seen in both England and the United States and was probably due to the fact that darker moths were better able to "blend in" to the dingy environment and hide from predators. In both countries, clean air laws were passed and decreases in pollution resulted. Now, in both countries, lighter-colored moths are again predominant. Dr. Douglas Futuyma, a biologist at the State University of New York at Stony Brook, reported that other insect species have shown increases in the proportion of darker-colored individuals in industrialized areas, a phenomenon called "industrial melanism." In those species, as well, the proportion of dark specimens drops as air quality improves.

In many cases, butterflies also help conservationists decide where to locate parks and nature refuges. Generally, the more varieties of butterflies that exist in an area, the more species of other animals and plants will live there too. Unfortunately, many butterfly species are disappearing around the world.

Monarch Butterfly

Historically, monarch butterflies migrated by the millions on a 3,000-mile journey up and down the North American continent. Over time, monarch butterfly populations have also become established in Australia and on the Pacific islands of Samoa and Tahiti. Other monarch populations have appeared in Hawaii and New Zealand.

TABLE 9.1

Endangered or threatened insects and spiders, February 2004

Status	Species name	Status	Species name
Insects		E	Butterfly, Uncompahgre fritillary (*Boloria acrocnema*)
E	Beetle, American burying (*Nicrophorus americanus*)	E	Dragonfly, Hine's emerald (*Somatochlora hineana*)
E	Beetle, Coffin cave mold (*Batrisodes texanus*)	E	Fly, Delhi Sands flower-loving (*Rhaphiomidas terminatus abdominalis*)
E	Beetle, Comal Springs dryopid (*Stygoparnus comalensis*)	E	Grasshopper, Zayante band-winged (*Trimerotropis infantilis*)
E	Beetle, Comal Springs riffle (*Heterelmis comalensis*)	E	Ground beetle, [unnamed] (*Rhadine exilis*)
T	Beetle, delta green ground (*Elaphrus viridis*)	E	Ground beetle, [unnamed] (*Rhadine infernalis*)
E	Beetle, Helotes mold (*Batrisodes venyivi*)	E	Moth, Blackburn's sphinx (*Manduca blackburni*)
E	Beetle, Hungerford's crawling water (*Brychius hungerfordi*)	T	Moth, Kern primrose sphinx (*Euproserpinus euterpe*)
E	Beetle, Kretschmarr cave mold (*Texamaurops reddelli*)	T	Naucorid, Ash Meadows (*Ambrysus amargosus*)
E	Beetle, Mount Hermon June (*Polyphylla barbata*)	E	Skipper, Carson wandering (*Pseudocopaeodes eunus obscurus*)
E	Beetle, Tooth cave ground (*Rhadine persephone*)	E	Skipper, Laguna Mountains (*Pyrgus ruralis lagunae*)
T	Beetle, valley elderberry longhorn (*Desmocerus californicus dimorphus*)	T	Skipper, Pawnee montane (*Hesperia leonardus montana*)
T	Butterfly, bay checkerspot (*Euphydryas editha bayensis*)	T	Tiger beetle, northeastern beach (*Cicindela dorsalis dorsalis*)
E	Butterfly, Behren's silverspot (*Speyeria zerene behrensii*)	E	Tiger beetle, Ohlone (*Cicindela ohlone*)
E	Butterfly, callippe silverspot (*Speyeria callippe callippe*)	T	Tiger beetle, Puritan (*Cicindela puritana*)
E	Butterfly, El Segundo blue (*Euphilotes battoides allyni*)	**Arachnids**	
E	Butterfly, Fender's blue v*caricia icarioides fenderi*)	E	Harvestman, Bee Creek cave (*Texella reddelli*)
E	Butterfly, Karner blue (*Lycaeides melissa samuelis*)	E	Harvestman, Bone cave (*Texella reyesi*)
E	Butterfly, Lange's metalmark (*Apodemia mormo langei*)	E	Harvestman, Cokendolpher cave (*Texella cokendolpheri*)
E	Butterfly, lotis blue*v(Lycaeides argyrognomon lotis*)	E	Meshweaver, Braken bat cave (*Cicurina venii*)
E	Butterfly, mission blue (*Lcaricia icarioides missionensis*)	E	Meshweaver, Government Canyon bat cave (*Cicurina vespera*)
E	Butterfly, Mitchell's satyr (*Neonympha mitchellii mitchellii*)	E	Meshweaver, Madla's cave (*Cicurina madla*)
E	Butterfly, Myrtle's silverspot (*Speyeria zerene myrtleae*)	E	Meshweaver, Robber baron cave (*Cicurina baronia*)
T	Butterfly, Oregon silverspot v*Speyeria zerene hippolyta*)	E	Pseudoscorpion, Tooth cave (*Tartarocreagris texana*)
E	Butterfly, Palos Verdes blue (*Glaucopsyche lygdamus palosverdesensis*)	E	Spider, Government Canyon bat cave (*Neoleptoneta microps*)
E	Butterfly, Quino checkerspot (*Euphydryas editha quino [=E. e. wrighti]*)	E	Spider, Kauai cave wolf or pe'e pe'e maka 'ole (*Adelocosa anops*)
E	Butterfly, Saint Francis' satyr (*Neonympha mitchellii francisci*)	E	Spider, spruce-fir moss (*Microhexura montivaga*)
E	Butterfly, San Bruno elfin (*Callophrys mossii bayensis*)	E	Spider, Tooth cave (*Neoleptoneta myopica*)
E	Butterfly, Schaus swallowtail (*Heraclides aristodemus ponceanus*)		
E	Butterfly, Smith's blue (*Euphilotes enoptes smithi*)		

E = Endangered
T = Threatened

SOURCE: Adapted from "U.S. Listed Invertebrate Animal Species Report by Taxonomic Group as of 02/17/2004," Threatened and Endangered Species System (TESS), U.S. Fish and Wildlife Service, Washington, DC, 2004 [Online] http://ecos.fws.gov/tess_public/TESSWebpageVipListed?code=I&listings=0#F [accessed February 17, 2004]

For many years, naturalists sought to pinpoint the location where monarchs hibernate in January and February in preparation for their mating season and northward migration in March. In 1975, following an arduous search, a serene monarch hibernation area was located in the high altitude forests of the Michoacán Mountains in Mexico. Mexico declared the impoverished region a protected area. The inhabitants of the area turned the site into an ecotourist attraction in order to generate income for the economy. However, ecotourism not only failed to generate sufficient money to support the people of the area, but also caused severe habitat disruption. The onslaught of tourists affected habitats by introducing excessive noise, tobacco smoke, fire, and pollution. Monarch butterflies are now considered endangered by the IUCN. The U.S. Fish and Wildlife Service and the Mexican government have since attempted to nurture a self-sustaining economy in the monarch hibernation area by introducing fish breeding and horticulture.

In January 2002 a massive die-off of monarch butterflies in their wintering grounds in Mexico became major news worldwide. An estimated 250 million butterflies froze to death following a winter storm. As many as 80 percent of monarch colonies may have succumbed. While the storm may have been directly responsible for the deaths, deforestation and logging near the butterfly habitat are believed to have played a significant role. In particular, a fuller and healthier forest canopy would have better protected individuals from extreme weather. Despite the fact that butterfly hibernation areas are in protected reserves, logging continued there until recently. Although the massive die-off was a huge blow to monarch populations, many individuals did survive and it is hoped that the population will bounce back.

MONARCHS AND THE BIOPESTICIDES DEBATE. Monarch butterflies have also played an unwitting role in the recent debate regarding genetically modified foods. In an effort to reduce the amount of pesticides in the environment, plant geneticists have developed novel hybrid plants that are genetically altered to produce substances called biopesticides. These plants repel pests without additional application of pesticides. In order to create biopesticide-producing plants, scientists insert DNA for pesticidal proteins directly into plant genomes. The introduction of biopesticides generated continuing controversy in the 2000s. Proponents argued that biopesticides were much less toxic than chemical pesticides, and also claimed that biopesticides affected only targeted plant pests without affecting other consumer organisms. Opponents, however, feared that any genetically altered species posed potential and unknown threats.

These fears were substantiated when researchers discovered that one genetic hybrid of corn, called Bt corn, is poisonous to monarch butterflies. Bt corn is genetically modified to include genes from a known pesticidal bacterium, *Bacillus thuringiensis*. Pesticidal proteins were genetically spliced into the corn genome to create a hybrid that repelled an important pest, the European corn borer. Bt corn was believed to be safe for the environment because it lacked toxins. Researchers reported, for example, that Bt corn had no effect on honeybees, ladybugs, or other organisms that inhabit cornfields. However, a new study reported in 1999 that in laboratory tests involving monarch caterpillars, as many as 44 percent of the caterpillars died after exposure to Bt corn.

Sacramento Mountains Checkerspot Butterfly

The Sacramento Mountains checkerspot butterfly has a highly specialized habitat—it occurs only in meadows at elevations of between 8,000 and 9,000 feet in southern New Mexico. Furthermore, the species is only found where there are native flowering plants, and is absent from meadows where invasive species have taken over. This is because Sacramento Mountains checkerspot caterpillars feed solely on native plant species such as the New Mexico penstemon. The Sacramento Mountains checkerspot is characterized by brown, red, orange, and white checked wings.

The Sacramento Mountains checkerspot is currently proposed for listing as endangered in its entire range. The species was first petitioned for listing by the Center for Biodiversity in 1999. Surveys of population sizes took place between 1997 and 2000 and revealed that the species occurs only in fragmented populations within a 33-square-mile area in New Mexico. The butterfly was officially proposed for listing in 2001; it remained a proposed species as of 2004. It is threatened primarily by loss of habitat due to urban development and destruction of habitat by off-road vehicles and overgrazing. In addition, several invasive plant species are taking over meadows once occupied by native plant species used by Sacramento Mountains checkerspot caterpillars. Finally, over-collection of specimens has harmed populations. A critical habitat of 5,000 acres is being proposed for the species, half of which is on federal property and half of which lies on private property.

Karner Blue Butterfly

The Karner blue butterfly was listed as endangered in 1992. It once occupied habitats in the eastern United States from Minnesota to Maine as well as Ontario, Canada. At present, the species occurs in portions of Minnesota, Wisconsin, Indiana, Michigan, New York, New Hampshire, and Ohio. Most Karner blue butterfly populations are very small and in danger of extinction.

The caterpillars of the Karner blue butterfly rely for food on a species of lupine that is now found primarily on roadsides, military bases, and some forest areas. (See Figure 9.1 for a description of the Karner blue butterfly life cycle.) The primary reason for endangerment of the Karner blue butterfly is habitat loss due to land development for human use and forest maturation. Table 9.2 shows the recovery objectives, recovery criteria, recovery actions needed, total cost of recovery, and expected date of recovery as set out in the recovery plan for the species completed in September 2003. Figure 9.2 shows the recovery units, or populations, of the species, sites for potential recovery units, as well as other sites where the species has historically been found.

As is the case with other endangered species, conservation measures protecting the habitat of the Karner blue butterfly are expected to benefit numerous others rare species as well. Table 9.3 lists other rare species that overlap with the Karner blue butterfly in habitat in the state of Michigan. These include mammals, birds, reptiles, other insects and invertebrates, and a large number of plants. This is one of many examples of how the Endangered Species Act, despite focusing on individual species, contributes to the conservation of many species and to entire ecosystems.

Blackburn's Sphinx Moth

Blackburn's sphinx moth was first listed as an endangered species in February 2000 and is found exclusively in Hawaii. This moth species is threatened by factors such as urban development, conversion of land for agricultural use, invasive plant species, non-native ungulates (hoofed animals), and invasive predators and parasites. Figure 9.3 shows the estimated pre-human contact range of the species in Hawaii, current points of Blackburn sphinx moth occurrence, and current points of occurrence of the native host plant on which the moth depends. Some of the invasive predators and parasites that impact the species, and the islands on which they are found, are listed in Table 9.4. Conservation recommendations in the species recovery plan, which was drawn up by the Fish and Wildlife Service in October 2003, include habitat conservation and restoration, planting of the moth's host plant in new habitats, and a captive breeding and reintroduction program. The total cost for recovery of the species is estimated at $5.5 million.

OTHER ENDANGERED INSECTS

Santa Cruz Mountain Insects

Insects, like numerous other species, suffer from diminished habitat as a result of encroaching develop-

FIGURE 9.1

Life history stages of the Karner blue butterfly

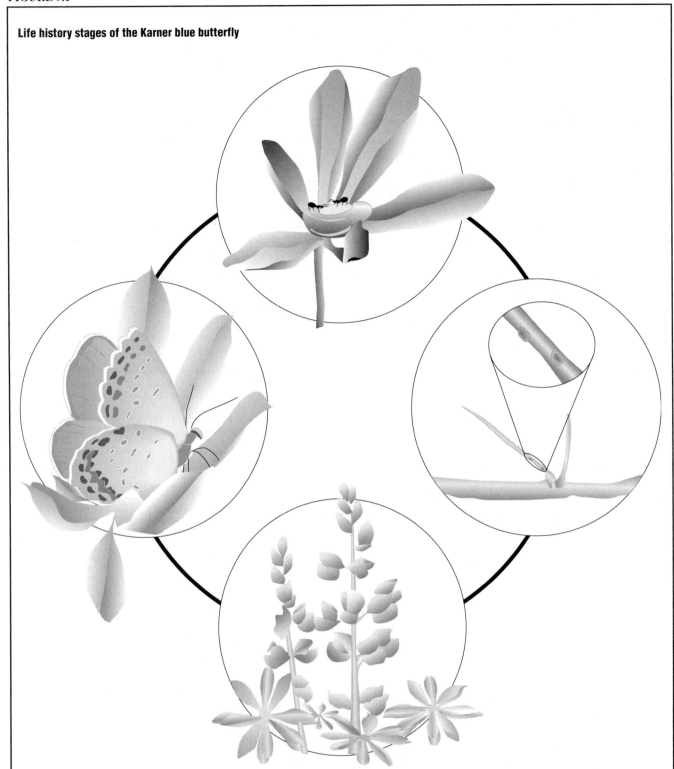

The Karner blue butterfly produces two broods of young each year, a spring brood and a summer brood. Larvae emerge in April from eggs that have overwintered and feed on wild lupine, *Lupinus perennis*, the only known larval food plant of the butterfly. the larvae are often attended by ants, which collect a sugary solution secreted by the larvae and in turn may protect the larvae from predation and/or parasitism. Near the end of May, the larvae pupate, and adults emerge in late May or early June. The butterfly then mates and lays eggs on the lupine plant. The second brood of butterflies emerges mid-July to early August. Their eggs overwinter to hatch in April.

SOURCE: Karner Blue Butterfly Recovery Team, "Figure 3. Illustration of Life History Stages of the Karner Blue," in *Karner Blue Butterfly Recovery Plan (Lycaeides melissa samuelis)*, Department of the Interior, U.S. Fish & Wildlife Service, Great Lakes-Big Rivers Regions (Region 3), Fort Snelling, MN, September 2003

TABLE 9.2

Karner blue butterfly recovery plan overview

Recovery objectives: The objective of this recovery plan is to restore viable metapopulations of Karner blues across the species extant range so that it can be reclassified from endangered to threatened. The long-range goal is to remove it from the federal list of endangered and threatened wildlife and plants.

Recovery criteria: The reclassification criteria will be met when a minimum of 27 metapopulations [19 viable metapopulations (supporting 3,000 butterflies each), and 8 large viable metapopulations (supporting 6,000 butterflies each)] are established within at least 13 recovery units across the butterfly's range and are being managed consistent with the recovery objectives outlined in this plan. Delisting will be considered when a minimum of 29 metapopulations (13 viable and 16 large viable metapopulations) have been established within at least 13 recovery units and are being managed consistent with the plan.

Actions needed:

1. Protect and manage Karner blue and its habitat to perpetuate viable metapopulations.
2. Evaluate and implement translocation where appropriate.
3. Develop rangewide and regional management guidelines.
4. Develop and implement information and education program.
5. Collect important ecological data on Karner blue and associated habitats.
6. Review and track recovery progress (includes re-evaluation of recovery goals for Wisconsin).

Total estimated cost of recovery (in $1,000s):

Year	Need 1	Need 2	Need 3	Need 4	Need 5	Need 6	* Total
2003	872.5	75	7	133	391	7	1,485.5
2004	964.5	55	26	63	423	27	1,558.5
2005	974	100	27	48	400	15	1,564
Total	2811	230	60	244	1,214	49	4,608

*Does not include land acquisition costs.

Date of recovery: Full recovery of the species is anticipated to require at least 20 years, until about 2023.

SOURCE: Adapted from Karner Blue Butterfly Recovery Team, "Executive Summary: Karner Blue Butterfly Recovery Plan," in *Karner Blue Butterfly Recovery Plan (Lycaeides melissa samuelis),* Department of the Interior, U.S. Fish & Wildlife Service, Great Lakes-Big Rivers Regions (Region 3), Fort Snelling, MN, September 2003

ment, industrialization, and changing land use patterns. In California's Santa Cruz Mountains, the tiny Zayante band-winged grasshopper, barely half an inch long, occupies areas containing abundant high-quality silica sand, known as Zayante or Santa Margarita sand. This sand is valuable for making glass and fiberglass products, and several businesses have entered the area in the hope of capitalizing on this. The Zayante band-winged grasshopper joined the ranks of listed endangered species in January 1997. In 2000, as a result of a lawsuit filed by the Center for Biological Diversity, the Fish and Wildlife Service proposed the establishment of critical habitat for the grasshopper.

The Ohlone tiger beetle was listed as endangered in October 2001. The species was discovered in 1987 and is found only in Santa Cruz County, California. The Ohlone tiger beetle is a small species, about half an inch long, with spotted metallic green wings and copper-green legs. Both adults and larvae hunt invertebrate prey. The Ohlone tiger beetle occupies a total of less than twenty acres of remnant native coastal prairie habitat on state land, private land, and property belonging to the University of California at Santa Cruz. The species declined due to habitat loss and habitat fragmentation resulting from urban development, as well as over-collection, pollution from pesticides, and the increasing encroachment of invasive plant species. The petition to list the Ohlone tiger beetle with

the Fish and Wildlife Service was originally made by a private citizen in 1997.

In 1998 the Fish and Wildlife Service completed a recovery plan for the Zayante band-winged grasshopper, the Ohlone tiger beetle, as well as other insect and plant species found in the Santa Cruz Mountains. Table 9.5 summarizes a range of conditions that cause harm to a variety of Santa Cruz Mountain threatened and endangered species. Factors leading to endangerment include sand mining, urban development, conversion of land to agricultural uses, recreational use (such as hiking, horseback riding, off-road vehicle use, bicycling, and camping), competition with non-native species, fire suppression, pesticides, logging, and over-collection.

Hine's Emerald Dragonfly

The Hine's emerald dragonfly has been listed as an endangered species since 1995 and is found in federal and state preserves and National Forest lands in Illinois, Wisconsin, Michigan, and Missouri. In earlier times, its range extended through portions of Ohio, Alabama, and Indiana as well. The Hine's emerald dragonfly has a metallic-green body and emerald-green eyes. It is considered a biological indicator species because it is extremely sensitive to water pollution. The decline of this dragonfly species has resulted primarily from loss of suitable wetland habitat, such as wet prairies, marshes, sedge meadows, and

FIGURE 9.2

Range-wide recovery units for the Karner blue butterfly

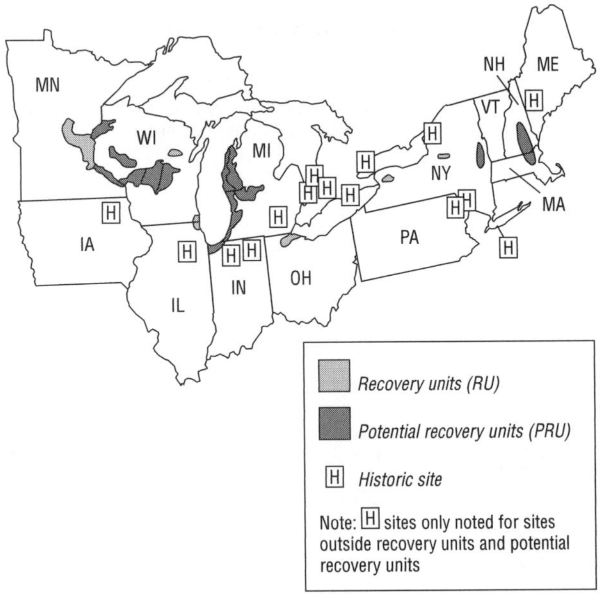

SOURCE: Karner Blue Butterfly Recovery Team, "Figure B-1. Map Showing Range-Wide Recovery Units for the Karner Blue Butterfly," in *Karner Blue Butterfly Recovery Plan (Lycaeides melissa samuelis)*, Department of the Interior, U.S. Fish & Wildlife Service, Great Lakes-Big Rivers Regions (Region 3), Fort Snelling, MN, September 2003

FIGURE 9.3

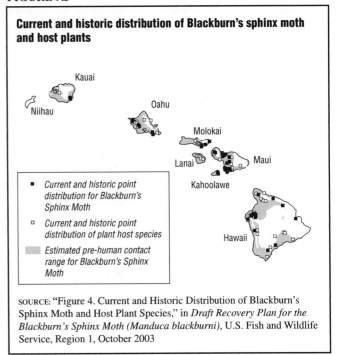

Current and historic distribution of Blackburn's sphinx moth and host plants

SOURCE: "Figure 4. Current and Historic Distribution of Blackburn's Sphinx Moth and Host Plant Species," in *Draft Recovery Plan for the Blackburn's Sphinx Moth (Manduca blackburni)*, U.S. Fish and Wildlife Service, Region 1, October 2003

fens occurring over dolomite rock. (The lakeside daisy is another species damaged by the decline of these habitats—it is listed as threatened.)

Wetland habitats support dragonflies during their aquatic larval period, which lasts some three to four years. Adult dragonflies occupy open areas and forest edges near wetland habitats, where they feed on invertebrate species such as mosquitoes. Hine's emerald dragonflies also serve as prey for a variety of bird and fish species. The recovery plan for the dragonfly includes measures to protect current habitat as well as reintroduction of the species to portions of its former range. Private companies that own land supporting dragonfly populations have aided conservation efforts by monitoring populations and preserving important habitat areas.

ENDANGERED SPIDERS

Kauai Cave Wolf Spider

The Kauai cave wolf spider is a blind species found only in special caves on the southern part of the island of Kauai in Hawaii. Several cave areas were proposed as critical habitat for this and other endangered cave species, including the Kauai cave amphipod, in 2002. Caves occupied by the Kauai cave wolf spider and Kauai cave amphipod are formed by young lava flows.

Unlike most other spiders, the Kauai cave wolf spider hunts prey directly. Its prey includes the (also highly endan-

gered) Kauai cave amphipod. The Fish and Wildlife Service originally listed both species as endangered in January 2000. Female cave wolf spiders lay some fifteen to thirty eggs per clutch, and carry young on their backs after hatching. Cave species are extremely sensitive to changes in temperature and light. It is feared that official designation of critical habitat by the Fish and Wildlife Service will make the delicate cave systems more prone to human use, resulting in damage from activity including light pollution, garbage (which may attract new species to the caves), and cigarette smoke.

Spruce-fir Moss Spider

The Spruce-fir moss spider is an endangered spider related to the tarantula. It was placed on the Endangered Species List in 1995. Spruce-fir moss spiders live in moss mats found only in the vicinity of Fraser fir trees. Its populations have declined largely due to the introduction in the United States of an invasive European insect species, the balsam-wooly adelgid. The balsam-wooly adelgid infests Fraser fir trees, causing them to die within a time period of two to seven years. With the death of numerous fir trees, other forest trees have also blown over. The resulting increase in light level and temperature causes the moss mats on which spruce-fir moss spiders depend to dry up. The Fish and Wildlife Service designated critical habitat for the species in 2001, including areas in the Great Smoky Mountains National Park and the Pisgah and Cherokee National Forests, as well as a preserve managed by The Nature Conservancy. This designation of critical habitat followed a lawsuit against the Fish and Wildlife Service, which had previously deemed designating critical habitat "not prudent" because it believed the spider would be more vulnerable to collectors.

TABLE 9.3

Michigan imperiled species associated with habitats of the Karner blue butterfly

Scientific name	Common name	State status	Federal status
Rare mammals			
Cryptotis parva	least shrew	T	
Microtis pinetorum	woodland vole	SC	
Rare birds			
Buteo lineatus	red-shouldered hawk	T	
Haliaeetus leucocephalus	bald eagle	T	T
Nycticorax nycticorax	black-crowned night heron	SC	
Rare reptiles & amphibians			
Clemmys guttata	spotted turtle	SC	
Clemmys insculpta	wood turtle	SC	
Clonophis kirtlandii	Kirtland's snake	E	FSC
Elaphe o. obsoleta	black rat snake	SC	
Sistrurus c. catenatus	eastern massasauga	SC	C
Terrapene c. carolina	eastern bow turtle	SC	
Rare invertebrates			
Atrytonopsis hianna	dusted skipper	T	
Erynnis p. persius	Persius dusky wing	T	
Hesperia ottoe	Ottoe skipper	T	
Incisalia henrici	Henry's elfin	SC	
Lepyronia gibbosa	Great Plains spittlebug	T	
Incisalia irus	frosted elfin	T	
Oecanthus pini	pinetree cricket	SC	
Orphulella p. pelidna	barrens locust	SC	
Papaipema sciata	Culvers root borer	SC	
Pygarctia spraguei	Sprague's pygarctia	SC	
Schinia indiana	phlox moth	E	FSC
Scudderia fasciata	pine katydid	SC	
Spartiniphaga inops	spartina moth	SC	
Speyeria idalia	regal fritillary	E	FSC
Rare vascular plants			
Arabis missouriensis var. *deamii*	Missouri rock cress	SC	FSC
Aster sericeus	western silvery aster	T	
Bouteloua cutipendula	side-oats gramma grass	T	
Carex albolitescens	greenish-white sedge	SC	
Carex festucacae	fescue sedge	SC	
Cirsium hillii	Hill's thistle	SC	FSC
Cyperus flavescens	yellow nut grass	SC	
Echinodorus tenellus	dwarf burhead	E	
Eleocharis atropurpurea	purple spike rush	E	
Eleocharis engelmannii	Engelman's spike rush	SC	
Eleocharis melanocarpa	black-fruited spike rush	SC	
Eleocharis microcarpa	small-fruited spike rush	T	
Eleocharis tricostata	three-ribed spike rush	T	
Festuca scaberlla	rough fescue	T	
Fuirena squarossa	umbrella grass	T	
Gentiana puberulenta	downy gentian	E	
Geum triflorum	prairie smoke	T	
Hemicarpha micrantha	dwarf bulrush	SC	
Hibiscus moscheutos	swamp rose mallow	SC	
Hypericum gentianoides	gentian-leaved St. John's wort	SC	
Isoetes engelmannii	Engelman's quilwort	E	
Juncus biflorus	two-flowered rush	SC	
Juncus brachycarpus	short-fruited rush	T	
Juncus scipoides	scirpus-like rush	T	
Juncus vaseyi	Vasey's rush	T	
Lechea pulchella	Leggett's pinweed	T	
Linum sulcatum	furrowed flax	SC	
Lycopodium appressum	appressed bog clubmoss	T	
Panicum longifolium	long-leaved panic grass	T	
Platanthera ciliaris	yellow fringed orchid	T	
Polygala cruciata	cross-leaved milkwort	SC	
Polygonium careyi	Carey's smartweed	T	
Potemogeton bicupulatus	waterthread pondweed	T	
Prunus allechaniensis var. *davisii*	Alleghany plum	SC	FSC
Psilocarya scirpoides	bald rush	T	
Pycnathemum verticillatum	whorled mountain mint	SC	

TABLE 9.3

Michigan imperiled species associated with habitats of the Karner blue butterfly [CONTINUED]

Scientific name	Common name	State status	Federal status
Rare vascular plants			
Rhexia virginica	meadow beauty	T	
Rhexia mariana var *mariana*	Maryland meadow beauty	T	
Rhynchospora macrostachya	tall beak rush	SC	
Rotata ramosior	tooth cup	SC	
Scirpus hallii	Hall's bulrush	E	FSC
Scirpus torreyi	Torrey's bulrush	SC	
Scleria pauciflora	few-flowered nut rush	E	
Scleria reticularis	netted nut rush	T	
Scleria triglomertata	tall nut rush	SC	
Sisyrinchium atlanticum	Altantic blue-eyed grass	T	
Sisyrinchium strictum	blue-eyed grass	SC	
Sporobolus heterolepis	prairie dropseed	T	
Trichostema dichotomum	bastard pennyroyal	T	
Triplasis purpurea	sand grass	SC	

State status codes:
SC = special concern
T = threatened
E = endangered
Federal status codes:
E = endangered
T = threatened
FSC = federal species of concern (these are the former federal C2 candidate species)
C = candidate

SOURCE: Karner Blue Butterfly Recovery Team, "Table D3. Michigan Imperiled Species Associated with Karner Blue Habitats. Data provided by the Michigan Natural Features Inventory," in *Karner Blue Butterfly Recovery Plan (Lycaeides melissa samuelis),* Department of the Interior, U.S. Fish & Wildlife Service, Great Lakes-Big Rivers Regions (Region 3), Fort Snelling, MN, September 2003

TABLE 9.4

Some potential non-native insect predators and parasites of Blackburn's sphinx moth

Order/family	Genus/species:	Island(s) on which the species has been reported:	Island(s) on which the species has not been reported:
Diptera Tachinidae	*Chaetogaedia monticola* (tachinid fly)	Hawaii, Kauai, Lanai, Maui, Molokai, Oahu	Kahoolawe
Diptera Tachinidae	Lespesia archippivora (tachinid fly)	Hawaii, Kauai, Maui, Molokai, Oahu	Kahoolawe, Lanai
Hymenoptera Formicidae	*Anoplolepis longipes* (long-legged ant)	Hawaii, Kauai, Maui, Oahu	Kahoolawe, Lanai, Molokai
Hymenoptera Formicidae	*Linepithema humilis* (Argentine ant)	Hawaii, Kahoolawe, Kauai, Lanai, Maui	Molokai, Oahu
Hymenoptera Formicidae	*Ochetellus glaber* (no common name)	Hawaii, Kahoolawe, Kauai, Maui, Oahu	Lanai, Molokai
Hymenoptera Formicidae	*Pheidole megacephala* (big-headed ant)	Hawaii, Kahoolawe, Kauai, Lanai, Maui, Molokai, Oahu	—
Hymenoptera Formicidae	*Solenopsis geminita* (fire ant species)	Hawaii, Kauai, Lanai, Maui, Molokai, Oahu	Kahoolawe
Hymenoptera Formicidae	*Solenopsis papuana* (fire ant species)	Hawaii, Kauai, Lanai, Maui, Molokai, Oahu	Kahoolawe
Hymenoptera Vespidae	*Vespula pennsylvanica* (yellow jacket wasp)	Hawaii, Kauai, Maui, Oahu	Kahoolawe, Molokai, Lanai
Hymenoptera Ichneumonidae	*Hyposoter exiguae* (no common name)	Hawaii, Kauai, Maui, Molokai, Oahu	Kahoolawe, Lanai
Hymenoptera Trichogrammatidae	*Trichogramma chilonis* (no common name)	Kauai, Oahu	Hawaii, Maui, Kahoolawe, Lanai, Molokai
Hymenoptera Trichogrammatidae	*Trichogramma minutum* (no common name)	Hawaii, Lanai, Molokai, Oahu	Kauai, Kahoolawe, Maui

SOURCE: "Table 2. Some of the Potential Non-Native Insect Predators and Parasites of Blackburn's Sphinx Moth," in *Draft Recovery Plan for the Blackburn's Sphinx Moth (Manduca blackburni),* U.S. Fish and Wildlife Service, Region 1, October 2003

TABLE 9.5

Summary of threats to imperiled insects and plants in the Santa Cruz Mountains in California

Species	Sand mining	Urban development	Agricultural conversion	Recreational use*	Competition with nonnative plants	Altered fire cycles	Forest or chaparral succession	Other
Mount Hermon June beetle	X	X	X	X		X	X	Pesticides Overcollection X
Zayante band-winged grasshopper	X	X	X	X		X	X	pesticides overcollection X
Ben Lomond spineflower	X	X	X	X	X	X	X	
Scotts Valley spine flower		X						herbicides pesticides fertilizers altered hydrologic regimes
Ben Lomond wallflower	X	X	X	X		X	X	
Scotts Valley polygonum		X						
Ohlone tiger beetle		X	X	X	X			overcollection pesticides X
Santa Cruz cypress		X	X			X		logging

*Recreational use includes a variety of activities, including hiking, equestrain use, off-road vehicles, bicycling, and camping. Each of these activities varies in the type and intensity of impacts caused.

SOURCE: Connie Rutherford and Kim Touneh, "Table 1. Summary of Threats to the Taxa Included in this Plan," in *Recovery Plan for Insect and Plant Taxa from the Santa Cruz Mountains in California,* U.S. Fish & Wildlife Service, Region 1, Portland, OR, 1998

CHAPTER 10
COMMERCIAL TRADE OF WILDLIFE

Humans have used wild animal and plant products for numerous purposes since prehistoric times. Clothing was made from animal skins, and tools from bones. In many societies, products from rare species symbolized wealth and success. For example, flashy feathers from South American birds were given as a tribute to Inca chiefs by their subjects, and women in nineteenth-century Europe sported ostrich feathers in their hats. In East Asia, animal parts have been used to prepare medicines and aphrodisiacs. Exotic species have also been kept as pets—cheetahs and falcons, for example, were kept for hunting. In addition, species such as dogs, cats, apes, monkeys, frogs, guinea pigs, rats, and mice are used in scientific research.

Sadly, overexploitation of wild species for commercial gain is the second most important cause of animal extinction, after habitat loss. According to the World Conservation Union's *2000 IUCN Red List of Threatened Species*, hunting, collection, and trade affect 37 percent of all bird species, 34 percent of mammals, and 8 percent of surveyed plant species. Once non-domesticated animal species are considered commodities, they have an extremely high likelihood of becoming endangered. A small subset of endangered species currently affected by trade include whales hunted for meat and blubber; exotic birds captured for the illegal pet trade; rhinos poached for their horns; minks killed for their pelts; snakes, alligators, and lizards hunted for their skins; and elephants slaughtered for their ivory tusks. The argalis (see Figure 10.1) is a species of wild sheep endangered because trophy hunters seek its massive horns.

THE FUR, FEATHERS, AND LEATHER TRADE

Numerous wild animal species are hunted for their fur pelts or leather hides. These are used to make coats, hats, shoes, gloves, belts, purses, and other accessories. This has led to the near extermination of mammals and reptiles such as minks, foxes, beavers, seals, alligators and croco-diles, chinchillas, otters, and wild cats. Birds were once hunted for fashion as well—species of egrets, herons, spoonbills, and songbirds were slaughtered by the thousands to supply plumes for women's hats during the nineteenth century.

Beginning in the nineteenth century, the fur industry turned increasingly to domestically raised animals, not because of environmental concerns but because they found it too economically risky to leave the acquisition of pelts to chance. Fur farms opened on Prince Edward Island in Canada in 1887 and quickly spread across the country. At their height, there were well over 10,000 fur farms. By 1939, however, rising costs, the loss of European markets, and changes in fashion reduced fur demand. Canadian fur farms were reduced to less than 2,000 primarily mink farms by the middle of the twentieth century. In August 1998 animal rights activists in England, unhappy with fur farm practices, released thousands of minks from cages. The minks escaped into the district of New Forest, where they wrought havoc on natural habitats and attacked chicken farms. Many were eventually trapped and killed.

In 2000 the world market for shahtoosh, the wool of the Tibetan chiru antelope, came under scrutiny by both the U.S. Fish and Wildlife Service and the Convention on International Trade in Endangered Species of Wild Fauna and Flora (CITES). Measures were adopted at the CITES meeting in Nairobi, Kenya that year to reduce chiru poaching. The Fish and Wildlife Service also proposed listing the chiru as an endangered species, but this is still pending in 2004. The chiru is listed as vulnerable by the IUCN.

Crocodilian Leathers

Among the most biologically costly of fashion trends is the use of reptilian hide for leather shoes, belts, wallets, and other accessories. High fashion has never tired of the look and feel of tanned crocodilian leather, with alligator skin the most popular of all reptile hides. Louisiana's

FIGURE 10.1

The argalis is prized by hunters for its massive horns. *(Corbis Corporation)*

Department of Agriculture estimates that 90 percent of alligator hide originates in the United States, particularly from the bayou regions of Louisiana. Finished products are costly, with alligator purses selling for $200–$1,000 apiece.

Largely because of the demand of European designers for alligator hide, the American alligator was first listed as an endangered species in 1967. It was reclassified as threatened in the 1970s as populations recovered in response to conservation efforts. The American alligator was finally delisted in 1987. As a result of their one time endangerment, Fish and Wildlife representatives continue to monitor alligator egg harvesting and hunting, particularly in Louisiana.

Huia Birds—Plucked to Extinction

Unlike American alligators, which were brought back from endangerment, the fate of the Huia bird was more tragic. The beautiful Huia, native to New Zealand, was hunted to extinction during the 1920s, primarily because of demand for adornments made from its luxurious feathers. The species was characterized by black plumes with striking white tips. In addition, Huia feathers figured prominently in the native Maori culture of New Zealand, and Maoris hunted the species as well. The Huia was declared extinct in 1930.

COLLECTORS OF RARE AND EXOTIC SPECIES

Many wild species are valued by collectors, including spiders, insects such as beetles or butterflies, and plants, particularly orchids and cacti. Rare species are particularly sought after. For that reason Fish and Wildlife biologists are sometimes reluctant to reveal the critical habitats of threatened and endangered species in the United States. Despite strict prohibition under the Endangered Species Act, however, the poaching of numerous imperiled species thrives.

Exotic species including wild birds, reptiles, and mammals are also valued in the illegal pet trade. According to CITES, approximately 40,000 primates were illegally traded annually in the 1990s. Animal smuggling is an extremely lucrative business, and international efforts to halt it have not been successful. This is attributed in large part to shoddy or nonexistent inspection due to lack of funds and manpower.

The Reptile Trade

The reptile trade is extremely lucrative, with large profits and low transport costs. In addition, trade in reptiles is less closely controlled and monitored than that of mammals and birds. Illegally collected reptiles are used primarily for food, although some species also bring in huge sums in the pet trade.

In 1998 decades of effort by U.S. and Mexican agents culminated in the apprehension of a Malaysian reptile smuggler in Mexico City. He was convicted of heading a large smuggling operation that procured live threatened and endangered reptiles from the wild for sale as exotic pets. Animals were transported from Asia into North America via Mexico. Between 1995 and 1998 this smuggling ring was estimated to have brought in over three hundred protected animals worth about $500,000. These included a Chinese alligator that sold for $15,000 on the black market, monitor lizards that brought in $3,000 apiece, and a ten-foot Komodo dragon from Indonesia that sold for $30,000.

In March 2001 the Malaysian Department of Wildlife and National Parks and the Royal Customs and Excise announced the interception of two large shipments of threatened reptiles. The first included 1,100 animals, and the second included sixty rare snakes, tortoises, and spiders.

Some exotic reptiles, including green iguanas and boa constrictors, can be legally obtained and kept as pets. However, many of the owners who acquire these animals fail to realize the responsibilities involved. Giant green iguanas, a favorite of reptile collectors, may grow to six feet in length, a size many owners find unmanageable. Giant green iguanas are also particularly susceptible to metabolic bone disease (MBD), which results from calcium deficiency and causes severe deformity or death. Although MBD can be cured, treatment is costly, and pet owners frequently decide to get rid of their pets rather than seek veterinary care. In addition some owners dispose of overgrown or diseased reptilian pets in sewers or other public conduits, creating dangers for native species. (This is the source of long-time rumors that alligators inhabit New York City sewers.)

Illegal Trade of Wild Birds

Human desire for exotic pets is emptying the skies of some of Earth's most colorful creatures. (See Figure 10.2.) Numerous bird species, particularly parrots, are endangered due to overexploitation for the illegal pet trade. Approximately 75 percent of the exotic birds sold as pets in the United States were caught in the wild rather than bred in captivity. Demand for exotic pets results in very high prices, as much as $10,000 or more for certain species. In the United States, a single parrot can easily command a thousand dollars or more. Table 10.1 shows some of the potential profits to be made in the rare bird trade.

Illegal trade in birds is thriving worldwide. Due to a lack of financial resources, most countries are only rarely able to enforce laws designed to control trade. The European community has no enforcement agency to deal with the issue, and the Fish and Wildlife Service is grossly underfunded in this respect. Illegal traders often use legal trade as a cover, relying on falsification of documents, under-declaration of the number of birds in a shipment,

FIGURE 10.2

Many tropical birds, including this scarlet macaw, are sought as exotic pets. *(Field Mark Publications)*

concealment of illegal birds in legal shipments, capture in excess of quotas, and misdeclaration of species. The United States, the largest importer of wild birds in the world, legally brings half a million exotic birds into the country each year. An estimated 100,000 more may be smuggled into the country, with as many as 60 percent of the birds dying in transit because of terrible shipping conditions. Illegal smuggling continues despite the passage of the Wild Bird Conservation Act in 1992, which banned the import of ten species of threatened birds. In 1993 the law was expanded to include almost all CITES-listed bird species.

Bird trapping varies from country to country. Most methods are indiscriminate and result in the capture of untargeted species. In liming, a "teaser" bird lures other birds to trees, where they become stuck on limes, or glued sticks. Liming causes great stress to captured birds. In addition, limes are sometimes set and left, with the result that birds break legs or wings struggling to get loose. Nets are also used to capture wild birds in Latin America and Africa. Decoy birds are used to attract the target species. In night capture, birds are immobilized using a bright light and caught. Nylon loops are sometimes strung around

TABLE 10.1

Profits to be made in the rare-bird trade

Country and species	Price for trapper	Exporter declared value	Exporter price list	Retail value in importing country
Senegal				
Quelea	$0.09	N/A	0.50	22
Senegal parrot	$1.82	4	2.70	115
Tanzania				
Meyer's parrot	$2.10	7	17.25	105
Guyana				
Blue and Gold macaw	$5.00	175	325	750
Orange-winged Amazon	$2–3.00	25	32	298
Argentina				
Blue-fronted Amazon	$1.20–3.50	23	70–136	340
Red lory	$2.52	18	15–20	230
White cockatoo	$6.50	85	100	800–900

SOURCE: "Profits to Be Made in the Rare-Bird Trade," in *Flight to Extinction—The Wild-Caught Bird Trade*, Animal Welfare Institute and Environmental Investigation Agency, Washington, DC, 1997

perches to entangle birds. As with liming, nylon loops are indiscriminate in their capture of birds, and many birds are seriously injured attempting to escape. In fact, in Indonesia 10 to 30 percent of cockatoos caught with nylon loops are rendered commercially nonviable because of injuries to their legs and feet. In wing shooting, pellets are shot into a flock, rendering some birds unable to fly and easy to capture. More birds are killed than captured in the process, and many of the captured individuals die later. Finally, young birds are sometimes taken from the nest. This method, also called tree-felling, is used to acquire parrots from the wild because pet dealers prefer young birds that can more easily be trained to "talk." The parrots' nesting tree is often cut down or hacked apart, rendering it useless as future habitat. Consequently, this is one of the most environmentally destructive methods of capture.

Tropical Fish

Collection of tropical fish species for the aquarium trade has harmed numerous species. In Hawaii, a major supplier of saltwater species for the aquarium market, fish depletion has led to conflicts between tropical reef fish collectors, scuba diving operations, and subsistence fishers. Lisa Choquette, the owner of a scuba tour business, explains that "areas that we take divers to all the time, and that once had rivers of fish swimming in and out of the corals, are now quite barren." In addition, several tropical species collected as tiny juveniles for the aquarium trade ultimately grow into large fish sought by subsistence fishermen. Exploitation of reef fish for trade has increased over the past decades, from 90,000 fish taken in 1973 to over 423,000 in 1995. Aquarium species collected most commonly in Hawaii include the yellow tang, kole, Achilles tang, longnose butterfly fish, Moorish idol, orangespine unicornfish, and Potter's angelfish. Fish populations have declined significantly in locations where aquarium collection occurs. For example, the Achilles tang has declined by 63 percent and the longnose butterfly fish by 54 percent.

In response to these declines, Hawaii passed a bill establishing several Fish Replenishment Areas where collecting is prohibited. Biologists are also trying to develop captive breeding programs, so that aquarium species can be raised in captivity rather than collected from the wild.

HEALTH REMEDIES AND FADS

Numerous populations of both animals and plants are being depleted for medicinal purposes. The World Health Organization reports that 80 percent of the world population depends largely on animal or plant-based medicines. In addition, plant and animal derivatives are frequently used as components of modern medicines or herbal remedies.

At the top of wildlife contraband lists are aphrodisiacs and arthritis cures made from rhinoceros and tiger parts (none of which has been shown to be effective). In 1992 the Fish and Wildlife Service seized over $500,000 worth of East Asian medicines containing endangered species parts at the Port of Newark in New Jersey. According to a 1996 report from the Environmental News Network, illicit trade in medicinal substances is a booming business in Hong Kong, where there is little that money can't buy. Table 10.2 shows a list of endangered animal parts found in a single market in Golden Rock, Myanmar during a brief study in 2000. The study was conducted by TRAFFIC, a wildlife advocacy and monitoring organization sponsored jointly by the World Wildlife Fund and the World Conservation Union (IUCN). Table 10.2 also lists the reasons why these animal products are valued by locals. Most of the documented animal products at Golden Rock were from mammals, though some were derived from reptiles or birds.

Threats to African Wildlife

Numerous African species are seriously threatened by demand for medicinal ingredients. Of East African and South African wildlife alone, a total of 131 plant and ani-

TABLE 10.2

Observations during survey of Golden Rock, Myanmar, April 16–17, 2000

Species		Part	Quantity	Use	Price	National law	CITES
Asiatic Black Bear	*Ursus thibetanus*	skins	5			P	I
		paws	29	Oil for treating aching joints	K 2000 each		
		rendered fat	numerous	To improve hair condition and white skin patches	K 600/bottle		
		skulls	8	Drink made from the paste to treat children's mouth diseases			
Cat	*Felis sp?*	gall bladder	5	Oil for treating aching joints	K 5000 each		I/II
Leopard	*Panthera pardus*	small skulls	numerous				I
		paws	20				
		head	2				
		skin	1				
		penis and testes	1	Stimulate sex hormones			
Leopard	*Panthera pardus*	skeleton	5			TP	I
or Clouded Leopard	*Neofelis nebulosa*	canines	2	To protect the home		TP	I
Tiger	*Panthera tigris*	bone pieces	4	unknown	K 2500 each	TP	I
		horns	2				
		skins	7				
		head	13	Oil for treating aching joints			
Common Palm Civet	*Paradoxurus hermaphroditus*	skin	1	Ornament		P	III
		stuffed	1				
Civet?		skin	4			?	I/II
Dolphin	Cetacea	skin with fins	2	Oil for treating aching joints		*TP	I
Elephant	*Elephas maximus*	and fat layer	6	Paste applied to skin to cure hernias			
		sole of foot	25	To cure fungal skin infections			
		skin (pieces)	numerous	Rings worn to protect against supernatural attack/to attract women			
		tail hair	2	Hung in the home to bring business success			
		tail	1.5	Carving material. Paste to cure piles			
		leg bones	numerous	Carved into beads for Buddhist prayer necklaces	K 100 each		
		bones	5	Carved into figurines			
		molars	22				

TABLE 10.2

Observations during survey of Golden Rock, Myanmar, April 16–17, 2000 [CONTINUED]

Species		Part	Quantity	Use	Price	National law	CITES
Macaque	*Macaca* sp.	skull	33	Oil/ornamental purposes			II
Otter	*Lutra* or *Aonyx* sp.	charred body	1	Oil for treating aching joints		TP	I/II
Pangolin	*Manis* sp.	head	1	Treatment for children's diseases: scales hung on a string around a child's neck		TP	II
		skins	3				
Porcupine	*Hystrix* sp.	head	1				III
		quills	numerous	Quills dipped in lime are used in light acupuncture (without breaking skin) on back of neck to cure headaches			
Serow	*Capricornis sumatraensis*	heads	34	Manufacture of traditional buttons		not protected	I
		skulls	10	Oil for treating aching joints			
		legs	4	Oil for treating aching joints			
Wild Pig	*Sus* sp.	skull	3	Ornament and possibly medicine		TP	
Squirrel		tails	20	Key-chains			
Squirrel	*Callosciurus* sp.	stuffed	1	Ornament			
Giant Flying Squirrel	*Petaurista* sp.	charred body	2	Oil for treating aching joints		not protected	–
Treeshrew	*Tupia* sp.	stuffed	3	Ornament		not protected	–
Giant squirrel	*Ratufa* sp.	stuffed	2	Ornament		P	II
Reticulated Python	*Python reticulatus*	skins	26	Sold to visiting middlemen for onward sale to leather factories	Approx. K 700/metre	not protected	II
Rock Python	*Python molurus*	skins	8	As above		TP	II
Python	*Python* sp.	meat	15	Oil for treating aching joints		P	II
Elongated Tortoise	*Indotestudo elongata*	shell	1	Manufacture of combs according to dealer, although this is questionable		P	II
Great Hornbill	*Buceros bicornis*	head	4	Ornament		TP	I
		skin	2	Ornament			
		shell	1	Oil applied to white skin blotches			

TP: totally protected; P: protected; SP: seasonally protected; *unless a domesticated elephant

K: Kyat (currency)

CITES: Convention of International Trade in Endangered Species

SOURCE: "Table 1. Observations during survey of Golden Rock, 16–17 April, 2000," in "Observations on Wildlife Trade at Golden Rock, Myanmar," *TRAFFIC Bulletin*, Vol. 19, No. 1, 2001

mal species required attention by conservation management organizations in 1998.

Over 100 African plant species were cited by TRAFFIC as overexploited and in need of conservation management. This included the Sudanese *Aloe sinkatana*, whose leaves and leaf excretions are used for treating skin disorders and diseases of the digestive system. *Adansonia digitata*, a tree, is also in decline because its fruit and bark are used in treating dysentery. The bark of the afromontane tree species, *Prunus africana*, is also overexploited for treatment of prostate gland diseases. Over one thousand tons of *P. africana* bark were exported from Kenya between 1990 and 1998. France imported four tons of *P. africana* extract from Madagascar. CITES initiated international trade control of this tree species in 1994.

At least 100 animal species are used in traditional medicine in eastern and southern Africa. Among the animals most threatened by medicinal trade is the African rock python, whose skin contains an agent used in the treatment of sexually transmitted diseases and back pain. The Cape pangolin, a rare species of horny "scaled" mammal, is prized by shamans who use the scales to make charms and talismans. The African wild ass is exploited for blood, meat, and fat, all of which are valued for a variety of curative powers by the Eritreans of northeastern Africa. The green turtle, found in Kenya, is illegally traded for the pharmaceutical effects of its oil and genitalia.

Traditional Chinese Medicine

Numerous Chinese medicines are made from the parts of endangered species. The true extent of this trade is unknown—however, informed sources estimate that the industry is worth several billion dollars a year. In Taiwan, for example, rhinoceros horns are twice as valuable as gold. Although no studies have ever demonstrated the medicinal value of rhinoceros horn, numerous Asians believe it has magical curative powers. Rhino populations have declined worldwide as a result of poaching for the medicinal trade.

In the United States, at least 430 different East Asian medicines containing body parts of endangered or threatened species have been documented. According to a study by the World Wildlife Fund, such products are in fact more readily available on store shelves in the United States than in China. The products seen most frequently are tiger bone-containing remedies for arthritis and other muscular ailments. In 1994 the United States passed the Rhinoceros and Tiger Conservation Act to curtail trade of these products. A 1998 amendment to the act, the Rhino and Tiger Labeling Law, closed a loophole in the original legislation by empowering the Fish and Wildlife Service to remove products from store shelves based solely on labeling claims and without forensic proof that the content included tiger or rhinoceros parts. The revised statute

also established prison terms of up to six months and fines of up to $12,000 for violations. Additionally, the amendment called for the establishment of outreach programs to promote public awareness of this issue.

BUSH MEAT

"Bush meat" refers to meat obtained from wild species. Trade in wild meat threatens numerous species in Africa, South America, and Asia. According to a 2001 report by TRAFFIC, wild meat in Africa is obtained from species such as "elephants, gorillas, chimpanzees and other primates, forest antelopes (duikers), crocodiles, porcupines, bush pigs, cane rats, pangolins, monitor lizards, and guinea fowl." Most of the trade occurs on a regional to national scale. However, some meat is exported, particularly to European countries. Officials have seized several illegal shipments at European airports including meat from protected monkeys, pangolins, tortoises, and antelopes. In addition, two London shopkeepers were convicted in 2001 for selling meat from CITES-listed species such as monkeys, savanna monitors, and African pythons. At the 2000 CITES meeting, a group was established to address the issue of unsustainable bush meat exploitation.

ANIMALS USED FOR MEDICAL OR SCIENTIFIC RESEARCH

The use of animals for scientific and medical research is both common and controversial. Under the Animal Welfare Act (AWA) of 1966 and its amendments, the Animal and Plant Health Inspection Service (APHIS) of the U.S. Department of Agriculture is responsible for reporting on species used in research. APHIS reported that in 2001 over 1.2 million animals were used for research purposes in the United States. (See Figure 10.3.) However, this figure does not include rats, mice, birds, or farm animals used exclusively in agricultural research, as the AWA does not require that these be tracked. The AWA requires that animals kept for research purposes be treated humanely. However, it places no restrictions on how animals can be used in valid experiments. The law does call for the limitation of pain and suffering if doing so will not interfere with the experiment.

For decades, some animal rights organizations have protested the use of animals in research. Activists argue that the vast majority of animal research, if not all of it, is cruel and unnecessary. Activists also argue that, despite laws like the AWA, many research animals live in inhumane environments. Although large-scale animal research continues, animal rights and anti-cruelty organizations have had some successes. Many businesses have stopped testing their products on animals and advertise them as "cruelty-free."

Most animal research is conducted on domesticated species, whose numbers are adequate to support this use. A major exception, however, is the primates.

FIGURE 10.3

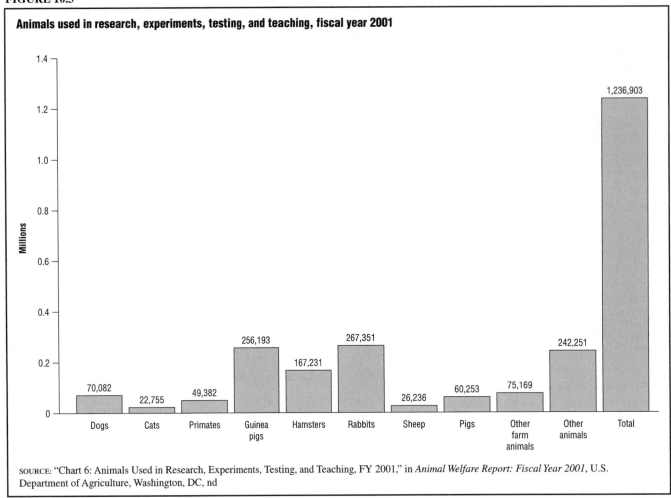

Animals used in research, experiments, testing, and teaching, fiscal year 2001

SOURCE: "Chart 6: Animals Used in Research, Experiments, Testing, and Teaching, FY 2001," in *Animal Welfare Report: Fiscal Year 2001*, U.S. Department of Agriculture, Washington, DC, nd

Research and the Primate Trade

The primate trade dates back thousands of years. Mesopotamians used monkey bones to make drugs, and Egyptians trained baboons to harvest figs. Today, however, primates are particularly valued by medical researchers because they are closely related to humans. Because of this, primates such as chimpanzees and rhesus monkeys are regularly used for medical, chemical, and even nuclear testing. In 2001 scientists in the United States used 49,382 primates for research. (See Figure 10.3.)

According to CITES, 40,000 primates are traded internationally every year for biomedical research. Most of this takes place in industrial nations—the United States, United Kingdom, and Japan are the top primate-importing countries. While the results of this research are sometimes of medical value, numerous animals suffer, and many primate populations are in severe decline. All non-human primate species are listed under either CITES Appendix I (Species in Danger of Extinction) or Appendix II (Species Threatened in the Absence of Trade Controls).

The discovery of acquired immunodeficiency syndrome (AIDS) in the 1980s made primates, particularly chimpanzees, even more valuable to the medical research industry. Pressure on chimpanzee populations due to collection for medical research prompted primatologists to petition the Fish and Wildlife Service to upgrade chimpanzees from threatened to endangered. Fearing opposition from the medical community, the Fish and Wildlife Service compromised, declaring in 1990 that wild chimpanzees in their natural range in Central and West Africa would be listed as endangered, while captive populations outside the natural range would be listed as threatened.

BREEDING PRIMATES FOR SCIENCE AND RESEARCH. Since the 1970s most countries harboring wild primate populations have restricted the export of these animals. Indonesia and the Philippines, which once supplied 50 to 80 percent of all internationally traded primates, adopted export bans in 1994. These bans have helped restore native populations. As a result, the demand for primates for medical research is increasingly being met through captive breeding. China has been a major source of captive-bred rhesus monkeys for the United States and Europe since 1988. Barbados, which has the largest monkey colony in the Northern Hemisphere, supplies a steady flow of primates for research purposes. Vietnam has also developed as an export center for captive-bred primates.

However, some officials claim that many primates shipped from Vietnam were actually caught in the wild.

TRAFFIC'S PRIORITY SPECIES AND ECOREGIONS

TRAFFIC is a leading wildlife trade monitoring network sponsored jointly by the World Wildlife Fund and the World Conservation Union (IUCN). It works closely with the Secretariat of the Convention on International Trade in Endangered Species (CITES). Regarding threatened species, TRAFFIC states its objective as: "To ensure that wildlife trade does not result in the endangerment of any wild animal or plant species." As of 2004, TRAFFIC's priority species included:

- Elephants—Elephant tusks are highly valuable in the illegal ivory trade.

- Tigers—Tiger bones and other parts are used in traditional Asian medicine. Tiger skins are also valuable in illegal markets.

- Tibetan antelope—This species is poached for its precious wool, known as shahtoosh.

- Sharks—The highly endangered whale sharks are hunted for meat, fins, liver, skin, and cartilage.

- Marine turtles—Demand for meat, eggs, and turtle shells has resulted in the overexploitation of numerous species, including the Caribbean hawksbill turtle.

- Rhinos—Rhinoceros are poached for their horns, which are used in traditional Asian medicine.

- Sturgeon—Sturgeon are overexploited for their eggs, which make up the luxury food caviar, as well as for their meat.

- Freshwater turtles—The number of critically endangered freshwater turtle species has increased rapidly in the early 2000s. Softshell turtles represent a luxury food in Asia, and turtle shells are used in traditional Chinese medicine.

- Mahogany—Mahogany tree species are exploited for timber that is used to make furniture, boats, musical instruments, expensive wood paneling, and other products.

- Agarwood—Agarwood is the fragrant heartwood of certain tree species and is used for medicine, perfume, and incense in Ayurvedic, Tibetan, and traditional East Asian medicine.

TRAFFIC also listed the following priority ecoregions in 2004:

- Asian forests

- Southeast Asian mangroves

- Lower Mekong Basin

- Russian Far East

- Eurasia-Central Asia

- Altai-Sayan region

- East African coastal marine environments

- East African coastal forests

- North America's Chihuahuan Desert

- North America's high arctic

- Amazonian flooded forests

- Amazonian freshwater environments

- The Andes

WORLD "LEADERS" IN WILDLIFE TRADE

The United States—A Consuming Giant

In 1994 the Fish and Wildlife Service reported that U.S. wildlife trade represented a $20 billion market, including an estimated $5 billion in illegal trade—this is despite U.S. claims to leadership in the protection of threatened plant and animal species. Although the U.S. undeniably has some of the most promising legislation in the world regarding wildlife trade, the insatiable demand of American consumers, plus inadequate resources for law enforcement, has created a booming trade. The most alarming aspect of this trade is Americans' desire for exotic birds—particularly Amazonian parrots, African gray parrots, and Indonesian cockatoos—precisely those bird species most endangered by trade.

Bird smuggling is a particular problem along the Texas-Mexico border. In 1994 federal officials uncovered what they believed to be one of the nation's largest parrot-smuggling operations and seized $70,000 worth of smuggled birds from a Mexican gang. However, this represented only a tiny part of a huge smuggling market responsible for the illegal importation of between 25,000 and 150,000 birds each year. In 1996 a parrot expert named Tony Silva was convicted of smuggling $1.4 million worth of endangered parrots. This included the highly endangered hyacinth macaw, of which only 2,000–5,000 individuals remain in the wild. Because of their rarity, hyacinth macaws are valued at $12,000 each by unscrupulous collectors. In 1997 Adolph Pare of Miami, Florida was sentenced to a year in prison and fined $300,000 for attempting to smuggle 4,000 African gray parrots illegally collected in the Democratic Republic of Congo (formerly Zaire) into the United States. He had obtained fake CITES permits for the parrots.

In 1996 the Fish and Wildlife Service also uncovered an illegal trade operation involving bald eagles. The investigation culminated in the arrest of eight men. Citations were also issued against eight tourist shops in the

Four Corners region of Arizona, Colorado, New Mexico, and Utah, where bald eagle carcasses were being sold for $1,000 apiece. FWS also reported that more than 60 bald and golden eagles were shot or trapped that winter to feed the demand for feathers, wings, tails, and talons. Numerous tourist centers were fined for selling eagle feathers, prohibited under the Bald and Golden Eagle Protection Act. This law, originally passed in 1940, prohibits all trade in bald and golden eagle parts without a permit. A 1972 amendment to the act raised the maximum fine for some crimes to half a million dollars.

Asia and the Pacific Rim—A Black Hole for Endangered Species

The failure of some Asian countries—particularly China, Japan, South Korea, and Taiwan—to curtail illegal trade has combined with economic growth in the Far East to produce a huge demand for numerous endangered species and their products. Although some effort has recently been made to enforce CITES regulations within Asia, officials have had difficulty combating entrenched organized crime networks. Nor are cultural habits, such as the use of endangered species products in many traditional Chinese medicines, easily changed.

CHINA. With a population in excess of 1.29 billion in 2004, China has become one of the world's largest consumers of wildlife and endangered species. The massive growth in wildlife consumption in China is matched by growth in the export and import of endangered species, their parts, and medicines derived from them. Despite the threat of sanctions by CITES and the United States, the Chinese government has largely turned its back on the growing illegal trade. Furthermore, corruption is widespread. A number of investigations have revealed the involvement of government stores and officials in the sale of restricted products.

INDONESIA. Indonesia legally exports between 58,000 and 91,000 birds each year, primarily cockatoos, lories, and other psittacines (birds belonging to the parrot family). Countless others are exported illegally. Approximately 126 avian species native to Indonesia are threatened because of trade or habitat destruction. In July 2003, the World Parrot Trust, a non-profit organization dedicated to protecting threatened birds worldwide, reported that the Indonesian government had pledged to ban the export of parrots illegally captured in the wild.

JAPAN. With a population in excess of 127 million in 2004, Japan has one of the highest per capita levels of wildlife consumption in the world. Japan also persists in aggressively campaigning for increased consumption of some types of endangered wildlife. At the 2000 meeting of the International Whaling Commission (IWC), for example, it joined forces with Norway in an effort to eliminate bans against commercial whaling. Moreover, Japan

has lobbied CITES for increased wildlife trade. Japan's population of black bears is listed on CITES Appendix I, and its brown bear on Appendix II. Domestic trade in bears (not regulated by CITES, which only deals with international trade) is nonetheless both legal and completely unregulated. Up to one-fifth of Japan's black bear population is killed each year.

VIETNAM. In the late 1990s Vietnam was one of the worst offenders in the trade of rare and endangered species. Although the country joined CITES in 1994, little change resulted in the absence of rigid enforcement policies. As other countries in Southeast Asia tightened controls on wildlife smuggling, Vietnam welcomed trade and turned itself into the largest endangered species market in the world. In market stalls in Ho Chi Minh City, a wide variety of wildlife, both dead and alive, fills the streets.

The Americas

ARGENTINA. Argentina is one of the world's largest suppliers of wild psittacines (birds related to parrots), shipping between 63,000 and 183,000 individuals each year and threatening the continued survival of numerous species. The extent of illegal traffic is difficult to determine. In addition, tree-felling, a method for collecting young birds from nests, is causing extensive habitat destruction. The blue-fronted Amazon parrot accounts for 27 percent of the country's bird trade.

GUYANA. Guyana officially exports between 15,000 and 19,000 birds each year, including some valuable macaws. The country ranks, along with Senegal, Tanzania, Argentina, and Indonesia, among the top five exporters of wild birds for the international market. National legislation in Guyana allows for the capture of any species, regardless of its conservation status, and inspectors have documented the trade of dozens of rare scarlet macaws.

Africa

NIGERIA. Poachers trap or shoot gorillas for their heads, which are sold as trophies to tourists, and their hands, which are sold as ashtrays. In Nigeria, more lowland gorillas are being killed each year than are being born, creating an imminent threat of extinction for this species.

NAMIBIA. Despite protests from animal rights groups, commercial sealing endures as a flagship industry in Namibia, where the penises of baby seal pups are sold as aphrodisiacs to markets in the Far East. Sealskin is also used for shoes, wallets, and accessories. Large-scale sealing, a successful industry in the job-starved Namibian economy, brings approximately $500,000 into that country each year.

SENEGAL. Senegal exports between 1 and 10 million birds each year and derives approximately 65 percent of the value of its bird exports from a single species, the African gray parrot. This species does not occur naturally in Senegal but is imported from other African countries for trading with third parties.

TANZANIA. Tanzania supplies the international market with a variety of songbirds, including the popular Fischer's lovebird, a native species whose numbers have declined drastically. Tanzania exports somewhere between 200,000 and 3 million birds per year. Despite government attempts to control trade, protected species are routinely exported.

TRADE POLICIES AND AGREEMENTS

The Lacey Act

In the United States, the indiscriminate slaughter of wildlife in the nineteenth century brought about the extinction of numerous species. The Lacey Act was passed in 1900 and represented the first national conservation law. The Lacey Act prohibited interstate transport of wildlife killed in violation of a state law, and also allowed individual states to prohibit import of wildlife or their products even if killed lawfully. For example, egret plumes taken in a state where the bird was protected could not be shipped to other states; in addition, a state could outlaw entry of the plumes even if collection was legal in the exporting state. In 1908 the scope of the Lacey Act was expanded to include wildlife imported from abroad. The Lacey Act contributed to the elimination of the meat markets where the last Labrador ducks were sold, and of the plume trade that nearly led to extinction for the snowy and common egrets as well as other water birds.

Two comprehensive amendments to the Lacey Act in 1981 and 1988 added important new restrictions and increased the fines for illegal trade of wildlife. The amended Lacey Act now covers all CITES- and state-protected species. Its regulations apply to species, their parts, and products made from them. Illegal import or export of wildlife-related contraband is now a federal crime. The amended Lacey Act also makes it illegal to provide guide or outfitting services for would-be poachers. The Lacey Act authorizes fines and jail time for offenders. Fines and penalties, authorized at $10,000 maximum by the amendment of 1981, were increased more than tenfold by the Criminal Fines Improvement Act of 1987, with penalty limits now as high as $250,000 for misdemeanors and $500,000 for felonies. Lacey Act enforcement agents are authorized to carry firearms under the amended act, and rewards are authorized for those who provide tips to law enforcement.

The North American Free Trade Agreement

The North American Free Trade Agreement (NAFTA) was signed in 1993 by the United States, Mexico, and Canada. Its goal was to remove trade barriers among the three nations by eliminating most tariffs, investment restrictions, and quotas. Conservationists feared that the passage of NAFTA would weaken U.S. species and environmental protection laws. This had resulted earlier from the signing of another free trade agreement, the General Agreement on Tariffs and Trade (GATT). Under GATT, laws for wildlife protection were sometimes judged to be "technical barriers to trade." For example, in 1991, Mexico used GATT to successfully challenge U.S. tuna-import restrictions intended to protect dolphins. Similarly, U.S. loggers successfully sued under GATT to prevent the British Columbian government from subsidizing the replanting of forests, arguing that it was an unfair subsidy for Canadian loggers.

The Environmental Investigation Agency, a watchgroup for environmental issues, concluded that NAFTA's elimination of trade barriers would stimulate the already high demand for wildlife products from Mexico. It added that trade liberalization among the U.S., Mexico, and Canada would result in increased border crossings, facilitating illegal trade and placing an even greater burden on overworked FWS inspectors and agents.

The World Trade Organization

The World Trade Organization (WTO) is a global trade association that promotes trade among nations and possesses broad authority to rule on trade disputes. The original WTO agreements were signed at Marrakech, Morocco in April 1994. As of April 2004 the organization included 147 member nations.

Environmentalists have frequently been critical of the WTO, charging that it is unconcerned about environmental issues when these conflict with trade and development. Conservationists also fear that the WTO could force the U.S. to back down on environmentally friendly laws that restricted trade, just as GATT had done. This fear was realized when India, Thailand, Pakistan, and Malaysia petitioned the WTO on U.S. shrimp import legislation. In particular, these countries objected to U.S. laws prohibiting importation of shrimp from countries without turtle excluder device (TED) regulations for the protection of endangered sea turtles. In April 1998 the WTO ruled that the U.S. laws were discriminatory. Conservation groups called on the U.S. government to defy the WTO decision, fearing the environment would take a back seat whenever a direct conflict arose with free trade. The United States attempted a compromise, requiring environmentally friendly fishing practices from foreign nations only when shrimp was earmarked for export to the United States.

A similar compromise was proposed with regard to dolphin-safe tuna fishing, and the federal government agreed to disregard its own policy in order to maintain its standing in the WTO. Critics alleged that the United States had placed the fate of the American environment in the hands of other nations. Many critics considered the move a serious blow to environmental protection.

In the wake of these decisions, a series of WTO meetings held in Seattle, Washington from November 29 through December 4, 1999, erupted in massive civil unrest. Over 50,000 protesters from around the globe participated, protesting vehemently against diverse policies of the WTO, including its attitudes towards the environment, human rights, sweatshops, labor unions, wages, and the price and quality of food. Special-interest groups engaged in the protests included the Humane Society, the Sierra Club, the Center for Science and the Public Interest, Global Exchange, the United Auto Workers, and numerous others. An estimated $6 million in damages resulted from the demonstrations, and over 600 protesters were arrested. The WTO meeting was entirely shut down, if only temporarily.

THE CONVENTION ON INTERNATIONAL TRADE IN ENDANGERED SPECIES (CITES)

The Convention on International Trade in Endangered Species of Wild Fauna and Flora (CITES) is an international treaty established to regulate commerce in wildlife. CITES, first ratified in 1975, was developed to block both the import and export of endangered species as well as to regulate trade in vulnerable species. CITES maintains three levels of control. Appendix I, the most stringent, includes species that are in immediate danger of extinction. CITES generally prohibits international trade of these species. Appendix II lists species that are likely to become in danger of extinction without strict protection from international trade. Permits may be obtained for the trade of Appendix II species only if trade will not harm the survival prospects of the species in the wild. Appendix III includes species identified by individual countries as being subject to conservation regulations within its borders.

CITES is generally regarded as the most important legislation regulating trade in endangered or vulnerable species. The treaty nations hold a meeting, called a Conference of Parties (or COP), approximately every two to three years. There were 164 member nations party to CITES in 2004.

Among the most hotly contested topics at the 2000 CITES meeting (COP 11) was the listing status of the African elephant. The African elephant population, which stabilized during the 1990s after a drastic 20-year decline, served as an example of the beneficial nature of CITES protection. Indeed, some wildlife experts surmised that the market for ivory products in North America and Western Europe evaporated after CITES imposed a ban on ivory trafficking in 1989, and that the Japanese market for these products dropped by 50 percent. The error of that assumption was exposed, however, following the 1997

CITES conference in Harare, Zimbabwe. When delegates at that conference authorized the export of 60 tons of stockpiled ivory from three African countries—Zimbabwe, Botswana, and Namibia—the ivory sold for over $5 million on the international market. This occurred in 1999. Soon after, ivory poaching increased more than fourfold in Kenya. Tanzania and Zimbabwe reported increases in illegal elephant slaughter as well.

In 2000 South Africa, Zimbabwe, Namibia, and Botswana once again petitioned CITES for authorization to sell stockpiled ivory. In addition, these nations declared that they were now overrun by elephants because of the ivory ban and petitioned for the approval of a culling system in which elephants from overpopulated areas would be moved to less populated regions. The South African contingency requested an allowance for some trade, both in ivory and in elephant leather. In the ongoing debate, India and Kenya responded by petitioning for a total ban on elephant ivory trade. India and Kenya also proposed that the elephant be moved to CITES Appendix I. In the end, the opposing factions reached a compromise in which both proposals were withdrawn—elephants remained listed under Appendix II, and the ban on ivory sales remained in effect.

At CITES' COP 12 meeting (held in Santiago, Chile in November 2002), member nations adopted trade controls for a number of new species which were added to CITES Appendix II. These included:

- mahogany, which suffers from overexploitation for timber

- whale sharks and basking sharks, which are hunted for the meat, fins, and liver oil

- 26 species of Asian turtles, which are exploited for traditional Asian medicine, the pet trade, and for food

- all 32 seahorse species, which are declining due to overexploitation for the aquarium market and for traditional medicines, fishing practices, and pollution

The listing of the two shark species was considered a landmark decision because CITES had not previously addressed fisheries. In addition, species of parrots, chameleons, orchids, and frogs were transferred from Appendix II to Appendix I due to their continued decline. In the continuing battle over ivory sales, CITES also conditionally approved a narrow range of future ivory sales. These can only take place after studies on elephant poaching and population sizes are complete.

CITES has a number of shortcomings. First, many countries lack the funds and expertise to determine the endangerment status of their species. As a result, numerous species that require protection have yet to be listed with the convention. Some experts also argue that CITES listing serves to advertise a species' rarity, thereby boosting its trade. However, the primary criticism of CITES is that its regulations are notoriously difficult to enforce. Wildlife protection organizations such as TRAFFIC estimate that 30 percent of the total value of the global wildlife trade occurs in violation of either CITES or national laws. Other problems include the absence of laws to implement CITES, weak penalties for violators, and widespread corruption among public officials. Many nations are not even party to the CITES convention, making them potential wildlife bazaars where animals and plants illegally exported from CITES nations can be "laundered." Numerous biologically rich nations have not signed the CITES treaty. Finally, CITES addresses only trade across international borders. It does not address the problem of trade within countries, which is detrimental to many endangered and vulnerable species.

THE INTERNATIONAL WHALING COMMISSION

The campaign to save endangered whales has perhaps made greater progress than any other international effort to protect endangered species. In 1946, long before the creation of CITES, the International Whaling Commission (IWC) was established to regulate whaling. The IWC, a loosely governed consortium, included fifty-two nations in 2004. The primary function of the IWC is to conserve whale stocks through measures such as: the complete protection of endangered whale species; designation of whale sanctuaries; limiting of the numbers and sizes of whales that can be taken; designation of open and closed seasons for whaling; and prohibition of takes of whale calves as well as females accompanied by calves. Unfortunately, the IWC is powerless to enforce its resolutions, and depends largely on international pressure and the enforcement policies of individual nations. Member countries that are unwilling to comply with restrictions imposed by any IWC agreement may refuse to participate or may simply quit the IWC.

In order to protect dwindling whale populations, the IWC began by setting quotas on whale kills. As populations continued to decline, however, the IWC declared a moratorium on commercial whaling in 1986, with certain exceptions. In 1994 the IWC banned whaling within the 11 million square miles around Antarctica, an area called the Southern Ocean Sanctuary. The sanctuary, which must be reauthorized at ten-year intervals, is intended to create a safe harbor for the 90 percent of world whales that feed there. There is also an IWC whale sanctuary in the Indian Ocean, originally established in 1979. At the IWC conference in 2002, Mexico, which boasts a large whale watching industry, declared it would establish a 1.15 million square mile whale sanctuary along Mexican coastal waters in the Atlantic and Pacific Oceans.

Despite international pressure to obey the moratorium on commercial whaling, Japan, Norway, Russia, and Iceland, among other nations, continue to whale. Additionally, although the IWC has condemned whaling for research purposes, it nonetheless tolerates a self-allocated annual kill for research. Japan, which, along with Norway, continues to campaign for the reinstatement of commercial whaling, has killed numerous whales under the auspices of research. In 2002 Japan allocated itself a research quota of 700 whales, including 590 minke whales, 10 sperm whales, 50 Bryde's whales, and 50 sei whales. Selling the whale meat, Japan claims, is required by a commission rule prohibiting the waste of research byproducts. The IWC condemned this as a thinly veiled ruse to continue commercial whaling, and called on Japan to use nonlethal research methodologies. Moreover, some environmentalist groups charge that this "research" trade provides a cover for illegal trade in the meat of protected species. In 1997, Earthtrust, a conservation group based in Hawaii, announced the results of several years of tests on whale meat obtained from Japanese markets and restaurants. DNA tests revealed that a large proportion were from endangered species such as humpback and blue whales, rather than from "research" specimens. The Earthtrust project involved conservation biologists Steve Palumbi of Harvard University and C. Scott Baker of the University of Auckland. The illegal trade in whale meat—which brings in as much as $300 per pound—is hypothesized to involve large organized crime groups in Japan.

At the IWC meeting in 2003, Japan continued to argue that whales deplete fisheries, a claim not substantiated by patterns of fish catch in recent years. Norway has also objected to the IWC moratorium on commercial whaling and set itself a quota of 711 whales in 2003. Much of the Norwegian catch ends up being sold in Japan. In addition, Japanese and Taiwanese companies have been caught smuggling large amounts of whale meat.

Subsistence Whaling

In response to the IWC's moratorium on whaling, several groups—including the Makah of Washington State, the Inuits of Alaska (formerly known as Eskimos), and the Chukchi of Siberia—requested a special exemption to hunt bowhead whales, arguing that whales were necessary for their subsistence, in addition to being a significant part of their culture and tradition. These hunts have occurred for over 8,000 years. Critics of the exemptions argued that these groups were no longer dependent on whaling for food. Furthermore, critics charged that traditional whaling in these cultures had involved spears—resulting in a much smaller kill than is possible today with harpoon guns. The IWC granted permission for aboriginal subsistence whaling in 1997 but also established quotas to limit the annual take. In particular, only 280 whales could be taken in a five-year period, with no more than 67 takes in a single year. Since then, subsistence hunting permits have also been issued to Greenlanders (for fin whales and minke whales) as well as inhabitants of St. Vincent and the Grenadines (for humpback whales).

In 2002 the IWC rejected the United States' request that Alaskan Inuits be allowed to continue their whale hunts. The U.S. had requested fifty-five bowhead whales over a period of five years. This was the first time aboriginal hunting quotas were denied. The decision was attributed in the U.S. press to Japanese retaliation—the U.S. had led efforts against allowing Japanese coastal whaling towns to hunt a total of fifty minke whales.

CHAPTER 11

WILDLIFE AS RECREATION

One of the reasons frequently given for conserving wildlife and habitat is the aesthetic and recreational value of natural places. Human beings derive pleasure from natural places in large numbers, and in a wide variety of ways.

NATIONAL SURVEY OF FISHING, HUNTING, AND WILDLIFE-ASSOCIATED RECREATION

Americans have a rich tradition of enjoying nature. In fact, several of the country's most popular recreational activities involve wildlife and wild places. As part of its effort to conserve species and natural habitats, the U.S. Fish and Wildlife Service publishes a periodic report on how Americans use these natural resources. The data come from interviews conducted by the U.S. Bureau of the Census. The most recent report is the *2001 National Survey of Fishing, Hunting, and Wildlife-Associated Recreation*, published in October 2002. In this survey, the Fish and Wildlife Service found that over 80 million Americans over the age of 16—39 percent of the population—participated in some form of wildlife-related activity in 2001. They spent a total of $108 billion on those activities—about 1.1 percent of the nation's Gross Domestic Product. (See Figure 11.1.)

During 2001, 34 million people in the United States fished, 13 million hunted, and over 66 million enjoyed some form of wildlife-watching recreation, including photography and feeding or observing animals. Many participants in one of these wildlife-related activities engaged in the others as well. The prevalence of wildlife-watching from 1980–2001 is shown in Figure 11.2.

Wildlife watching attracted over 66 million Americans in 2001, 31 percent of the total population. (See Figure 11.3.) These included residential participants who took a special interest in wildlife near their homes (62.9 million) as well as nonresidential participants who went on a trip the primary purpose of which was wildlife-watching (21.8 million).

FIGURE 11.1

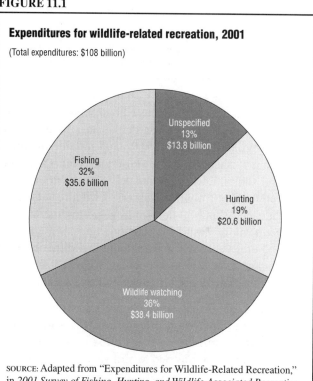

Expenditures for wildlife-related recreation, 2001

(Total expenditures: $108 billion)

Unspecified
13%
$13.8 billion

Fishing
32%
$35.6 billion

Hunting
19%
$20.6 billion

Wildlife watching
36%
$38.4 billion

SOURCE: Adapted from "Expenditures for Wildlife-Related Recreation," in *2001 Survey of Fishing, Hunting, and Wildlife-Associated Recreation*, U.S. Fish and Wildlife Service, Washington, DC, October 2002

Figure 11.4 shows the percent of total residential participants by wildlife-watching activity. The largest number participated by feeding wild birds or observing wildlife. As shown in Figure 11.5, a large majority of residential wildlife observers were interested in birds—96 percent. However, other animal groups, such as mammals, insects and spiders, reptiles and amphibians, and fish, also drew wildlife-watchers. People from non-metropolitan areas, or small metropolitan areas, were most likely to engage in residential wildlife watching. (See Figure 11.6.) Figure 11.7 shows the age breakdown of residential wildlife-watchers.

FIGURE 11.2

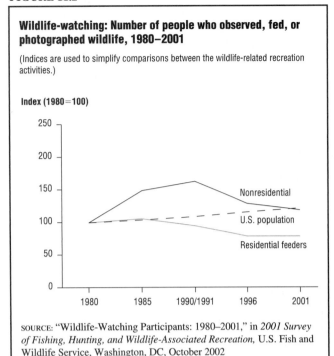

Wildlife-watching: Number of people who observed, fed, or photographed wildlife, 1980–2001

(Indices are used to simplify comparisons between the wildlife-related recreation activities.)

SOURCE: "Wildlife-Watching Participants: 1980–2001," in *2001 Survey of Fishing, Hunting, and Wildlife-Associated Recreation*, U.S. Fish and Wildlife Service, Washington, DC, October 2002

FIGURE 11.3

Wildlife watching is a popular activity among Americans. More than 66 million Americans watched birds or other wildlife in 2001. *(Field Mark Publications)*

Nonresidential participants who observed, fed, or photographed wildlife showed particular interest in birds and land mammals. However, fish and marine mammals (including whales) were also well-represented. (See Figure 11.8 and Table 11.1.) Approximately 83 percent of all nonresidential wildlife observers observed wildlife in their state of residence. About 30 percent traveled to other states to engage in wildlife-watching activity. Figure 11.9 shows the types of sites visited by nonresidential wildlife observers. Woodlands were the most popular, followed by lake or streamsides, open fields, brush-covered areas, and wetlands.

Table 11.2 focuses on the activities of birdwatchers. There were almost 46 million birdwatchers in 2001. Of these, over 40 million observed birds around the home, and over 18 million traveled to birdwatch.

ECOTOURISM

Tourism is one of the largest industries worldwide, generating 200 million jobs globally. The World Tourism Organization (WTO) estimated that there were some 663 million international travelers in 1999, and that these spent a total of more than $453 billion. Nature tourists perhaps account for 40–60 percent of all international tourists, with 20–40 percent focusing on wildlife in particular. In addition, nature tourism is increasing at an annual rate of 10–30 percent.

Ecotourism is a special form of nature travel that The International Ecotourism Society (TIES) defines as "responsible travel to natural areas which conserves the environment and sustains the well-being of local people."

The World Conservation Union (IUCN) defines ecotourism as "environmentally responsible travel and visitation to relatively undisturbed natural areas, in order to enjoy and appreciate nature (and any accompanying cultural features—both past and present) that promotes conservation, has low negative visitor impact, and provides for beneficially active socioeconomic involvement of local populations."

The United Nations General Assembly designated 2002 the International Year of Ecotourism. Programs run collaboratively by United Nations Environment Programme (UNEP), the WTO, and TIES focused on ecotourism's capacity to aid in the conservation of natural and cultural heritage, promote the exchange of ideas in ecotourism management, and allow for exchanges of experiences in ecotourism.

According to TIES, ecotourists are most often between the ages of thirty-five and fifty-four, are evenly split between males and females, and are usually college graduates (82 percent). However, recent increases in ecotourism among people with less education suggest that

FIGURE 11.4

Percent of total residential wildlife activity participants, by activity, 2001

(Total: 62.9 million participants)

SOURCE: "Percent of Total Residential Participants, by Activity," in *2001 Survey of Fishing, Hunting, and Wildlife-Associated Recreation,* U.S. Fish and Wildlife Service, Washington, DC, October 2002

FIGURE 11.5

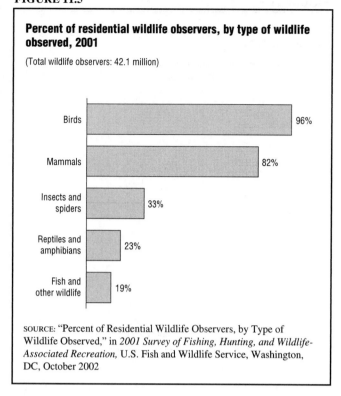

Percent of residential wildlife observers, by type of wildlife observed, 2001

(Total wildlife observers: 42.1 million)

SOURCE: "Percent of Residential Wildlife Observers, by Type of Wildlife Observed," in *2001 Survey of Fishing, Hunting, and Wildlife-Associated Recreation,* U.S. Fish and Wildlife Service, Washington, DC, October 2002

ecotourism is expanding into more mainstream markets. The majority of ecotourists (60 percent) prefer to travel as a couple, though others like to travel either with their families (15 percent) or alone (13 percent). In surveys, ecotourists ranked their top priorities as "wilderness setting," "wildlife viewing," and "hiking/trekking."

TIES' list of popular ecotourism destinations and activities includes hiking and camping in U.S. National Parks (more than 424 million visitations in 2001), visiting nature reserves in South Africa (5,898,000 visitors in 1998), going on safari in Kenya (826,000 visitors in 1993), visiting national parks in Australia (1.7 million visitors in 1998), birdwatching in Peru (642,336 visitors in 1999), visiting national parks in Brazil (3.5 million visitors in 1998), trekking in Nepal (50,708 international trekkers in 1997), visiting parks and reefs in Belize, and viewing wildlife in the Galapagos Islands (60,000 visitors per year on average).

A nationwide survey conducted by TIES in 1998 asked the question, "What type of nature-based activities did you participate in during your last nature-based vacation?" The top twelve answers in order were: visiting parks, hiking, exploring a preserved area, observing wildlife (non-birds), walking nature trails in ecosystems, viewing unique natural places (sinkholes, dunes), participating in environmental education, birdwatching, biking,

freshwater fishing, snorkeling or scuba diving, and exploring a major protected swamp or marsh.

BIRDING

Birding is a wildlife-related recreational activity that enjoys worldwide appeal—there are countless national and regional birding organizations. More than 46 million Americans engage in birdwatching every year. Important conservation studies such as the U.S. Breeding Bird Survey rely largely on volunteer birders to help document long-term population trends and distributions of over 400 North American breeding bird species.

The American Birding Association (ABA) is the largest association of amateur birders in the U.S. Membership has grown steadily since its founding in 1968 and stood at nearly 22,000 in 2004. In terms of birding activity, a 1997 ABA survey showed that 16 percent of members bird more than 80 days a year, and 24 percent bird between 40 and 80 days a year. In addition, 17 percent of members traveled more than 10,000 miles to go birdwatching, while another 20 percent traveled between 5,000 and 10,000 miles. Birdwatchers see diverse species on their outings—21 percent reported identifying 401 species or more in the last year, 17 percent identified 301–400 species, 25 percent identified 201–300 species, and 22 percent identified 101–200 species. A large majority—over 80 percent—of members maintain a "life list" of all the bird species they have ever seen. Among other activities, 82 percent feed birds in their backyards, 67 percent participate in bird counts, 36 percent photograph

FIGURE 11.6

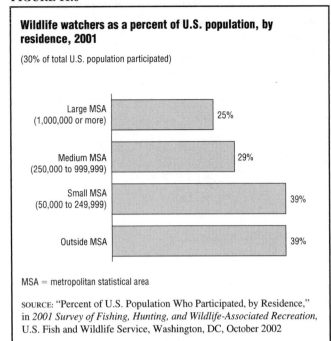

Wildlife watchers as a percent of U.S. population, by residence, 2001

(30% of total U.S. population participated)

MSA = metropolitan statistical area

SOURCE: "Percent of U.S. Population Who Participated, by Residence," in *2001 Survey of Fishing, Hunting, and Wildlife-Associated Recreation,* U.S. Fish and Wildlife Service, Washington, DC, October 2002

FIGURE 11.7

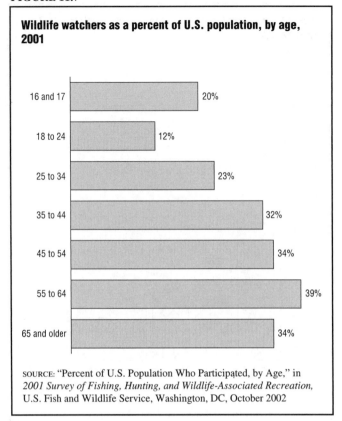

Wildlife watchers as a percent of U.S. population, by age, 2001

SOURCE: "Percent of U.S. Population Who Participated, by Age," in *2001 Survey of Fishing, Hunting, and Wildlife-Associated Recreation,* U.S. Fish and Wildlife Service, Washington, DC, October 2002

birds, 6 percent record bird songs, and 41 percent are active with a local bird club.

WHALE WATCHING

Whale watching has become increasingly popular in recent years, contributing to coastal economies worldwide. (See Figure 11.10.) In 1995 the Whale and Dolphin Conservation Society, based in Bath, England, estimated the industry's value at $504 million. In August 2000 the International Fund for Animal Welfare reported that the industry had grown to $1.049 billion by 1998. It also reported that over 9 million people in 87 countries went on whale-watching expeditions in 1998—an increase of over 3.5 million people since 1994 and more than double the figure of 4 million people in 1991. According to the report, the number of whale watchers increased by an average of more than 12 percent each year during the late 1990s. In 1998 nearly 48 percent of all whale watching occurred in the United States, with an estimated 4.3 million people participating.

A few American cities—Provincetown, Massachusetts, and Lahaina, Hawaii, in particular—reap significant economic benefits from whale watching. Countries such as Canada, New Zealand, South Africa, Argentina, Iceland, and Mexico have also developed lucrative whale-watching industries. Smaller nations, including St. Lucia, Namibia, Oman, and the Solomon Islands, also run profitable whale-watching operations. By 1998 whale-watching programs featured not only the most popular species—humpback whales, fin whales, minke whales, and pilot whales—but eighty-three additional cetaceans, including orcas, or killer whales, and highly endangered northern right whales. The California gray whale, recently removed from the Endan-gered Species List, is the star of the whale-watching industry on the U.S. West Coast. In addition, commercial whale-watching vessels frequently serve as forums for educational outreach and scientific research.

CANNED HUNTING

In the 1980s a controversial form of hunting known as "canned hunting" swept the United States. Originating in Texas, canned hunting now occurs in most states.

In a canned hunt, the hunter pays a set fee and steps onto private property where an animal—most often a boar, ram, bear, lion, tiger, zebra, buffalo, rhinoceros, or antelope—is confined. The hunter then kills the animal with the weapon of his or her choice. The animals are easily cornered—some have been domesticated or raised in facilities where they've become friendly to humans. A 1994 Humane Society investigation found that there may be several thousand canned-hunting facilities in the United States.

There are no federal laws restricting canned hunts. A 2001 survey by Laura J. Ireland revealed that only California, Delaware, Georgia, Montana, New York, Oregon, Wisconsin, and Wyoming had laws prohibiting or regulating canned hunts of exotic species or big game mammals. Zoos frequently sell "surplus" animals either directly to canned-hunt facilities or to dealers who then sell animals at auctions attended by canned-hunt organizers. Some pressure has been exerted on zoos to acknowledge their responsibility for the animals they discard.

TABLE 11.1

Nonresidential (away from home) wildlife-watching participants by wildlife observed, photographed, or fed and place, 2001

(Population 16 years old and older. Numbers in thousands)

| Wildlife observed, photographed, or fed | Total participants | | Participation by place | | | | | |
| | | | Total | | In state of residence | | In other states | |
	Number	Percent	Number	Percent	Number	Percent	Number	Percent
Total, all wildlife	**21,823**	**100**	**21,823**	**100**	**18,041**	**83**	**6,570**	**30**
Total birds	**18,580**	**85**	**18,580**	**100**	**16,150**	**87**	**5,855**	**32**
Songbirds	12,878	59	12,878	100	11,182	87	3,860	30
Birds of prey	12,495	57	12,495	100	10,596	85	4,060	32
Waterfowl	14,432	66	14,432	100	12,384	86	4,258	30
Other water birds (shorebirds, herons, pelicans, etc.)	10,314	47	10,314	100	8,474	82	3,229	31
Other birds (pheasants, turkeys, road runners, etc.)	7,907	36	7,907	100	6,640	84	2,248	28
Total land mammals	**15,506**	**71**	**15,506**	**100**	**13,207**	**85**	**4,844**	**31**
Large land mammals (deer, bear, etc.)	12,226	56	12,226	100	10,047	82	3,784	31
Small land mammals (squirrel, prairie dog, etc.)	12,958	59	12,958	100	10,911	84	4,200	32
Fish	6,330	29	6,330	100	5,019	79	2,000	32
Marine mammals	3,013	14	3,013	100	1,982	66	1,233	41
Other wildlife (turtles, butterflies, etc.)	9,409	43	9,409	100	7,929	84	3,071	33

Note: Detail does not add to total because of multiple responses. Column showing percent of total participants is based on the "Total, all wildlife" number. Participation by place percent columns are based on the total number of participants for each type of wildlife.

SOURCE: "Table 40: Nonresidential (away From Home) Wildlife-Watching Participants by Wildlife Observed, Photographed, or Fed, and Place: 2001," in *2001 Survey of Fishing, Hunting, and Wildlife-Associated Recreation,* U.S. Fish and Wildlife Service, Washington, DC, October 2002

FIGURE 11.8

Percent of nonresidential wildlife-activity participants who observed, fed, or photographed wildlife, 2001

(Total participants: 21.8 million)

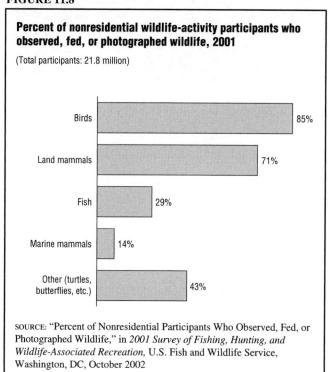

SOURCE: "Percent of Nonresidential Participants Who Observed, Fed, or Photographed Wildlife," in *2001 Survey of Fishing, Hunting, and Wildlife-Associated Recreation,* U.S. Fish and Wildlife Service, Washington, DC, October 2002

FIGURE 11.9

Type of site visited by nonresidential wildlife-activity participants, 2001

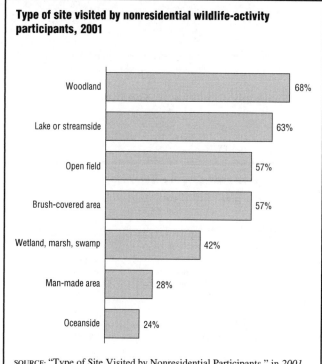

SOURCE: "Type of Site Visited by Nonresidential Participants," in *2001 Survey of Fishing, Hunting, and Wildlife-Associated Recreation,* U.S. Fish and Wildlife Service, Washington, DC, October 2002.

FIGURE 11.10

A humpback whale, seen off the coast of Massachusetts. *(AP/Wide World Photos)*

TABLE 11.2

Wild bird observers and days of observation, 2001

(Population 16 years old and older. Numbers in thousands)

Observers and days of observation	Number	Percent
Observers		
Total bird observers	**45,951**	**100**
Residential (around the home) observers	40,306	88
Nonresidential (away from home) observers	18,342	40
Days		
Total days observing birds	**5,467,841**	**100**
Residential (around the home)	5,159,259	94
Nonresidential (away from home)	308,583	6

Note: Detail does not add to total because of multiple responses.

SOURCE: "Table 41: Wild Bird Observers and Days of Observation: 2001," in *2001 Survey of Fishing, Hunting, and Wildlife-Associated Recreation*, U.S. Fish and Wildlife Service, Washington, DC, October 2002

IMPORTANT NAMES AND ADDRESSES

American Zoo and Aquarium Association
8403 Colesville Rd., Suite 710
Silver Spring, MD
20910-3314
(301) 562-0777
FAX: (301) 562-0888
URL: http://www.aza.org

American Rivers
1025 Vermont Ave. NW, Suite 720
Washington, DC 20005
(202) 347-7550
FAX: (202) 347-9240
E-mail: amrivers@amrivers.org
URL: http://www.amrivers.org

AmphibiaWeb
U.C. Berkeley 3101 Valley Life Sciences
Building #3160
Berkeley, CA 94720
URL: http://amphibiaweb.org

Animal Protection Institute
P.O. Box 22505
Sacramento, CA 95822
(916) 447-3085
FAX: (916) 447-3070
E-mail: info@api4animals.org
URL: http://www.api4animals.org

Animal Welfare Institute
P.O. Box 3650
Washington, DC 20027
(703) 836-4300
FAX: (703) 836-0400
URL: www.awionline.org

**Biological Resources Discipline
(BRD—USGS)**
Western Regional Office
909 First Avenue, Suite #800
Seattle, WA 98104
E-mail: brd_wro@usgs.gov
URL: http://biology.usgs.gov

BirdLife International
Wellbrook Court

Girton Rd.
Cambridge, CB3 ONA, UK
44(0) 1223 277 318
E-mail: birdlife@birdlife.org
URL: http://www.birdlife.net

Center for Plant Conservation (CPC)
P.O. Box 299
St. Louis, MO 63166-0299
(314) 577-9450
E-mail: cpc@mobot.org
URL: http://www.mobot.org/CPC/welcome.
html

Coral Reef Alliance (CORAL)
417 Montgomery St. Suite 205
San Francisco, CA 94104
(415) 834-0900
FAX: (415) 834-0999
Toll-free: 1-888-CORAL-REEF
E-mail: info@coral.org
URL: http://www.coral.org

**Declining Amphibians Populations Task
Force (DAPTF)**
Department of Biological Sciences
The Open University, Walton Hall
Milton Keynes, MK7 6AA UK
FAX: 44 (0)1908 654167
E-mail: daptf@open.ac.uk
URL: http://www.open.ac.uk/daptf/

Defenders of Wildlife
1130 17th St., NW
Washington, DC 20036
(202) 682-9400
E-mail: info@defenders.org
URL: http://www.defenders.org

Desert Tortoise Preserve Committee, Inc.
4067 Mission Inn Ave.
Riverside, CA 92501
(909) 683-3872
FAX: (909) 683-6949
URL: http://www.tortoise-tracks.org

Duke University Primate Center
3705 Erwin Rd.
Durham, NC 27705
(919) 489-3364
E-mail: primate@duke.edu
URL: http://www.duke.edu/web/primate/
home.html

Environmental Defense Fund
257 Park Ave. S
New York, NY 10010
(212) 505-2100
FAX: (212) 505-2375
E-mail: members@environmentaldefense.
org
URL: http://www.edf.org

Florida Panther Society, Inc.
377 Northwest Stephen Foster Dr.
White Springs, FL 32096
E-mail: karenhill@panthersociety.org
URL: http://www.panthersociety.org

Friends of the Earth
1717 Massachusetts Ave., NW, 600
Washington, DC 20036
Toll-free: 1-877-843-8687
FAX: (202) 783-0444
E-mail: foe@foe.org
URL: http://www.foe.org

Greenpeace U.S.A.
702 H St. NW
Washington, DC 20001
Toll-free: 1-800-326-0959
URL: http://www.greenpeaceusa.org

Humane Society of the United States
2100 L. St. NW
Washington, DC 20037
(202) 452-1100
URL: http://www.hsus.org

**Intergovernmental Panel on
Climate Change**
IPCC Secretariat

C/O World Meteorological Organization
7bis Avenue de la Paix
C.P. 2300
CH-1211
Geneva 2, Switzerland
41 (22) 730-8208
FAX: 41 (22) 730-8025
E-mail: ipcc-sec@wmo.int
URL: http://www.ipcc.ch

Izaak Walton League of America
707 Conservation Ln.
Gaithersburg, MD 20878
(301) 548-0150
FAX: (301) 548-0146
Toll-free: 1-800-453-5463
E-mail: general@iwla.org
URL: http://www.iwla.org

National Audubon Society
700 Broadway
New York, NY 10003
(212) 979-3000
FAX: (212) 979-3188
URL: http://www.audubon.org

National Wildlife Federation
11100 Wildlife Center Dr.
Reston, VA 20190-5362
Toll-free: 1-800-822-9919
URL: http://www.nwf.org

Natural Resources Defense Council
40 West 20th St.
New York, NY 10011
(212) 727-2700
FAX: (212) 727-1773
E-mail: nrdcinfo@nrdc.org
URL: http://www.nrdc.org

Nature Conservancy
4245 North Fairfax Drive, Suite 100
Arlington, VA 22203-1606
(703) 841-5300
FAX: (703) 841-1283
Toll-free: 1-800-628-6860
E-mail: comment@tnc.org
URL: http://nature.org

Ocean Conservancy
1725 DeSales St. NW, Suite 600
Washington, DC 20036
(202) 429-5609
FAX: (202) 872-0619
URL: http://www.oceanconservancy.org

**People for the Ethical Treatment of
Animals (PETA)**
501 Front St.
Norfolk, VA 23510
(757) 622-7382
FAX: (757) 622-0457
E-mail: info@peta.org
URL: http://www.peta-online.org

Rachel Carson Council
P.O. Box 10779
Silver Spring, MD 20914
(301) 593-7507
FAX: (301) 593-6251
E-mail: rccouncil@aolcom
URL: http://members.aol.com/rccouncil/
ourpage/rcc_page.htm

Sierra Club
85 Second St., 2nd Floor
San Francisco, CA
94105-3441
(415) 977-5500
FAX: (415) 977-5799
E-mail: information@sierraclub.org
URL: http://www.sierraclub.org

TRAFFIC International
219a Huntingdon Rd.
Cambridge, CB3 0DL, UK
(44) 1223 277427
FAX: (44) 1223 277237
E-mail: traffic@trafficint.org
URL: http://www.traffic.org

**TRAFFIC North America—
Regional Office**
1250 24th St. NW
Washington, DC 20037
(202) 293-4800
FAX: (202) 775-8287
E-mail: tna@wwfus.org
URL: http://www.traffic.org

Union of Concerned Scientists
2 Brattle Square
Cambridge, MA 02238
(617) 547-5552
URL: http://www.ucsusa.org

**U.S. Fish and Wildlife Service
Division of Endangered Species**
U.S. Department of the Interior
4401 N. Fairfax Dr., Rm. 420
Arlington, VA 22203
URL: http://endangered.fws.gov

United Nations Environment Programme
United Nations Avenue, Gigiri
P.O. Box 30552
Nairobi, Kenya
(254-2) 621234
FAX: (254-2) 624489/90
E-mail: eisinfo@unep.org
URL: http://www.unep.org

The Wilderness Society
1615 M St. NW
Washington, DC 20036
Toll-free: 1-800-843-9453
E-mail: member@tws.org
URL: http://www.wilderness.org

Wildlife Management Institute
1146 19th Street, NW, Suite 700
Washington, DC 20036
(202) 371-1808
FAX: (202) 408-5059
URL: http://www.wildlifemanagement
institute.org

World Conservation Union
Rue Mauverney 28
Gland, 1196, Switzerland
41 (22) 999-0000
FAX: 41 (22) 999-0002
E-mail: mail@iucn.org
URL: http://www.iucn.org

World Wildlife Fund
1250 24th St. NW
Washington, DC 20037
(202) 293-4800
FAX: (202) 293-9211
E-mail: PIResponse@wwfus.org
URL: http://www.worldwildlife.org

Worldwatch Institute
1776 Massachusetts Ave., NW
Washington, DC 20036-1904
(202) 452-1999
FAX: (202) 296-7365
E-mail: worldwatch@worldwatch.org
URL: http://www.worldwatch.org

RESOURCES

A first source of information on endangered species is the U.S. Department of the Interior's Fish and Wildlife Service. Their Endangered Species Program Web site (http://endangered.fws.gov/) includes news stories on threatened and endangered species, information about laws protecting endangered species, regional contacts for endangered species programs, and a searchable database with information on all listed species. Each listed species has an information page that provides details regarding the status of the species (whether it is listed as threatened or endangered and in what geographic area), federal register documents pertaining to listing, information on Habitat Conservation Plans and National Wildlife Refuges pertinent to the species, and, for many species, links to descriptions of biology and natural history. Particularly informative for those interested in the nuts and bolts of conserving species are the recovery plans published for a large number of listed species. These detail the background research on the natural history of endangered species and also list measures that should be adopted to aid in conservation. The Fish and Wildlife Service also maintains updated tables of the number of threatened and endangered species by taxonomic group, as well as lists of U.S. threatened and endangered species. Finally, the Fish and Wildlife Service publishes the bimonthly *Endangered Species Bulletin* (available online at http://endangered. fws.gov/bulletin.html), which provides information on new listings, delistings, and reclassifications, in addition to news articles on endangered species.

The World Conservation Union (IUCN) has news articles on a wide array of conservation issues at its Web site (http://www.iucn.org). Information from the *2003 IUCN Red List of Threatened Species* is also available online at http://www.redlist.org. This site includes an extensive database of information on IUCN-listed threatened species. Species information available includes Red List endangerment category, the year the species was assessed, the countries in which the species is found, a list of the habitat types the species occupies, major threats to continued existence, and current population trends. Brief descriptions of ecology and natural history and of conservation measures for protecting listed species are also available. Searches can also be performed by taxonomic group, Red List categories, country, region, or habitat.

The Convention on International Trade in Endangered Species of Wild Fauna and Flora (CITES) has information on international trade in endangered species at http://www.cites.org. This includes a species database of protected fauna and flora in the three CITES appendices, as well as information on the history and aims of the convention and its current programs.

Aside from the above three rich sources of species information, numerous organizations are dedicated to the conservation of particular listed species. Readers with interest in a particular endangered species are advised to conduct Internet searches to locate these groups. The Save the Manatee Club (http://www.savethemanatee.org), which focuses on West Indian manatees, and the Save Our Springs Alliance (http://www.sosalliance.org), which focuses on protection of the endangered Barton Springs salamander, are only two of many examples.

Information on federal lands and endangered species management can be found at the National Wildlife Refuge Web site (http://refuges.fws.gov), the National Park System Web site (http://www.nps.gov), and the National Forest Service Web site (http://www.fs.fed.us/). National Wildlife Refuge brochures are available at http://library. fws.gov/refuges/index.html.

The Intergovernmental Panel on Climate Change has a wealth of global warming-related resources available online at http://www.ipcc.ch. Particularly valuable are periodic "Summary for Policymaker" reports, which summarize the extent of global warming as well as predicted impacts. The U.S. Environmental Protection Agency

(EPA) also maintains a site dedicated to global warming issues at http://www.epa.gov/globalwarming. Finally, the "GLOBAL WARMING: Early Warning Signs" Web site is a joint production of the Environmental Defense Fund, Natural Resources Defense Council, Sierra Club, Union of Concerned Scientists, U.S. Public Interest Research Group, World Resources Institute, and World Wildlife Fund, and can be found at http://www.climatehotmap.org. This site provides a graphical interface for examining the numerous documented effects global warming has already had on the world. Early warning signs are divided into "fingerprints"—"direct manifestations of a widespread and long-term trend toward warmer global temperatures," and "harbingers"—"events that foreshadow the types of impacts likely to become more frequent and widespread with continued warming." Fingerprints include heat waves, sea level rise, coastal flooding, melting glaciers, and Arctic and Antarctic warming. Harbingers include spreading disease, earlier arrival of spring, plant and animal range shifts and population declines, coral reef bleaching, downpours, heavy snowfall, flooding, droughts, and fires.

"Endangered Ecosystems of the United States—A Preliminary Assessment of Loss and Degradation," a 1995 publication from the National Biological Service, remains the most up-to-date assessment of U.S. ecosystems. Information on water quality in the United States is available at the EPA Web site, http://www.epa.gov/water. Information on wetlands can be found at the Fish and Wildlife Service's "National Wetlands Inventory" page at http://www.nwi.fws.gov.

The World Conservation Union's *1997 IUCN Red List of Threatened Plants* is a valuable resource on threatened plant species.

BirdLife International (http://www.birdlife.net) provides diverse resources on global bird conservation. It is an association of non-governmental conservation organizations that has over 2 million members worldwide.

AmphibiaWeb (http://amphibiaweb.org) provides detailed information on global amphibian declines. It maintains a watch list of recently extinct and declining species, discusses potential causes of amphibian declines and deformities, and also provides detailed information on amphibian biology and conservation. AmphibiaWeb also sponsors a discussion board where readers can submit questions regarding amphibians.

TRAFFIC (http://www.traffic.org) was originally founded to help implement the CITES treaty but now addresses diverse issues in wildlife trade. It is a joint wildlife trade monitoring organization of the World Wildlife Fund (WWF) and the World Conservation Union (IUCN). The TRAFFIC Web site contains articles on current topics related to wildlife trade. In addition, TRAFFIC also publishes several periodicals and report series on wildlife trade, including the *TRAFFIC Bulletin*, *TRAFFIC Online Report Series*, and *Species in Danger Series*. These publications are available online at http://www.traffic.org/publications/index.html.

The International Whaling Commission has a Web site at http://www.iwcoffice.org/. Information on whaling regulations, whale sanctuaries, and other issues associated with whales and whaling can be accessed there.

The *2001 National Survey of Fishing, Hunting, and Wildlife-Associated Recreation* provides extensive data on wildlife recreation in the United States. It is published by the Fish and Wildlife Service using data collected by the U.S. Bureau of the Census.

Information Plus sincerely thanks all of the organizations listed above for the valuable information they provide.

INDEX

International Whaling Commission (IWC)
    establishment of, 11
    issues of, 165–166
    Japan and, 162
    moratorium on whale hunting, 101
Inuits of Alaska, 165, 166
Invasive species
    amphibian decline from, 107
    aquatic, 90–91
    birds threatened by, 133
    endangered mammals from, 116
    examples of, 2004, 8*t*
    impact of, 9*f*
    invasive insects/plants, threat to forests,
      72
    species endangerment from, 8–9
Invasive Species Council, 8–9
Invertebrate species, 14–15
Iowa, extinct species in, 2*t*
IPCC (Intergovernmental Panel on Climate
    Change), 42, 45–46
Ireland, Laura J., 170
Island species, 132
    See also Hawaii
IUCN. *See* World Conservation Union
1997 IUCN Red List of Threatened Plants
    (World Conservation Union), 55–58
IUCN Red List of Threatened Species (World
    Conservation Union), 2–3
2003 IUCN Red List of Threatened Species
    (World Conservation Union)
    birds report in, 131
    on endangered amphibians, reptiles, 105
    on endangered mammals, 115–116
    fish report in, 93
    on insects, endangered/threatened, 145
2000 IUCN Red List of Threatened Species
    (World Conservation Union)
    on invasive species, 8
2003 IUCN Red List of Threatened Species
    (World Conservation Union)
    plant findings in, 58–61
2000 IUCN Red List of Threatened Species
    (World Conservation Union)
    on trade of wildlife, 153
Ivory-billed woodpecker, 137
Ivory trade
    CITES listing status of African elephants,
      164
    controversy over, 125, 126
    elephants as priority species and, 161
IWC. *See* International Whaling
    Commission

J

Jaguars, 123
Japan
    animals used in research in, 160
    whaling and, 165, 166
    wildlife trade in, 162
Japanese giant salamander, 108
Jessica oil spill, 84
Journal of Heredity, 145

K

Karner blue butterfly
    life history stages, 148*f*

Michigan imperiled species associated
    with habitats of, 151*t*
    overview of, 147
    range-wide recovery units, 150 (*f*9.2)
    recovery plan overview, 149*t*
Kauai cave wolf spider, 150
Kemp's ridley turtle, 111
Kenai Peninsula (Anchorage, AK), 51
Kentucky, 136–137
Kenya
    ecotourism in, 169
    ivory trade in, 164
Khan, Kublai, 11
Klamath Basin, 94–95, 97
Klamath Marsh National Wildlife Refuge,
    97
Komodo dragon, 114, 155
Kraus, Scott, 101
Krausman, Paul R., 7
Kyoto Protocol, 52

L

Lacey Act, 103, 163
Lake Erie watersnake
    endangered, 112
    historic range on western Basin Lake
      Erie islands, 113*f*
    threats to, 113*t*
Lakes
    Aral Sea, 89
    lake acres/river miles under advisory,
      1993-2002, 88 (*f*5.6)
    lakes under advisory for various
      pollutants, trends in number of, 1993-
      2002, 86*f*
Lambert, Thomas, 20, 23
Land, 131
    See also Critical habitat; Federal lands
Land management, U.S., 23
Landowners
    bighorn sheep and, 127
    Endangered Species Act and, 20, 23
    Habitat Conservation Plans and, 15–16
Larsen B ice shelf
    collapse of, 47
    photograph of retreat of, 50*f*
Larvae, butterfly, 145
Laws, 103–104
    See also Legislation and international
      treaties
Leather trade, 153–154
Leatherback turtles, 111*f*
Legislation and international treaties
    Animal Welfare Act, 159
    Bald and Golden Eagle Protection Act,
      162
    Bald Eagle Protection Act of 1940, 142
    Clean Water Act, 132
    Convention on International Trade in
      Endangered Species, 11, 34, 36–37,
      164–165
    Criminal Fines Improvement Act, 163
    Endangered Species Conservation Act of
      1969, 11
    Endangered Species Preservation Act,
      1966, 11
    Everglades Forever Act, 78

Executive Order 13112 on Invasive
      Species, 8
    Helsinki Declaration, 43
    International Dolphin Conservation Act,
      102
    Kyoto Protocol, 52
    Lacey Act, 103, 163
    Magnuson Fishery Conservation and
      Management Act of 1976, 90, 103
    Marine Mammal Protection Act, 101,
      102, 103–104
    Migratory Bird Conservation Act, 131
    Montreal Protocol on Substances That
      Deplete the Ozone Layer, 42
    National Invasive Species Act of 1996,
      90
    Nonindigenous Aquatic Nuisance
      Prevention and Control Act of 1990, 90
    North American Free Trade Agreement,
      163
    oil drilling in Arctic National Wildlife
      Refuge bills, 28
    Rhino and Tiger Labeling Law, 159
    Rhinoceros and Tiger Conservation Act,
      159
    trade policies and agreements, 163–164
    Water Resources Development Act of
      2000, 78
    Wild Bird Conservation Act, 155
    Wilderness Act, 26
    World Trade Organization agreements,
      163–164
    See also Endangered Species Act
Liming, 155
Little Tennessee River, 99–100
Living organisms, 1
Lizards
    reptile trade, 155
    Texas horned lizard, 114 (*f*6.7)
    threatened or endangered, 112–114
Logging
    habitat destruction from, 7
    NAFTA and, 163
    within National Forests, 25
    northern spotted owl and, 4
    primates and, 127
    rainforest deforestation, 70, 71
    spotted owls habitat loss from, 137
    in Tongass National Forest, 73
    U.S. endangered forests and, 72
    woodpeckers threatened by, 136
Long-leaf pine ecosystem
    at-risk species living in longleaf pine or
      wiregrass habitats in southern coastal
      plain, 66*t*–67*t*
    endangered species in, 62, 64
Long-line fishing, 90, 131
Loon, yellow-billed, 132
Los Angeles (CA)
    distribution of six endangered plant
      species in mountains surrounding Los
      Angeles Basin, 68*f*
    endangered plants in mountains
      surrounding, 67–68
Lost River sucker, 97
Louisiana, 154

M

Macaw
hyacinth macaw, 161
scarlet macaw, 155*f*
trade of, 162
Madagascar, 127
Magnuson Fishery Conservation and
Management Act of 1976, 90, 103
Mahogany, 161, 164
Makah of Washington State, 165
Malaria, 47
Mammals, endangered
bears, 121
big cats, 122–124
bighorn sheep, 127
bison, 128, 128*f*
black-footed ferret, 116–117, 117*f*
elephants, 125–126, 126*f*
endangered or threatened mammals,
February 2004, 17*t*, 116*t*
grizzly bear recovery zones, 121 (*f7.6*)
human encounters, 115
levels of endangerment, 115–116
marine mammals, 101–103
Northern Idaho ground squirrel, 117
Northern Idaho ground squirrel, listing
factors/threats for, 118*t*
Northern Idaho ground squirrel probable
historical distribution and
primary/secondary metapopulation
sites, 2003, 118*f*
pandas, 121–122
primates, 126–127, 127*f*
quagga, 128–129, 129*f*
rhinoceros, 124–125, 125*f*
Siberian tiger, 124*f*
threatened and endangered animal
species found on National Wildlife
Refuge System, 2004, 33*t*
wolf breeding pairs in Northern Rocky
Mountain states, 1979-2002, 119*f*
wolf recovery areas, central Idaho,
northwest Montana, Greater
Yellowstone, 2002, 120*f*
wolves, 117–121
wolves, red wolf, 121 (*f7.5*)
Manatees
endangered, 101–102
photograph of, 101*f*
Mangrove forests, 78–79
Maoris, 154
Marine food chain, 93 (*f5.11*)
Marine iguanas, 84
Marine Mammal Authorization Program, 103*t*
Marine Mammal Protection Act (MMPA)
protection of dolphins, 102
protection of whales, 101
protections of, 103–104
Marine turtles, 161
Marine waters, 83–84
Mass extinction
debate over, 4
occurrences of, 1–2
Maximum sustainable yield, 89
MBD (metabolic bone disease), 155
Mead's milkweed
endangered, 68

present/historic distribution of, by
county, 69 (*f4.4*)
threats, recommended recovery actions, 70*t*
Meat trade
bush meat, 159
whale meat, 165
Medical research
animals used in, 159–161
animals used in research, experiments,
testing, teaching, fiscal year 2001, 160*f*
whaling and, 165
Medical waste, ocean dumping, 84
Medications, plant-derived, 79–80
Medicinal plants, 80
Medicine
animals/plants used in, 156, 159, 162
observations during survey of Golden
Rock, Myanmar, April 16-17, 2000,
157*t*–158*t*
plants used in, 55
Merck (pharmaceutical company), 80
Mercury
biomagnification in food chain, 85*f*
Florida Everglades and, 78
water pollution from, 84–85
Metabolic bone disease (MBD), 155
Metamorphosis
of amphibians, 105
of butterflies, 145
Methane
emissions, 43
greenhouse effect and, 41
rise in levels of, 42
sources, 2001, 48 (*f3.10*)
Mexican gray wolf, 119
Mexican spotted owl, 137
Mexico
El Chichon volcano, 44
illegal animal trade in, 155
Kemp's ridley turtles in, 111
monarch butterflies in, 146
North American Free Trade Agreement,
163
whaling sanctuary, 165
wildlife trade with U.S., 161
Michigan
extinct species in, 2*t*
moths in, 145
Migration
Convention on Migratory Species of
Wild Animals, 37–38
whooping crane migration routes and
nonessential experimental population
area, 2002, 139*f*
of whooping cranes, 138
Migratory Bird Conservation Act, 131
Migratory Bird Conservation Commission,
131
Migratory songbirds
endangered, 134–135
North American Breeding Bird Survey,
135–136
MIKE (Monitoring of Illegal Killing of
Elephants), 125
Milankovitch Cycles, 41
Miller, Mary Beth, 115
Mining, habitat destruction from, 7

Minke whales, 170
Minnesota, 2*t*
Missouri, 2*t*
Missouri River, 97
MMPA. *See* Marine Mammal Protection Act
Monarch butterfly
biopesticides and, 146–147
die-off in Mexico, 146
history of, 145–146
Money
for ecosystem conservation, 29–30
endangered or threatened species with
highest reported expenditures, fiscal
years 1998-2000, 23*t*
from exotic animal trade, 155
expenditures for wildlife-related
recreation, 2001, 167*f*
trade, profits to be made in rare-bird
trade, 156*t*
from wildlife trade, 161
See also Funding
Monito gecko, 112–113
Monito Island, 112–113
Monitor lizards
endangered, 114
trade of, 155
Monitoring of Illegal Killing of Elephants
(MIKE), 125
Monkeys, 160–161
Montana
wolf breeding pairs in Northern Rocky
Mountain states, 1979-2002, 119*f*
wolf recovery areas, 2002, 120*f*
See also Yellowstone National Park (WY
and MT)
Monteverde Cloud Forest Reserve (Costa
Rica), 106
Montreal Protocol on Substances That
Deplete the Ozone Layer, 42
Mosquitoes
in Hawaii, 138–139
mosquito-borne diseases, 46, 47
range shifts of, 50
Moths
Blackburn's sphinx moth, 147
as indicator species, 145
pollution and, 145
Motor vehicles, 43
Mount Pinatubo eruption (Philippines), 44
Mountain gorillas, 127
Mountain lions
characteristics of, 122
encounters with humans, 115
Florida panther, 122–123
"Multispecies Conservation Plan", 16
Murres, 132
Mussels
freshwater mussels, endangered, 91–92
Higgins eye, 94 (*f5.13*)
pearly-mussels in upper Mississippi
River drainage, decline of, 1920-2000,
93 (*f5.10*)
zebra mussel distribution, 1998 and 2003,
91*f*–92*f*
zebra mussels, 90, 92
Myanmar
animals/plants used in medicine, 157